From Symbolism to
Socialist Realism

CULTURAL SYLLABUS
SERIES EDITOR:
 MARK LIPOVETSKY *(University of Colorado - Boulder)*

FROM SYMBOLISM TO SOCIALIST REALISM

A Reader

Compiled, edited and with introductions
by Irene MASING-DELIC

BOSTON / 2012

Library of Congress Cataloging-in-Publication Data:
A catalog record for this book as available from the Library of Congress.

The book is supported by Mikhail Prokhorov Foundation
(translation program TRANSCRIPT).

Copyright © 2011 Academic Studies Press
All rights reserved

ISBN - 978-1-936235-42-1, Hardback
ISBN - 978-1-618112-32-3, Paperback

Book design by Ivan Grave

Published by Academic Studies Press in 2012
28 Montfern Avenue
Brighton, MA 02135, USA
press@academicstudiespress.com
www.academicstudiespress.com

To IURA

TABLE OF CONTENTS

Acknowledgments   12
Editor's Preface   13

Section One
Russian Culture before the October Revolution

Introduction   16

Historical-Cultural Contexts

Walter Sablinsky,   26
    "Father Gapon and the St. Petersburg Massacre of 1905,"
    from *The Road to Bloody Sunday*

Boris Savinkov,   31
    "The Assassination of Grand Duke Sergei,"
    from *Memoirs of a Terrorist*

Modernist Views on Art in Essays and Manifestos, Criticism

Valerii Briusov,   40
    "Keys to the Mysteries" from *The Russian Symbolists*

Viktor Zhirmunskii,   56
    "Two Tendencies of Contemporary Lyric Poetry,"
    from *The Silver Age of Russian Culture*

Viktor Shklovskii,   64
    "Art as Technique"
    from *Russian Formalist Criticism: Four Essays*

David Burliuk, Aleksandr Kruchenykh,
    Vladimir Maiakovskii, Viktor Khlebnikov,   82
    "Slap in the Face of Public Taste,"
    from *Words in Revolution: Russian Futurist Manifestoes 1912-1928*

Aleksandr Kruchenykh,   85
    "Declaration of Transrational Language,"
    from *Words in Revolution, Russian Futurist Manifestoes 1912-1928*

Richard Peace, 88
 "The Cherry Orchard,"
 from *Chekhov: A Study of the Four Major Plays*

Joan Delaney Grossman, 121
 "'The Marble Bust' and Briusov's Vision of Art,"
 from *Depictions: Slavic Studies in the Narrative and Visual Arts*

Vignettes

Valerii Briusov, 132
 "The Marble Bust: A Tramp's Story,"
 from *The Republic of the Southern Cross and other Stories*

Aleksandr Blok, 137
 "The Stranger,"
 from *Modern Russian Poetry*

Anna Akhmatova, 139
 "When in a Suicidal Anguish,"
 from *Modern Russian Poetry*

Nikolai Gumilev, 140
 "The Lost Streetcar,"
 from *Modern Russian Poetry*

Section Two
From Civil War to Stalinism via NEP

Introduction 143

Everyday Life: Reality and Dreams

Marina Tsvetaeva, 155
 "Attic Life,"
 from *Earthly Signs: Moscow Diaries, 1917-1922*

Aleksandra Kollontai, 160
 "Make Way for Winged Eros:
 A Letter to Working Youth. Love as a Socio-psychological Factor,"
 from *A Great Love: Selected Writings*

Andrei Siniavskii, 173
"The New Way of Life,"
from *Soviet Civilization: A Cultural History*

Evgenii Zamiatin, 180
"On Literature, Revolution, Entropy, and Other Matters,"
from *A Soviet Heretic: Essays by Yevgeny Zamyatin*

Literary Criticism

Kathleen Lewis and Harry Weber, 187
"Zamyatin's *WE*, the Proletarian Poets and Bogdanov's *Red Star*,"
from *The Ardis Anthology of Russian Futurism*

Irene Masing-Delic, 206
"Bright Hopes and Dark Insights: Vision and Blindness
as Cognition Tropes in Babel's *Red Cavalry*,"
from *For SK, In Celebration of the Life and Career of Simon Karlinsky*

Diana L. Burgin, 223
"Bulgakov's Early Tragedy of the Scientist-Creator:
An Interpretation of *The Heart of a Dog*,"
from *Slavic and East European Journal*

Victor Erlich, 241
"The Masks of Mikhail Zoshchenko,"
from *Literature, Culture, and Society in the Modern Age,
in Honor of Joseph Frank, Part II*

Nils Åke Nilsson, 256
"Through the Wrong End of Binoculars:
An Introduction to Iurii Olesha,"
from *Scando-Slavica*

Edward J. Brown, 280
"Two Plays,"
from *Mayakovsky. A Poet in the Revolution*

Vignettes

Osip Mandel'shtam, 289
"Brothers, Let's Glorify the Twilight of Freedom,"
from *Modern Russian Poetry*

Mikhail Zoshchenko,   290
"A Dogged Sense of Smell,"
from *The Galosh and Other Stories*

Mikhail Zoshchenko,   293
"Nervous People"
from *The Galosh and Other Stories*

Vladimir Maiakovskii,   296
"Brooklyn Bridge,"
from *Modern Russian Poetry*

Section Three
The Stalinist Period and World War II

Introduction   302

Memoirs

Iurii Olesha,   320
"1930: How Meierkhol'd Put on My Play,"
from *A Book of Farewell*

Ivanov-Razumnik,   323
from *The Memoirs of Ivanov-Razumnik*

Antonina Pirozhkova,   329
from *At His Side: The Last Years of Isaac Babel*

Cultural Contexts

Andrei Siniavskii,   340
"The Mystery and the Magic of Stalin's Power,"
from *Soviet Civilization: A Cultural History*

Daniel E. Collins,   348
"The Tower of Babel Undone in a Soviet Pentecost:
A Linguistic Myth of the First Five-Year Plan,"
from *Slavic and East European Journal*

Alexander Poznansky,   357
"Tchaikovsky as Communist Icon,"
from *For SK, In Celebration of the Life and Career of Simon Karlinsky*

Beth Holmgren,   367
"Power Relationships and Authorship,"
from *Women's Works in Stalin's Time, On Lidiia Chukovskaia and Nadezhda Mandelstam*

Leona Toker,   393
"Soviet Labor Camps: A Brief History,"
from *Return from the Archipelago: Narratives of Gulag Survivors*

Socialist Realism

Maksim Gor'kii,   407
"Soviet Literature: Address Delivered
to the First All-Union Congress of Soviet Writers,
August 17, 1934,"
from *Maxim Gorky on Literature*

Katerina Clark,   419
"Socialist Realism in Soviet Literature,"
from *The Routledge Companion to Russian Literature*

Boris Groys,   433
"The Typology of the Nonexistent,"
from *The Total Art of Stalinism*

War Diary

Vasilii Grossman,   440
Excerpts from *A Writer at War:
Vasily Grossman with the Red Army, 1941-1945*

Vignettes

Osip Mandel'shtam,   448
"We Exist in a Country Grown Unreal and Strange,"
from *Modern Russian Poetry*

Georgii Ivanov,   449
"Russia, Our Happiness. Russia, Our Light,"
from *Modern Russian Poetry*

Marina Tsvetaeva,   450
"This Thing Called Homesickness! A Fable,"
from *Modern Russian Poetry*

Vladimir Nabokov,   452
"No Matter How the Soviet Tinsel Glitters,"
from *Modern Russian Poetry*

Vasilii Lebedev-Kumach,   453
    "Song About Our Motherland,"
    from *Modern Russian Poetry*

Mikhail Isakovskii,   455
    "A Word to Comrade Stalin,"
    from *Modern Russian Poetry*

Epilogue
After WWII and after Stalin

Comments on the Epilogue Selections   457

A Denunciation

Andrei Zhdanov,   460
    "The Central Committee Resolution
    on the Journals *Zvezda* and *Leningrad*,"
    from *The Central Committee Resolution and Zhdanov's Speech
    on the Journals* Zvezda *and* Leningrad

Memoir

Evgenii Evtushenko,   466
    from *Yevtushenko's Reader: The Spirit of Elbe;
    A Precocious Autobiography; Poems*

Acknowledgements

I gratefully acknowledge The Ohio State University's Arts & Humanities Grant-in-Aid funding for supporting the preparation of this manuscript.

I thank graduate student Daria G. Safronova from The Department of Slavic and East European Languages and Cultures at Ohio State University for her invaluable help in preparing this manuscript. Without her efficient assistance and generosity with her time, this Reader would have taken considerably longer to complete. Graduate student Justin Wilmes, also from The Department of Slavic and East European Languages and Cultures at Ohio State University, made a fine translation of an excerpt from Iurii Olesha's *Book of Farewell* ("Kniga proshchaniia"), and I appreciate his contribution greatly.

Thanks are also due to Mark Lipovetsky for the helpful discussions we had on drafts of this collection.

Many authors and copyright holders kindly allowed reprinting of their works for no fee. I am greatly indebted to: Diana Burgin, Daniel Collins, Henry Erlich, Barbara Frenchi, Vladimir Kollontai, Vladimir Markov and Merrill Sparks, Eja Nilsson, Alexander Poznansky, and Yevgeny Yevtushenko.

Finally, I would like to express my appreciation to The Academic Studies Press for entrusting me with this engaging project.

Preface

This Reader, entitled *From Symbolism to Socialist Realism*, is aimed at upper division undergraduate students and beginning graduate students of Russian and comparative literature. Its purpose is to provide cultural and critical contexts to literary texts and movements of the first half of the twentieth century: modernist "Silver Age" literature, early Soviet prose, and socialist realist works of the Stalinist period. It contains literary criticism and theory, memoirs, (propaganda) speeches, manifestos, excerpts from historical works, and some "vignettes," or very short prose pieces, as well as poems from the time period under discussion. Other items include pieces on music history, Soviet philosophy of language, and Socialist Realism in literature and art.

The volume is divided into three main sections: Russian Culture before the October Revolution, From Civil War to Stalinism via NEP, and The Stalinist Period and the World War II era. Each of these sections has an Introduction by the editor that summarizes the main events and cultural trends of the given time period and introduces the selected items. There is also a brief Epilogue section that gives a few glimpses from post-war and post-Stalinist Russia.

I chose materials that would provide background for the most frequently studied writers. For the pre-revolutionary period these, in my estimation, would be: Anton Chekhov, some symbolist prose authors, and the futurist avant-garde (above all Maiakovskii). For post-revolutionary literature, writers such as Evgenii Zamiatin, Isaak Babel, Iurii Olesha, Mikhail Zoshchenko, and Mikhail Bulgakov are perhaps the best known names. Andrei Siniavskii's book chapters on NEP-culture and Stalin's "magic," Katerina Clark's article on Socialist Realism, Gor'kii's speech at the First Writers' Congress, and Zhdanov's "denunciations" of Akhmatova and Zoshchenko illuminate the literary climate of high Stalinist literature.

To reduce this volume to manageable proportions, some cuts had to be made to longer articles (such as Richard Peace's "The Cherry Orchard," Nils Åke

Nilsson's "Through the Wrong End of Binoculars," Aleksandra Kollontai's "Winged Eros," and others). All such cuts have been marked in the text (by ellipsis). The number of footnotes was also reduced and many notes condensed for most articles; short bibliographies of works relevant to each section were added instead. Sometimes I added small items of information; this information of the type "Iur'ev" [now Estonian Tartu] is given in square brackets.

One item was translated from the Russian (by OSU graduate student Justin Wilmes): an excerpt from Iurii Olesha's *Book of Farewell* ("Kniga proshchaniia"). Hopefully it will inspire further translations of this remarkable work. I was unable to trace the name of the translator of Valerii Briusov's "The Marble Bust" ("Mramornaia golovka"). It is not given on the cover of the 1922 edition of *The Republic of the Southern Cross and Other Stories*.

Transliteration issues are always problematic. I have used the Library of Congress system everywhere except for authors' names in reference matter. For example, I keep the spelling Mayakovsky or Yevtushenko in the Table of Contents, if this is the transliteration used by the translator. I also use translators' versions in titles and bibliographies so that an item can be found in library catalogues. I use Maiakovskii and Evtushenko in the subsequent text, taking the liberty of changing the transliteration used by the translator. For the sake of consistency, I have transliterated Tchaikovsky as Chaikovskii and Gorky as Gor'kii, however much better known the standard transliteration is. For émigré artists I have however provided the way their names were usually spelt in the West, in brackets. Spelling was Americanized in articles written in British English.

I hope this collection of contextualizing materials will find readers who appreciate the diversity of perspectives, genres and topics found in it, as well as the chronological blend of "old classics" of literary and cultural criticism and recent contributions. Of course the picture of the first half of the twentieth century presented here is far from complete, and as editor I take responsibility for any essential lacunae. I hope that the target audience, upper division students of Russian, nevertheless will find the Reader useful and illuminating.

—*Irene Masing-Delic*
October 2011

Section One

Russian Culture before the October Revolution

- Introduction
- Historical-Cultural Contexts
- Modernist Views on Art in Essays and Manifestos, Criticism
- Vignettes

Introduction

> *The Romanovs had no contact whatsoever with the modern world and continued, in spite of repeated warnings, to live like a seventeenth-century dynasty ... The end of this royal family marked the end of an epoch.*
> —Greg King

> *A Social-Revolutionary without a bomb is no longer a Social-Revolutionary.*
> —Ivan Kaliaev

The turn of the century saw a great deal of both urban and rural unrest in Imperial Russia. This situation was the result of the rapid industrialization of an essentially agrarian society and its traditional corollary, exploitation of the labor force. It was combined with continued peasant poverty, which the liberation of the serfs in 1861 had not alleviated and which the ruling elites were unable and/or unwilling to tackle by bringing about major social reforms. There was devastating rural famine in the 1890s while the State continued to sell grain abroad; the private initiative of Lev **Tolstoi** and his family did more to help the starving peasants than any public institution. Famine was followed by a series of industrial strikes and student protests in the 1900s. In 1904, the last Russian tsar, **Nikolai II** (ruling period: 1894-1917) engaged in an ill-conceived war against Japan, grossly underestimating its military might and skills. Virtually the entire Russian fleet was lost at Tsushima in 1905, and Nikolai soon had to acknowledge complete defeat at the hands of the "yellow" enemy. In addition, "Bloody Sunday" in early 1905 did much to damage tsarist prestige—a peaceful workers' march to the Winter Palace to petition for minimum wages and better labor

Introduction

conditions led to a massacre of the petitioners by tsarist troops. This event caused public outrage outside of Russia as well as within it, and became an important factor in the strikes that followed soon after and the ensuing revolutionary uprising that was quenched only in late December, 1905. The Tsar was forced to institute the **Duma**, a legislative body in which different political parties were represented. The Duma was restricted by needing the pro-Tsarist **State Council** to approve its proposals, however, and the Tsar himself could veto its legislation. He could also dissolve the Duma altogether, and did so twice.

Social unrest and protest movements were not new phenomena in Russian public life. For several decades of the second half of the previous century, the socialist **Populist** (*Narodnik*) movement engaged in social and enlightenment activities among the rural population, encouraging protest and rebellion but usually meeting with little understanding among the peasants. State persecution ended in trials and exiles of the narodniks. Impatience with the status quo led to the formation of an underground terrorist faction, the *People's Will*, which targeted powerful government officials for "liquidation." Their greatest "success" was the killing of **Aleksandr II** in 1881. His inheritor, **Aleksandr III**, steered a marked anti-liberal course, which suppressed protest movements but did not eliminate them. A few decades after Aleksandr II's assassination, the *Socialist Revolutionary Party*, through its underground "Combat Organization," blew up Prince **Sergei**, the Tsar's uncle, as well as numerous other members of the ruling elite. Other political parties also formed at the same time and attained legal status after the Constitution of 1905 and the formation of the Duma. In addition to the already mentioned Socialist Revolutionaries, the inheritors of the agrarian Populists, there was the *Marxist Social-Democratic Labor Party*, which sought support in the urban working class. There was also a smaller liberal party, the *Constitutional Democrats* (usually referred to as *kadety*, as **k** and **d** formed the initial letters in the Russian party name *Konstitutsionnye Demokraty*). All of them wanted to abolish the autocracy. The *Social-Democratic Labor Party*, which was formed in 1899, split into two factions in 1903: the *Mensheviks* (the minority faction) and the *Bolsheviks* (the majority faction;

the semantics of "bigger" was to their advantage). The Bolsheviks were led by the uncompromising Vladimir Il'ich **Lenin** (real name **Ul'ianov;** most revolutionaries operated under pseudonyms), who was already projecting the "revolutionary democratic dictatorship of the proletariat and the peasantry," and also "anticipating the use of terror in order to establish the dictatorship" (Service).

In spite of these far-reaching political developments, serious military defeats, and frequent assassinations, the Tsar was not persuaded to abandon his "God-given" power, but was rather confirmed in his determination to maintain the autocracy. He did not "play by the rules," and stalled Duma activities whenever and in any way he could. Nikolai II was convinced that the Russian Tsar was ordained by God to be the all-powerful "father of his people." Being "divinely ordained" made him responsible to no one but God.

The lavish "fairytale" commemoration of three hundred years of Romanov rule, celebrated in Petersburg in 1913, marks a peak of self-deception in the world of make-believe that the country's ruling elite inhabited at the time. Four or five years later, most of the Romanovs were either executed or exiled, and their empire annihilated; two other European empires—the Austro-Hungarian and German ones—also collapsed soon after theirs.

The immediate cause of the these three empires' disappearance from the map was World War I (1914-1918). Pitted against Germany and Austria, Russia initially saw nationalist enthusiasm and support for the dynasty, but disastrous defeats and huge losses of life led to mass desertion and anarchy, fanned by revolutionary propaganda. Food was becoming scarce in the capital and there were mass strikes. These events deprived even Nikolai of his illusions, and he abdicated in early 1917. The "February Revolution" led to the formation of a provisional government under the leadership of Aleksandr **Kerenskii,** who was a lawyer of moderate Socialist Revolutionary leanings. After the Lenin-led Bolshevik takeover in late 1917, which received the name the **Great October Revolution**, Kerenskii fled abroad. On Lenin's orders, Nikolai II and his family were sent out of Petersburg, kept under house arrest, and eventually executed in 1918 in the city of **Ekaterinburg**. Austria-Hungary and Germany, defeated by France, Great Britain, and the US, ceased to be monarchies also, but they did not embark on the "great Socialist experiment" that Bolshevik Russia did.

The Russian **intelligentsia,** on the whole, actively supported the decline of imperial Russia, with hope, trepidation, or a mixture of both, but mostly with few regrets for the past. Many had great expectations of a better post-tsarist world. There was a general sense that the outmoded tsarist state was no longer viable and had to be replaced by a new social order that would befit the remarkable achievements of Russian contemporary culture. Indeed, the so-called **Silver Age** (1890s-1910s; some include the 1920s) was a remarkably rich, innovative and diverse period in which the arts flourished. Russian science could also demonstrate great achievements since the second half of the nineteenth century, with the creator of the periodic table of the elements, chemist Dmitrii **Mendeleev,** and the physiologist Ivan **Pavlov** as perhaps its best known representatives. The latter came up with the concept of the "conditioned, or conditional, reflex" (using dogs for his experiments), which impacted **behaviorism.**

The "Silver Age"

A veritable cultural revolution…
—Martin Malia

In stark contrast to the bleak decline of tsarist Russia's political and social structures, the so-called **Silver Age** culture of the turn-of-the-century and pre-World War I eras demonstrated a superabundance of achievements in both arts and sciences. Literature, traditionally regarded as the foremost Russian art, flourished in prose and drama, but even more so in poetry, which had been in decline ever since the **Golden Age** of Aleksandr **Pushkin** (d. 1837). **Symbolist** poets Valerii **Briusov,** Aleksandr **Blok,** and Viacheslav **Ivanov** created refined poetry inspired by the cult of beauty, mystical visions, and syncretic religious quests, all of which were seen as paths to "other worlds" (Fedor **Dostoevskii**). This brilliant group of symbolists, which also included the prose writer of genius Andrei **Belyi**, was soon followed by the **Acmeists,** technically refined poets steeped in the concrete manifestations of world culture and less interested in elusive "other worlds." The **Futurist** poets "transcended" language itself by creating "trans-sense" language based on the magical potency of sound and the "true" roots of language: Velimir **Khlebnikov**'s famous "laughnik-poem" (entitled "Incantation") literally wanted to destroy the Old World by laughing it out of existence. His fellow futurist Vladimir **Maiakovskii** wrote tragic love poetry using extravagant metaphors and creating intriguing, but decipherable, neologisms.

The other arts were also rich in innovative genius, with remarkable achievements in the visual arts by modernist painters such as Mikhail **Vrubel'**, Valentin **Serov**, Vasilii **Kandinskii** (Wassily/ Vasily **Kandinsky**), Mark **Shagal** (Marc **Chagall**), Kazimir **Malevich,** and many others. Music composition continued the great achievements of Petr **Chaikovskii** and Modest **Musorgskii** from the second half of the nineteenth century, notably represented by Nikolai **Rimskii-Korsakov**, Sergei **Rakhmaninov** (Sergei **Rachmaninov/ Rachmaninoff)**, Aleksandr **Skriabin** and Igor' **Stravinskii** (Igor **Stravinsky)**. The performing arts had outstanding directors, actors, singers, and dancers, as well as impresarios, such as Sergei **Diagilev** (Sergei/Serge **Diaghilev)**, who introduced Russian ballet and opera to the Parisians. The stage became the space where many of the arts met: ballet dancers such as Anna **Pavlova**, Tamara **Karsavina,** and Vatslav **Nizhinskii** (Vaslav **Nijinsky)**, and opera singers such as the bass Fedor **Shaliapin** (Feodor **Chaliapin**), performed in costumes and with décor that were works of art rather than mere props. The drama theater presented experimental staging, mainly inspired by the anti-realist Vsevolod **Meierkhol'd**. The more traditional theater director Konstantin **Stanislavskii** created his famous acting "method," which changed acting techniques all over the world, especially in the United States. He and his director colleague Vladimir **Nemirovich-Danchenko** were the ones to introduce Anton **Chekhov's** plays to Moscow and the world, as well as those of the "stormy petrel" of Revolution, Maksim **Gor'kii**. There were "revolutions" in literally all spheres of life, and not least in gender relations. Gender roles were being reconsidered, and behavioral patterns changed markedly at this time, when "all values were being re-evaluated" (as Friedrich **Nietzsche** put it). As if in confirmation of changed gender relations, great woman poets such as Anna **Akhmatova** and Marina **Tsvetaeva** came to the fore. They clearly transcended the pretty "female poet" (*poetessa*) images that had dominated in the past. The art considered perhaps the most important of all was "life creation," however. This form posited the transformation of prosaic everyday life (*byt*) into lived art. Life was aesthetically organized by artists who created "scenarios" for their lives and roles for themselves that belonged to another time period, for example, or who gave much thought to their appearance—not trying to be fashionable, but to transform themselves aesthetically. There were multiple strategies for how to incarnate art and transcend the "merely human." Sometimes this kind of life creation was paid for dearly in terms of "ordinary" happiness, as the poet Vladislav **Khodasevich**, a late symbolist, made poignantly clear in his essayistic memoirs (see, for example, "Konets Renaty," "The End of Renata").

There was also a pronounced receptiveness to Western cultural impulses in Russia at the time, and literary curiosity went beyond French and English Decadence, French painting, and German philosophy. Scandinavian writers, for example, were widely read. Many Russian modernist writers translated a great deal from different literatures (a good case in point is the symbolist poet Konstantin **Bal'mont,** who traveled as far as India and translated poetry from that continent), or engaged in explorations of ancient cultures (such as Egyptian, Ancient Greek, and Roman). There was, to use acmeist poet Osip **Mandel'shtam's** famous phrase, "a yearning for world culture." A larger than usual interest in Russian culture was also prevalent in Western Europe, and was apparent in its main cultural center, Paris, as already mentioned. Cultural cross-pollination and interactive dialogue stimulated innovative cultural productivity, and Russia was certainly not "lagging behind" in regard to daring artistic renewal, but shared fully in developing and creating various modernist trends. There was a new emphasis on the unique individual vision, not excluding attempts to reach "beyond" the "merely real" to something "more real," as the symbolists liked to put it, but the "more real" was not necessarily limited to purely spiritual realms. The Ultimate for all was life-transforming Art creating palpable Beauty. A subjective and free vision of reality was preferred to a "pedestrian positivism" that bound man to the material world, offering no escape from causality and temporality. Religious mysticism—often "heretic," including occult movements—the cult of art, a new emphasis on unconventional erotic experience and sensual beauty, philosophical speculation, and many more cultural pursuits of the times together evoked the spirit of the Italian Renaissance, another age of daring departures from and creative rediscoveries of the past. The Russian Silver Age did indeed aspire to being another major epoch of cultural "rebirth," based on syncretism.

Not all turn-of-the-century art was modernistic exploration of the expressive potential of new art forms and hitherto taboo thematics. There also existed the more traditionally Russian **Realism,** which continued alongside mystical **Symbolism**, yearning to reach "other worlds." In some cases, this Realism offered a realism that differed from that of the nineteenth century, whose favorite genre was the thick novel: it could be impressionistic and sparse, as in Anton **Chekhov**'s short prose (he never wrote a novel with the exception of one in the small format), or formally perfect but thematically subversive, as in Ivan **Bunin**'s lyrical prose, or stridently heroic-romantic, as in Gor'kii's early work. Modernism dominated, however, as represented by the refined but earthbound and culturally concrete **Acmeism**, and radically innovative **Futurism**, heavily backed by literary theoreticians such as the **Formalist** Viktor **Shklovskii** and the linguist Roman **Jakobson**. Gor'kii would soon reach international fame as the "Voice of Revolution" and, as such, launch the politically-oriented literature that would combat modernism, and eventually culminate in **Socialist Realism**. Allying himself to Lenin and his Bolshevism and later to Stalin and his gigantic projects (paid for by millions of lives), he created a model for the close alliance between Writer (Artist) and State that would prevail from the onset of Stalinism in the 1930s and last, to varying degrees of closeness until the fall of the Soviet Union in 1991.

Introduction

The Selections

Some of the ferment in all spheres of public and cultural life is captured in the first section of the Reader. It opens with Walter *Sablinsky*'s discussion of reactions to Bloody Sunday and the ruling elite's inability to understand realities and thus to part with illusions about "Holy Russia's" special path, which had no need of democracy, parliamentary debates, a party system and other "Western" institutions. This political blindness called forth another form of political blindness: terrorism. Boris **Savinkov**, the well-known plotter of assassinations as member of the Socialist Revolutionary **Combat Organization**, also had writerly aspirations, authoring the novel *Pale Horse* (*Kon' blednyi*, 1909) and the *Memoirs of a Terrorist* (1917). In these works, he raises the moral implications of breaking the "thou shalt not kill" commandment, resolving the issue in favor of transgressing that commandment. In the excerpt chosen here, he describes the stalking and assassination of the Tsar's uncle, **Grand Duke Sergei Romanov**, an anti-Semitic arch-conservative. Three essays by the Symbolist poet Valerii **Briusov**, the theoretician of Formalism Viktor **Shklovskii** and the scholar Viktor **Zhirmunskii** expound on the new ideas about literature that came to the fore at this time—ideas that differed markedly from the traditional Russian approach to literature as social engagement and psychological analysis. Two radical Futurist manifestos representing the avant-garde position follow.

The next two articles, by literary scholars Richard *Peace* and Joan *Grossman*, present Chekhov's famous last play "The Cherry Orchard" (1904) and Briusov's short but intriguing story "The Marble Bust." Peace offers insightful explanations for the oft-debated question as to why it should be "funny" to lose one's estate and face financial ruin, for Chekhov insisted it was a "comedy" he had written about the financial and social decline of an aristocratic family. The spectacle of the aristocracy's—or any class's or individual's—inability to adapt to change, and their clinging to delusions and self-deception, is undoubtedly always both "comical" and not so comical, and Chekhov emphasized that aspect. Silver

Age scholar Grossman discerns the crux of Briusov's fantastic story—the narrator "recognizes" his lost beloved in a marble bust created centuries before she lived—in ontological issues, including the questions of what is more "real," life or art, and which creates which? The **Vignettes** offer that very story, as well as three poems. "The Stranger" by Aleksandr **Blok** offers a romantic, yet "decadent," vision of otherworldly Beauty. It too raises the question of the real versus the "more real," adding the disillusioning touch that the vision the poet has may well be the result of ample wine consumption rather than a mystical experience emanating from another world. The **Acmeists** Anna **Akhmatova**, Nikolai **Gumilev** and Osip **Mandel'shtam** challenged the Symbolists, as already mentioned, stating that the mysteries of the other world belonged *there* and not to this world, which should be poetically described on its own terms. Anna Akhmatova was better known for her love of poetry than for civic themes during the Silver Age period of her career, but in the poem from 1917 selected for this section of the Reader she declares her firm decision not to join the emigration and not to abandon her country, regardless of what was happening in it. Her later poetry, including the cycle *Requiem*, which was written during the 1930s Stalinist repressions, deepens the "civic" strand that already emerges in "When in Suicidal Anguish." Gumilev was executed by the Bolsheviks in 1921 for his alleged participation in an anti-government conspiracy. His "surreal" "Lost Streetcar," written in 1921, seems to anticipate this event. Time is clearly "out of joint" in the poem, with the lyrical subject traveling into the past as well as the future, encountering terror in the name of Revolution in both time dimensions.

Introduction

SUGGESTED FURTHER READINGS

Anemone, Anthony, editor and author of the Introduction. *Just Assassins: The Culture of Terrorism in Russia*, Evanston, IL: Northwestern University Press, 2010.

Kataev, Valentin. *If only we Could Know: an Interpretation of Chekhov*, Chicago: Ivan R. Dee, 2002.

Kelly, Catriona. *A History of Russian Women's Writing, 1820-1992*, Oxford: Clarendon Press, New York: Oxford University Press, 1994.

Matich, Olga. *Erotic Utopia: the Decadent Imagination in Russia's fin-de-siecle.* Madison, Wisconsin: University of Wisconsin Press, 2005.

Pyman, Avril. *A History of Russian Symbolism,* Cambridge: Cambridge University Press, 1994.

Volkov, Solomon. *The Magical Chorus, A History of Russian Culture, from Tolstoy to Solzhenitsyn,* translated from the Russian by Antonina WW. Bouis, New York: Alfred A. Knopf, 2008.

HISTORICAL-CULTURAL CONTEXTS

FATHER GAPON AND THE ST. PETERSBURG MASSACRE OF 1905

by Walter SABLINSKY*

* From *The Road to Bloody Sunday* Princeton University Press, Princeton, New Jersey, 1976, pp. 274-278. Studies of the Russian Institute, Columbia University.

. . . .
The most significant effect of Bloody Sunday was this dramatic change in the attitude of the heretofore loyal lower classes. The wanton firing on unarmed workers had an overwhelming psychological impact. Until 1905 the bulk of the Russian masses had remained steadfastly devoted to their sovereign, but after Bloody Sunday even the most religious monarchists among the workers tore portraits of the tsars from the walls of their homes. Some removed the icons also. The tsar was no longer distinguished from the hated bureaucrats surrounding him; he was held personally responsible for the tragedy in front of his palace. Lenin's sister [A. Elizarova-Ul'ianova] recalled a marked change in mood among the most conservative and

politically backward elements in the capital. Cab drivers, who were usually hostile to and uncommunicative with the intelligentsia, openly discussed the events. She recalled a typical peasant driver recounting to her the shooting at Narva Arch. He was particularly indignant at the firing upon a religious procession carrying icons and portraits of the tsar. Feigning innocence, she led him on: "Hey, it would seem the tsar's portrait might also get hit?" "Yes, and he got it right in the nose," was the terse reply. From this surprising response she concluded, "I was witnessing the extinction of the faith in the tsar among those most loyal to him, the lowest strata of the masses."

All of Russian society was repulsed by the brutal suppression of the peaceful demonstration. The strikes in St. Petersburg continued and spread to other cities. In the words of the Kolpino workers [the town of Kolpino, near St. Petersburg, had ironworks and an iron foundry], "After these bloody events, no one can return to work." Assemblies of nobility, zemstvos [organs of rural self-government], city dumas [councils], faculties of universities, and other public bodies issued strongly worded statements deploring the government actions. University students voted to go on strike; theater performances were canceled; and the Merchants' Club of St. Petersburg refused to admit officers of the Guard. The regime was indeed in trouble when even students of theological academies voted overwhelmingly to go on strike. Students of the St. Petersburg Theological Academy unanimously condemned the government action, offered a prayer for the victims of the massacre, and called for a "modern regime" with national representation. The general reaction of the Russian public was perhaps best expressed in the anguished invocation of Bishop Sergii of St. Petersburg:

> Let that day be darkness! . . . That night—let thick darkness seize it! Let it not rejoice among the days of the year, let it not come into the number of the months. (Job 3:4)
>
> Oh, if only that day was not in our history!

The editorial in the official newspaper of the Church added: "There can be no two opinions about the ninth of January. That day is recognized by all as grievous and lamentable...." The wave of protests reverberated throughout the world, and mass demonstrations took place in major cities around the globe. Nowhere were the demonstrations more outspoken than in France, Russia's principal ally. Jean Jaures [French socialist politician] and Georges Clemenceau [French prime minister 1906-1909] thundered their denunciations from the floor of the National Assembly. Anatole France and many others spoke before mass meetings. Even the conservative *Times* of London editorialized:

> There is but one sentiment excited throughout the civilized world by the events in St. Petersburg—a sentiment of horror at the brutal butchery of unarmed people whose only offense—at least in the case of the vast majority—was a display of their pathetic faith in the goodness of the Tsar."[1]

For the government officials who were to varying degrees responsible for the tragedy, the most lamentable fact was the ease with which the confrontation could have been avoided. The general consensus was that a close relative of the tsar, or a high official in full uniform, could have accepted the petition on behalf of the tsar and thereby pacified the workers. As it was, Nicholas II had missed an excellent opportunity to reaffirm the faith of the masses. Grand Duke Paul, an uncle of the tsar, was in the company of Maurice Paleologue, future French ambassador to Russia, when he received news of the shootings. The grand duke exploded: "Why in heaven didn't the emperor receive the strikers' deputation? There was nothing seditious about their attitude.... What has happened is both unpardonable and irreparable ... we would have been saved!" An English lord, seeing Russia in the throes of the revolution of 1905, commented that the tsar had "forfeited the confidence of his people and lost an opportunity offered him which, if seized, would have made him the most popular sovereign in the world."

Despite their private acknowledgments that Bloody Sunday had been a grievous and avoidable error, the public expressions of regret which many officials hastened to deliver defended the use of troops and tried to gloss over the effects of the massacre. Sviatopolk-Mirskii [Russian Minister of the Interior] insisted that he could not have permitted the huge gathering without risking an outbreak of large-scale disorders. In an interview, Grand Duke Vladimir [an uncle of Tsar Nikolai II] lamented the shooting and stated that he had personally attempted to prevent it. Yet he justified the use of troops to prevent a march on the Winter Palace, which he likened to the march on Versailles in 1789. Behind the demonstration, he said, was an "anarchistic and socialist plot." Carefully understating the import of the workers' claims, the grand duke assured his interviewers that reforms were forthcoming. As one defender of the regime asserted, the assumption underlying the government's response was that "to allow the manifestation was to capitulate without a struggle." Only after the blood had been shed did the tsarist officials question this assumption.

Tsar Nicholas II, on whose shoulders the final responsibility rested, seemed curiously aloof from the disastrous events in the capital. He passed the day quietly with his family in the pleasant surroundings of [his summer palace] Tsarskoe Selo. The brief entry in his diary spoke of Bloody Sunday as though it had been a tragic natural calamity. Though he expressed grief over the day's events, he seemed unaware of their fatal implication and quickly passed on to more mundane affairs:

> January 9, Sunday: A grievous day! Serious disorders occurred in St. Petersburg because workers sought to reach the Winter Palace. Troops were compelled to fire in several parts of the city; many were killed and wounded. God, how painful and heartbreaking!
> Mama [i.e. the Empress] came from the city straight to church. Had lunch with everyone. Went for a walk with Misha. Mama stayed overnight.

The immediate response of the regime's defenders was to blame revolutionaries and hostile foreign governments for instigating the demonstration. Reactionary vigilante groups, abetted by the police, attacked members of the intelligentsia on the streets of St. Petersburg, and a number of students were badly beaten. Various governmental agencies spread rumors that the disorders were instigated by foreign agents, and a government-supported public relations firm based in Europe and directed by General Cherep-Spiridovich, former president of the Moscow Slavonic Society, sent a series of telegrams to this effect. An unsigned telegram to the ministry of the interior stated that Gapon [the priest who had led the peaceful demonstration][2] was a paid enemy agent supplied with "pounds of sterling." The General Staff received a telegram stating that enormous sums of Japanese and English money were spent to foment disorders in Russia. The message concluded, "Explain the truth to the Russian people. Any sympathy with the disorders is crime and treason." Harried officials, only too glad to find excuses for their actions, gave these telegrams wide circulation. The acting prefect of Moscow had them printed and posted throughout the city, and pro-government newspapers gave the allegations prominent coverage.

SELECTED NOTES

[1] *The London Times*, January 24, 1905.

[2] Possibly he was a double agent; he was murdered by Socialist Revolutionaries in 1906 [IMD].

The Assassination of Grand Duke Sergei

by Boris SAVINKOV*

* From *Memoirs of a Terrorist.* Translated by Joseph Shaplen, New York: Albert and Charles Boni, 1931, pp. 98-105.

....

We hesitated as to the day on which to kill the Grand Duke [Grand Duke Sergei Aleksandrovich was one of Nikolai II's uncles and the Governor General of Moscow]. Through the newspapers I[1] learned that on February 2 there would be a performance at the Bol'shoi Theater for the benefit of the Red Cross, under the patronage of the Grand Duchess Elizabeth [Elisaveta, *sic*] Fedorovna [wife of Grand Duke Sergei and sister of Empress Aleksandra]. The Grand Duke was bound to visit the theater on that occasion. We picked February 2 for the assassination. Shortly before that Dora Brilliant [responsible for explosives in the group] had gone to Iur'ev [now Estonian Tartu], where she kept our dynamite. I went to see her and on February 1 our entire organization was again in Moscow, including [Boris] Moiseenko who had continued driving his cab without interruption [his job was to act as cab-sleigh driver and to monitor the victim's movements].

Dora Brilliant stopped on the Nikolskaia [Street], at the "Slavianskii Bazaar" hotel. Here in the morning, on February 2, she prepared two bombs, one for Kaliaev[2] and another for [P. A.] Kulikovskii [a founding member of the Socialist Revolutionary Party]. We did not know at what time of day the Grand Duke would drive to the theater. We decided, therefore, to lie in wait for him from the beginning of the performance, i. e. from eight o'clock. At seven o'clock I came to the "Slavianskii Bazaar" hotel and at that very moment Dora Brilliant appeared at the entrance with two bombs, wrapped in a blanket under her arm. Together we turned into Bogoiavlenskii Lane, removed the blanket and placed the bombs in a briefcase I had brought with me. In Bol'shoi-Cherkasskii Lane we met Moiseenko. I got into his sleigh and drove to the Ilynka [Street], where I met Kaliaev. I gave him his bomb and drove off to find Kulikovskii, who was to wait for me on Varvarka [Street]. At seven-thirty both bombs had been delivered. At eight o'clock Kaliaev took up his station on Voskresenskii Square, before the City Duma, and Kulikovskii at the entrance to the Aleksandrovskii Gardens. There were thus but two roads open for the Grand Duke to the Bol'shoi Theater from the Nikolskii Gate—to Kaliaev or to Kulikovskii. Both Kaliaev and Kulikovskii were dressed as peasants in long cloaks, caps and high boots. Their bombs were wrapped in their handkerchiefs. Dora Brilliant returned to her hotel. In the event of failure, we had agreed to meet at midnight, after the performance. Moiseenko went to his livery stable. I entered the Aleksandrovskii Gardens and waited for the explosion.

It was bitter cold. A storm was beginning. Kaliaev stood in the shadow of the city Duma doors, facing the dark, deserted square. Shortly after eight o'clock the Grand Duke's carriage appeared at the Nikolskii Gate. Kaliaev recognized it immediately by its bright green lights. The carriage turned into Voskresenskii Square, and in the darkness Kaliaev thought he recognized the Grand Duke's coachman, Rudinkin. Without hesitation he dashed forward, straight across the path of the carriage. He had already raised his hand to hurl the bomb. But suddenly he perceived that in addition to the Grand Duke there was also in the carriage the Grand Duchess Elizabeth and the children of the Grand Duke Paul—Marie and Dmitrii. Kaliaev let his hand fall and withdrew. The carriage stopped at the entrance of the Bol'shoi Theater.

Kaliaev proceeded into the Aleksandrovskii Gardens. Approaching me, he said:

"I think I have done the right thing. How can one kill children?"

He was so excited he could hardly proceed. He realized the danger of having deliberately missed this one, big chance of killing the Grand Duke. He not only risked his own life but the life of the entire organization. He could have been arrested at the carriage with bomb in hand, and then the assassination would have had to be indefinitely postponed. I told him, however, that far from blaming him I applauded his conduct. He then suggested that we decide the question of whether in seeking to kill the Grand Duke we should not hesitate, if necessary, to kill also his wife and the children. We had never discussed or even raised the question. Kaliaev said that if we decided to kill the whole family, he would agree to hurl the bomb into the carriage on its way back from the theater, regardless of who was in it. I expressed the opinion that this was quite out of the question.

During our conversation we were joined by Kulikovskii. From his station he observed how the Grand Duke's carriage turned toward Kaliaev, but he did not hear any explosion. For this reason he thought that the assassination had failed and that Kaliaev was arrested.

I expressed some doubt as to whether the Grand Duke had actually been in the carriage and wondered whether Kaliaev had not mistaken the carriage of the Grand Duchess for that of the Grand Duke. We decided to check up on the matter. Kaliaev was to go to the place where the carriages were parked and investigate. It was possible that both carriages were there. I was to go into the theater and look for the Grand Duke.

I went to the box office. The house was sold out. A band of ticket speculators hurled themselves upon me. I realized that I might not be able to pick out the Grand Duke in the theater. Therefore, without purchasing a ticket, I asked the speculators:

"Is the Grand Duchess in the theater?"

"Yes. She arrived fifteen minutes ago."

"And the Grand Duke?"

"He arrived together with Her Highness."

Kaliaev and Kulikovskii waited for me in the street. Kaliaev's investigation revealed there was only one carriage, the Grand Duke's. The Grand Duke had come to the theater with his family.

All three of us went for a walk and found ourselves, without realizing where we were going, along the embankment of the Moscow River. Kaliaev walked alongside of me, his head bowed, and holding his bomb in one hand. Kulikovskii walked a short distance behind. Suddenly his steps were silenced. I turned around. He stood supporting himself against the granite pillars. It seemed he would collapse at any moment. I walked over to him. He muttered:

"Take the bomb. I'm going to let it fall!"

I took his bomb. He remained standing, immovable, for a long time. It was evident his strength had left him.

At the conclusion of the performance, Kaliaev returned to the theater and walked over to the Grand Duke's carriage. Again, the Grand Duchess and the children of Grand Duke Paul entered the carriage. Kaliaev came back to me and returned the bomb. At midnight I met Dora and gave her both bombs. Silently she heard my story of what had occurred. I asked her what she thought of Kaliaev's conduct and of our decision.

She lowered her eyes.

"The 'poet' [Kaliaev's nickname] did as he should have done."

Kaliaev and Kulikovskii had no passports, having left them with their things at the railway station. I had the receipts. It was too late to return for the passports and too late to leave Moscow. They had to spend the night in the street. I was dressed as a wealthy Englishman, they as peasants. They were frozen and tired. Kulikovskii was hardly able to keep on his feet. I decided, despite the difference in our attires, to enter a restaurant.

We went into the restaurant "Alpine Rose" on the Sofiika [Street]. The porter would not let us in. I demanded to see the manager. After long negotiations we were admitted to a back room. It was warm here and one could rest.

Kaliaev livened up and in an excited voice began to recapitulate the scene before the city Duma. He said he feared he had committed a crime against the organization and was happy that the comrades did not blame him. Kulikovskii was silent. He seemed weak and broken. I still do not understand how he survived the rest of the night in the street.

At about four o'clock, after the "Alpine Rose" was closed, I bid them good-bye. We decided to try again during the same week. February 2 was Wednesday. Moiseenko declared that Monday was the last time the Grand Duke had driven to his office. Knowing the Grand Duke's habits we concluded that on February 3, 4, or 5 he would certainly drive to the governor-general's palace on the Tverskaia [Street]. We could not even think of assassinating him on February 3, the day after our failure. Kaliaev and Kulikovskii could not apparently rely upon themselves. The assassination was postponed to the fourth or fifth. On the morning of February 3 Kaliaev and Kulikovskii were to leave Moscow, to return the next day. This gave them an opportunity to get some rest. To save time on the day of the assassination we decided where they were to meet me to get the bombs. Dora Brilliant had unloaded the bombs. She was thus compelled to load them again. On Friday, February 4, at one o'clock in the afternoon, I came to the "Slavianskii Bazaar" and received the bombs, wrapped, as on the first occasion, in a blanket.

I got into Moiseenko's sleigh, but we had hardly gone a few steps when he turned to me and said:

"Have you seen the 'poet'?"

"Yes."

"Well, how is he?"

"What do you mean how? He's all right."

"Well, and I have seen Kulikovskii."

"Well?"

"Very bad."

From his coach box he told me that Kulikovskii had arrived in Moscow in the morning and told him he could not take part in the assassination. Kulikovskii said he had overestimated his powers and realized now, after what had taken place February 2, that he could not engage in terrorist work. Moiseenko told me this without comment.

The situation looked difficult. It was necessary to choose; either I or Moiseenko had to take part in the assassination or let Kaliaev be the only one to hurl the bomb.

Moiseenko was a cab driver. His arrest would have exposed our methods to the police. I had an English passport. My arrest would have caused much trouble for James Halley, the Englishman who gave it to me. So, we could not take part in a new assassination immediately—at least not until Moiseenko had sold his horse and sleigh and changed his passport, or until I had obtained another. This meant it would be necessary for Dora Brilliant again to unload and load the bombs. Remembering Pokotilov's death I was not keen on permitting this any oftener than was absolutely necessary.[3]

On the other hand, it seemed rather risky to stage the assassination with Kaliaev alone. We knew the Grand Duke's route. He was to drive through the Nikolskii and Iverskii Gates along the Tverskaia to his home in the square. I feared that with but one man in action the Grand Duke might only be wounded. The attempt would then have to be regarded as a failure.

I had to make the decision immediately, while in the sleigh, for Kaliaev awaited me a short distance away, in Iushkov Lane. Kulikovskii failed to appear for his bomb. On the same day, in the evening, he left town and was arrested in Moscow several months later. He escaped from the Prechistenka police station, and on June 28, 1905, while being sought by the police all over Russia, appeared openly at a reception of Count Shuvalov, Mayor of Moscow, and shot him. For this killing he was sentenced to death by the Moscow military tribunal. The sentence was commuted to an indeterminate term at hard labor. He had proven, contrary to his own opinion, that his lack of "nerve" in the case of the Grand Duke Sergei was no evidence that he was unfit for terrorist activity.

On approaching Kaliaev I decided to postpone the assassination to such time as either I or Moiseenko could take direct part in it, and when he entered the sleigh I told him of Kulikovskii's refusal and suggested the postponement. Kaliaev became excited:

"Not under any circumstances. We can't subject Dora again to this danger. I take everything upon myself."

I pointed out that he alone was not enough, that there was the possibility of failure, of an accidental explosion or arrest, but he would not listen to me.

"You say one man is not enough? And were we really two the day before yesterday? I was in one place and Kulikovskii in another. Where was the reserve? Why not today?"

I replied we had dynamite for only two bombs, that on February 2 we were compelled to place two men in different spots because we did not know how the Grand Duke would drive to the theater, that the situation was different today, that it would be best to take no chances but to wait a few days and arrange the assassination with two men.

Kaliaev replied:

"Don't you really trust me? I tell you I can handle it myself."

I knew Kaliaev. I knew that none of us could be so confident of himself as he. I knew he would hurl the bomb only in the very front of the carriage, and not before, and that he would be master of himself to the end. But I was afraid of accidents.

I said:

"Listen here, Ianek, I do think it would be better to have two men. Imagine, if we fail! What then?"

He said:

"Failure is out of the question."

His self-confidence moved me. He continued:

"If the Grand Duke appears I will surely kill him. You may be quite sure of that."

At this moment Moiseenko turned to us from his coach box:

"Make up your mind, quick. It's time."

I made the decision: Kaliaev was to meet the Grand Duke single-handed.

We got out of the sleigh and walked together along the Ilynka to the Red Square. As we approached the place the clock on the Kremlin tower struck two. Kaliaev stopped.

"Good-bye, Ianek."

"Good-bye."

He kissed me and turned toward the Nikolskii Gate. I passed through Spasskii Tower into the Kremlin and stopped before the monument of Alexander II. From this point the Grand Duke's palace could be seen. The carriage stood at the entrance. I recognized the coachman Rudinkin. I realized the Grand Duke would soon be on his way to his office.

I walked past the palace and the carriage and through the Nikolskii Gate to the Tverskaia. I had an appointment with Dora Brilliant in a pastry shop on Kuznetzkii Bridge and was hurrying to meet the appointment in time to return to the Kremlin at the moment of the explosion. When I reached Kuznetzkii Bridge I heard a muffled sound in the distance, but paid no attention to it because it did not seem to me like the detonation of an explosion. I met Dora in the pastry shop. We walked out to the Tverskaia and in the direction of the Kremlin. At the Iverskaia [Gate] we were met by a street urchin, without cap, shouting:

"The Grand Duke has been killed. His head was torn off."

Crowds of people were running toward the Kremlin. At the Nikolskii Gate the crowd was so large it was impossible to pass. Dora and I stopped. Suddenly I heard:

"Here, *barin*, a cab."

I turned around. Moiseenko, pale, was offering us his sleigh. Slowly we drove away from the Kremlin. Moiseenko asked:

"Did you hear it?"

"No."

"I was standing here and heard the explosion. The Grand Duke is killed."

At that moment Dora let her head fall on my shoulder and, unable to restrain her tears any longer, broke out weeping. Her entire body shook in a spasm. I tried to comfort her, but she wept even louder, repeating:

"We have killed him.... I killed him.... I ..."

"Whom?" I asked, thinking she was referring to Kaliaev.

"The Grand Duke."

Historical-Cultural Contexts • *Boris Savinkov*

NOTES [IMD]

1. The narrator is Boris Savinkov (1879-1925), a prominent member of the Socialist-Revolutionary Party's *Battle Organization* that engaged in anti-Tsarist terrorism. He planned the assassinations of the Minister of the Interior V. K. von Plehve (Pleve) and of Grand Duke Sergei, described here. He also was a minor writer, author of the novel *The Pale Horse* (1909 written under the pseudonym Ropshin), as well as of the *Memoirs of a Terrorist* (1917) from which the above excerpt is taken. One of his main themes in the novel, as well as in the *Memoirs* is the psychological and spiritual effect terrorist activity has on those engaged in it, especially those with religious convictions (as Ivan—Ianek—Kaliaev in the excerpt). Savinkov fought against the Bolsheviks during the Civil War, escaping to France after the defeat of the Whites. He died in a Soviet prison after returning—remorsefully—to the Soviet Union. It is unclear whether his death was suicide, accident or murder

2. Ivan Kaliaev (1877–1905) threw the bomb that killed Grand Duke Sergei, in 1905, as described here. He was executed refusing the reprieve that Grand Duchess Elizabeth, the wife of the Grand Duke, a very pious woman, offered him on the condition he would make a statement of repentance. French writer Albert Camus made him the hero of his play *The Just Assassins (Les Justes)*. Kaliaev wrote religious poetry. He is also portrayed in Savinkov's novel *The Pale Horse* where he is Vania.

3. He accidentally killed himself while making a bomb.

MODERNIST VIEWS ON ART
IN ESSAYS AND MANIFESTOS, CRITICISM

KEYS TO THE MYSTERIES

by Valerii BRIUSOV*

* Valerii Bryusov
** From *The Russian Symbolists: An Anthology of Critical and Theoretical Writings*, Ronald E. Peterson, ed. and trans. Ann Arbor: Ardis, 1986. Pp. 52-64.

I

When unsophisticated people are confronted with the question "What is art?" they do not try to comprehend where it came from, what place it holds in the universe, but accept it as a fact, and only want to find some application for it to their lives. Thus arise the theories of useful art, the most primitive stage in the relationship between man's thought and art. It seems natural to people that art, if it exists, should be suitable for their dearest small needs and necessities. They forget there are many things in the world that are completely useless in terms of human life, like beauty, for example, and that they themselves constantly commit acts that are totally useless—they love and they dream.

It seems ridiculous to us now, of course, when [the Italian poet] Tasso assures us that poetic inventions are similar to the "sweets" that are used to coat the edge of a dish with bitter medicine; we read, with a smile, Derzhavin's poems to Catherine the Great, in which he compares poetry to sweet lemonade.[1] But did not Pushkin, partially under the influence of echoes of Schelling's philosophy and partially arriving at the same opinions independently, reproach the dark masses for seeking "usefulness" and say that they were worth less than a "cooking pot," and didn't his tongue slip in "Monument" [*Pamiatnik*] when he wrote these verses:

> And I will long be the favorite of the people,
> Because I aroused good feelings with my lyre.[2]

And didn't Zhukovskii,[3] adapting Pushkin's poems for print, furnish the following line in a more direct way: "That I was useful because of the vital charm of my verses...," which gave [the advocate of utilitarianism] Pisarev cause for rejoicing.[4]

In the greater public, the public that knows art in terms of serialized novels, operatic productions, symphonic concerts, and exhibits of paintings, the conviction that art's function is to provide noble diversion prevails, indivisibly, to this day. Dancing at balls, skating, playing cards—these are also diversions, but less noble ones; and people who belong to the intelligentsia, meanwhile, read Korolenko,[5] or even Maeterlinck [Belgian playwright], listen to [the bass] Shaliapin, go to the *Peredvizhnaia* [mobile art exhibitions of realist painters, usually depicting social issues], and to decadents' exhibits. A novel helps to pass the time in a train or in bed, before falling asleep; you meet acquaintances at the opera, and find diversion at art exhibits. And these people attain their goals, they really relax, laugh, are entertained and fall asleep.

None other than Ruskin, an "apostle of beauty," speaks out in his books as a defender of "utilitarian art."[6] He advised his pupils to draw olive leaves and rose petals, in order to discover for themselves and to give others more information than we have had up to now about Grecian olives and England's wild roses. He advised them to reproduce cliffs, mountains, and individual rocks, in order to obtain a more complete understanding of the characteristics of mountainous structure. He advised them rather to depict ancient, disappearing ruins, so that their images could be preserved, at least on canvas, for the curiosity of future ages. "Art," says Ruskin, "gives

Form to knowledge, and Grace to utility; that is to say, it makes permanently visible to us things which otherwise could neither be described by our science, nor retained by our memory." And more: "the entire vitality of art depends upon its being either full of truth or full of use. Great masters could permit themselves in awkwardness, but they will never permit themselves in uselessness or unveracity."

A very widespread, if not prevailing, school of literary historians treats poetry in the same way that Ruskin does the plastic arts. They see in poetry only the exact reproduction of life, from which it is possible to learn the customs and mores of that time and country where the poetic work was created. They carefully study descriptions of the poet, the psychology of the characters he has created, his own psychology, passing on then to the psychologies of his contemporaries and the characteristics of his times. They are totally convinced that the whole sense of literature is to help in the study of life in this or that century, and that readers and poets themselves fail to realize this, as uneducated people, and simply remain in error.

Thus the theory of "useful art" has rather eminent supporters, even in our time. It is more than obvious, however, that it is impossible to stretch this theory to cover all the manifestations of art, that it is ridiculously small for it, as a dwarf's caftan would be for the Spirit of the Earth. It is impossible to limit all art to Sudermann and Bourget, just to please the good bourgeois, who want "noble diversions" from art.[7] Much in art does not come under the concept of "pleasure," if one considers this word only in its natural sense, and does not put the term "aesthetic pleasure" under it, because it does not say anything and itself demands an explanation. Art terrifies, it shakes us, it makes us cry. In art there is an Aeschylus, an Edgar Allen Poe, a Dostoevskii. Just recently L. Tolstoi, with his customary accuracy of expression, compared those who seek only pleasures in art to people who would try to convince us that the only goal of eating is the pleasure of taste.

It is also just as impossible to please science and knowledge by seeing only reflections of life in art. Although the most divine Leonardo wrote essays about *come lo specchio e maestro de' pittori,*[8] and although until recently in literature and the plastic arts, "realism" seemed to be the final word (that is what is written in today's textbooks)—art has never reproduced but has always changed reality: even in da Vinci's pictures, even among the most ardent realist authors, like [Honorée] Balzac, our Gogol', and [Émile] Zola. There is no art that can repeat reality. In the external world, nothing exists that corresponds to architecture and music. Neither the Cologne cathedral nor Beethoven's symphonies can reproduce what surrounds us. In sculpture there is only a form without any paint, in a painting there are only colors without form, but in life, however, the one and the other are inseparable. Sculpture and painting give immobile moments, but in life everything flows in time. Sculpture and painting repeat only the exterior of objects: neither marble nor bronze is able to render the texture of skin; a statue has no heart, lungs, or internal organs; there are no hidden minerals in a drawing of a mountain ridge. Poetry is deprived of any embodiment in space; it snatches up only separate moments and scenes from countless feelings, from the uninterrupted flow of events. Drama unites the means of painting and sculpture with the means of poetry, but beyond the decoration of the room there are no other parts of the apartment, no streets, no city; the actor who goes off into the wings stops being Prince Hamlet; what in actuality lasted twenty years can be seen on the stage in two hours.

Art never deceives people, with the exception of anecdotal cases, like the foolish birds pecking at fruits painted by Zeuxis.[9] No one believes a picture is a view through an open window, no one greets the bust of his acquaintance, and not one author has been sentenced to prison for an imaginary crime in a story. Besides, we refuse to call artistic precisely those works which reproduce reality with a singular resemblance. We recognize neither panoramas nor wax statues as art. And what has been accomplished if art succeeds in mimicking nature? Of what use can the doubling of reality be? "The advantage of a painted tree over a real one," says August Schlegel [one of the writers and theoreticians of the German Romantic movement], "is only that there won't be any caterpillars on it." Botanists will never study a plant according to drawings. The most expertly depicted marina will never replace a view of the ocean for the traveler, if only because a salty breeze will not blow in his face and the sounds of waves crashing against the beach rocks will not be heard. We will leave the reproduction of reality to photography and the phonograph—technicians' inventions. "Art belongs to reality as wine does to grapes," [Franz] Grillparzer [Austrian playwright]) said.

The defenders of "utilitarian art" have, it's true, one refuge. Art does not serve the goals of science. But it can serve society, the social order. The use of art could be that it unites separate personalities, transfusing one person's feelings into another so that it welds the classes of society into one whole and helps their historic struggle among themselves. Art from this point of view is only one means of communication for people among a number of different means, which are, first of all, the word, then writing, the press, the telegraph, the telephone. The common word and prose speech render thoughts, art renders feelings... Guyau defended such a sphere of thought with force and wit.[10] Here in Russia, L. Tolstoi has recently preached the same ideas, in a slightly altered form.

But does this theory really explain why artists create and why audiences, readers, and viewers seek artistic impressions? When sculptors knead clay, when painters cover canvases with paints, when poets seek the right word in order to express what they have to—not one of them sets his mind on transmitting his feelings to others. We know of artists who have scorned humanity, who have created only for themselves, without a goal, without the intention of making their works public. Is there really no self-satisfaction in creation? Did not Pushkin say to the artist: "Your work is your reward?"[11] And why don't the readers cut this telegraph line between themselves and the soul of the artist? What is there for them in the feelings of someone they don't know, who may have lived many years ago, in another country? The task of scholarship about art is to solve the riddle of what consolidates the artist's dark cravings and the corresponding cravings of his listeners and viewers. And there is no solution in the scholastic answer: "art is useful because it facilitates the intercourse of feelings; and we want intercourse by feelings because we have a special instinct for communication."

• *Valerii Briusov*

The stubbornness of the advocates of "utilitarian art," despite all attacks on them by European thinkers of the last century, has not weakened yet and will probably not run dry as long as arguments about art continue to exist. There is always the possibility of pointing to its usefulness in one way or another. But how easy it is to use this object—that force! Archeologists learn about ancient life from the remains of buildings, but we don't build houses so that their ruins can help archeologists in the twenty-fifth century. Graphologists affirm that it is possible to learn about the character of a person from his handwriting. But the Phoenicians (according to the myth) invented writing for an entirely different purpose. The peasant in Krylov's fable condemned the ax to cut chips. The ax noted with justification that it was not guilty of being dull.[12] In Mark Twain's book about the prince and pauper, poor Tom, once he is in the palace, uses the state seal to crack nuts. Perhaps Tom cracked nuts very successfully, but the state "seal was meant to be used for other things.

II

People who think differently, who put aside the question of what art is needed for, what use it is, have asked themselves another metaphysical question: What is art? Separating art from life, they examine its creations as something self-important, self-contained. Thus arose the theories of "pure art"—the second stage in the relationship between man's thought and art. Carried away by the struggle with the defenders of applied, utilitarian art, these people have gone to the other extreme and have affirmed that art need never have any kind of utility, that art is diametrically opposed to all profit, all purpose: art is purposeless. Our [Ivan] Turgenev has expressed these thoughts with merciless frankness: "Art has no purpose other than art itself." And in a letter to [the poet] [Afanasii] Fet, he is even more explicit: "It's not that useless art is rubbish; uselessness is precisely the diamond in its crown." When the supporters of these views asked: what unites into one class the creations that people recognize as artistic, the pictures of Raphael, and Byron's verses, and Mozart's melodies—why is all of this art?—what do they have in common? They answered—Beauty!

....

When the theory of pure art had just been created, it was possible to understand that beauty meant exactly what it means in the language. It was possible to apply the word "beautiful" to almost every work of ancient art and to art of the time of pseudo-classicism. The nude bodies of statues, the images of gods and heroes were beautiful; tragedies' myths were sublimely beautiful. There were, however, hanged slaves, incest... in Greek sculpture and poetry—which did not fit too well with the concept of beauty. Aristotle and his later imitator [Nicolas] Boileau [literary "law-giver" of French classicism] had to advise artists to depict ugliness in such a way that it seemed, nevertheless, attractive. But the Romantics and their successors, the realists, rejected this embellishment of reality. All the world's ugliness invaded artistic works. Deformed faces, rags, the pitiful conditions of reality stepped out into pictures; novels and poems changed their place of action from regal castles to dank cellars and smoky attics. Poetry took on the hustle and bustle of everyday life, with the vices, horrors, and vanity of the petty, commonplace, little people of today...

....

In addition, even the very concept of beauty is not immutable. There is no special, universal measure of beauty. Beauty is no more than an abstraction, a common notion, similar to the notions of truth, good, and many other widespread generalizations of human thought. Beauty varies with the centuries. Beauty is different for different centuries. What was beautiful to the Assyrians seems ugly to us; fashionable clothes, which captivated Pushkin by their beauty, arouse laughter in us; what the Chinese now consider beautiful is foreign to us. But in the meantime, works of art from all ages and all nations conquer us equally. History was recently a witness to how Japanese art subjugated all of Europe, even though beauty in these two worlds is completely different. There is inalterability and immortality in art, which beauty doesn't have. And the marble statues of the Pergamon altar[13] are eternal not because they are beautiful, but because art has inspired its own life in them, independent of beauty.

In order to reconcile the theory of "pure art" with the facts somewhat, its defenders have had to violate the notion of beauty in every possible way. Since ancient times, when speaking about art, they began to give the concept of "beauty" different, often rather unexpected meanings. Beauty was identified with perfection, with unity in diversity; it was sought in undulating lines, in softness, in moderateness of dimensions. "The unfortunate notion of beauty," says a German critic, "has been stretched in all directions, as if it were made of rubber...they say that, in relation to art, the word 'beauty' should be understood in a broader sense, but it would be better to say too broad a sense. To affirm that Ugolino is beautiful in a broader sense is the same as avowing that evil is good in a broader sense and that a slave is a master in a broader sense."[14]

The substitution of the word "typicality" for "beauty" has enjoyed particular success. People have assured us that works of art are beautiful because they represent types. But if you lay these two concepts one on top the other, they are far from congruent. Beauty is not always typical, and not everything typical is beautiful. *Le beau c'est rare*,[15] says one whole school of art. Emerald green eyes seem beautiful to many people, although they are rarely encountered. Winged human figures in Eastern pictures are striking because of their beauty, but they are the fruit of fantasy and themselves create their own types. On the other hand, are there not animals that are ugly by their very distinguishing marks, which are impossible to depict typically in any other way than ugly? Such as cuttle-fish, skates, spiders, and caterpillars? And the types of all inner ugliness, all vices, all that is base in a man, or stupid, or trite—how could they become beauty? And isn't the new art, more and more boldly entering into the world of individual, personal feelings, sensations of the moment and of just this moment, breaking absolutely and forever with the specter of typicality?

In one place Pushkin speaks about the "science of love," about "love for love," and notes:

> ... this important amusement,
> Praised in our forefathers' time,
> Is worthy of old apes.[16]

These same words can be repeated about "art for art's sake." It separates art from life, i.e., from the only soil on which something can grow into humanity. Art for the sake of aimless Beauty (with a capital letter) is dead art. No matter how irreproachable the sonnet's form, no matter how beautiful the marble face of a bust, if there is nothing beyond these sounds, beyond the marble, what will attract me to it? Man's spirit cannot be reconciled with static peace. *"Je hais le movement qui deplace les lignes"* —I hate any movement that displaces lines," says [the French poet] Baudelaire's Beauty. But art is always seeking, always an outburst, and Baudelaire himself poured not deathly immobility, but whirlpools of grief, despair, and damnation into his chiseled sonnets. The same state seal that Tom used to crack nuts in the palace probably sparkled very prettily in the sun. But even its beautiful shine was not its purpose. It was created for something greater.

III

People of science have approached art in completely different ways. Science has no pretensions about penetrating the essence of things. Science knows only the relations of the phenomena, knows only how to compare and contrast them. Science cannot examine anything without knowing its relation to another thing. Science's conclusions are observations about correlations between objects and phenomena.

Relying on this truth, science has naturally discovered two ways of studying art: studying the emotional excitement that seizes the viewer, reader, or listener when he surrenders to artistic impressions, and studying the emotional excitement that prompts an artist to create. Science started out on these two paths, but almost from the first step it lost its way.

We must recognize as hopelessly unsuccessful the attempt to connect the study of aesthetic excitement, those impressions that works of art give us, with physiology. The connection between psychological and physiological facts poses a riddle for science even in the most elementary phenomena. It still cannot explain the transition between the prick of a pin to the sensation of pain. The desire to reduce immeasurably complex artistic emotions to something like the pleasant or unpleasant movement of the eyeball cannot provide us with anything but a subject for ridicule. Every physiological explanation of aesthetic phenomena goes no further than dubious analyses. We could achieve the same measure of success looking for answers to the questions of higher mathematics in physiology (at its present stage of development).

Psychology could do no more here. But even this science, which Maeterlinck said had "usurped the beautiful name of Psyche," is also still far from maturity. Up to now it has investigated only the simplest phenomena of our spiritual life, although with a flippancy characteristic of children, it hastens to affirm that it already knows everything, that there is nothing else in the human spirit, and if there is, it is carried out according to the same models. Finding itself confronted by one of the most mysterious phenomena of human spiritual existence, the sphinx-like riddle of art, psychology began to solve this complex mathematical problem, which demands the most refined methods of advanced analysis, using only the four principles of arithmetic. The problem remained unresolved, of course, the answer obtained was most arbitrary. But psychology announced that the work had been done. And if the facts themselves did not fit the pattern, so much the worse for the facts!

Psychological aesthetics gathered a number of phenomena, which it recognized as "direct producers of aesthetic sensation," such as, for example, in the area of vision: combinations of chiaroscuros, harmonies of colors and their unification with luster, the beauty of complex movements and forms, the proportions of parts, the firm and soft support of weight,—or in the area of sound: special combinations of tones called melody and harmony, tempo, emphasis, cadence. It added various pleasant sensations, procured by means of association, to these "producers." And psychological aesthetics now intends to solve the question of art with addition and subtraction, without even using "multiplication and division." They seriously think that every artistic creation can be divided, in its crudest sense, into these basic elements: brilliance, curvature, and melody, and that after this division there is no remainder.

Without even saying that the simplicity of many of these quasi-elements is extremely dubious, the whole matter comes down to the fact that only in art do these impressions evoke "aesthetic excitement." We all know the brilliance of the sun, it is often pretty, pleasant, one can find pleasure in it; but there is none of that unique thrill in it that works of art pour into everyone who truly knows how to cling to it. But in a poem, where the same sun is depicted, although it is made of verses and "does not enlighten" (Lotze's expression)—it shines for us with an entirely special brilliance, the brilliance of a work of art. And it is like this everywhere.

....

Another path has led science to study the emotional excitement that causes man to sculpt statues, to paint pictures, to compose poems. Science has begun to try to find out what kind of desires attract the artist, compel him to work—sometimes to exhaustion—and find self-satisfaction in his work. And that spirit that wafted over science in the century just past, which in its time removed things and phenomena from their places, even though they seemed immobile to the philosophical eighteenth century, turned them into an uncontrollable stream of the eternally changing, eternally evolving world, the spirit of evolutionism—this spirit fixed the researchers' attention on the origin of art. As in many other cases, science substituted the word to "become" for the word to "be" and began to investigate not "What is art" but "Where did art come from," thinking that it was answering one and the same question. And so detailed research appeared about the origin of art among aboriginal people and savages, about the crude powerless rudiments of ornament, sculpture, music, poetry... Science thought it would solve the mystery of art by analyzing its genealogical tree.

In its own way, the theory of heredity was applied here, with the assurance that a child's soul depends entirely on the combination of his ancestors' spiritual characteristics.

The investigation of art's ancestors led to the theory that was first expressed by [the German poet] Schiller with complete definiteness. Spencer picked up and developed this theory in passing, but with overwhelming scientific detail. The forefather of art was recognized as: the game. Lower animals do not play games at all. Those who, thanks to better nutrition, have a surplus of nervous energy, feel the need to expend it—and they spend it on games. Mankind spends it on art. A rat that gnaws on things that are not good for it, a cat that plays with a ball of yarn, and especially children playing are already indulging in artistic activity. It seemed to Schiller that he was not debasing the significance of art at all with this theory. "Man," he says, "plays only when he is a person in the full sense of the word, and he is only a person when he plays." This theory adjoins, of course, to the theories of useless art, which Spencer realizes: "To seek an end, which would serve life, i. e., good and utility," he writes, "inevitably means to lose sight of its aesthetic character."[17]

Similar to the other scientific solution to the enigma of art, this theory is also too broad to accurately define art, as the theories of "utilitarian" and "pure" art were too narrow. In its search for the simplest elements that make up aesthetic excitement, science has offered elements that are often not art and which completely fail to explain the idiosyncratic, unique influence of art. In its search for what causes us to be attracted to a creation, it has also named things that often do not lead to art at all. If all art is a game, then why is not every game art? How can we draw a boundary between them? Are not children playing with a ball more like adults playing cards than Michelangelo creating David? And why was this Michelangelo an artist when he sculpted his statues and was not an artist when he played knuckle bones? And why do we recognize aesthetic excitement when we listen to the flight of the Valkyries [in Wagner's opera *The Valkyrie*] but are only amused when we watch kittens playing? How, finally, do we explain that admiration which artists of all ages arouse in mankind: we see them as prophets, as life's leaders, as teachers. Are [Norwegian playwright] [Henrik] Ibsen and L. Tolstoi only organizers of the great, universal games of our days?

....

IV

The most striking thing is that all these theories have irrefutable facts behind them. Art gives us pleasure—who's going to argue! Art teaches—we know this from thousands of examples. But together with this there are often no easily attainable goals, no use, in art— only fanatics can deny this. Finally, art unites people, opens the heart, makes everyone communicants of the artist's creation. What is art? How can it be both useful and useless? serve Beauty and often be ugly? be a means of communication and seclude the artist?

The only method that can hope to answer these questions is intuition, inspired guessing—the method that philosophers and thinkers, who have sought the solution to the mystery of existence, have used in all ages. And I will point to one solution to the enigma of art that belongs precisely to a philosopher, which—it seems to me—gives an explanation to all those contradictions. This is the answer of [Arthur] Schopenhauer. The philosopher's own aesthetics are too closely tied to his metaphysics. But, tearing his guessing loose from the restricting chains of his thought, freeing his teachings about art from his accidentally entangled teachings about "ideas," the intermediaries between the worlds of *noumena* and *phenomena*— we arrive at a simple and clear truth: art is the comprehension of the world by other, non-rational ways. Art is what in other areas we call revelation. Works of art are doors half-opened to Eternity.

The world's phenomena, as they open up to us in the universe— extended in space and flowing in time, subject to the law of causality—must be studied by the methods of science, by rationality. But this study, based on the indications of our higher senses, gives us only approximate knowledge. Our eyes deceive us, attributing characteristics of a sunny ray to a flower that we are looking at. Our ears deceive us, reckoning vibrations of air as characteristics of a ringing bell. All our consciousness deceives us, transferring its characteristics, the conditions of its activity, to external objects. We live in the midst of an eternal, primordial lie. A thought, and consequently science, are powerless to expose this lie. The most that they could do is to point it out, to explain its inevitability. Science only brings order to the chaos of false concepts and arranges them according to rank, making it possible, making it easier to learn about them, but not to have cognition of them.

But we are not hopelessly locked in this "blue prison," using Fet's image. Signs are those moments of ecstasy, of super-sensible intuition, that offer different comprehensions of worldly phenomena, that penetrate more deeply under their external covering, into their core. The primordial task of art consists of fixing forever these moments of insight, of inspiration. Art begins at the instant when the artist tries to make his dark, mysterious sensations clear to himself. Where there is none of this clarification, there is no artistic creation. Where there is no mystery in a feeling, there is no art. A person for whom everything in the world is simple, clear, attainable, cannot become an artist. Art is only where there is audacity beyond the edge, breaking through the boundaries of the cognizable with the craving to scoop up "at least a drop" of

An alien element, from the beyond.[18]

"The gates of Beauty lead to cognition," said the same Schiller. In all the centuries of their existence, unconsciously, but unchangingly, artists have carried out their mission: to explain the mysteries revealed to them, and at the same time they have sought other, more perfect means of attaining cognizance of the universe. When the savage drew zigzags on his shield and affirmed that it was a "Serpent," he had already performed an act of cognition. In the same way the ancient marble statues, the images of Goethe's *Faust*, Tiutchev's poems—all of these are precisely renderings, in a visible, tangible form, of those insights that the artist had. True cognitions of things in them was revealed to the degree of completeness that the imperfect materials of art (marble, paints, sounds, words...) allowed.

But in the course of long centuries, art has not given a clear and definite account of its purpose. Various aesthetic theories knocked artists off the path. And they raised idols, instead of praying to the true god. The history of the new art is primarily a history of its liberation. Romanticism, Realism, and Symbolism are three stages in the struggle of artists for freedom. They have finally thrown off the chains of enslavement to different random goals. Now art is finally free.

Now it is consciously devoted to its highest and singular purpose: to be the world's cognition beyond rational forms, beyond thinking about causality. Don't hinder this new art in its task, which at another time might seem useless and alien to present-day needs. You measure its use and modernity with standards that are too short. Our personal benefit is tied to the benefit of mankind. All of us live in eternity. Those questions of existence that art can answer will never stop being topical. Art is perhaps the greatest power that mankind possesses. At the same time when all the crowbars of science, all the axes of public life, are not able to break down the walls and doors that enclose us—art conceals within itself awesome dynamite, which can shatter those walls, and moreover it is the *sesame* that makes doors open by themselves. Let contemporary artists consciously forge their works in the shape of keys to the mysteries, in the shape of mystical keys that will unlock for mankind the doors of its "blue prison" to eternal freedom.

1904

RONALD E. PETERSON'S NOTES

1. *Derzhavin*—Gavriil Derzhavin (1743-1816), Russian poet; the reference about "lemonade" is from his ode "Felitsa," published in 1783.

2. *Pushkin*—Aleksandr Pushkin (1799-1837), Russia's greatest poet; the "cooking pot" statement is from Pushkin's "Poet i tolpa" (The Poet and the Crowd), 1828; the two lines quoted are from his "Ia pamiatnik sebe vozdvig nerukotvornyi" (I Built a Monument for Myself— the monument is his poetry), 1836.

3. *Zhukovskii*—Vasilii Zhukovskii (1783-1868), Russian poet and translator; Zhukovskii was compelled to change certain lines in Pushkin's "Monument" poem, because of the censors, when he published the poem after Pushkin's death.

4. *Pisarev*—Dmitrii Pisarev (1840-1868), Russian writer and critic; Briusov is referring to Pisarev's article about Pushkin's lyrics in the book *Pushkin i Belinskii* (1865).

5. *Korolenko*—Vladimir Korolenko (1853-1921), Russian author who was popular at the time.

6. *Ruskin*—John Ruskin; see his *Lectures on Art*, delivered at Oxford University in 1870, especially the lecture "The Relation of Art to Use."

7. *Sudermann* and *Bourget*. [H.] Sudermann (1857-1928), German dramatist, and P. Bourget (1852-1935), French Naturalist writer; both were quite popular in Russia at the time.

8. *Come lo specchio e maestro de' pittori*—"how the mirror is the teacher of the artists."

9. *Zeuxis*—Greek painter (420-380 B.C.), who according to the legend painted grapes so realistically that birds pecked at them.

10. *Guyau*—Jean Marie Guyau (1854-1888), French philosopher.

11. *Pushkin*—the quotation is from Pushkin's unfinished novel in verse, "Ezerskii" (1833).

12. *Krylov*—Ivan Krylov (1768-1844), author of numerous fables; the one Briusov has in mind is Krylov's "Krest'ianin i topor" (The Peasant and the Ax), 1816.

13. *Pergamon*—a city in Greece; the altar (second century B.C.) was dedicated to Zeus and depicts mythological themes.

14. *Ugolino*—Count Ugolino, a character in Dante's *Inferno* (Canto XXXIII).

15. *Le beau c'est rare*—"Beauty is rare."

16. *Pushkin*—the quotation is taken from Pushkin's novel in verse *Evgenii Onegin* (4, VIII), published as a book first in 1833.

17. *Spencer*—Herbert Spencer (1820-1903).

18. *Fet*—the reference to a "blue prison" is from Fet's "Pamiati N. Danilevskogo" (To the Memory of N. Danilevskii), written in 1886; the line quoted is from Fet's "Lastochki" (Swallows), 1885.

Two Tendencies of Contemporary Lyric Poetry[1]

by Viktor ZHIRMUNSKII*

Translated by *John Glad*

* V.M. Zhirmunsky

**From *The Silver Age of Russian Culture*, Carl Proffer and Ellendea Proffer, eds. Ann Arbor: Ardis, 1975. Pp. 60-65.

Russian lyric poetry of the last quarter of the (nineteenth) century developed under the banner of Symbolism. Although the overcoming of Symbolism has long been a topic of discussion, it is only recently—just shortly before the (First World) War—that a poetic school has arisen that broke with the precepts of Symbolism in its very foundations. The poetic progenitor of this school was M. A. Kuzmin. The participants in the new movement gave their artistic faith the bizarre and meaningless name of "Acmeism." In their poetic manifestos they renounced the romantic mysticism which had dominated the poetic work and world-view of the older poets. Instead of a poetry of hints, allegories and symbols, the vaguely disturbing quality of which had a musical effect, they demanded clarity, completeness and firmness of poetic images, logical exactitude and concreteness (*veshchestvennost'*) in words and word combinations. Whereas the Symbolists loved to repeat the words of Verlaine—"Music above all else!"—the theoretician of the new poetic school, [Nikolai] Gumilev, quoted the demand of Theophile Gautier: "Creation is the more perfect/The more passionless the material!/ Be it verse, marble or metal..."

In this collision of two literary generations we are not witnessing an accidental competition of minor, uninteresting literary cliques, but rather a deep break in poetic feeling—perhaps still deeper than the transition from the lyric poetry of the 1880s to the art of the Symbolists. [Konstantin] Bal'mont continues the tradition of [Afanasii] Fet; [Aleksandr] Blok is internally connected to the lyricism of Vladimir Solov'ev. Bal'mont and Kuzmin, Blok and [Anna] Akhmatova, contemporaries by chance who are often close to each other in poetic themes, belong to artistic worlds that differ essentially and represent two types of art that are nearly opposites.

We will attempt to show this difference in a comparison of two poems of Blok and Akhmatova which are similar in theme but differ entirely in thematic treatment; a particular instance of such comparison will serve to illustrate our general conclusions more convincingly. Blok's poem is entitled "In the Restaurant."

> Never shall I forget (did it take place or not—
> This evening); in a blaze of dawn[2]
> The pale sky flamed out and was shoved aside,
> And in the yellow dawn were lanterns.
> I sat at the window in the overfilled hall.
> Somewhere were bows singing of love,
> I sent you a black rose in a goblet
> Of "Ai" that was as gold as the sky.
> You looked. Confused and bold,
> I met Your haughty gaze and bowed.
> Turning to your escort, with intentional harshness
> You said: "This one's head over heels too."
> And immediately the strings thundered something in reply,
> The bows sang out hysterically...
> But you were with me in your young contempt,
> In the hardly noticeable quiver of your hand...
> You tore away like a frightened bird,
> You passed—light as my dream...
> And perfumes sighed, lashes dreamed,
> Anxiously silks began to whisper.

> But from the depths of mirrors you cast glances at me,
> And casting them, shouted: "Catch."
> And the necklace tinkled, and the gypsy danced
> And howled to the dawn of love.

Akhmatova's poem is entitled "In the Evening."

> The music grated in the garden
> With such inexpressible grief.
> The iced oysters on the plate
> Smelled freshly and sharply of the sea.
> He said to me: "I am a true friend!"
> And touched my dress...
> How unlike caresses
> Are the touches of these hands.
> As if one were patting cats or birds...
> Or watching graceful circus riders...
> Only laughter in his calm eyes
> Under the light gold of the lashes.
> But the mournful voices of the violins
> Sing behind the floating smoke:
> "Bless the heavens;
> You are alone with your beloved for the first time."

Both poems are written on a similar theme; the country garden, the restaurant, the music, and the meeting with the loved one are repeated in both. The more particular features showing similarity, such as the "voices of the violins" which "sing" ("Somewhere bows were singing of love"), are evidence of a possible influence on Akhmatova, particularly in view of the fact that Blok's poem is one of his more famous ones. But there is a deep underlying difference behind the thematic similarity. Blok is depicting an event of mystical content, saturated with boundless significance; Akhmatova has produced a simple everyday meeting, although it is subjectively significant. What devices are used to create this difference of impressions?

Blok begins with the words: "Never shall I forget (did it take place or not—this evening)." Thus he immediately creates the impression of unity, unusualness, and the exclusiveness of this rendezvous. But is he relating a dream or did this actually happen? The same doubt as to the reality of the image of the beautiful is expressed in "The Stranger" ("Neznakomka"):

> And every evening, at the appointed hour,
> (Or do I only dream this?)
> A girl's figure, swathed in silks,
> Moves in the murky window...

And the same consciousness of the singularity of the beautiful object and doubt as to its reality are repeated below: "You passed—light as my dream." Akhmatova, however, knows that this happened, not in a dream, but in living reality, recalled in all its details: "The iced oysters on the plate smelled freshly and sharply of the sea."

Blok frames his poem with the use of the symbolic image of "dawn," with which we are already acquainted from most of his other verse as an accompaniment of the wonderful appearance of the stranger ("Neznakomka"). But this is not the bright dawn of his youthful verses of the beautiful lady—roses and gold in the bright azure of the sky; this is the "sick" dawn of his "gypsy" verses—yellow, smoky, inflamed: "The pale sky flamed out and was shoved aside, and in the yellow dawn were lanterns." The metaphorical verbs, "flamed out" and "shoved aside," lend grandiose mythological outlines to this picture of a yellow sick sky. The same is true of the last lines: "And the necklace tinkled, and the gypsy danced and howled to the dawn of love." In Akhmatova's poem this symbolic framing, repeated in the beginning and at the end, is of course absent. In the composition of her verse, the music "grating in the garden"—"the mournful voices of the violin"—play an identical role.

As has already been shown, these violins are present in both verses. In Blok's, however, they are in the unknown vague distance: "Somewhere bows were singing of love"; and the content of the song is just as unknown and incomprehensible to the poet: "And immediately the strings thundered something in reply" ... "Somewhere" and "something" are significant words for the romantic poet. In Akhmatova's poem the expression is exact: "the music grated in the garden," "(violins) sing behind the floating smoke." Exact localization of the sounds corresponds to an exact statement of their emotional content—sad, mournful sounds: "The music grated in the garden with such inexpressible grief." This lyrical empathy with the mood of the song is expressed in the words of common everyday speech. And at the same time, as is always the case with Akhmatova, there is a surprising exactness and individuality in the selection of the epithet and in connecting it (synthetic union) with the corresponding word: "But the mournful voices of violins..."

Both poets describe the subject of their love. Blok says of his loved one: "You tore away like a frightened bird, you passed—light as my dream... and perfumes sighed, lashes dreamed,/ Anxiously silks began to whisper..." Before us again passes the image of the stranger [from the poem "The Stranger"]: "She sits down at the window, wafting perfumes and mists. And from her supple silks emanate ancient superstitions." By the same devices the poet accomplishes the transformation of the image of the loved one into a wonderful and magical otherworldly phenomenon which has entered into this world. Also used is a series of animating metaphors and comparisons: "perfumes breathe," "eyelashes dream," "silks whisper anxiously"; she rushed from her place "with the frightened movement of a bird." Also, the comparison which has already been pointed out leads us out beyond the borders of the world of external reality: the stranger is like a "dream." This differs from Akhmatova's description of the loved one. It communicates an intimate and delicate sensual observation in an epigrammatically exact verbal formula: "How unlike caresses are the touches of these hands." "Only laughter in his calm eyes under the light gold of the lashes." Here again the art of Akhmatova is primarily a new and creative combination of words that are simple as far as their logical and material meanings are concerned; as a result the union of the words is irreplaceable, individual, synthetic. The metaphorical images of Blok, however, grow out of a lyrical melodic mood. Hence the repetitions of parts of words and whole words, vowels and consonants, syntactic parallelism, even internal rhymes: "And perfumes sighed, lashes dreamed, anxiously silks began to whisper" particularly in the last strophe.

What composes the factual content of the two verses? When told "in one's own words," in prosaic exposition, one feels that Blok's poem is being exposed, it loses its poetic meaning. The meeting with the unknown woman in the restaurant, the poet addressing her, her "haughty" and contemptuous reply, and—abruptly during the sounds of the music, when their eyes meet in the mirror—the sudden feeling of nearness that seized both of them. Only in poetic treatment will we comprehend the mystic significance of this occurrence for the poet ("Never shall I forget!")—the significance of the appearance of the stranger, the only real loved one, in the earthly image of the unknown beauty. And for this reason the first words signifying this singular meeting ("I sent you a black rose in a goblet of 'Ai' that was gold as the sky") sound so romantically solemn. In Akhmatova's poem the content is simple and easily defined, and the external sense of the story corresponds completely to the internal sense. This is the first meeting with the beloved. She recognizes that he does not love her and never will; he is only a "true friend." "He said to me: 'I am a true friend!' and touched my dress... How unlike caresses are the touches of these hands."

On the basis of this example we can express, in general form, the difference between the art of Blok and that of Akhmatova—between the mystical lyricism of the Symbolists and contemporary poetry which has "overcome Symbolism."

The lyrical poetry of the Symbolists is of a primarily mystical nature. The presence of the infinite in each experience inserts a peculiar deeper meaning, communicates a new estimation of everything that occurs. We feel that the experience is somehow born from the very depths of the soul—still whole, undivided—frequently chaotic. With Akhmatova and poets of her circle we observe a return to feeling on a finite human scale; it is complete in itself, as if outlined and limited on all sides. The separateness and distinctness of each emotional experience, the graceful and strict order in "emotional housekeeping" is to be understood in this connection. The Symbolists are typified by an exclusive self-centered quality and an internal adhesion to one's own experience.

In Akhmatova we have an interest in the external world, its sensual, objective, visual details, and an ability to exactly observe the external signs of emotional experience; each experience is connected with some external fact as its cause or felt sign.

The peculiarities of poetics are inevitably connected with these peculiarities of poetic feeling. Among the Symbolists music is born from the spirit of music; the words call forth a vague mood with their sounds rather than with their meaning; repetitions of sounds, words, and entire lines are common, as in songs. The words become metaphorical allegories, hints at other meanings; their logical and material sense is clouded, but their emotionally lyrical effectiveness is all the stronger. In the new generation of poets, however, the emotional element in immediate musical expression is absent; and at the same time the peculiarities of melodic, lyrically musical style disappear. In return, the poetic images acquire a graphic defined quality; the logical and material sense of the words is restored to its rights; the connection of words is determined primarily by the meaning and is consolidated by an exact, strict, epigrammatic formula; division and completion are expressed in syntactic construction and in the very composition of the poem. A return to the classical art of Pushkin is being accomplished in the poetics of the new school.

Throughout the nineteenth century the Romantic tradition dominated Russian lyrics, tracing its origins back to [Vasilii] Zhukovskii, [Fedor] Tiutchev, Fet, and Solov'ev. The Russian Symbolists attached themselves to this tradition. We first observe a return to Classicism in the lyric poetry of Mikhail Kuzmin. In Anna Akhmatova's *White Flock* it is expressed quite clearly. For this reason we assert that in the poetic creation of recent years we see a new poetic art which profoundly differs from the lyric poetry of the Symbolist poets.

Modernist Views on Art in Essays and Manifestos, Criticism

• *Viktor Zhirmunskii*

TRANSLATOR'S AND EDITOR'S NOTES

[1] This essay of 1920 was a critical landmark for Russian poetry of the period. It gave substance to the Acmeists' claim to have founded a new poetic school distinct from Symbolism. Zhirmunskii's ties with formalist scholarship are strongly evident here. The concept of artistic evolution as a reaction against immediate predecessors in favor of more distant ones results in Zhirmunskii uniting Acmeism with Classicism and contrasting the former to Symbolism-Romanticism. (Trans.)

[2] "Sunset" would be the more adequate translation for the word *zaria* used in the poem even thought the word means "dawn" as well. The event clearly takes place in the evening, however. "Ai" [Ay] a few lines further down is a French champagne. [IMD].

ART AS TECHNIQUE

by Viktor SHKLOVSKII*

*Victor Shklovsky

** From Russian Formalist Criticism, Four Essays. Translated and with an Introduction by Lee T. Lemon and Marion J. Reis. Lincoln and London: University of Nebraska Press, 1965. Pp. 3-24.

Viktor Shklovskii is certainly the most erratic and probably the most important of the Formalist critics. A charter member of the group, he had that rare combination of brilliant originality, combativeness, and theoretical flexibility required of a propagandist during the early years of a movement. As [Boris] *Eikhenbaum shows ("The Theory of the 'Formal Method'"), Shklovskii touched most of the fundamentals of Formalist theory, was often the first to define a problem, and frequently pointed towards its solution. He saw issues clearly and stated them sharply — perhaps too sharply. Like* [modernist critic and poet] *T. E. Hulme or* [poet and critic] *T. S. Eliot, he was a master of the kind of statement that disciples make slogans of and opponents find embarrassingly easy to attack. Because he was the most obvious and the most vulnerable target for the Marxists and because his attitude toward the Russian Revolution was unusually complex, he was one of the first of the Formalists to attempt a compromise. By 1926 he was trying to include sociological material in his study of literature; his work on Tolstoi in 1928 analyzes* War and Peace *as a product of two irreconcilable forces — the social class Tolstoi represented and the novel as a genre.*

Modernist Views on Art in Essays and Manifestos, Criticism
• Viktor Shklovskii

"Art as Technique" (1917) [Iskusstvo kak priem] *is the most important statement made of early Formalist method, partly because it announces a break with the only other "aesthetic" approach available at that time and in that place, and partly because it offers a theory of both the methodology of criticism and the purpose of art... Shklovskii attacks the views... that "art is thinking in images" and that its purpose is to present the unknown (most often the abstract or transcendent) in terms of the known. Theoretically, the views recognized neither the richness of poetry nor its intrinsic value. Empirically, the views were inadequate, as Shklovskii points out. To use an example from* [the English Romantic poet] [William] Wordsworth, *the lines*

> The world is too much with us; late and soon,
> Getting and spending, we lay waste our powers:

are certainly poetic, yet it would be rash to argue that the poetic quality comes from the deeply latent imagery. And at the end of his sonnet, Wordsworth resurrects Proteus and Triton as images to evoke a feeling that many persons have had first hand; the image here is less familiar than the thing it stands for...

At this time the Formalists needed a critical formula that would define the difference between literature and non-literature more precisely and more generally than had been done, and that would at the same time state the purpose of literature. Shklovskii's concept of "defamiliarization"[1] *did both.... Shklovskii's argument, briefly stated, is that the habitual way of thinking is to make the unfamiliar as easily digestible as possible. Normally our perceptions are "automatic," which is another way of saying that they are minimal. From this standpoint, learning is largely a matter of learning to ignore. We have not really learned to drive an automobile, for example, until we are able to react to the relevant stoplights, pedestrians, other motorists, road conditions, and so on, with a minimum of conscious effort. Eventually, we may even react properly without actually noticing what we are reacting to—we miss the pedestrian but fail to see what he looks like. When reading ordinary prose, we are likely to feel that something is wrong if we find ourselves noticing the individual words as words. The purpose of art, according to Shklovskii, is to force us to notice. Since perception is usually too automatic, art develops a variety of techniques to impede perception or, at least, to call attention to themselves.* Thus "Art is a way of experiencing the artfulness of an object; the object is not important." *The object is unimportant because as art the poem does not have to point to anything outside itself; the poem must "not mean/ But be."*

This is not the place to debate the merits of conflicting aesthetic systems, but we should note that Shklovskii's position is more subtle than its opponents would admit. To the extent that a work of art can be experienced, to the extent that it is, it is like any other object. It may "mean" in the same way that any object means; it has, however, one advantage—it is designed especially for Perception, for attracting and holding attention. Thus it not only bears meaning, it forces an awareness of its meaning upon the reader. Although Shklovskii did not follow this line, it does widen the range of his theory without inconsistency. He prefers to argue, as does [English literary theoretician] *I. A. Richards, that perception is an end in itself, that the good life is the life of a man fully aware of the world. Art, to paraphrase Richards and to summarize Shklovskii, is the record of and the occasion for that awareness.*

According to Shklovskii, the chief technique for promoting such perception is "defamiliarization." It is not so much a device as a result obtainable by any number of devices. A novel point of view, as Shklovskii points out, can make a reader perceive by making the familiar seem strange. Wordplay, deliberately roughened rhythm, or figures of speech can all have the same effect. No single device, then, is essential to poetry. Poetry is recognized not by the presence of a certain kind of content or of images, ambiguities, symbols, or whatever, but by its ability to make man look with an exceptionally high level of awareness.

....

"Art is thinking in images." This maxim, which even high school students parrot, is nevertheless the starting point for the erudite philologist who is beginning to put together some kind of systematic literary theory. The idea, originated in part by [linguist, folklorist and literary theoretician] [Aleksandr/Oleksandr] Potebnia, has spread. "Without imagery there is no art, and in particular no poetry," Potebnia writes. And elsewhere, "Poetry, as well as prose, is first and foremost a special way of thinking and knowing."

• *Viktor Shklovskii*

Poetry is a special way of thinking; it is, precisely, a way of thinking in images, a way which permits what is generally called "economy of mental effort," a way which makes for "a sensation of the relative ease of the process." ... Potebnia and his numerous disciples consider poetry a special kind of thinking—thinking by means of images; they feel that the purpose of imagery is to help channel various objects and activities into groups and to clarify the unknown by means of the known. Or, as Potebnia wrote:

> The relationship of the image to what is being clarified is that: (a) the image is the fixed predicate of that which undergoes change—the unchanging means of attracting what is perceived as changeable.... (b) the image is far clearer and simpler than what it clarifies.

In other words:

> Since the purpose of imagery is to remind us, by approximation, of those meanings for which the image stands, and since, apart from this, imagery is unnecessary for thought, we must be more familiar with the image than with what it clarifies.

It would be instructive to try to apply this principle to Tiutchev's comparison of summer lightning to deaf and dumb demons or to Gogol's comparison of the sky to the garment of God.[2] "Without imagery there is no art"—"Art is thinking in images." These maxims have led to far-fetched interpretations of individual works of art. Attempts have been made to evaluate even music, architecture, and lyric poetry as imagistic thought. After a quarter of a century of such attempts [Dmitrii] Ovsianiko-Kulikovskii [one of Potebnia's disciples] finally had to assign lyric poetry, architecture, and music to a special category of imageless art and to define them as lyric arts appealing directly to the emotions. And thus he admitted an enormous area of art which is not a mode of thought. A part of this area, lyric poetry (narrowly considered), is quite like the visual arts; it is also verbal. But, much more important, visual art passes quite imperceptibly into non-visual art; yet our perceptions of both are similar.

Nevertheless, the definition "Art is thinking in images," which means (...) that art is the making of symbols, has survived the downfall of the theory which supported it. It survives chiefly in the wake of Symbolism, especially among the theorists of the Symbolist movement.

Many still believe, then, that thinking in images—thinking in specific scenes of "roads and landscape" and "furrows and boundaries"[3]—is the chief characteristic of poetry. Consequently, they should have expected the history of "imagistic art," as they call it, to consist of a history of changes in imagery. But we find that images change little; from century to century, from nation to nation, from poet to poet, they flow on without changing. Images belong to no one: they are "the Lord's." The more you understand an age, the more convinced you become that the images a given poet used and which you thought his own were taken almost unchanged from another poet. The works of poets are classified or grouped according to the new techniques that poets discover and share, and according to their arrangement and development of the resources of language; poets are much more concerned with arranging images than with creating them. Images are given to poets; the ability to remember them is far more important than the ability to create them.

Imagistic thought does not, in any case, include all the aspects of art nor even all the aspects of verbal art. A change in imagery is not essential to the development of poetry. We know that frequently an expression is thought to be poetic, to be created for aesthetic pleasure, although actually it was created without such intent—e.g., [the poet] [Innokentii] Annenskii's opinion that the Slavic languages are especially poetic and Andrei Belyi's ecstasy over the technique of placing adjectives after nouns, a technique used by eighteenth-century Russian poets. Belyi joyfully accepts the technique as something artistic, or more exactly, as intended, if we consider intention as art. Actually, this reversal of the usual adjective-noun order is a peculiarity of the language (which had been influenced by Church Slavonic). Thus a work may be (1) intended as prosaic and accepted as poetic, or (2) intended as poetic and accepted as prosaic. This suggests that the artistry attributed to a given work results from the way we perceive it. By "works of art," in the narrow sense, we mean works created by special techniques designed to make the works as obviously artistic as possible.

Potebnia's conclusion, which can be formulated "poetry equals imagery," gave rise to the whole theory that "imagery equals symbolism," that the image may serve as the invariable predicate of various subjects. (This conclusion, because it expressed ideas similar to the theories of the Symbolists, intrigued some of their leading representatives—Andrei Belyi, Merezhkovskii and his "eternal companions" [the title of a collection of essays by this writer] and, in fact, formed the basis of the theory of Symbolism.) The conclusion stems partly from the fact that Potebnia did not distinguish between the language of poetry and the language of prose. Consequently, he ignored the fact that there are two aspects of imagery: imagery as a practical means of thinking, as a means of placing objects within categories; and imagery as poetic, as a means of reinforcing an impression. I shall clarify with an example. I want to attract the attention of a young child who is eating bread and butter and getting the butter on her fingers. I call, "Hey, butterfingers!" This is a figure of speech, a clearly prosaic trope. Now a different example. The child is playing with my glasses and drops them. I call, "Hey, butterfingers!" This figure of speech is a poetic trope. (In the first example, "butterfingers" is metonymic; in the second, metaphoric—but this is not what I want to stress.)

Poetic imagery is a means of creating the strongest possible impression. As a method it is, depending upon its purpose, neither more nor less effective than other poetic techniques; it is neither more nor less effective than ordinary or negative parallelism, comparison, repetition, balanced structure, hyperbole, the commonly accepted rhetorical figures, and all those methods which emphasize the emotional effect of an expression (including words or even articulated sounds).[4] But poetic imagery only externally resembles either the stock imagery of fables and ballads or thinking in images—e.g., the example in Ovsianiko-Kulikovskii's *Language and Art* in which a little girl calls a ball a little watermelon. Poetic imagery is but one of the devices of poetic language. Prose imagery is a means of abstraction: a little watermelon instead of a lamp-shade, or a little watermelon instead of a head, is only the abstraction of one of the object's characteristics, that of roundness. It is no different from saying that the head and the melon are both round. This is what is meant, but it has nothing to do with poetry.

The law of the economy of creative effort is also generally accepted. [Positivist philosopher] [Herbert] Spencer wrote:

> On seeking for some clue to the law underlying these current maxims, we may see shadowed forth in many of them, the importance of economizing the reader's or the hearer's attention. To so present ideas that they may be apprehended with the least possible mental effort, is the desideratum towards which most of the rules above quoted point.... Hence, carrying out the metaphor that language is the vehicle of thought, there seems reason to think that in all cases the friction and inertia of the vehicle deduct from its efficiency; and that in composition, the chief, if not the sole thing to be done, is to reduce this friction and inertia to the smallest possible amount.

And R(ichard) Avenarius [a positivist thinker and representative of *empiriocriticism*]:

> If a soul possess inexhaustible strength, then, of course, it would be indifferent to how much might be spent from this inexhaustible source; only the necessarily expended time would be important. But since its forces are limited, one is led to expect that the soul hastens to carry out the apperceptive process as expediently as possible—that is, with comparatively the least expenditure of energy, and, hence, with comparatively the best result.

....

These ideas about the economy of energy, as well as about the law and aim of creativity, are perhaps true in their application to "practical" language; they were, however, extended to poetic language. Hence they do not distinguish properly between the laws of practical language and the laws of poetic language. The fact that Japanese poetry has sounds not found in conversational Japanese was hardly the first factual indication of the differences between poetic and everyday language. [Formalist critic] Lev Iakubinskii has observed that the law of the dissimilation of liquid sounds does not apply to poetic language. This suggested to him that poetic language tolerated the admission of hard-to-pronounce conglomerations of similar sounds. In his article, one of the first examples of scientific criticism, he indicates, inductively, the contrast (I shall say more about this point later) between the laws of poetic language and the laws of practical language.

We must, then, speak about the laws of expenditure and economy in poetic language not on the basis of an analogy with prose, but on the basis of the laws of poetic language.

If we start to examine the general laws of perception, we see that as perception becomes habitual, it becomes automatic. Thus, for example, all of our habits retreat into the area of the unconsciously automatic; if one remembers the sensations of holding a pen or of speaking in a foreign language for the first time and compares that with his feeling at performing the action for the ten thousandth time, he will agree with us. Such habituation explains the principles by which, in ordinary speech, we leave phrases unfinished and words half expressed. In this process, ideally realized in algebra, things are replaced by symbols. Complete words are not expressed in rapid speech; their initial sounds are barely perceived. [The philologist] Aleksandr Pogodin offers the example of a boy considering the sentence "The Swiss mountains are beautiful" in the form of a series of letters: T, S, m, a, b.

This characteristic of thought not only suggests the method of algebra, but even prompts the choice of symbols (letters, especially initial letters). By this "algebraic" method of thought we apprehend objects only as shapes with imprecise extensions; we do not see them in their entirety but rather recognize them by their main characteristics. We see the object as though it were enveloped in a sack. We know what it is by its configuration, but we see only its silhouette. The object, perceived thus in the manner of prose perception, fades and does not leave even a first impression; ultimately even the essence of what it was is forgotten. Such perception explains why we fail to hear the prose word in its entirety (...) and, hence, why (along with other slips of the tongue) we fail to pronounce it. The process of "algebrization," the over-automatization of an object, permits the greatest economy of perceptive effort. Either objects are assigned only one proper feature—a number, for example—or else they function as though by formula and do not even appear in cognition:

> I was cleaning a room and, meandering about, approached the divan and couldn't remember whether or not I had dusted it. Since these movements are habitual and unconscious, I could not remember and felt that it was impossible to remember—so that if I had dusted it and forgot—that is, had acted unconsciously, then it was the same as if I had not. If some conscious person had been watching, then the fact could be established. If, however, no one was looking, or looking on unconsciously, if the whole complex lives of many people go on unconsciously, then such lives are as if they had never been.[5]

And so life is reckoned as nothing. Habitualization devours works, clothes, furniture, one's wife, and the fear of war. If the whole complex lives of many people go on unconsciously then such lives are as if they had never been." And art exists that one may recover the sensation of life; it exists to make one feel things, to make the stone stony. The purpose of art is to impart the sensation of things as they are perceived and not as they are known. The technique of art is to make objects "unfamiliar," to make forms difficult, to increase the difficulty and length of perception because the process of perception is an aesthetic end in itself and must be prolonged. *Art is a way of experiencing the artfulness of an object; the object is not important.*

....

After we see an object several times, we begin to recognize it. The Object is in front of us and we know about it, but we do not see it—hence we cannot say anything significant about it. Art removes objects from the automatism of perception in several ways. Here I want to illustrate a way used repeatedly by Lev Tolstoi...

Modernist Views on Art in Essays and Manifestos, Criticism
• Viktor Shklovskii

Tolstoi makes the familiar seem strange by not naming the familiar object. He describes an object as if he were seeing it for the first time, an event as if it were happening for the first time. In describing something he avoids the accepted names of its parts and instead names corresponding parts of other objects. For example, in "Shame" Tolstoi "defamiliarizes" the idea of flogging in this way: "to strip people who have broken the law, to hurl them to the floor, and to rap on their bottoms with switches," and, after a few lines, "to lash about on the naked buttocks." Then he remarks:

> Just why precisely this stupid, savage means of causing pain and not any other—why not prick the shoulders or any part of the body with needles, squeeze the hands or the feet in a vise, or anything like that?

I apologize for this harsh example, but it is typical of Tolstoi's way of pricking the conscience. The familiar act of flogging is made unfamiliar both by the description and by the proposal to change its form without changing its nature. Tolstoi uses this technique of "defamiliarization" constantly. The narrator of "Kholstomer," for example, is a horse, and it is the horse's point of view (rather than a person's) that makes the content of the story seem unfamiliar. Here is how the horse regards the institution of private property:

> I understood well what they said about whipping and Christianity. But then I was absolutely in the dark. What's the meaning of "his own," "his colt"? From these phrases I saw that people thought there was some sort of connection between me and the stable. At the time I simply could not understand the connection. Only much later, when they separated me from the other horses, did I begin to understand. But even then I simply could not see what it meant when they called me "man's property." The words "my horse" referred to me, a living horse, and seemed as strange to me as the words "my land," "my air," "my water."
>
> But the words made a strong impression on me. I thought about them constantly, and only after the most diverse experiences with people did I understand, finally, what they

meant. They meant this: In life people are guided by words, not by deeds. It's not so much that they love the possibility of doing or not doing something as it is the possibility of speaking with words, agreed on among themselves, about various topics. Such are the words "my" and "mine," which they apply to different things, creatures, objects, and even to land, people, and horses. They agree that only one may say "mine" about this, that, or the other thing. And the one who says "mine" about the greatest number of things is, according to the game which they've agreed to among themselves, the one they consider the most happy. I don't know the point of all this, but it's true. For a long time I tried to explain it to myself in terms of some kind of real gain, but I had to reject that explanation because it was wrong.

Many of those, for instance, who called me their own never rode on me—although others did. And so with those who fed me. Then again, the coachman, the veterinarians, and the outsiders in general treated me kindly, yet those who called me their own did not. In due time, having widened the scope of my observations, I satisfied myself that the notion "my," not only in relation to us horses, has no other basis than a narrow human instinct which is called a sense of or right to private property. A man says "this house is mine" and never lives in it; he only worries about its construction and upkeep. A merchant says "my shop," "my dry goods shop," for instance, and does not even wear clothes made from the better cloth he keeps in his own shop.

There are people who call a tract of land their own, but they never set eyes on it and never take a stroll on it. There are people who call others their own, yet never see them. And the whole relationship between them is that the so-called "owners" treat the others unjustly.

There are people who call women their own, or their "wives," but their women live with other men. And people strive not for the good in life, but for goods they can call their own.

I am now convinced that this is the essential difference between people and ourselves. And therefore, not even considering the other ways in which we are superior, but considering just this one virtue, we can bravely claim to stand higher than men on the ladder of living creatures. The actions of men, at least those with whom I have had dealings, are guided by words—ours, by deeds.

• *Viktor Shklovskii*

The horse is killed before the end of the story but the manner of the narrative, its technique, does not change:

> Much later they put Serpukhovskii's [the horse-owner's] body, which had experienced the world, which had eaten and drunk, into the ground. They could profitably send neither his hide, nor his flesh, nor his bones anywhere.
>
> But since his dead body, which had gone about in the world for twenty years, was a great burden to everyone, its burial was only a superfluous embarrassment for the people. For a long time no one had needed him; for a long time he had been a burden on all. But nevertheless, the dead who buried the dead found it necessary to dress this bloated body, which immediately began to rot, in a good uniform and good boots; to lay it in a good new coffin with new tassels at the four corners, then to place this new coffin in another of lead and ship it to Moscow; there to exhume ancient bones and at just that spot to hide this putrefying body, swarming with maggots, in its new uniform and clean boots, and to cover it over completely with dirt.

Thus we see that at the end of the story Tolstoi continues to use the same technique even though the motivation for it (the reason for its use) is gone.

In *War and Peace* Tolstoi uses the same technique in describing whole battles as if battles were something new. These descriptions are too long to quote; it would be necessary to extract a considerable part of the four-volume novel. But Tolstoi uses the same method in describing the drawing room and the theater:

> The middle of the stage consisted of flat boards; by the sides stood painted pictures representing trees, and at the back a linen cloth was stretched down to the floor boards. Maidens in red bodices and white skirts sat on the middle of the stage. One, very fat, in a white silk dress, sat apart on a narrow bench to which a green pasteboard box was glued from behind. They were all singing something. When they had finished, the maiden in white approached the prompter's box. A man in silk with tight-fitting pants on his fat legs approached her with a plume and began to sing and spread his arms in dismay. The man in the tight pants finished his

song alone; then the girl sang. After that both remained silent as the music resounded; and the man, obviously waiting to begin singing his part with her again, began to run his fingers over the hand of the girl in the white dress. They finished their song together, and everyone in the theater began to clap and shout. But the men and women on stage, who represented lovers, started to bow, smiling and raising their hands.

In the second act there were pictures representing monuments and openings in the linen cloth representing the moonlight, and they raised lamp shades on a frame. As the musicians started to play the bass horn and counter-bass, a large number of people in black mantles poured onto the stage from right and left. The people, with something like daggers in their hands, started to wave their arms. Then still more people came running out and began to drag away the maiden who had been wearing a white dress but who now wore one of sky blue. They did not drag her off immediately, but sang with her for a long time before dragging her away. Three times they struck on something metallic behind the side scenes, and everyone got down on his knees and began to chant a prayer. Several times all of this activity was interrupted by enthusiastic shouts from the spectators.

The third act is described:

> ... But suddenly a storm blew up. Chromatic scales and chords of diminished sevenths were heard in the orchestra. Everyone ran about and again they dragged one of the bystanders behind the scenes as the curtain fell.

In the fourth act, "There was some sort of devil who sang, waving his hands, until the boards were moved out from under him and he dropped down."[6]

In *Resurrection* Tolstoi describes the city and the court in the same way; he uses a similar technique in "Kreutzer Sonata" when he describes marriage—"Why, if people have an affinity of souls, must they sleep together?" But he did not defamiliarize only those things he sneered at:

> Pierre stood up from his new comrades and made his way between the campfires to the other side of the road where,

it seemed, the captive soldiers were held. He wanted to talk with them. The French sentry stopped him on the road and ordered him to return. Pierre did so, but not to the campfire, not to his comrades, but to an abandoned, unharnessed carriage. On the ground, near the wheel of the carriage, he sat cross-legged in the Turkish fashion, and lowered his head.

He sat motionless for a long time, thinking. More than an hour passed. No one disturbed him. Suddenly he burst out laughing with his robust, good natured laugh—so loudly that the men near him looked around, surprised at his conspicuously strange laughter. "Ha, ha, ha," laughed Pierre. And he began to talk to himself.

"The soldier didn't allow me to pass. They caught me, barred me. Me—me—my immortal soul. Ha, ha, ha," he laughed with tears starting in his eyes.

Pierre glanced at the sky, into the depths of the departing, playing stars. "And all this is mine, all this is in me, and all this is I," thought Pierre. "And all this they caught and put in a planked enclosure." He smiled and went off to his comrades to lie down to sleep.

Anyone who knows Tolstoi can find several hundred such passages in his work. His method of seeing things out of their normal context is also apparent in his last works. Tolstoi described the dogmas and rituals he attacked as if they were unfamiliar, substituting everyday meanings for the customarily religious meanings of the words common in church ritual. Many persons were painfully wounded; they considered it blasphemy to present as strange and monstrous what they accepted as sacred. Their reaction was due chiefly to the technique through which Tolstoi perceived and reported his environment. And after turning to what he had long avoided, Tolstoi found that his perceptions had unsettled his faith.

The technique of defamiliarization is not Tolstoi's alone. I cited Tolstoi because his work is generally known.

Now, having explained the nature of this technique, let us try to determine the approximate limits of its application. I personally feel that defamiliarization is found almost everywhere where form is found. In other words, the difference between Potebnia's point of view and ours is this: An image is not a permanent referent for those mutable complexities of life which are revealed through it; its purpose is not to make us perceive meaning, but to create a special perception of the object—*it creates a "vision" of the object instead of serving as a means for knowing it.*

....

In studying poetic speech in its phonetic and lexical structure as well as in its characteristic distribution of words and in the characteristic thought structures compounded from the words, we find everywhere the artistic trademark—that is, we find material obviously created to remove the automatism of perception; the author's purpose is to create the vision which results from that deautomatized perception. A work is created "artistically" so that its perception is impeded and the greatest possible effect is produced through the slowness of the perception. As a result of this lingering, the object is perceived not in its extension in space, but, so to speak, in its continuity. Thus "poetic language" gives satisfaction. According to Aristotle, poetic language must appear strange and wonderful; and, in fact, it is often actually foreign: the Sumerian used by the Assyrians, the Latin of Europe during the Middle Ages, the Arabisms of the Persians, the Old Bulgarian of Russian literature, or the elevated, almost literary language of folk songs. The common archaisms of poetic language, the intricacy of the sweet new style (*dolce stil nuovo*),[7] the obscure style of the language of Arnaut Daniel with the "roughened" (*harte*) [hard] forms which make pronunciation difficult—these are used in much the same way. Lev Iakubinskii has demonstrated the principle of phonetic "roughening" of poetic language in the particular case of the repetition of identical sounds. The language of poetry is, then, a difficult, roughened, impeded language. In a few special instances the language of poetry approximates the language of prose, but this does not violate the principle of "roughened" form.

Her sister was called Tat'iana.

> For the first time we shall
> Wilfully brighten the delicate
> Pages of a novel with such a name

wrote Pushkin. The usual poetic language for Pushkin's contemporaries was the elegant style of Derzhavin; but Pushkin's style, because it seemed trivial then, was unexpectedly difficult for them. We should remember the consternation of Pushkin's contemporaries over the vulgarity of his expressions. He used the popular language as a special device for prolonging attention, just as his contemporaries generally used Russian words in their usually French speech (see Tolstoy's examples in *War and Peace*).

Just now a still more characteristic phenomenon is under way. Russian literary language, which was originally foreign to Russia, has so permeated the language of the people that it has blended with their conversation. On the other hand, literature has now begun to show a tendency towards the use of dialects (Remizov, Kliuev, Esenin, and others,[8] so unequal in talent and so alike in language, are intentionally provincial) and of barbarisms (which gave rise to the Severianin group[9]). And currently Maksim Gor'kii is changing his diction from the old literary language to the new literary colloquialism of Leskov.[10] Ordinary speech and literary language have thereby changed places (see the work of Viacheslav Ivanov and many others). And finally, a strong tendency, led by Khlebnikov, to create a new and properly poetic language has emerged. In the light of these developments we can define poetry as *attenuated, tortuous* speech. Poetic speech is *formed speech*. Prose is ordinary speech—economical, easy, proper, the goddess of prose [*dea prosae*] is a goddess of the accurate, facile type, of the "direct" expression of a child. I shall discuss roughened form and retardation as the general law of art at greater length in an article on plot construction.[11]

Nevertheless, the position of those who urge the idea of the economy of artistic energy as something which exists in and even distinguishes poetic language seems, at first glance, tenable for the problem of rhythm. Spencer's description of rhythm would seem to be absolutely incontestable:

> Just as the body in receiving a series of varying concussions, must keep the muscles ready to meet the most violent of them, as not knowing when such may come: so, the mind in receiving unarranged articulations, must keep its perspectives active enough to recognize the least easily caught sounds. And as, if the concussions recur in definite order, the body may husband its forces by adjusting the resistance needful for each concussion; so, if the syllables be rhythmically arranged, the mind may economize its energies by anticipating the attention required for each syllable.

This apparently conclusive observation suffers from the common fallacy, the confusion of the laws of poetic and prosaic language. In The *Philosophy of Style* Spencer failed utterly to distinguish between them. But rhythm may have two functions. The rhythm of prose, or of a work song like "Dubinushka," permits the members of the work crew to do their necessary "groaning together" and also eases the work by making it automatic. And, in fact, it is easier to march with music than without it, and to march during an animated conversation is even easier, for the walking is done unconsciously. Thus the rhythm of prose is an important automatizing element; the rhythm of poetry is not. There is "order" in art, yet not a single column of a Greek temple stands exactly in its proper order; poetic rhythm is similarly disordered rhythm. Attempts to systematize the irregularities have been made, and such attempts are part of the current problem in the theory of rhythm. It is obvious that the systematization will not work, for in reality the problem is not one of complicating the rhythm but of disordering the rhythm—a disordering which cannot be predicted. Should the disordering of rhythm become a convention, it would be ineffective as a device for the roughening of language. But I will not discuss rhythm in more detail since I intend to write a book about it.[12]

Modernist Views on Art in Essays and Manifestos, Criticism
• Viktor Shklovskii

SELECTED AND (SOMETIMES) ABBREVIATED NOTES
by Lemon and Reiss

[1] The Russian word is *ostranenie;* it means literally "making strange."

[2] Fedor Tiutchev (1803-1873), a poet, and Nikolai Gogol' (1809-1852), a master of prose fiction and satire, are mentioned here because their bold use of imagery cannot be accounted for by Potebnia's theory. Shklovskii is arguing that writers frequently gain their effects by comparing the commonplace to the exceptional rather than vice versa.

[3] This is an allusion to Viacheslav Ivanov's *Borozdy i mezhi* [*Furrows and Boundaries*] (Moscow, 1916), a major statement of Symbolist theory.

[4] Shklovskii is here doing two things of major theoretical importance: (1) he argues that different techniques serve a single function, and that (2) no single technique is all-important. The second permits the Formalists to be concerned with any and all literary devices; the first permits them to discuss the devices from a single consistent theoretical position.

[5] Lev Tolstoi's *Diary*, entry dated February 29, 1897. (The date is transcribed incorrectly; it should read March 1, 1897.)

[6] The Tolstoi and Gogol' translations are ours.

[7] Dante, *Purgatorio*, 24:56. Dante refers to the new lyric style of his contemporaries.

[8] Aleksei Remizov (1877-1957) is best known as a novelist and satirist; Nikolai Kliuev (1885-1937) and Sergei Esenin (1895-1925) were "peasant poets." All three were noted for their faithful reproduction of Russian dialects and colloquial language.

[9] A group noted for its opulent and sensuous verse style.

[10] Nikolai Leskov (1831-1895), novelist and short story writer, helped popularize the *skaz*, or yarn, and hence, because of the part dialect peculiarities play in the *skaz*, also altered Russian literary language. *Ed.note*.

[11] Shklovskii is probably referring to his *Razvertyvanie siuzheta* [*Plot Development*].

[12] We have been unable to discover the book Shklovskii promised.

Slap in the Face of Public Taste[1]

by David BURLIUK,
Aleksandr KRUCHENYKH[2],
Vladimir MAIAKOVSKII,
Viktor KHLEBNIKOV*

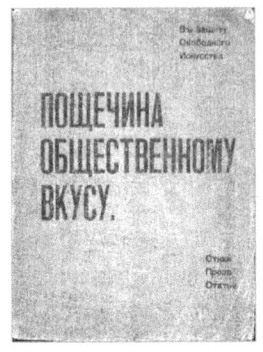

* D. Burliuk, Aleksandr Kruchenykh, V. Maiakovsky, Viktor Khlebnikov
** From *Words in Revolution: Russian Futurist Manifestos 1912-1928*, volume ed. Anna Lawton. Texts translated and edited by Anna Lawton and Herbert Eagle. Introduction by Anna Lawton and afterword by Herbert Eagle. Washington: New Academia Publishing, 2005. Pp. 51.

To the readers of our New First Unexpected.

We alone are the *face* of *our* Time. Through us the horn of time blows in the art of the word.

The past is too tight. The Academy and Pushkin are less intelligible than hieroglyphics.

Throw Pushkin, Dostoevskii, Tolstoi, etc., etc. overboard from the Ship of Modernity.

He who does not forget his *first* love will not recognize his last.

Who, trustingly, would turn his last love toward Bal'mont's perfumed lechery? Is this the reflection of today's virile soul?

Who, faintheartedly, would fear tearing from warrior Briusov's black tuxedo the paper armorplate? Or does the dawn of unknown beauties shine from it?[3]

Wash Your hands which have touched the filthy slime of the books written by those countless Leonid Andreevs.[4]

All those Maksim Gor'kiis, Kuprins, Bloks, Sologubs, Remizovs, Averchenkos,

Chernyis, Kuzmins, Bunins, etc.[5] need only a dacha on the river. Such is the reward fate gives tailors.

From the heights of skyscrapers we gaze at their insignificance!... We *order* that the poets' *rights* be revered:

1. To enlarge the *scope* of the poet's vocabulary with arbitrary and derivative words (Word-novelty).

2. To feel an insurmountable hatred for the language existing before their time.

3. To push with horror off their proud brow the Wreath of cheap fame that You have made from bathhouse switches.

4. To stand on the rock of the word "we" amidst the sea of boos and outrage.

And if *for the time being* the filthy stigmas of Your "Common sense" and "good taste" are still present in our lines, these same lines *for the first time* already glimmer with the Summer Lightening of the New Coming Beauty of the Self-sufficient (self-centered) Word.

D. BURLIUK, Aleksandr KRUCHENYKH,
V. MAIAKOVSKII, Viktor KHLEBNIKOV

NOTES

[1] "Slap in the Face of Public Taste" (*Poshchechina obshchestvennomu vkusu*) is the first and most famous manifesto of the Hylaea group (later renamed Cubo-Futurism). The manifesto opens the homonymous almanac, published in Moscow in 1912.

[2] The correct name is Aleksei Kruchenykh, but the poet at times and quite inconsistently used the name Aleksandr.

[3] These two paragraphs are a caustic attack on the Symbolist movement in general, a frequent target of the Futurists, and on two of its representatives in particular: Konstantin Bal'mont (1867-1943), a poet who enjoyed enormous popularity in Russia during the first decade of this century, was subsequently forgotten, and died as an émigré in Paris; Valerii Briusov (1873-1924), poet and scholar, leader of the Symbolist movement, editor of the *Scales* and literary editor of *Russian Thought*, who after the Revolution joined the Communist party and worked at Narkompros.

⁴ Leonid Andreev (1871-1919), a writer of short stories and a playwright, started in a realistic vein following Chekhov and Gor'kii; later he displayed an interest in metaphysics and a leaning toward Symbolism. He is at his best in a few stories written in a realistic manner; his Symbolist works are pretentious and unconvincing. The use of the plural here implies that, in the Futurists' eyes, Andreev is just one of numerous epigones.

⁵ Several disparate poets and prose writers are randomly assembled here, which stresses the radical position of the signatories of this manifesto, who reject indiscriminately all the literature written before them. The use of the plural, as in the previous paragraphs, is demeaning. Maksim Gor'kii (pseud. of Aleksei Peshkov, 1868-1936), Aleksandr Kuprin (1870-1938), and Ivan Bunin (1870-1953) are writers of realist orientation, although there are substantial differences in their philosophical outlook, realistic style, and literary value. Bunin was the first Russian writer to win a Nobel Prize, in 1933. Aleksandr Blok (1880-1921) is possibly the best, and certainly the most popular, Symbolist poet. His early poetry reflects his fascination with Vladimir Solov'ev's idealistic philosophy and the idea of the "eternal feminine"; his later poems reveal a concern for patriotic and nationalistic themes. Blok accepted the Revolution as an apocalyptic phenomenon and made an unsuccessful attempt to join the new order. Fedor Sologub (pseud. of Fedor Teternikov, 1863-1927) belongs to the first phase of Russian Symbolism, better known as Decadence. He was a refined poet but gained long-lasting fame from his novel *Petty Demon* (1907). Aleksei Remizov (1877-1957), a brilliant and very prolific prose writer, is a highly original stylist in the tradition of Gogol' and Dostoevskii. Arkadii Averchenko (1881-1925), a popular humorous writer, wrote short stories in a satirical vein. Sasha Chernyi (pseudo. of Aleksandr Glikberg, 1880-1932), poet-satirist and author of short stories, is also known for his children's prose and poetry. Mikhail Kuzmin (1875-1936) was the first post-Symbolist poet to oppose clarity of style and earthly aestheticism to vagueness and mysticism, both in a theoretical statement and in his creative output. The names Sologub and Kuzmin are incorrectly spelled in the original ("Sollogub" and "Kuz'min"), possibly to reinforce the sarcasm of the statement. The spelling "Sollogub" implies aristocratic origins, whereas Kuz'min implies plebeian ones.

Declaration of Transrational Language[1]

by Aleksandr KRUCHENYKH*

* A. Kruchenykh

** From *Words in Revolution: Russian Futurist Manifestos 1912-1928*, volume ed. Anna Lawton. Texts translated and edited by Anna Lawton and Herbert Eagle. Introduction by Anna Lawton and afterword by Herbert Eagle. Washington: New Academia Publishing, 2005. Pp. 182-183.

1. Thought and speech cannot keep up with the emotions of someone in a state of inspiration, therefore the artist is free to express himself not only in the common language (concepts), but also in a personal one (the creator is an individual), as well as in a language which does not have any definite meaning (not frozen), a *transrational* language. Common language binds, free language allows for fuller expression (Example: go osneg kaid etc.).[2]

2. Transreason is the (historically and individually) primordial form of poetry. At first it is a rhythmic-musical excitement, a protosound (the poet should write it down, because in further reworking he may forget it).

3. Transrational speech generates the transrational protoimage (and vice versa)—something not precisely defined, for example: the formless bogeymen Gorgo, Mormo; the misty beauty Ylayali; Avoska and Neboska, etc.[3]

4. One resorts to transrational language: **(a)** when the artist wants to convey images not fully defined (within himself or without himself), **(b)** when he does not want to name the object, but only to hint at it—a transrational feature: "he's kind of strange, he has a square soul"—here a usual word is given a transrational meaning. The invented first names and family names of literary heroes, names of peoples, localities, cities, etc. also belong here. For example: Oile, Bleiana, Vudras and Baryba, Svidrigailov, Karamazov, Chichikov, et al. (excluding, however, names which are explicitly allegorical, such as: Pravdin, Glupyshkin[4]—here the symbolism is clear and well defined).

(c) When one loses one's reason (hate, jealousy, rage...).

(d) When one does not need it—religious ecstasy, love. (The glossa of exclamation, interjection, murmurs, refrains, children's babble, pet names, nicknames—such transreason is plentiful among writers of all schools.)

5. Transreason awakens creative imagination and sets it free, without insulting it with anything concrete. Thought causes the word to contract, writhe, turn to stone; transreason, on the contrary, is wild, flaming, explosive (wild paradise, fiery languages, blazing coal).

6. Consequently, we have to distinguish three basic forms of word-creation:

    I. Transrational—
        a. The magic of songs, incantations, and curses.
        b. "Revelation (naming and depiction) of things unseen"[5]—mysticism.
        c. Musical-phonetic word-creation—orchestration, texture.

    II. Rational (its opposite is the language of the clinically insane, possessing its own laws as determined by science; but whatever is beyond scientific understanding must be included in the realm of the aesthetics of the random).

    III. Random (alogical, accidental, creative breakthrough, mechanical word combination: slips of the tongue, misprints, blunders; partially belonging to this category are phonetic and semantic shifts, ethnic accent, stuttering, lisping, etc.).

7. Transreason is the most compact art, both in terms of the time span between perception and expression, and in terms of its form, for example: Kuboa (Hamsun), Kho-bo-ro,[6] etc.

8. Transreason is the most universal art, although its origin and its initial character may be national, for example: Hurrah, Evan-evoe! etc.

Transrational works can provide a universal poetic language, born organically, and not artificially like Esperanto.

A. KRUCHENYKH
Baku, 1921

EDITOR'S NOTES

[1] The manifesto "Declaration of Transrational Language" (*Deklaratsiia zaumnogo iazyka*) appeared as a leaflet in Baku in 1921 and was subsequently reprinted in several of Kruchenykh's books. Besides reaffirming basic ideas, it sums up the poet's experience and intensive work while in Tiflis (1917-1920).

[2] This whole paragraph, article 1, is taken literally from "Declaration of the Word as Such," in this collection. The example is from one of Kruchenykh's poems, first published in *Union of Youth*, no. 3, and later in *Explodity*.

[3] Ylayali is a mythical figure from the novel *Hunger* (1890) by the Norwegian writer Knut Hamsun (1859-1952). Avos'ka and Nebos'ka are figures belonging to Russian folklore, and their approximate meaning is What-about and How-about.

[4] Oile is a mythical planet from a cycle of poems by F. Sologub, with the title "The Star Mair." This cycle was mainly written in 1898, with the last poem added in 1901. Oile is also the fantastic setting of the last part of Sologub's trilogy, *The Created Legend* (1908-12). Bleiana is another mythical country, from the short story "On the Road" by S. Miasoedov (...) Udras (rather than Vudras) and Baryba are two creatures from the collection of poems *Brightness* by Sergei Gorodetskii. They appear in the poems "They Celebrate Iarila" (1905) and "They Look for Baryba" (1907). Svidrigailov is a character from Dostoevskii's *Crime and Punishment*. Chichikov is the hero of Gogol's novel *Dead Souls*. Pravdin (Trueman) is a character from the comedy "The Young Hopeful" (1872 by D. Fonvizin (1745-92). Glupyshkin (Simpleton) is the Russian name for the character of Cretinetti from French silent movie comedies.

[5] See "New Ways of the Word,"...

[6] Kuboa, a word invented by the hero of Hamsun's novel *Hunger*. Kho-bo-ro is a transrational line from Kruchenykh's book *Learn Art* (1917).

"The Cherry Orchard"

by Richard PEACE*

* From *Chekhov: A Study of the Four Major Plays*. New Haven and London: Yale University Press, 1983. Pp. 117-153.

Chekhov's last play was written, with great pain and difficulty, in the year before his death. Yet despite the author's own tragic circumstances, he himself thought of the play as a comedy. The idea of writing a four-act vaudeville, or a comedy, for the Moscow Arts Theater goes back to 1901 and his own formulation of: "a funny play, where the devil would go about in a whirlwind" (i.e. "where all pandemonium might be let loose"), seems to hint at the sort of naive slapstick comedy associated with the early Gogol' of *Evenings in a Village near Dikanka*, as though Chekhov, at the end of his life, felt the need to go back to his own comic roots. Unlikely as it may seem, the influence of Gogol' can certainly be detected in the play.

As *The Cherry Orchard* was nearing completion, Chekhov forewarned Stanislavskii's wife (M. P. Lilina) in a letter of 15 September 1903: "Not a drama but a comedy has emerged from me, in places even a farce." The first person to read the play in Moscow was its recipient, Ol'ga Knipper [Chekhov's wife and a Moscow Art Theater actress], but in the telegram she sent to her husband expressing her delight with the play, she mentioned the tears it evoked in her. That very same day (18 October) Nemirovich-Danchenko read the play to a group of members of the Moscow Arts Theater company. By the fourth act they were in tears. The following day the manuscript was given to Stanislavskii. The first act he dutifully read as a comedy, but described himself as forcibly caught up by the second act, in a sweat in the third, and by the fourth he, too, was blubbering. In a letter to the author, he challenged the view which Chekhov had advanced to Lilina: "This is not a comedy or a farce, as you wrote, it is a tragedy, whatever way out you may have found for a better life in the last act."

The emotion which actors and producers alike felt in the play was further reinforced by the circumstances of its first performance. The *premiere* took place on 17 January 1904, a date which coincided with Chekhov's forty-fourth birthday, and was further marked out as a jubilee celebrating a quarter century of his career as a writer. At the end of the play, despite the fact that he was a terminally sick man, the author was called on stage to receive the tributes proper to such an occasion. Chekhov's ordeal was not lightened by the fact that the play had not only been badly acted but produced in a way contrary to his own intentions. The happy comedy which he had envisaged had turned into a valediction of tears. In a letter to Ol'ga Knipper of 10 April, Chekhov complained:

> Why is it that in posters and newspaper announcements my play is persistently called a drama? Nemirovich-Danchenko, and Stanislavskii see in my play something absolutely different from what I have written, and I am willing to stake my word on it that neither of them has once read my play through attentively. Forgive me, but I assure you, it is so.

This fundamental disagreement about the interpretation of *The Cherry Orchard* is one of the most intractable, yet intriguing problems in Chekhovian scholarship. It suggests, as a general issue, some irreconcilable cleavage between an "author's theater" and a "producer's theater" the implications of which go beyond the staging of Chekhov's own plays, yet, on a particular plane, it raises fundamental questions about the nature of Chekhov's humor. In spite of the tears that it evoked in those who first read and performed it, Chekhov defiantly sub-titled his play "A comedy in four acts" (*komediia v chetyrekh deistviiakh*). Is it possible "to read the play through attentively" and find out why?

At first sight it appears to be Chekhov himself who calls for tears from his actors: his own directions indicate that many of the speeches are to be delivered "through tears." Nevertheless as rehearsals were under way, Chekhov clarified his intentions in a letter to Nemirovich-Danchenko (23 October) stressing that these "tears" were not to be taken literally—they were merely an indication of mood. Yet this prescription for a mood which patently runs counter to the laughter expected of a "comedy" has its own resonance in the traditions of Russian literature: it suggests Gogol's well-known formula "laughter through tears."

....

...Chekhov, who once proclaimed Gogol' the greatest of Russian writers, showed a Gogolian sense of humor in many of his early stories. Thus in "The Death of a Civil Servant" he invites his readers to laugh at the circumstances which bring about the death of a figure traditionally treated as deserving compassion—the poor civil servant.

....

No situation is unequivocally comic in its own right. The basic device of "slapstick" contains pain and humiliation as well as comedy, so that a clown can exploit a fall either in the direction of laughter or the direction of pathos. Chekhov spoke of his last comedy as "in places almost a farce" and it is true that it contains pronounced elements of slapstick: an incensed and indignant Trofimov falls down the stairs; Varia, wishing to hit Epikhodov with a stick, hits Lopakhin instead: Epikhodov crushes a hat box, and has boots which squeak as he walks. Nevertheless these stock ingredients of farce are not as straightforward as they might at first seem. When in Act I Lopakhin pokes his head round the door and makes an unexpected mooing noise at Varia, her reaction is to threaten him with her fist, but Chekhov's accompanying directions read: [through tears]. When in Act IV Varia takes up an umbrella rather too violently and Lopakhin feigns fear that he is about to be beaten, the audience is aware not only of Varia's threatening fist in Act I (and the actual beating in Act III) but also of the poignancy of Lopakhin's non-proposal that preceded it and has injected its own tension into this second non-event. This final act, where the Moscow Arts Theater saw only tears, is in reality packed with comic detail. Even Lopakhin's failure to propose to Varia has its Gogolian antecedents in the ludicrous behavior of those reluctant bridegrooms Shpon'ka and Podkolesin (*Ivan Fedorovich Shpon'ka and his Aunty*, and *Marriage*) and overt comedy persists until the end in such details as the unexpected onset of Epikhodov's comic voice.

Throughout *The Cherry Orchard* Chekhov places the action on a knife edge between laughter and tears; but he intends no neutral balance. He expects pathos to weigh on the side of the comic, not against it, and comedy, thus reinforced, to tilt decisively in favor of laughter. The expectations of Stanislavskii were entirely different, and with equal ease he was able to incline the play's delicate mechanism in a contrary direction.

The "tearful" interpretation of the play derives almost entirely from a particular focus on a single character: Liubov' Andreevna. At the very beginning, before her entry on stage, Lopakhin characterizes her as: "a good person, easy to get on with, a person without affectation" (*khoroshii ona chelovek, prostoi chelovek*). Once on stage she easily captures an audience's sympathy; she is warm, full-blooded, romantic, generous (though some of these qualities, particularly the latter, may also be flaws). She can be seen as a tragic figure, who has suffered both in life and in love. Happy and excited though she is, in Act I, to return to the place of her birth, there is nevertheless a sadness which she cannot conquer: "If only one could take off this heavy stone from my breast and shoulders, if only I could forget my past." Later in Act III she will be more precise about the nature of this stone—it is her lover in Paris from whom she has parted: "I love, love... this stone round my neck. I am going down to the bottom with it, but I love this stone, and cannot live without it." The fact that the image here is one of drowning (*ia idu s nim na dno*) suggests yet another identification for this "stone" of the past—the grief and guilt associated with the drowning of her young son; a punishment, she feels, for having taken up with a lover.

It cannot be doubted that Liubov' Andreevna is at the very center of the play, and the conflict for possession of the cherry orchard might be interpreted as an opposition of her values to those of Lopakhin: the romantic and the generous opposed to the prosaic and the mercenary; the cultured and the vulnerable in hopeless combat with the philistine and the successful; the ancient and aristocratic ranged against the plebeian and the new. Conflict within the play, however, is not as straightforward as this.

Another possible opposition exists between Liubov' Andreevna and the "eternal student" Trofimov—a conflict between a depth of feeling which stems from a tragic past and a naive superficial optimism about the future, which shuns all emotion. Trofimov is the play's chief advocate for a complete break with the past. He successfully woos Ania, the representative of the younger generation of landowners away from all attachment to the cherry orchard, yet such wooing seems essentially ideological. Her mother mocks Trofimov for saying that he is "above love" castigating his smugness as lack of experience:

> You're able to solve all your problems in a resolute way—but, tell me, my dear boy, isn't that because you're young, because you're not old enough yet to have suffered on account of your problems.

This choice of verb: "to suffer through" (*perestradat'*) is typical of Liubov' Andreevna's emotional attitude to life with its emphasis on "love" and "suffering" (it seems significant that her very Christian name Liubov' actually means "Love"). Her emotionalism is in obvious contrast to Trofimov's purely intellectual attitude to life and its problems.

It cannot be denied that the play ranges Liubov' Andreevna against Lopakhin and Trofimov, but it does not do so in any crude diagrammatical way. If comic elements, which are a feature of the way her two "opponents" are presented, seem excluded from the portrayal of Liubov' Andreevna herself, we should not necessarily assume that she is the only serious character in the play, and that her attitude to life is the only one endorsed by the author himself.

....

If it were not for the figure of Liubov' Andreevna, no producer would hesitate to present the play as a comedy. She is surrounded by a retinue of genuinely comic characters, as well as by more serious figures who nevertheless are not allowed to escape implications of the comic. Liubov' Andreevna seems above all this, and yet the comedy is centered on her in a very real sense; for in those who surround her can be glimpsed traits and attitudes of Liubov' Andreevna herself—but parodied and exaggerated to the point where they become comic. The most obvious example of this is to be seen in her brother who acts a comic alter ego. Brother and sister share many attitudes and assumptions in common, but in Gaev they are taken to ludicrous extremes. It is because of this exaggeration that the oppositional relationship of both Lopakhin and Trofimov is, as we shall see, even more pertinent for Gaev than it is for Liubov' Andreevna herself.

The opening stage directions of Act I make clear the emotional and symbolic setting for Liubov' Andreevna's homecoming: [*A room which used to be the children's bedroom and is still referred to as the "nursery"*]. The Russian is even more piquant: the word: *detskaia*—"nursery" is derived from an adjective which can also mean "childlike," "infantile." Liubov' Andreevna's first utterance in the play is this one word *detskaia* in the form of an exclamation. Her next remarks develop the theme: "The nursery, my dear, my beautiful room! ... I used to sleep here when I was little.... [Cries.] And now I feel as if I were little again" (*I teper' ia kak malen'kaia*). The ambiguity of this last statement, which could also mean "even now I am like a small girl" seems significant. It is followed by her twice kissing her brother Gaev, who is in essence a child, and by once kissing Varia—the most adult member of the household.

The nursery as the setting for Act I is thus highly suggestive: both Liubov' Andreevna and Gaev have the characteristics of children incapable of looking after themselves or of living in any other world than that of make-believe. But it is in Gaev that the characteristics of the child are most pronounced—with his constant sucking of sweets (he jokes of having consumed his estate in the form of sweets); with his imaginary games of billiards; but above all through the way in which he allows [the servant] Firs to fuss over him, and scold him for not wearing the right clothes.

The tendency towards romantic effusion, evident in Liubov' Andreevna's opening speeches on the nursery, is taken to comic excess in Gaev. Towards the middle of Act I he causes embarrassment by his comically inappropriate declamation honoring the centenary of a family bookcase. Yet only shortly before this, his sister had addressed it, even kissed it: "You can laugh at me, I'm foolish.... My dear bookcase! [*Kisses bookcase.*] My own little table!" In spite of her invitation to laugh at this exhibition of emotion (indeed perhaps because of it) such an unsympathetic response from the audience is effectively blocked. We are merely allowed a glimpse of irony, when it is later discovered that this emotional symbol of the past has been guarding the telegrams from her lover in Paris, summoning her return.

When Gaev opens the window on to the cherry orchard in Act I he is permitted his one moment of poetry:

> GAEV [*opens another window*]. The orchard is all white. You haven't forgotten, Liuba? How straight this long avenue is— quite straight, just like a ribbon that's been stretched taut. It glitters on moonlit nights. Do you remember? You haven't forgotten?

This, however, is merely the prelude to a much longer speech from Liubov' Andreevna in her most exalted and poetic manner:

> LIUBOV' ANDREEVNA [*looks through the window at the orchard*]. O my childhood, My purity! In this nursery I slept, looked from here out of the window at the orchard, Happiness awoke along with me every morning. Even then it was exactly the same, nothing has changed. [*Laughs from happiness.*] All, all

white! O, my orchard! After a dark rainy autumn and a cold winter, you are again young, full of happiness. The heavenly angels have not forsaken thee....

Here in spite of the moments of potential bathos (the middle-aged Venus regretting lost "purity"; the "heavenly angels") Liubov' Andreevna's speech is not comic. Indeed one may argue, in view of what has already been said on the mixed nature of the comic and the pathetic, that the audience's awareness of potential bathos serves in effect to heighten the pathos. Yet what is possible for Liubov' Andreevna is not allowed her brother: his apostrophizing of Nature in Act II is treated as yet another absurd embarrassment:

> GAEV [*in a subdued voice, as if reciting a poem*]. Oh, glorious Nature, shining with eternal light, so beautiful, yet so indifferent to our fate ... you, whom we call Mother, uniting in yourself both Life and Death, you live and you destroy.

Much the same is true in Act IV. Gaev is once more silenced when he begins to talk in a rhetorical manner about his feelings on leaving the house, whereas earlier in the act his sister had been allowed to pour out her elevated feelings on the same subject, and even to personify the house as "old grandfather" (*staryi dedushka*): "Goodbye, dear house, old grandfather [house]. Winter will pass, spring will come again, and then you won't be here anymore, you'll be pulled down. How much these walls have seen!"

If Gaev is an obvious comic shadow for the childlike and naively romantic aspects of Liubov' Andreevna, it can also be seen that similar functions are carried out by other characters who surround her. Simeonov-Pishchik is the embodiment of her fecklessness over matters of money and estate affairs. When Liubov' Andreevna drops her purse in Act II the incident seems tragically symbolic (even though comedy is possible in the actions of [her servant] Iasha crawling around the stage to pick up her scattered gold). Nevertheless, the comic counter-weight comes in Act III, when Pishchik, who is similarly faced with the need to make mortgage repayments suddenly thinks he has lost his money, but finds it again in the lining of his coat. Liubov' Andreevna's incompetence in money results in the loss of her estate, but such fecklessness in Pishchik has the happy outcome of comedy. For Pishchik, something always turns up: Englishmen find china clay deposits on his estate, and at the end of the play he has money to pay everyone back.

The means by which Pishchik is saved is yet a further commentary on Liubov' Andreevna's romantic attitude to her estate and her cherry orchard. He is prepared to come to terms with modern commercial interests, be it the railway he allows to pass through his estates, or the mining of china clay. The business proposition put to her by Lopakhin is dismissed as "vulgar."

Pishchik is a comic deflator of such pretentiousness. In Act I he interrupts the discussion of former gastronomic delights prepared from the fruit of this orchard by asking Liubov' Andreevna whether she ate frogs in Paris, and she allows herself the comic retort: "I ate crocodiles." Shortly afterwards her hypochondria receives similar treatment, when Iasha reminds her that it is time to take her pills:

> PISHCHIK. Don't take medicines, my dear ... they don't do you any good ... or harm either. Let me have them. [Takes the box from her, pours the pills into the palm of his hand, blows on them, puts them all into his mouth and takes a drink of kvass.] There!

As a result, he later falls asleep whilst still speaking, snores, but suddenly wakes up and asks Liubov' Andreevna to lend him money for his own mortgage repayments.[1]

The tragic overtones of Liubov' Andreevna's life—the misfortunes which weigh on her like a stone—find a comic projection in the ridiculous figure of Epikhodov, nicknamed "Two-and-twenty misfortunes." He, like a truly tragic figure, is a stoic in the face of adversity: "Every day something or other unpleasant happens to me. But I don't complain; I'm accustomed to it, I even laugh at it." Liubov' Andreevna's unhappy, destructive love affair has its gross parallel at the level of the servants in the triangular relationship between Epikhodov, Duniasha and Iasha, and tragedy even seems threatened at the beginning of Act II, when Epikhodov reveals that he always carries a gun in case he feels like shooting himself.

Nevertheless, despite the subsequent behavior of Duniasha, he spends the rest of the act quietly strumming his guitar.

Two incongruously associated aspects of Liubov' Andreevna's character: on the one hand her cosmopolitan rootlessness, and on the other her immersion in the past and deafness to a changing world, are embodied in the antithetical figures of Sharlotta and Firs. Chekhov had originally ended Act II with a lyrical conversation between these two characters, but he dropped this idea on the advice of Stanislavskii; transferring some of Sharlotta's speeches to the beginning of the act instead.

There is more than a hint of the fairground in the passport-less wandering of Sharlotta, yet it serves as a comment on her mistress and benefactor, who has lived in Mentone and Paris, and who, once back in Russia, confesses almost immediately that she cannot sit still; her return to Paris in Act IV comes as no surprise. When Liubov' Andreevna expresses pleasure that Firs is still alive, and receives the incongruous reply "the day before yesterday," we may laugh at what this tells us about Firs, but at the same time be aware of an echo for his backward-looking mistress. There is more pathos in the presentation of Firs and Sharlotta than there is in the portrayal of the other comic characters. In Firs this stems from his age, but in the case of Sharlotta it is perhaps significant that she of all the characters is the nearest to the professional clown.

The comic characters perform a vital function in the delicate mechanism of the play's overall balance. They act as conductors of ridicule, drawing the comedy away from Liubov' Andreevna herself, allowing her to remain serious, tragic, poetic, yet at the same time they take up and comment on certain aspects of her personality, which if taken to excess, or if seen in a different perspective, are merely comic. The shadowy presence of such aspects can serve to heighten the pathos of her presentation, but if they are allowed more fully into the light, we may then indeed have something nearer to Chekhov's own intentions. A hair's breadth can separate the devices of pathos and comedy—at the shock of loss Liubov' Andreevna: [*would have fallen, if she were not standing beside a table and an armchair*]; whereas, in the elation of gain, Lopakhin: [*pushes a small table accidentally and nearly knocks over some candle-sticks*].

The play's dominant theme is social change. We are made aware of this from the very opening in the conversation between Lopakhin, the self-made man, and Duniasha, the maid with pretensions to gentility. Nearly every character is associated to some degree with social ambiguity. Liubov' Andreevna herself has lowered her status through marriage—her brother tells us at the end of Act I that she had married someone who was not a nobleman (...). Her elder daughter, Varia, is adopted and is of peasant or lower class origin (...) as she tells Lopakhin in Act II. In effect, Varia seems more like a housekeeper than a daughter of the house. She is characterized in Chekhov's stage directions by her keys, (i. e. *kliuchi* which suggests the Russian word for housekeeper *kliuchnitsa*)... Most telling of all, she always addresses her mother and uncle by the polite form of "you" (*vy*) whereas the true daughter Ania addresses them in the familiar form *ty*.

Ania herself will turn her back on the estate and the old life, under the influence of Trofimov, who, although his own father was a drug store owner, is comically referred to as a "shabby gentleman." The real gentry, as exemplified by Liubov' Andreevna, her brother Gaev and the neighbor Simeonov-Pishchik, are chronically short of money. The Gaev family estate will be sold, and Gaev himself will be offered a job in a bank.

Times are obviously changing. The younger servants, Iasha and Duniasha, give themselves airs and ape their masters. Duniasha dances at the ball in Act III as though she were a guest, and indeed the real guests are of low social status. Firs comments: "We used to have generals, barons, and admirals dancing at our balls, but now we send for the post-office clerk and the station-master, and even they don't come too willingly." The presence of such figures is in itself significant—they represent the modern world of rapid communication: the railway (newly built) and the telegraph (Liubov' Andreevna is constantly being summoned back by telegram to her lover in Paris). Thus Liubov' Andreevna's ball not only acknowledges social change, it invites the new forces which are disrupting the old way of life.

Lopakhin, the self-made merchant of peasant origin, stands at the center of this social change. He is the bridge between the old world and the new. The ambiguity of his social position is nicely judged; through his money he is the equal of the masters, yet he is also aware of his relationship to the lower orders. Thus on taking his leave in Act I he kisses the hand of Liubov' Andreevna, embraces the nobleman Pishchik, but does not forget to shake hands with the servants Iasha and Firs. Lopakhin merely says a polite farewell to Gaev, but this is understandable given Gaev's rather squeamish hostility to this upstart who is destined to replace him as owner of the estate.

The loss of a *dacha* is one of the first things we learn about Liubov' Andreevna. As Ania tells us: "She has already sold her *dacha* near Mentone. She has nothing left, nothing." It is, therefore, ironic that later in the same act Lopakhin should tell her of the transformation being effected in the Russian countryside because of the hunger for *dachas* among the new rising force of the urban middle class: "Up to now in the countryside there have been only masters and peasants, but now *dacha* owners have appeared as well. Every town, even the smallest, is surrounded by *dachas*."[2] Lopakhin rubs salt into the wound by suggesting that the Gaev estate should undergo the same fate.

Social change in Russian literature is often presented as a conflict between generations. Turgenev's *Fathers and Children* is perhaps the best known example, and the novel is typical in that it presents the struggle as one of ideas, which are identified by specific decades of the nineteenth century: it is the struggle of the "men of the sixties" against the "men of the forties." This theme, in essence the theme of the Russian intelligentsia, is also present in *The Cherry Orchard*. Gaev, who is of the generation of the "fathers" in the play, identifies himself towards the end of Act I as a "man of the eighties":

> GAEV. You know, I'm a man of the "eighties." People don't think much of that period, but all the same I can say that I've suffered quite a lot in the course of my life for my convictions. It's not for nothing that the peasants love me. You have to know the peasants! You have to know from which side...

At this point he is shut up by a representative of the "children," his niece Ania. Gaev is always silenced when he makes such speeches;

the others find it embarrassing—it is mere rhetoric. In fact words are the only mark of his claim to belong to the intelligentsia of the 1880s. When he says that no one praises that period, he is right. Alexander II had been assassinated in 1881 and the event had ushered in a period of great repression in Russian political and intellectual life. It was a time when all ideas and actions were suspect, a time of "petty deeds" (*malye dela*). Intellectually it was largely a cowed and demoralized generation, so that for Gaev to suggest that he has suffered for his convictions as a "man of the eighties" must strike a Russian audience as ludicrous. The role and nature of the peasant was a permanent preoccupation of the Russian intelligentsia, and at no time more than during the decade preceding the 1880s. There is no evidence in the play that Gaev has any real interest in the peasants, and (as we shall see) the attitude to serfdom will be the corner stone of the criticism voiced by the younger generation against the "fathers" in the play. Moreover it is curious that Gaev should seek to identify himself with the "eighties." As he is now fifty-one years old, it would seem more natural for him to consider himself a "man of the seventies"; for in 1881 he could not possibly have been younger than twenty-eight, and the period of the 1880s would therefore have largely coincided with his own thirties. Gaev's self-identification with the 1880s doubly proclaims his intellectual immaturity.

Gaev's earlier, embarrassing speech to the bookcase reveals the values of the "man of the eighties." Although he talks of "fruitful work" (*plodotvornaia rabota*), it appears to be books which, in his view have summoned the Russian intelligentsia to action throughout the whole century. There is no evidence that Gaev himself has read any books; his one passion is that sign of a misspent youth—billiards—and he frames his idea not in terms of books but of the bookcase. Thus books are substituted for action, and a bookcase for the books themselves:

> GAEV. Your silent summons to fruitful work has, not slackened through the course of a century, maintaining [*through tears*] in the generations of our kith and kin courage, a faith in a better future, and fostering in us the ideals of good and of social self-awareness.

Some forty years earlier, in his influential essay *What is Oblomovism?* the critic Nikolai Dobroliubov had assessed the tradition of gentry culture as it had developed up to that point. He claimed that for the gentry intelligentsia reading got in the way of deeds, that rhetoric replaced action, and that its leaders showed little more than self-regard: he saw the summation of its values in the hero of Goncharov's novel *Oblomov*. Gaev, in paying tribute to a full century of this tradition, seems cast in the role of an updated "Oblomov" (...) Little appears to have changed: Gaev is lazy, lives in a childish world of the imagination; he too is nannied by an elderly servant, who dresses him much as Zakhar dresses Oblomov. Gaev prefers rhetoric to books and most certainly to action; his social consciousness is merely self-regarding—the social self-awareness of a class. Nevertheless, Oblomov's friend Shtol'ts, the representative of a newly rising entrepreneurial class, had been Oblomov's constant support, but in Chekhov's play the activities of that entrepreneurial friend of the family, Lopakhin, are ultimately destructive.

Nobody takes the elevated thoughts of Gaev seriously, yet Trofimov is listened to. He is of the younger generation of the intelligentsia and his social origins are quite different from those of Gaev. In Act II Gaev's proclamation of aesthetic and romantic values, in the speech on nature which he is forced to abandon, follows hard on the heels of Trofimov's speech on the future and on the need for work. It is as though Gaev had been spurred into vying with the younger man; for, significantly, Trofimov's words are an indictment of Gaev himself:

> TROFIMOV. The vast majority of the intelligentsia that I know is not searching for anything, does nothing and, as yet, is unfitted for hard work. They call themselves an intelligentsia, but they address servants as "thou," treat peasants like animals. They do not learn well and they read nothing seriously. They do absolutely nothing; only talk about the sciences, and understand little in art.

Gaev, the "man of the eighties," who claims to love the peasants, is just such an intellectual charlatan. He, too, addresses the servant,

Iasha, as "thou" (*ty*), even though his sister addresses Iasha in the polite form: "you" (*vy*), and the pet name she reserves for Gaev himself—Lena—seems to confirm his laziness (*len'*).³

Chekhov's portrayal of Trofimov is not as explicit as he would have liked. The concept of "eternal student" has not necessarily the comic implications it assumes in the play, as Chekhov explained to his wife, in confiding the fears he had entertained about the play's success: "I was chiefly afraid about the lack of movement in the second act, and a certain lack of completeness in the student Trofimov. You see, Trofimov is constantly in exile, he is constantly being expelled from the university, and how can one depict things like that?"⁴ It would have been impossible for Chekhov to have depicted his student as a revolutionary, nevertheless, when Trofimov refuses Lopakhin's money, in Act IV, there can be no doubt as to his meaning:

> I'm strong, I'm proud, I can do without you, I can pass you by. Humanity is advancing towards the highest truth, the greatest happiness that it is possible to achieve on earth, and I am in the van[-guard]!

There is a naive, idealistic, purity about Trofimov which is reminiscent of the revolutionary heroes depicted by N. G. Chernyshevskii in his novel *What is to be done?* His sexual purity is mocked by Liubov' Andreevna, but by treating Trofimov's idealism and the involuntary protraction of his university career with humor, Chekhov manages to present him in a way acceptable to the censorship of the time. He did not deceive everybody. As *The Cherry Orchard* was in rehearsal, Gor'kii is reported to have said to its author: "Now I am convinced that your next play will be a revolutionary one."

Nevertheless Chekhov is polemicizing with Gor'kii in the play. Trofimov's words on being "strong and proud" pick up the pride advocated by Satin in Gor'kii's play *The Lower Depths*.⁵

....

[The discussion about "pride" continues the following day.]

LIUBOV' ANDREEVNA. No, let's continue what we were talking about yesterday.

TROFIMOV. What were we talking about?

GAEV. About pride.

TROFIMOV. We talked a lot yesterday, but we didn't agree on anything. The proud man, in the sense you understand him, has something mystical about him. Maybe you're right in a way, but if we try to think it out simply, without being too far-fetched about it, the question arises—why should he be proud? Where's the sense in being proud when you consider that Man, as a species, is not very well constructed physiologically, and, in the vast majority of cases is coarse, stupid, and profoundly unhappy, too? We ought to stop all this self-admiration. We ought to—just work.

GAEV. You'll die just the same, whatever you do.

TROFIMOV. Who knows? And anyway, what does it mean—to die? It may be that Man is possessed of a hundred senses, and only the five that are known to us perish in death, while the remaining ninety-five live on afterwards.

Trofimov, who begins by attacking the mysticism of Gor'kii's "proud man," is easily brought round in argument to propounding his own mystical ideas on mortal man, and although his next speech is his serious attack on the intelligentsia which, as we have already seen, is an implied criticism of Gaev, there is, nevertheless, a measure of unconscious irony at his own expense as a member of the intelligentsia:

> TROFIMOV. They all look very grave and go about with grim expressions on their faces, and they only discuss important matters and philosophize. Yet all the time anyone can see that our work-people are abominably fed and have to sleep without proper beds, thirty to forty to a room, with bed-bugs, bad smells, damp and immorality everywhere. It's perfectly obvious that all our nice-sounding talk is intended only to mislead ourselves and others.

Lopakhin, the practical business man, and Trofimov, the idealist intellectual, do not always see eye to eye, but in spite of their jibes there is a certain mutual respect. Lopakhin is impressed by

Trofimov's extolling of work, and through him the argument once more turns to the nature of man: he considers that the grand scale of Russia itself should produce native-born giants.[6] Significantly Liubov' Andreevna sees such supermen as a threat, whereas Chekhov himself, by suddenly forcing Epikhodov upon everyone's attention, appears to endorse Trofimov's original objection to the mysticism of "proud man"—the reality of man as he exists:

> LIUBOV' ANDREEVNA. Whatever do you want giants for? They're all right in fairy-tales, otherwise they're just terrifying.
> [EPIKHODOV *crosses the stage in the background, playing his guitar.*]
> LIUBOV' ANDREEVNA [*pensively*]. There goes Epikhodov...
> ANIA [*pensively*]. There goes Epikhodov...
> GAEV. The sun's gone down, ladies and gentlemen.

Here is Chekhov creating mood, but one, which for all its poetic wistfulness has hard ironic comment at its core.

....

If the guitar and person of "Two-and-twenty misfortunes" seem to add a melancholy, pessimistic note to hopes about the nature of man and the happiness to come through social change, there is yet another "sad" sound of a string to be heard in Act II, and it provides an even more ominous commentary on the theme. Again the mood is pensive: [*They all sit deep in thought; the silence is only broken by the subdued muttering of* FIRS. *Suddenly a distant sound is heard, coming as if out of the sky, like the sound of a string snapping, slowly and sadly dying away*]. Although the sound appears to come from above, Lopakhin suggests it might have an underground explanation—a pit accident. Even more improbably Gaev and Trofimov think of birds (a heron and an eagle owl). Liubov' Andreevna shudders, finding the sound "unpleasant somehow," but it is left to Firs, whose own mumblings the sound had disturbed, to interpret it as an omen: [*A pause.*] FIRS. "It was the same before the misfortune: the owl hooted and the samovar kept singing." When he is asked to what "misfortune" (*neschast'e*) he is referring, Firs replies: "before freedom." He has in mind the greatest social upheaval of nineteenth-century Russia — the liberation of the serfs in 1861, but he does not see this great reform which gave him the new status of a free man, as bringing happiness — it was "unhappiness" (i. e. misfortune).

....

The symbolism of the play, which on one level evokes a poetic penumbra of lyrical mood and pensive reflection, in reality exhibits the same mixed elements as the comedy — it contains an undercurrent which is ominous and disturbing. The central image of the cherry orchard is seen by different characters in different ways. It represents both happiness and suffering, and its fate also reflects the theme of social change. In Act I, the orchard, although off-stage, is an obvious presence; the windows of the nursery open directly on to it, and its beauty is a focal point of attention. Act II is set outside on the estate, but not in the cherry orchard. The opening directions indicate that the orchard begins beyond the poplars on one side of the set. During Act III, when the estate is being sold, there is little real evidence of the orchard's existence, and in Act IV the audience is aware of the cherry orchard through its negation in the off-stage sounds of the axes which are chopping it down. Thus with each successive act there is a sense of the cherry orchard receding further and further towards oblivion.

For Liubov' Andreevna the cherry orchard symbolizes her childhood and the past. It is the most remarkable phenomenon in the whole province, a thing of beauty, which also produces fruit (though not as often as it might, and now unfortunately it can no longer be put to use). Like Gaev's century-old bookcase it stands as a symbol for the flowering of nineteenth-century gentry culture, whose fruits and usefulness are now in the past.[7] Its existence is threatened by a more democratic age, in which every little bourgeois wants his *dacha* and his own plot of land, which, as their spokesman Lopakhin hopes, they will one day set about to cultivate.

....

[The tree symbolism of the play refers back] to the extended allegory of the forest in Dobroliubov's essay *What is Oblomovism?* Dobroliubov depicts the gentry intelligentsia as attempting to lead the ordinary people through a dangerous forest. They climb the trees to avoid the dangers and to spy the way ahead, but the trees are comfortable and they have found fruit there. They ignore the people below until the latter in desperation begin to hack down their trees:

> "Oh! Oh! Don't do that! Stop!' they howl when they see the people setting to work to cut down the trees on which they are ensconced. 'Don't you realize that we may be killed and that with us will perish those beautiful ideas, those lofty sentiments, those human strivings, that eloquence, that fervor, that love for all that is beautiful and noble that have always inspired us? Stop! Stop! What are you doing?"

The trees of Dobroliubov's allegory were to be taken as representing the institution of serfdom, which supported the gentry and yielded them fruit, whilst at the same time affording them an elevated position which they could claim was for the benefit of others, but axes remove this social myth as they remove the Gaevs' cherry orchard at the end of Chekhov's play.

For Liubov' Andreevna the orchard is still alive with happy ghosts. She looks out of the window in Act I and believes she sees her mother in a white dress. It is of course merely a tree. But for Trofimov the orchard is peopled with other ghosts, as he tells Ania towards the end of Act II:

> TROFIMOV. Just think Ania: your grandfather, great grandfather and all your ancestors were serf-owners, they owned living souls, and surely you are aware that from every cherry tree in the orchard, from every leaf, from every trunk, human beings are looking at you. Do you not hear the voices? To own living souls that has caused degeneration in us all, those who lived earlier and those living now, so that your mother, you, your uncle no longer notice that you are living on credit, on somebody else's account, at the expense of those people whom you do not allow beyond the entrance hall.... We are at least some two hundred years behind, we

still have absolutely nothing, no clearly defined attitude to the past, we only philosophize, complain of depression or drink vodka. It is, after all, so clear, that in order to begin to live in the present, we must first redeem our past, finish with it, but it can be redeemed only by suffering, only by unusual, unbroken labor. You must understand this, Ania.

This is undoubtedly the most important speech in the play. It begins with a broad vision, an exhortation to look beyond the narrow confines of the cherry orchard: "The whole of Russia is our orchard. The earth is great and beautiful and there are many, many wonderful places on it." Here Trofimov seems to be almost on the point of endorsing Lopakhin's earlier idea that the grand scale of nature in Russia should produce giants, but the body of the speech contains one of Chekhov's strongest indictments of Russia's past. It is a speech with many resonances. Thus it is significant that Trofimov projects the particular, legal situation of the orchard's present owners into the general and moral position of a whole class. They are in debt, but not to the bank: they are "living on credit, on somebody else's account, at the expense of those people whom you do not allow beyond the entrance hall." Similarly the "redemption" he proposes is no mere financial transaction—it is nothing less than the redemption of the entire past.

....

Lopakhin believes that he can forget his peasant past. In Act I he tells Liubov' Andreevna, that although her brother regards him as an oaf and a *kulak*, (a tight-fisted peasant) he feels that he has an affinity with her:

> LOPAKHIN. My father was your father's serf, and your grandfather's, too, but you did so much for me in the past that I forget everything and love you as if you were my own sister ... more than my own sister.

The word Lopakhin uses here is not "sister" but *rodnoi* (*Liubliu vas kak rodnuiu... bol'she chem rodnuiu*)—i. e. "I love you as kith and kin... more than kith and kin."

Liubov' Andreevna completely ignores this declaration of affection and kinship. Instead she proclaims her restlessness and almost immediately exhibits her affection for an inanimate object, using the very same kinship-like term of endearment—*rodnoi*: "My dear little bookcase" (*shkafik moi rodnoi*). She kisses it, then addresses her table.

There is no stage direction to indicate that Lopakhin might have taken this as a rebuff, but the next time he speaks, the comic juxtaposition of ideas suggests a certain irony: "I feel I'd like to tell you something nice, something jolly. [*Glances at his watch.*] I'll have to go in a moment, there's no time to talk." He then broaches his scheme for the cherry orchard.

Earlier, when the aged family retainer, Firs, had brought her a cushion, Liubov' Andreevna had extended the endearment *rodnoi* to him and kissed him, calling him "her dear little old Man" (*moi starichek*). In Act III she shows concern about his health and asks him where he will go if the estate is sold. Yet in Act IV, although she takes an emotional farewell of the house itself, and actually personifies it as "old grandad", she shows little concern for Firs, the real "old grandad" of the house, who is thoughtlessly left behind along with the furniture. Indeed there is unconscious irony in her words: "When we leave here there won't be a soul in the place."

This final act opens with Gaev and Liubov' Andreevna returning from saying farewell to the peasants. With typical lack of restraint in matters of money, she has given them her purse, but she is more thrifty with her attention when it comes to saying goodbye to her faithful old retainer. Firs is ill, she knows that she will not see him again, yet at the end of the act she looks impatiently at her watch and says she can spare him some five minutes. When she is told that he has already gone, she makes absolutely no comment but passes immediately to what she sees as her duties in respect of Varia.

There is a general lack of concern about Firs. In Act III the other servants enjoy themselves as guests at the ball, leaving Firs to do all the work, so that his complaint: "There's no one in the house but me" (*odin na ves' dom*) seems almost prophetic of the ending. Prophetic too is the apparent nonsense reply which Firs makes in Act II, when Gaev complains of being "fed up" with him for fussing over him about his clothes: "There's nothing to be done there... they went off in the morning without saying anything." Iasha, who ironically addresses Firs as "grandad" (*dedushka*) expresses his boredom more strongly in Act III: "How you weary me, Grandad! [*Yawns.*] I wish you'd go away and die soon." A similar unsympathetic sentiment is expressed by Epikhodov in Act IV at the very time that Ania is trying to find out whether Firs has already left:

> ANIA. Has Firs been taken to hospital?
>
> IASHA. I told them to take him this morning. He's gone, I think.
>
> ANIA [to EPIKHODOV, *who passes through the ballroom*]. Semen Panteleevich, will you please find out whether Firs has been taken to hospital?
>
> IASHA [offended]. I told Egor this morning. Need you ask ten times?
>
> EPIKHODOV. This superannuated Firs—candidly speaking, I mean he's beyond repair, he ought to go and join his ancestors. As for me, I can only envy him.

Saying farewell to Firs has been left to the unsympathetic, even hostilely disposed, younger generation of servants, and the fact that the letter, which should have accompanied him, is still in the house alerts neither Ania nor Varia to the possibility that he might not even yet have gone. It is Trofimov's point that serf-owning has corrupted everybody—masters and servants alike.

Firs, the human embodiment of the old order is left locked up in the old manorial house which is soon to be destroyed. Yet, although the masters have forgotten him, he, as ever, is solicitous for them:

> FIRS [walks up to the middle door and tries the handle]. Locked. They've gone.... [*Sits down on a sofa.*] They forgot about me. Never mind.... I'll sit here for a bit. I don't suppose Leonid Andreevich put on his fur coat, I expect he's gone in his light one.... [*Sighs, preoccupied.*] I didn't see to it... These youngsters!

The finer feelings of Leonid Andreevich (Gaev) himself seem reserved for such things as a bookcase... the house itself or even such abstract concepts as Nature, apostrophized as a person. The confusion of animate and inanimate is reflected even in his speech mannerisms. At moments of embarrassment he frequently asks: "whom?" (*kogo?*) instead of "what?" (*chto?*); and the billiard terminology which is constantly on his lips treats the billiard balls as grammatical animates rather than inanimate entities (e. g. *kladu chistogo, zheltogo v seredinu*, etc.).

....

...[The] estate is sold ... Nor, after all, is its sale [such an] irreparable loss ... When Gaev returns in Act III bearing the bad news, Chekhov's directions hint at comedy in their suggestion of "on the one hand, and yet on the other": [*Enter Gaev; he carries some parcels (i. e. purchases) in his right hand and wipes away his tears with his left*]. He makes no reply to his sister's anxious questions but, still crying, hands Firs "anchovies" and "Kerch herrings," and complains of not having eaten and of how much he has suffered. But his expression suddenly changes and he stops crying when he hears the sounds of Iasha playing billiards. In Act IV Gaev even seems to have caught some of Ania's optimism at the prospect of a new life:

> GAEV [*brightly*]. So it is indeed, everything's all right now. Before the cherry orchard was sold everybody was worried and upset, but as soon as it was all settled finally and once for all, everybody calmed down, and felt quite cheerful, in fact.... I'm an employee of a bank now, a financier.... I pot the red ... and you, Liuba, you're looking better, too, when all's said and done. There's no doubt about it.
> LIUBOV' ANDREEVNA. Yes, my nerves are better, it's true.[*someone helps her on with her hat and coat.*] I'm sleeping better, too.

It is true that the brother and sister are allowed their emotional leave-taking of the house, but then they both go off to their different lives: Liubov' Andreevna to her lover in Paris, and, symbolically, on money sent to redeem the estate to which she has no legal or moral right (in Act III she told us that the money had been sent to buy the estate in the aunt's name as she didn't trust them); money will also figure in Gaev's new life: he is to become a banker. Yet the improbability of such a career is suggested through oblique commentary. When Gaev first mentions the offer of this job in Act II his infantility is immediately stressed: Firs fusses over him with a coat. Moreover in the final act, as we have seen, Gaev refers to himself ironically as a financier, and adds a scrap of his perpetual play-talk: "I pot the red." In the leave-taking of these middle-aged children, one senses a pathos verging on the comic. It is aptly parodied in the ventriloquism and clowning of Sharlotta:

> GAEV. Sharlotta! She's singing.
> SHARLOTTA [*picks up a bundle that looks like a baby in swaddling clothes*]. Bye-bye, little baby. [*A sound like a baby crying is heard.*] Be quiet, my sweet, be a good little boy. [*The 'crying' continues.*] My heart goes out to you, baby! [*Throws the bundle down.*]

Hope seems to lie with the younger generation, represented by Ania (under the influence of Trofimov). For them the whole of Russia is their orchard, and an "ill-defined attitude to the past" is no longer possible. Ania rejects all the nostalgic ties of the estate, when she tells Trofimov at the end of Act II: "The house we live in hasn't really been ours for a long time. I'll leave it, I give you my word." But the ties of the past are ambiguous; its associations are also painful. Ania's mother had left the estate, in order never to see again the river where her little son had drowned. Ania ends Act II with a gesture of defiance, not only escaping from Varia, but more importantly exorcising specters of the past: "Let us go to the river. It's nice [i. e. "good"] there."

In the final act Ania and Trofimov make their farewells with the minimum of emotion:

> ANIA. "Good-bye, old house! Goodbye, old life!"
> TROFIMOV. "Greetings to the new life!" [*Goes out with* ANIA]....

In *The Cherry Orchard* Chekhov brings his theater of action without overt drama to its perfection. No one is killed, and, unlike the other three plays, no shots are fired either on or offstage, even though Act II opens with Sharlotta carrying a sporting gun and Epikhodov revealing that he has a revolver, about which he makes dark hints. As in the other plays drama inheres in the ready-made situation around which each act is built. For the most part, we have seen these situations before: arrival, departure, frustrated or misplaced festivities.

The first act opens not unlike *Uncle Vania*—with a servant and a friend of the family in conversation as they await the appearance of the family itself. But in *The Cherry Orchard* Lopakhin is waiting for a genuine homecoming, and the natural excitement which this event generates is sufficient to sustain the impetus of a whole act. There are discordant notes beneath the surface but what omens there are all seem to augur well. Thus, as in *The Seagull*, the dogs have been barking all night, but Duniasha interprets this as a sign that they know that the masters are coming. When she herself breaks a saucer (because of Iasha's advances), the usually strict housekeeper Varia says that it is a good sign; even the "ghost" which Liubov' Andreevna sees in the garden brings a moment of happiness, and the act ends on a peaceful, pastoral note, with a shepherd off-stage playing a reed pipe.

At first sight the set for Act II appears to be carrying on the pastoral theme, but there are disturbing features in this natural setting: a derelict shrine; large, old gravestones; and a well (which on land once used for burial can hardly indicate springs of purity). There is decay at the heart of this pastoral, and indeed it is almost immediately after Gaev's apostrophizing of Nature that the ominous sound of the breaking string is heard. This, in turn, is followed by a portent of dispossession. A shabby stranger passes through the estate, much as the wandering musicians had walked through the Prozorovs' garden in *The Three Sisters*. Although it is Varia who appears to be most affected (just as it is Ania who cries after the sound of the breaking string), nevertheless this figure of a "gentleman" who has seen better days has most relevance for Gaev. It is he who gives him directions and is rewarded by a poetic declamation, which seems a comic echo of his own earlier declamation to Nature. The stranger's scraps of recitation are both about suffering. In the first he almost appears to be addressing Gaev himself. "Oh, my brother, my suffering brother," whereas the second is about the universal suffering of the peasants.[8] The stranger is drunk and he wants to go to the station. Gaev's first words in Act II had been to comment on the convenience of the railway for going to the town to eat at a restaurant and he had been reproved by his sister for drinking too much and for making speeches. The shabby stranger can be seen as a premonition of the possible future awaiting Gaev himself.

Despite the would-be pastoral setting for Act II, the town itself is mentioned in the opening stage directions: [*Further away is seen a line of telegraph poles, and beyond them, on the horizon, the vague outlines of a large town, visible only in very good, clear weather*]. The suggestive detail of these directions reveals Chekhov the short-story writer rather than the practical dramatist. It is difficult to carry out these instructions to the letter. The town is more a presence which can be vaguely sensed, and amid these natural surroundings such a presence is a threat; for it is from the town that the new owners of little *dachas* will come, transported by the same railway which Gaev now finds so convenient for his trips of self-indulgence. The telegraph poles are another mark of the modern world. They, too, are a threat: they carry telegrams summoning Liubov' Andreevna back to Paris.

Act II is, therefore, full of omens. There are the guns displayed at its opening; there is Liubov' Andreevna's sense of impending disaster: "I keep expecting something dreadful to happen ... as if the house were going to fall down on us." Yet in terms of real action nothing dramatic happens, and the act ends with the undoing of omens on the part of the younger generation. Ania rejects the ancestral home and Trofimov tells her that if she has any keys she should throw them into the well—a symbolic act against the spiritual values of a poisoned past. Ania approves of his suggestion and they both happily flee to the river where her brother was drowned.

Like Acts II of both *Uncle Vania* and *The Three Sisters*, the third act of *The Cherry Orchard* is centered on would-be festivity. The opening stage directions call for light, music and movement, but they also convey a sense of misplaced celebration through the way in which Varia is to be portrayed: [*Varia cries quietly, and wipes away her tears as she dances*]. Here is an ambiguity of mood which will be picked up later in the arrival of Gaev with his tears and his purchases of *hors d'oeuvre*.

Festive entertainment is the dominant motif of the act, but it is all somehow wrong. Liubov' Andreevna comments: "The band came at the wrong time, and the party started 'at the wrong time'" (literally "We, too, have inopportunely contrived a ball"). The festive mood is all an illusion: the music comes from the local Jewish orchestra (four fiddles, a flute and a double bass); guests of no consequence have been drummed up merely for the numbers; billiards are being played — but only by the servants (Epikhodov breaks a cue and Iasha appears to have usurped the role of Gaev at the billiard table). The entertainments of Sharlotta, conjuring tricks and ventriloquism, emphasize illusion ...

....

Liubov' Andreevna's festivities are entirely misplaced; the music is not really for her, but for Lopakhin who enters towards the end of the act and announces that he has bought the estate:

> Hi! you musicians, come on now, play something, I want some music! Now then, all of you, just you wait and see Ermolai Lopakhin take an ax to the cherry orchard, just you see the trees come crashing down! We're going to build a whole lot of new villas, and our children and great-grandchildren are going to see a new living world growing up here.... Come on there, let's have some music!

The Cherry Orchard follows both *Uncle Vania* and *The Three Sisters* in basing its final act on departure and, as in the earlier plays, this final act is the undoing of the implications of Act I. The opening words of the stage directions take us straight back to the starting point: [*The same setting as for Act I*]. Yet the set is not the same: there are no curtains at the windows, no pictures, and what furniture there is has been piled into one corner as though waiting to be sold.

The parallels between this final act and Act I are striking: in both Lopakhin talks of leaving by train for Kharkov and keeps looking at his watch; in both Iasha is told that his mother is waiting to see him, but is obviously reluctant to see her; in both the characters comment on the cold; and both arrival in Act I and departure in Act IV leave the stage empty for a short time, but the locking of doors in Act IV contradicts the opening of windows in Act I. The play had opened with Lopakhin unintentionally left behind in the house, while the others had gone to the station. Then unrequited love had been lightly adumbrated as a comic theme in the relationship between Duniasha and Epikhodov, who hands her a bouquet of flowers (which he has just dropped), but says that the gardener has sent them to be placed in the drawing room. He mentions that the cherry trees are in blossom in spite of three degrees of frost. Towards the end of Act IV there is the non-proposal of Lopakhin to Varia in which three degrees of frost seem to assume a certain symbolic significance for their relationship. But the person left behind at the end is not Lopakhin—it is Firs. Lopakhin and Firs are in this and other respects antithetical characters: both are peasants but one represents the old life, the other the new possibilities. The parallelism with Firs also points to the true nature of Lopakhin's inhibitions concerning the marriage which has been arranged for him.

Lopakhin broaches the subject of his marriage at the very opening of the play, but it is a symbolic utterance, a saying which he attributes to Liubov' Andreevna. He describes how his drunken father had once beaten him as a boy and had burst his nose, but that Liubov' Andreevna had taken him inside and washed him, saying: "Don't cry, little peasant, It'll be better before you're old enough to get married" [literally "it will heal before your wedding"]. But for Lopakhin the wounds of the past life have never really healed—in spite of everything he feels he is still "a little peasant," and Liubov' Andreevna, although she may not intend it, is herself helping to keep these wounds open.

We have seen how in the opening act, she makes no comment on his confession of affection and his feeling that she is *rodnaia*, and when in Act II Liubov' Andreevna criticizes him for his way of life and his opinions, Lopakhin once more returns to the subject of his drunken peasant father and his terrible upbringing. At this Liubov'

Andreevna bluntly suggests that he should marry her adopted daughter Varia, stressing that she is of the right social origins: "She comes from the common folk, and she's a hard-working girl: she can work the whole day without stopping."

Shortly after this Firs enters and Lopakhin, in repeating the words just uttered by Liubov' Andreevna to the deaf old man, gets an unexpected reply: LOPAKHIN. "They say, you've aged a lot." FIRS. "I've been alive a long time. They were going to marry me off before your Dad was born." [*Laughs.*] Once more the question of marriage is obliquely linked to Lopakhin's origins—his father, but Firs is talking about enforced peasant marriage before the emancipation. Lopakhin teases him about the "good old days": "Oh, yes, it was a good life all right! At least, people got flogged!" Firs again mishears, but his reply only serves to confirm Lopakhin's point about the status of the peasant in the old days (while further suggesting the ambiguity of Lopakhin's present social position):

> FIRS [*not having heard him*]. Rather! The peasants belonged to the gentry, and the gentry belonged to the peasants; but now everything's separate, and you can't understand anything.

Later, after giving money to the vagrant, Liubov' Andreevna asks Lopakhin for a further loan. Then, virtually in the next breath, she tells Varia that she has arranged her marriage, and congratulates her. Varia is in tears at her lack of tact; it is as though she is being given away for money. Lopakhin, too, seems embarrassed, at least he counters by showing off his "culture" in a cruel jibe: "Okhmeliia, get thee to a nunnery." The quotation, though inaccurate, is apt. But the suggestion that Varia might be better suited to a religious life is one made not only by Liubov' Andreevna but also by Varia herself.

In Act III Liubov' Andreevna explains to Varia that no one is forcing her to marry Lopakhin, but the phrase she uses: "No one's trying to force you" (*nikto ne nevolit*) semantically evokes the specter of serfdom (i. e. *nevolia*). Here, as elsewhere, there is an "ill-defined attitude to the past," a submerged suggestion of the old ways: the marrying of serfs according to their masters' wishes. Indeed in Act

IV Liubov' Andreevna says that she is leaving with two cares on her mind, and both of them seem almost feudal. The first is care of the ailing Firs (and we see how well she copes with that); the second is to make arrangements for Varia. She prevails on Lopakhin to propose before she leaves, and he admits to feeling that once Liubov' Andreevna has left he will not be able to do so. The fact that Iasha has already drunk up the champagne does not augur well for a celebration. When Lopakhin is confronted with Varia, he is unable to bring himself to propose.

A certain lack of seriousness in Lopakhin's relationship with Varia is suggested in Act I when he suddenly peers round the door at Varia and Ania and makes a mooing sound, to which Varia responds with a tearful threat of violence. Later in the same act she "crossly" tells him that it is time he left. . . . When in Act III she aims a blow at Lopakhin, mistaking him for Epikhodov, the directions indicate that, at first, she apologizes [*angrily and sarcastically*] and when Lopakhin announces that he has bought the estate, Varia demonstratively throws her keys on the floor and walks out. It is clear that throughout the play there is constant tension between the couple. The adopted daughter's displays of anger stem from insecurity: in each case there lies behind them a linking of Lopakhin to the fate of the household. The self-made man Lopakhin, for his part, will not necessarily do what is expected of him, particularly if there is pressure from a lady for whom he entertains such ambiguous feelings, as he does for Liubov' Andreevna.

Lopakhin is one of the most interesting characters in the play. He has been given certain autobiographical features; for like the author he is the son of a petty shopkeeper, whose grandfather was a serf; like him he had an unpropitious childhood, but has made his own way in the world. Lopakhin's success, of course, has been in business but he also has certain pretensions to culture. At the opening of the play he has a book which he was trying to read before he fell asleep. In Act II he mentions a play which he has seen (though it might only be a vaudeville). He also "quotes" from *Hamlet*. At the same time he is aware of his own lack of education and of his terrible handwriting. Trofimov comments that he has fingers like an artist, and that he has a subtle and gentle soul. Nor is Lopakhin blind to beauty; he speaks enthusiastically of the poppy crop which he sowed in the spring. Here was beauty which he created, but beauty, which unlike the cherry orchard, could also be made to yield a profit. Besides the man of practical affairs there is also something of the idealist in Lopakhin, and Trofimov is perhaps right in suggesting that he goes too far in believing that the *dacha* owners will one day engage in productive farming.

Gaev calls him a boor, and there are certainly aspects of his behavior which might suggest this. In Act III he displays insensitivity when he boasts to its owners of having bought their estate, and a lack of tact in Act IV, when he allows his workmen to start felling the orchard before the family has left. Yet, as we have seen, Liubov' Andreevna is not always tactful in her dealings with Lopakhin, and her brother at times is downright rude.

Lopakhin's delight in purchasing the estate is understandable. He, too, has his ghosts, and his speech in Act III picks up many of the points made by Trofimov about the evils of serfdom:

> LOPAKHIN. Don't laugh at me! If only my father and grandfather could rise from their graves and see everything that's happened... how their Ermolai, their much-beaten, half-literate Ermolai, the lad that used to run about with bare feet in the winter ... how he's bought this estate, the most beautiful place on God's earth! Yes, I've bought the very estate where my father and grandfather were serfs, where they weren't even admitted to the kitchen!

The old order has certainly changed. Lopakhin, the new owner of the cherry orchard will have none of the old manorial life, but the axes which ring out its destruction in the final act have a particularly ominous sound for a Russian audience—the ax was the traditional weapon of peasant rebellion: "Your play can be called a terrifying, bloody drama, which God preserve, if it should ever break out. How awful and terrifying it is when the muffled strokes of axes ring out off-stage."[9] The curtain falls on three different but equally potent symbols of change: Firs left behind, forgotten in the deserted house; the ring of axes outside; and once more the strange sound of the breaking string.

• *Richard Peace*

Chekhov called *The Cherry Orchard* a comedy but it is not a comedy with a happy ending. Two years before his death, Chekhov told a young student:

> You say that you have wept over my plays. Yes, and not only you alone. But I did not want to write them for this purpose, it is Alekseev [Stanislavskii] who has made such crybabies out of them. I wanted something different. I only wished to tell people honestly: "look at yourselves, see how badly and boringly you live!" The principal thing is that people should understand this, and when they do, they will surely create for themselves another and a better life. I will not see it, but I know it will be entirely different, not like what we have now. And as long as it does not exist, I'll continue to tell people: See how badly and boringly you live! Is it that which they weep over?

Here is Chekhov himself speaking with the voice of Trofimov; here too is Lopakhin telling Liubov' Andreevna: "Oh, if only we could be done with all this, if only we could alter this distorted unhappy life somehow!" At the same time it is also Liubov' Andreevna reproaching Lopakhin: "I'm sure it wasn't at all amusing. Instead of going to see plays, you should take a good look at yourself. Just think what a drab kind of life you lead, what a lot of nonsense you talk!" The play's sympathies are far from one-sided, and it is given to Liubov Andreevna to utter the words which Chekhov himself could well have taken as an epigraph for his "comedy."

SELECTED NOTES

1. Liubov's addiction to pills and her incessant coffee-drinking suggest obliquely something disturbed and guilty about her worldliness."... In Act II we learn that she has already attempted to poison herself.
2. At the time of writing the play Chekhov was himself building a *dacha*.
3. In Act IV Lopakhin predicts that Gaev will not stay at the bank: *leniv ochen'* ("he is very lazy").
4. Letter to Ol'ga Knipper, 19 October 1903.
5. Gor'kii's play was produced by the Moscow Arts Theater in December 1902. The words referred to are: "Man! That is marvelous! It sounds ... Proud! Man!" Satin calls for the elevation of man, not for his humbling through pity.
6. Lopakhin's words on the size of Russia and native-born giants seem a conscious echo of a famous passage in Gogol's *Dead Souls*: "Should there not be a prodigious knight here where there is room for him to spread himself and pace up and down?"... Epikhodov appears on the stage at this moment as Chekhov's answer to Gor'kii's "proud man."
7. Stanislavskii comments on two possible stresses of the adjective for "cherry" (*vishnevyi*) in the play's title. Chekhov said that it should be pronounced *vishnevyi sad* not *vishnevyi sad*. "This time I understood the subtlety: *vishnevyi sad* is a business-like commercial orchard which brings a profit. Such an orchard is necessary even now. But a *vishnevyi sad* brings no profit. It preserves within itself and its blossoming whiteness the poetry of a bygone gentry life. Such an orchard grows and blossoms for a whim, for the eyes of pampered aesthetes. It is a pity to destroy it, but it is necessary since the process of the country's economic growth demands it."
8. The first is a garbled version of S. Ia. Nadson's poem of 1880: "My friend my brother, my weary, suffering brother/ Whoever you are do not lose heart" (*Drug moi, brat moi, ustalyi stradaiushchii brat/ Kto by ni byl, ne padai dushoi*).... The second fragment comes from a well-known poem by N. A. Nekrasov about the suffering of the common people of Russia, *Reflections at a Front Door* (*Razmyshleniia u paradnogo pod"ezda*).
9. From a letter which Chekhov received from a student in Kazan'.

'THE MARBLE BUST'
AND BRIUSOV'S VISION OF ART

by Joan DELANEY GROSSMAN*

When Valerii Briusov's "'The Marble Bust.' A Tramp's Story" (1902) first appeared in the Moscow daily *Russian Leaflet*, its title and subtitle may have struck some readers as an example of oxymoron. Briusov, the Symbolist poet of marble and bronze, flirting with the "tramp fiction" trend begun by Maksim Gor'kii may have seemed a Decadent joke. But Briusov's seriousness about fiction, both short and long, is well attested. While for him poetry was paramount, fiction-writing had a considerable share in his endeavor. The interplay of themes and even method between Briusov's fiction and poetry has been remarked, not least in the seven stories published in 1907 in the volume *The Earth's Axis*. Moreover, some of these stories illuminate central elements, not only in his own *oeuvre*, but in Symbolism generally. "The Marble Bust" can thus be read as an early study in miniature in Briusov's and Symbolism's conceptions of art and the artist.

The story is brief and briefly told. Drawn by curiosity, the narrator visits a prisoner convicted of attempted burglary and elicits his story. "You are right, I have seen better days," begins

* From *Depictions: Slavic Studies in the Narrative and Visual Arts, In Honor of William E. Harkins.* Edited by Douglas M. Greenfield. Ann Arbor: Ardis, 2000. Pp. 87-91.

the old tramp. A technical education and some money supported him during a wild youth. However, falling in love with the wife of a minor railroad official changed all that. Despite her modest circumstances, Nina possessed refinement and an artistic nature. Their love elevated him, but after a time, behaving as expected of young men of his kind, he abandoned her. Suppressing his memories, he lost sight of Nina and only later heard of her death. He traveled abroad, married, had children, prospered. Then came a change in his fortunes. His wife died, his children went into relatives' keeping, once again he began to drink and gamble and sank rapidly to the "lower depths." However, one day a servant seeing him loitering in a courtyard shouted out, "Hey, are you by any chance a locksmith?" Admitted to a luxurious apartment he set to work on the task. Just after completing it, he caught sight of a marble bust on a stand and was transfixed: Nina! But, as the lady of the house proudly explained, this very precious piece was sculpted in the fifteenth century and brought from Italy with no end of difficulty. He wandered away, his whole life changed as he came to understand the baseness of his actions and the depth of his fall.

However, his greatest pain came from the impossibility of retrieving any but fragmentary memories of his time with Nina. If only he could see the bust once again! It might help him remember. At last in desperation he broke into the house and was apprehended. Hearing his story the narrator wants to help him, but the old man asks: what difference does it make where I think of Nina? Prison is as good a place as any. Yet one thing troubles him: "What if Nina never existed, but my poor mind, weakened by alcohol, imagined the whole story of that love when I gazed at the marble bust?

Memory is well known for the tricks it plays with narrative as well as with experience. This tale that began as a "tramp story" progresses quickly through several prose genres as the old man's memory selects and rejects from its subconscious inventory. The tramp in fact disdains most of his life story as too trivial and hackneyed for many words. This is especially so in regard to those segments dealing with his life as a young man "in society":

> Of course I threw her over. All my comrades did the same: they started an intrigue with a married woman and after a certain time threw her over. I only behaved as everyone behaved, and it never even entered my mind that I had acted badly.... I had a brilliant future, and I could not tie myself down with some kind of romantic love. It was very painful but I overcame myself.

The shades of Constant's Adolphe, Tolstoi's Vronskii, and dozens of lesser literary lovers from plots of romantic intrigue are evoked and dismissed: in its triteness his behavior seems to him in retrospect only the latest variation on a tired old society tale. But when his memory strains to call up the image of Nina, another model from nineteenth-century fiction is briefly engaged: in his reflections there glimmers something of Turgenev's remorseful nostalgic heroes—N. N. in "Asia," Sanin in "Spring Torrents." Then suddenly and unexpectedly, with the story's closing sentence, a new generic frame is imposed: that of the fantastic story, so often, at least in the tradition stemming from E.T.A. Hoffmann, concerned with art and the artist.

The interplay of two worlds—natural and supernatural, or rational everyday and irrational—and the disturbance of the one by the seeming intrusion of the other, have long been the marks of this genre. Hoffmann's fantastic world has often been characterized as so intimately interconnected with everyday reality as to make one realm the "double" of the other, with the line between in considerable doubt. Indeed, the best exemplars often leave their readers in uncertainty about the relation of the two worlds and about the nature of reality itself.[1] Readers of "The Marble Bust" are left with such uncertainties, some of which are shared by the protagonist: "By what miracle could an artist in the fifteenth century shape those same tiny, crookedly placed ears that I knew so well ...? By what miracle could two identical women live, one in the fifteenth century, the other in our day?" And finally: "What if my poor mind ... imagined the whole story of that love when I gazed at the marble bust?" Beyond these lie other questions for the reader concerning the "truth" of art and ultimately the relation of two intermingling "worlds," life and art.

If the old man's final troubling doubt is accepted as an explanation of what occurred, the question arises: could the alcohol-sodden mind of an old tramp in fact produce such a fantasy? If so, is he not possessed of amazing poetic talent? And was the unknown fifteenth-century sculptor an artist of such power that his creation could transform this derelict into an imaginative artist, the creator of Nina? Or does the power somehow reside in the bust itself, the work of art which resurrects the derelict and seems to recreate a living woman? Or did the power lie in the elusive Nina of whom her lover recalled that "out of her cheap dresses she created a marvelous delirium. Yes, and everything from daily life on touching her became fantastic?" If we are to believe him, twice in his life this man was lifted from a sordid existence and cleansed by a vision of art. Or is it his own act of artistic creation that transforms him?

Several features of the tramp's narrative bear on one or another of these questions. Initially the old man is distressed by the gap in his memory. He returned her letters and has no portrait to help him. "She was called Nina, sir, yes, Nina, I am sure of that." Is he shoring up his memory—or is he naming his creation? There are hints of the latter in the recurrence throughout his story of words linked to artistic creation. "Separate pictures emerge from the darkness. There we are in the theater. She ... drinks in every word of the play, she smiles at me... I remember her smile." The only other physical feature he can recall without the aid of the marble bust is her hands, which are "as if chiseled."[2] Once having seen the bust and then able to visualize Nina's face in detail, he intensified his efforts. "To return the past is impossible. But I began hungrily to gather memories of Nina as one gathers the fragments of a precious shattered vase. One must ask whether this is a labor of re-creation or whether the creative process itself is being described.

The subject of artistic creation was never far from Briusov's thoughts. One of his earliest published poems dealt with this process, though from the conscious artist's point of view. The lyric "Creation" [*Tvorchestvo*], greeted with derision and incomprehension when first published in *Russian Symbolists*, in fact "bares the device" of Symbolist poetic creation as Briusov then understood it. Concrete reality is perceived by the poet who is in a state of creative readiness. Once stimulated, his fancy begins its hidden transforming activity. Out of "Shadows of uncreated creations/ Trembling in dream, /Like the fronds of latania /On an enameled wall" sounds take shape, sketched on that wall by "violet hands." The moon outside, casting its reflection on the enameled wall, creates its double which, in the poet's artistic imagination, overlays and then subsumes its original. In the final stage the poet's sensibility luxuriates in the "mysteries of the created creation," the finished work of art, while ordinary reality resumes its separate, everyday identity.

In "The Marble Bust" the protagonist's first encounter with Nina could have awakened his latent creative powers. His fancy would then clothe her in images drawn from art, which overlaid her actual presence so as to produce in her a reflection of his artistic ideal. Ultimately his imagination may thus have transformed an ordinary woman into the magical being embedded in his memory. If so, the image he carries away from his encounter with the marble bust, which has long outlived its model, could have constituted the final stage in a creative process.

The mystery of artistic genius and its creative power lay at the center of Symbolism's mythology of art, forming one of the strongest links between it and Romanticism. In this connection a powerful and productive myth was that of Pygmalion and Galatea. Ovid's story of the sculptor Pygmalion who falls in love with his statue and by his love brings her to life spoke volumes about art's transforming power. Briusov's tale begs to be considered in the light of this myth, though interpretation is rendered deliberately ambiguous. The three features of the narrative that indisputably exist on the plane of *realia* are the old tramp, the marble bust, and the tramp's story. At one significant remove—on the level of *realiora*?—is Nina. The passive "model" for the old man's story, his beloved, the nameless model for a fifteenth-century Italian sculptor: "she" is surely also the vision of ideal beauty that awakens the artistic power in both the sculptor and the tramp. That vision in turn empowers them both to bring her to life in their various arts.

There are many hints that "Nina" was her lover's creation. But when, at what juncture, and out of what raw material? Was she, as he fears, a mere figment of an imagination inflamed by the sight of this perfect work of art? He recalls how on one of those remembered evenings together she leaned toward him and said, "I know that you are not my happiness for long; but so be it—all the same, I have lived." "I remember those words," he says, underlining their significance. Or was she perhaps an ordinary woman pathetically eager to adorn her drab existence with a fleeting love that gives it temporary meaning? A possibility the old man may not have wished to consider. Was her desire to "live" so strong as to cast a temporary spell over her fickle lover? A spell that turns out not to be so ephemeral after all. In this story the locus of the transforming power and the initiator of its creative action are matters of uncertainty for both protagonist and audience. In the case just proposed the object of transformation, Nina, is a partner in the artistic act: Galatea and Pygmalion are sharers in the mystery.

Was the living woman Galatea on a higher or a lower level of being than the sculpted statue? The myth is perhaps ambiguous on this point, since only art could produce a living woman worthy of Pygmalion's creative love. The Pygmalion myth was pervasive in Romanticism. It figured vividly in Russia, where Pushkin exploited the motif of animated statues in his own poetic mythology, and where, in the Romantic discussion of art's relation to life, [Evgenii] Baratynskii's re-telling of it in the lyric "The Sculptor" [*Skul'ptor*, 1837] came to be considered programmatic.[3] The ongoing debate between adherents of the "art for art's sake" and the "art as instrument" schools of thought was heavily influenced in Russia in the 1890s by the philosophers Nikolai Fedorov and Vladimir Solov'ev. They, in effect, sought a reconciliation of these views, with art prophesying and helping to bring about a perfected mankind. Among Symbolists of the theurgic persuasion this reconciliation took the form of theories of "life creation," or the perfection of life through the instrumentality of art.

One of the earliest examinations of this question by a Symbolist writer was Dmitrii Merezhkovskii's widely discussed novel *The Gods Resurgent* (*Leonardo da Vinci*), published two years before Briusov's story.[4] This novel and the trilogy of which it is the second part diffused some of the central themes of European

Decadence and anticipated many issues that would feature in Russian Symbolism over the next decade. The episode of particular relevance here presents the climactic achievement of Leonardo's life and simultaneously his failure as an artist in the Pygmalion mold, the painting of the *Mona Lisa*. During the three years of their association, a mysterious relationship of spiritual interpenetration developed between the artist and his model Mona Lisa Gioconda. Leonardo treasures this deep, non-carnal union that nourishes his art. He suppresses feelings of human sexual love, though sensing that by so doing, he in some way diminishes her living being. "And every time that he killed this living beauty of Mona Lisa that he had called forth, the spectral image of her upon the canvas ... would become still more imbued with life, still more actual. And it seemed to him that she knew this and submitted, and helped him—and yielded up her soul to him and rejoiced." At last, as the portrait nears completion, he faces the stark choice: "Which would he choose: the living or the immortal Gioconda? He knew that, having chosen one, he would lose the other." Of course he chooses the immortal one. Mona Lisa leaves on a journey with her husband, falls ill and dies—a death Leonardo believes is not accidental. Sometime later he returns to his studio and uncovers the painting, which he had not viewed since their last meeting. "And such a force of life did he feel in that face, that he was awestruck before his own creation. He recalled superstitious stories of magical portraits, which, upon being pierced by a needle, cause the death of the one portrayed. Here, he reflected, it was just the contrary: he had taken life from the living so as to bestow it upon the unliving.[5] Art without vital creative love has immortalized its subject but has failed in its purpose of transformation. Merezhkovskii portrays Leonardo as achieving perfection in his painterly art while remaining incapable of yielding or unwilling to yield to art's higher power and purpose. In so portraying him, Merezhkovskii clearly was also striking a blow at the Decadent branch of Symbolism, of which Briusov was the foremost Russian spokesman.

Briusovian Decadence differed essentially from other strains of Symbolism in its view of the relation of art to life.[6] Early on and often Briusov asserted the superiority of art to life, but his notion of art was not the pure, lifeless perfection of form with whose worship he is often charged. He made this clear in his 1904 essay "The Keys to the Mysteries" where he wrote: "However faultless the form of a sonnet, however splendid the face of a marble bust, if beyond these sounds, beyond this marble there is nothing, what draws me to them? The human spirit cannot reconcile itself to repose.... Art is always search, always transport (*poryv*)." Life and art are intimately intertwined, but life is more limited, more fragile, perhaps more passive. Life—not to say beauty—fades and decays unless it is caught and transformed into art. But once so transformed, its higher existence and activity are assured. Further in the same essay Briusov cites from Schopenhauer the basis of his own belief about art: "Art is the penetration of the world by other than rational means. Art is what in other spheres we call revelation. Works of art are open doors into Eternity."

With all this in mind, it is possible to read "The Marble Bust" as an artistic statement of Briusov's position in the Symbolist debate over art. Applied to the Pygmalion myth Briusov's view might seem to question the ultimate benefit bestowed on the sculpted nymph by her artist-lover in bringing her to life. Certainly he must have held that Pygmalion's greatest achievement lay in perceiving within a piece of ivory the potential life that awaited the creative action of his art. In "The Marble Bust" Briusov conceives a kind of double "Pygmalion effect" that corresponds to his hierarchy of values. The original Nina (assuming her actuality) had a limited, pallid, and fragile existence. Happy to have come alive at all, she resigned herself to the brief period of "life" that her lover's powers could bestow on her. However much he observed her and committed her modest charms to memory, his powers were not yet creative and did not enable him to discern the essential being within her. Meanwhile, the marble bust from Renaissance Italy awaits its unveiling in Briusov's narrative, like the marble antique Venus unearthed by Leonardo at the beginning of Merezhkovskii's novel. Briusov's anonymous fifteenth-century artist and his model clearly had achieved that spiritual communion that existed between Leonardo and Mona Lisa, and the power radiating from the resultant work of art produces an instant of creative revelation five centuries later. The vision of the marble bust transforms the old tramp into an artist with the power to bring Nina to life again in a more perfect and "truer" form. His narrative re-creation is another work that gives another audience — his hearer — that instant of revelation that for Briusov constituted the essence of art.

In 1880 the poet-philosopher Vladimir Solov'ev published along with his translation of Hoffmann's literary fairytale "The Golden Pot" a brief preface in which this godfather of Russian Symbolism analyzed the peculiar Hoffmannesque view of reality. Hoffmann's hero Anselmus is a dreamer and misfit in the "real" world who finds his true destiny through the love of the little green snake Serpentina. Daughter of the exiled Prince of the Salamanders, Serpentina draws Anselmus into her father's realm where he is transformed into a true artist and forgets forever Serpentina's double Veronica and the world of burghers and officials where he might have found an uneasy niche. In Hoffmann's works material "reality" is so interpenetrated with the "fantastic" that, taken separately, it conveys a sense of incompleteness and two-dimensionality. "In Hoffmann's fantastic tales all persons live with a double life, appearing now in the fantastic, now in the real world." Consequently they are not bound to one sphere or the other. It is most often art's mysterious action on life that brings the two spheres together.

Solov'ev's translation and foreword anticipated by some years the growth of attention to Hoffmann during the Symbolist period. Though Briusov never explicitly declared an interest in the German Romantic, he was keenly aware of the new art's fruitful links with the earlier period and doubtless also of Hoffmann's treatments of art and the artist. "The Golden Pot" in particular held much of interest for Briusov. Whether or not it was a source of inspiration for "The Marble Bust," a persistent pattern of parallels is worth observing, beginning with the roles of Nina and Serpentina. Though she appears temporarily in the "real-life" role of wife of a petty official, Nina's true habitat is art. Her lover, whose artistic nature is at first mired in a life of triviality, goes through a period of trial in which he fails and falls to the lowest rung. (Anselmus, too, failed a crucial trial and found himself encased in a glass bottle in the study of Serpentina's father, along with other young men who, though similarly condemned, were completely unaware of their plight and continued to "live" in their ordinary way.) Serpentina's love, whose emblem is the Golden Pot, resurrects Anselmus's spirit. He repents and is taken with her to the land of poesy.

Solov'ev noted the extreme naturalism of Hoffmann's "reality." Moreover, many of his artists were drunkards and hallucinators, hardly aware of the power they carried within them or of any boundaries between their ordinary lives and their fantasy. "The essential character of Hoffmann's poetry ... consists in the constant inner link and mutual penetration of fantastic and real elements, by which fantastic images, notwithstanding their strangeness, emerge not as apparitions from another, alien world, but as the other side of that same reality, that very same real world, in which the living personages created by the poet live and suffer" [Solov'ev]. The old tramp, his "poor brain weakened by alcohol," might indeed have been capable of "creating (or re-creating) the whole story of this love," once he was transported in spirit to the "land of poesy" by the vision of art. Briusov's genre choice—fantastic tale disguised as tramp story—was eminently suited to expressing his own vision of art.

Modernist Views on Art in Essays and Manifestos, Criticism

• *Joan Delaney Grossman*

SELECTED NOTES

[1] For a definition of the fictional fantastic in which the element of doubt is obligatory, see Tsvetan Todorov, *The Fantastic. A Structural Approach to a Literary Genre*.

[2] The Russian word is "vytochennye." The last word of the previous sentence, which speaks of her elegance and refinement, is "utonchennoi"—a case of inexact rhyme.

[3] See Roman Jakobson, "The Statue in Pushkin's Poetic Mythology."

[4] *Voskresshie bogi* (*Leonardo da Vinci*), the second volume of D.S. Merezhkovskii's trilogy, appeared in *Mir bozhii* 1-12 (1900).

[5] Both Merezhkovskii and Briusov were readers and translators of Edgar Allan Poe and could not have been unaware of his story "The Oval Portrait" in which the artist-bridegroom, absorbed in the portrait he is creating, fails to note the ebb of life from his bride's countenance until, perfect painting completed, he turns to discover her a corpse. See Edgar Allan Poe, "The Oval Portrait."

[6] This difference arguably provides the basic cause of the split within the Symbolist movement that began as early as 1905 and was consummated in 1910 in the journal *Apollon*.

VIGNETTES

THE MARBLE BUST: A TRAMP'S STORY

by Valerii BRIUSOV* **

* Valery Brussof

** From *The Republic of the Southern Cross and Other Stories*. Translator unknown, with an Introductory Essay by Stephen Graham. London: Constable and Company, 1918. Pp. 33-40.

....

He had been tried for burglary, and sentenced to a year's imprisonment. I was struck by the behavior of the old man in court and by the circumstances under which the crime had been committed. I obtained permission to visit the prisoner. At first he would have nothing to do with me, and would not speak; but finally he told me the story of his life.

"You are right," he said. "I have seen better days, and I haven't always been a miserable tramp, nor always slept in night-hostels. I had a good education. I am an engineer. In my youth I had a little money and I lived a gay life: every evening I went to a party or to a ball and ended up with a drinking bout. I remember that time well, even trifling details I remember. And yet there is a gap in my recollections that I would give up all the rest of my unworthy life to fill: everything which has anything to do with Nina.

"She was called Nina, dear sir; yes, Nina. I'm sure of that. Her husband was a minor railway official. They were poor. But how clever she was at appearing elegant and somehow especially refined in the pitiful surroundings of her life! She herself did the cooking, but her hands were as if chiseled. Of her cheap clothes she made marvelous dream creations. Yes, and the whole prosaic everyday world, on contact with her, became fantastical. I myself, meeting her, became other than I was, better, and I shook off, as rain from my clothes, all the sordidness of life.

"May God forgive her sin in loving me. Everything around her was so coarse that she couldn't help falling in love with me, young and handsome as I was and knowing so much poetry by heart. But when I first made her acquaintance, and how—this I am unable to reconstruct in my memory. Only separate pictures emerge from the darkness. There we are in the theater. She, happy, gay (this was so rare with her), is drinking in every word of the play, and she is smiling at me.... I remember her smile. Afterwards, we were together at some place or other. She bent her head down to me, and said: "I know that you will not be my happiness for very long; never mind, I shall have lived." I remember these words. But what happened directly afterwards, and whether it is really true that all this happened when I was with Nina, I don't know.

"Of course, it was I who first gave her up. This seemed so natural to me. All my companions acted in this way: they flirted with some married woman, and then, after a while, cast her off. I only acted as everybody else did, and it didn't even enter my mind that I was behaving badly. To steal money, not to pay one's debts, to turn informer—this was bad, but to cast off a woman whom one has loved was only the way of the world. A brilliant future was before me, and I could not bind myself to some sort of romantic love. It was painful, very painful, but I overcame myself, and I even saw a heroic sacrifice in my resolution to endure this pain.

"I heard that Nina went away afterwards with her husband to the South, and that soon after she died. But my memories of Nina were so tormenting that I avoided all news of her at that time.

I tried to know nothing about her and not to think of her. I had not kept her portrait, I had returned her letters, we had no mutual acquaintances—and so, little by little, the image of Nina was erased from my soul. Do you understand? I gradually came to forget Nina, forget her entirely, her face, her name, and all her love. It was as if she had actually never existed at all in my life.... Ah, there's something shameful for mankind in this ability to forget!

"The years went by. I won't tell you now how I made a career. Without Nina, of course I dreamed only of external success, of money. At one time I had nearly obtained the complete success I had been striving for. I could spend thousands, could travel abroad. I married and had children. Afterwards, everything turned to loss; the enterprises I engaged in were unsuccessful; my wife died; finding myself left with children on my hands, I sent them away to relatives, and now, God forgive me, I don't even know if my little boys are alive. As you may guess, I drank and played cards... I started a business—it did not succeed; it swallowed up my last money and energy. I tried to get straight by gambling, and only just escaped being sent to prison—and, yes, not entirely without reason. My friends turned against me and my downfall began.

Little by little I got to the point where you now see me. I, so to speak, dropped out of intellectual society and fell into the abyss. What position could I aspire to take, badly dressed, almost always drunk? During the last years I worked for months, when not drinking, as a laborer in various factories. And when I had a drinking bout, I would turn up in the Khitrovo Thieves' Market and doss-houses. I passionately detested the people I met, and was always dreaming that suddenly my fate would change and I would be rich once more. I expected to receive some sort of non-existent inheritance or something of that kind. And I despised my companions because they had no such hope.

"Well, one day, all shivering with cold and hunger, I wander into someone's yard without knowing why, and something happens. Suddenly the cook calls out to me, "Hey, you there, are you by any chance a locksmith?" "Yes, I'm a locksmith," I said. They wanted someone to mend the lock of a writing-table. I found myself in a luxurious study, gilded knick-knacks all around, and pictures.

I began to work and did what was wanted, and the lady gave me a ruble. I took the money, and, all of a sudden, I saw on a little white pedestal, a marble bust. At first I felt faint. I don't know why. I stared at it and couldn't believe my eyes. Nina! I tell you, dear sir, I had quite forgotten Nina, and at this particular moment, for the first time, I fully understood, understood that I had forgotten her. Suddenly her image swam before my eyes and a whole world of feelings, dreams, thoughts, buried in my soul as in some sort of sunken Atlantis, woke, rose again, and lived again.

I look at the marble bust, all trembling, and I say: "Permit me to ask, Ma'am, whose bust is that?" "Oh, that," she said, "is a very valuable item; it was made five hundred years ago, in the fifteenth century." She told me the name of the sculptor, but I didn't catch it, and she said that her husband had brought this bust from Italy, and that because of it there had arisen a whole diplomatic correspondence between the Italian and Russian governments. "But," says the lady to me, "you don't mean to say it pleases you? What an up-to-date taste you have! Don't you see that the ears," says she, "are not in the right place, and the nose is irregular...?" And on and on she went.

"I rushed out as if I were suffocating. This was not a likeness, but an actual portrait; more than that—it was a sort of recreation of life in marble. Tell me, by what miracle could an artist in the fifteenth century make those same tiny ears, set awry, which I knew so well, those same eyes, just a tiny bit aslant, that irregular nose, and the high sloping forehead, out of all of which, unexpectedly, you got the most beautiful, the most captivating woman's face? By what miracle could there live two women so much alike—one in the fifteenth century, the other in our own day? And that she whom the sculptor had modeled was absolutely the same, and like to Nina not only in face but in character and in soul, I could not doubt.

"That day changed the whole of my life. I understood all the meanness of my behavior in the past and all the depth of my fall. I understood Nina as an angel, sent to me by Destiny and not recognized by me. To bring back the past was impossible. But I began eagerly to gather together my remembrances of Nina as one might gather up the shattered bits of a precious vase. How few they were! Try as I would I could not make something whole. All were fragments, splinters. But how I rejoiced when I succeeded in pulling some new shard out of my soul! I would spend whole hours thinking over these things and remembering; people laughed at me, but I was happy. I was old, it was late for me to begin life anew, but I could still cleanse my soul from base thoughts, from malice towards my fellow beings and from grumbling against my Creator. And in my remembrances of Nina I found this cleansing.

I wanted desperately to look once more at the bust. I wandered whole evenings near the house where it was and I tried to see the little marble head, but it stood a long way from the windows. I spent whole nights in front of the house. I knew all the people who lived there, how the rooms were arranged, and I made friends with a servant. In the summer the owners went away to the country. And then I could no longer fight against my desire. I thought that if I could see the marble Nina once again, I should at once remember everything, all of it to the end. And that would be ultimate bliss for me. So I made up my mind to do that for which I've been sentenced. You know that I didn't succeed. They caught me in the hall. And at the trial it came out that I'd been in the rooms on pretense of being a locksmith, and that I'd often been seen near the house... I was a beggar and I had forced the locks.... However, the story's finished now, dear sir!"

"But we'll make an appeal for you," I said. "They will acquit you."

"But why?" objected the old man. "No one grieves over my sentence, and no one is dishonored by it, and isn't it just the same where I shall think about Nina—in a doss-house or in a prison?" I didn't know what to answer, but the old man suddenly looked up at me with his strange and faded eyes and went on: "Only one thing worries me. What if Nina never existed, and it was merely my poor mind, weakened by alcohol, which invented the whole story of this love whilst I was looking at the little marble head?"

1902

THE STRANGER

by Aleksandr BLOK*

Above the restaurants on evenings
Wild, heavy air lumbers about.
And on the breath of Spring and rotting things
There rides the sound of drunks who shout.

And farther on, beyond the boredom of
Town houses, dusty alleys—shines
Faintly the modest gilded sign above
The bakery. And a child whines.

And every evening—past the railroad track
Their derby hats cocked rakishly,
The practiced wits stroll with their ladies back
And forth by ditches—fancy-free.

Upon the lake the creaking oarlocks sing,
A woman shrieks, while in the sky
That disk of moon, inured to everything,
Looks down and leers its stupid eye.

And every evening—this one friend of mine
Is mirrored in the glass he's raised.
Like it does me—the tart, mysterious wine
Leaves him also subdued and dazed.

And by adjoining tables all around.
The drowsy waiters stick—like dross.
While drunkards with their rabbit-eyes expound
Their shout, "*In vino veritas!*[1]"

---

[1] In wine there is truth. (*Latin*)

And every evening—like a punctual guest
(Is this a dream I entertain?)
The figure of a girl, by silk caressed,
Crosses the misty windowpane.

She edges through the drunks that fill the room,
Is always by herself, unknown.
And breathing scented mists from her perfume,
She picks a window-seat—alone.

Her rich, resilient silks, her black-plumed hat,
Her narrow hands with rings exhale
An atmosphere of wonder such as that
Of some old legendary tale.

Bewitched by this strangeness so near at hand,
I look through her dark veil and see
Appear a most enchanted shoreline and
Enchanted distances for me.

Vague mysteries are given me to tend;
A sun is left in my control.
And the tart wine has pierced into each bend
And convolution of my soul.

And those black drooping ostrich feathers rise
And fall in my brain evermore...
Together with two blue fathomless eyes
That bloom upon the distant shore.

A treasure lies in my soul—far from sight;
The key to it is only mine.
And you, you drunken monster, you are right.
I know: truth lies in wine.

24 April 1906, Ozerki

* 1880-1921. From *Modern Russian Poetry: An Anthology with Verse Translations*, edited and with an Introduction by Vladimir Markov and Merrill Sparks. Macgibbon & Kee, Printed in Great Britain, 1966. Pp. 159-163.

WHEN IN A SUICIDAL ANGUISH

by Anna AKHMATOVA*

When in a suicidal anguish
People expected German guests
And that austere Byzantine spirit
Flew from the Russian Church, once blessed...
I heard a voice. It called to soothe me.
Consolingly, it said, "Come here.
Leave your remote and sinful country.
Leave Russia now for good, my dear.

I'll wash your hands free of all bloodstains,
I'll rid your heart of this black shame.
And I'll conceal the pain of insults
And your defeats with a new name."
But not caring to hear, I calmly
Shut my ears tight, a hand on each,
So that my saddened soul would not be
Profaned by this unworthy speech.

1917

---

*1889-1966. From *Modern Russian Poetry: An Anthology with verse Translations*, edited and with an Introduction by Vladimir Markov and Merrill Sparks. Macgibbon & Kee, Printed in Great Britain, 1966. P. 275.

The Lost Streetcar

by Nikolai GUMILEV *

I was walking along the street as a stranger
And suddenly heard the cawing of crows,
The playing of lutes and distant thunder...
Before me a rushing streetcar arose.

How I managed to jump on the step as it passed me
Has remained a riddle to this day,
For it left a path in the air that was flaming
Even in daylight as it went its way.

It rushed like a storm that was dark and winged,
Lost in the depths of time somehow.
Stop the streetcar! Stop, stop, driver!
Stop the streetcar! Stop right now!

Too late. We had passed the wall already,
Slipped through the grove where the palm trees toss,
The Neva, the Nile, the Seine beneath us,
Three bridges we thundered across.

The face of an old beggar flashed past the window,
And his glance studied us, following us from the rear...
The same man, of course, the very same beggar,
Who died in Beirut sometime last year.

Where am I? My heart beats in replying
(Filled with a languor and care past control).
Do you see a station in which one can purchase
A ticket to the India of the soul?

Signboard... And the VEGETABLE SHOP letters
Are painted with blood. I know here instead
Of cabbages, instead of rutabagas,
They sell only heads that are dead.

---

* 1886-1921. From Modern Russian Poetry. An Anthology with Verse Translatios, Edited and with an Introduction by Vladimir Markov and Merrill Sparks. Macgibbon & Kee, Printed in Great Britain, 1966. Pp. 248-253.

Vignettes • *Nikolai Gumilev*

A man in a red shirt, face like an udder,
Cuts my head off too on the blocks.
It is lying together with the others
On the very bottom in a slippery box.

And there is a board fence in the alley,
A house with three windows and a lawn grown gray.
Stop the streetcar! Stop, stop, driver!
Stop the streetcar right away!

Now, Mashenka, you lived and sang here,
Wove carpets for me, the man you would wed.
Where now then is your voice and body?
Is it conceivable you are dead?

How you cried in your room so tiny!
And I in a powdered wig at the door
Was going to be presented to the Empress.
And I never saw you anymore.

I understand it now: Our freedom
Is only a light striking us from out-there.
People and spirits stand at the entrance
To a zoological garden of planets somewhere.

The sweet and familiar wind comes swiftly—
And across the bridge toward me full force
Flies the iron-gloved hand of the rider—
And two hoofs of his rearing horse.

The faithful fortress of orthodoxy,
Saint Isaac's, rises heavenly.
There I'll say a prayer for the health of Mashenka
And a simple "Rest in peace" for me.

To breathe is hard; to live is painful...
My desolate heart is forever sad.
Mashenka, I never thought it possible
To love one so much and to feel so bad.

1921

Section Two

From Civil War to Stalinism via NEP

- Introduction
- Everyday Life: Reality and Dreams
- Literary Criticism
- Vignettes

Introduction

> *Dictatorship was thought desirable, terror unobjectionable.*
>
> —Service

Political Contexts

The Bolshevik takeover in late fall of 1917 was a brief and relatively uneventful affair. With the battleship **Aurora** stationed near the Winter Palace where the **Provisional Government** was meeting, and with the leftist urban councils (*soviets*) in control of most of the city, the virtually unprotected palace was stormed by a faction known as the **Red Guards** (which later became the **Red Army**). Prime Minister Kerenskii fled **Petrograd**, as the capital was called then; it had received this russified form of the German name **Petersburg** during WWI, when the country was at war with Germany.

This coup d'état, later named the **Great Proletarian October Revolution,** actually took place in November, according to the **Gregorian** calendar that the new state soon adopted, replacing the old **Julian** calendar, which "lagged behind" the Gregorian one. The name "October Revolution," or just "[Great] October," remained, however. Petrograd would soon be renamed again. In 1924, after Lenin's death, it became **Leningrad**. Today it is once more **St. Petersburg**.

While the October Revolution itself was not very dramatic, it was soon followed by events that were. The period of so-called **War Communism** (1918-1921) saw the dissolving of the **Constituent Assembly** (in January 1918) and the formation of the **Sovnarkom** (Council of People's Commissars), i. e. a total Bolshevik takeover;

a separate peace treaty with the Central Powers in 1918 and the ensuing loss of large territories (the three Baltic countries of Estonia, Latvia and Lithuania, Poland, Finland, and other territories of the tsarist empire); the creation of the **Cheka** (the "Commission with Extraordinary Powers," i. e., the Secret Police) and its launching of the **Red Terror** in 1918; the separation of the Church from the State, soon to be replaced with the persecution of the Church and all religion; appropriations of grain imposed on the peasantry; expropriations of urban living space; famine; mutinies; and, above all, the **Civil War** (1918-1921).

Both the forcible dissolving of the Constituent Assembly, which had gathered to form the future government, and the separate peace treaty with Germany and Austria, which Lenin insisted upon and Lev **Trotskii** negotiated, evoked mixed reactions. The peace treaty was won at the cost of heavy territorial losses, as already mentioned, but was probably a wise move on the part of the Bolsheviks, since enthusiasm for the war had evaporated by 1917; certainly the peasantry yearned for one thing only: to return to the land. In the summer of 1918 there was an attempt on Lenin's life, which was answered by the **Red Terror;** according to some estimates, it claimed as many as 300,000 lives during the period 1918-1920. These mass executions (graphically shown in the 1992 Russian film *The Chekist*, by Aleksandr **Rogozhkin**) were not only a retaliation for the attempted killing of Lenin but also a manifestation of the inner conflicts that soon became as a new class war within the civil war that broke out in 1918. Members of the forcibly dispersed Constituent Assembly set up an alternative government on the Volga, and officers of the former Imperial Army collected and organized troops to oppose communist rule. These forces became known as the **White Armies**. Unable to rally under a shared political program and unable to renounce dreams of regaining the lands of the tsarist empire, as well as replicating it in other ways, the "Whites" were defeated by the "Reds" in 1921. The three-year-long, exceptionally brutal civil war brought heavy losses of life to both sides, in terms of military deaths and in terms of the atrocities committed by both sides and inflicted not only on each other but also on the civil population. Disease caused by post-revolutionary conditions killed a vast number of people in the armies and among civilians. Typhus especially claimed many lives.

War Communism attempted to "ban all private trade, nationalized almost all industrial establishments, [and] tried to achieve central control over production and allocation of goods" (A. Nove). Grain requisitions were merciless on the peasantry and led to wide-spread famine and peasant uprisings in the countryside. In the cities, there was collapse of urban structures, terror, strikes, and unrest. Even the sailors at the **Kronshtadt Naval Base** on an island in the Gulf of Finland west of Petersburg, who had backed the February Revolution and supported the Bolsheviks later, rose up against Communist domination in 1921, but they were defeated. Those rebels and civilians from the city who did not manage to flee to newly independent Finland were largely executed, jailed, and sent to hard labor camps.

One of the expectations of the Communist leadership, including Lenin, had been that industrialized countries would join Russia in bringing about the World Revolution. Particularly high hopes had been pinned on Germany following the Russian example. Such expectations apparently were part of Lenin's decision to launch the **Polish Campaign (1919-1921)** that is the setting for Isaak **Babel**'s *Red Cavalry* stories. In addition to challenging Polish independence (gained after the Brest-Litovsk peace treaty of 1918), as well as thwarting Polish efforts to capture Ukrainian territories, Lenin also seems to have wanted a free passage to Germany, where he expected a second revolution to take place at any moment. There were revolutionary movements operating in Germany, but these were quelled by 1923. Poland retained its independence, however, and repulsed the Red Army, which already was approaching **Warsaw**.

Defeat in the Polish campaign, discontent among the "pillars of revolution," the Kronshtadt sailors, and, above all, total economic devastation after three years of fratricidal war and ruthless grain confiscations convinced Lenin that a compromise was inevitable. He instigated the so-called New Economic Policy, **NEP**, with its partial return to capitalist market principles. His decision was met with relief by most people, not least the peasants who could again sell their surplus grain. There were disillusioned "idealists" too, however, and the Bolshevik Party certainly saw NEP only as a temporary measure. Under Stalin, NEP would end, to be replaced in 1928 by "dekulakization" and collectivization of agriculture. The entire planned economy of "five-year plans" was meant to make the Soviet Union a leader in heavy industry among the countries of the world—Stalin was determined that the Soviet Union never again would "lag behind" the West. With the dreams of worldwide Revolution abandoned, Stalin also launched the notion of "socialism in one country." The "five-year plans," incidentally, were supposed to be completed in less time and "over-fulfilled" as well.

> *The promise of a new order attracted many who were not necessarily Bolsheviks*
> —Milner-Gulland

Cultural Contexts

The reaction of the political intelligentsia to "Great October" was polarized. Liberals, Mensheviks, and many Socialist Revolutionaries who had wanted a New Russia under some form of democratic government rejected the Bolshevik takeover, but the victorious Bolsheviks and their sympathizers saw their own anti-democratic coup as the decisive action the country had needed to be saved from collapse. Eventually, Liberals, Mensheviks, and Socialist Revolutionaries were eliminated as parties and their leaders forced to emigrate or, subjected to persecution, and elimination. The reaction of the creative intelligentsia was equally divided. A large part of the old intelligentsia soon left Russia, or was expelled (for example, the "Philosophers' Ship" took non-Marxist philosophers and writers abroad). They formed poverty-stricken and nostalgic, but culturally productive, émigré centers in Berlin, Paris, Belgrade, Prague, Riga, Harbin (Manchuria-China), and elsewhere. In addition to artists, philosophers and writers, this so-called "First Wave" of Russian emigration (two more "waves" would follow) comprised defeated white guards, deposed tsarist civil servants, anti-Bolshevik politicians (such as Vladimir **Nabokov**'s father, a liberal and a former member of the Provisional Government), non-Marxist journalists, academics and many more diverse groups, including various left-wing political grouping, which rejected the Communist regime and feared persecution at home. The most prominent political émigré was Lev Trotskii, who was a Bolshevik, but nonetheless contracted Stalin's displeasure; he eventually sought refuge in Mexico, but was murdered there in 1940 by Stalin's agents. Others, however, including some of the most outstanding writers and artists of the modernist movement, glorified the "apocalyptic" event of "October." They saw the Revolution as marking the birth of a New World and new humankind, that were bound to be superior to anything as yet seen. Marxist utopians even saw the future as making the promises of religion—which had never materialized—finally come true; they would create an earthly paradise without God, but lacking in nothing thanks to the incessant labor of omnipotent humankind. Perhaps even death would be "abolished" by Soviet science—the preservation of Lenin's body in the mausoleum on **Red Square** to this day points to such utopian expectations of a "scientific" (non-religious) resurrection. Religious overtones were frequent in literature of the times, even when reinterpreted in terms of materialist philosophy. The writers of the so-called **Proletkul't** movement (Proletarian culture) in their poems exalted collective labor in such ecstatic terms that one can speak of a religious mood in them. Its founder was Sergei **Bogdanov**, who believed that the Proletarians were the "Redeemer class," since they were victims of exploitation, but themselves never had exploited anyone. They should therefore create their own culture founded on labor and collectivism. Lenin soon eliminated this group, which he thought acted too independently of the Bolshevik Party.

The poet Blok greeted "October" enthusiastically, at least initially. His "scandalous" and highly innovative narrative poem, *The Twelve* (1918), presents a patrol of twelve red guards as the "apostles" of a new era. Christ appears in the last lines of the poem, apparently blessing their unstoppable forward march into the future—or, possibly, mocking them. The young poet Boris **Pasternak** wrote his collection of poetry *My Sister Life* (1917; published in 1921), inspired more by the February Revolution than "October" and filled with hopes for the triumph of Life, Love and Art in a cleansed world where life would be "forever new" and everyone's "Sister." In his novel *Doctor Zhivago* (1957), he would still let his hero nostalgically re-experience that spring of 1917, which had seemed to promise so much. "October" would shatter most of those promises, as Zhivago recognizes.

The **Futurists,** renaming themselves **LEF** (Left Front and later New Left Front), celebrated their "victory," virtually identifying their literary program with the goals of the new state. They believed that a revolutionary state needed revolutionary art, and that they were the ones who could produce it. Futurist Vladimir **Maiakovskii**'s poems of the time "took the general position that the art of the past is of no use to factories, the streets and the working-class quarters of the city, and therefore should be eliminated" (Brown). He and many other avant-garde artists were convinced that "philistinism" would disappear from a world in which the bourgeoisie had lost its influence. In the cultural myths of this time, it was the bourgeois class which was seen as the carrier of greed, vulgarity, and smug self-satisfaction, whereas the proletariat was believed to be free of those vices. Others, such as the avant-garde writer Evgenii **Zamiatin,** pointed out that matters were more complicated. He wrote his famous dystopian novel *We* (1921) to demonstrate that triteness and smugness may well penetrate even a socialist state. In this work, which strongly impacted both Aldous **Huxley** and George **Orwell**, he also shows how radical and rationalist utopias claiming to have discovered the infallible guidelines for the construction of the perfect society inevitably end in (hypocritical) dictatorships that must rely on terror. In his essays, he outlined what he thought Revolution should be: never dogmatic, always open to the New, rejecting the stagnation of "*We* have the only truth there is" in favor of asking, "What revolution comes next and how can *I* contribute?" Seeing that the Bolsheviks were turning into "super-philistines," he wrote to Stalin and asked permission to leave the Soviet Union, which, surprisingly, he was allowed to do.

NEP may have disappointed the fanatics of pure Revolution, but it facilitated literary life by offering publishing venues not (entirely) controlled by the State. Ideological pluralism, within limits, was

Introduction

possible in the "market economy" of NEP. A talented group of mainly prose writers, which called itself the **Serapion Brothers** (after a work by the German Romantic E.T.A. **Hoffmann**), took advantage of the relative freedom available in the 1920s to write works of artistic merit which did not serve propaganda purposes but expressed their individual vision of life and art. Even several decades later, when most of them had "adapted" to **Socialist Realism,** Soviet critics attacked their "apolitical" stance of the 1920s. Other so-called "fellow travelers" also emerged, keen on writing in a style that would, as they saw it, match their revolutionary times. To this group belonged, for example, Boris **Pil'niak,** whose *The Naked Year* (1921) caused a sensation by both its experimental form and its "brutal" content, which did not hide the high price of suffering that launching the new world had cost. In all, the 1920s was a decade during which there appeared many talented new writers who were as yet unaware that the Revolution was getting ready to declare itself the "last one," and to state that no others were possible or desirable (to refer once more to Zamiatin's *We*). By the end of the 1920s, fellow-travelers were hounded by various Proletarian groups which, in their turn, were dissolved in 1932, by which time they had outlived their usefulness to the Communist Party. It was becoming increasingly clear that the Party (through its cultural organizations) had assumed the right to prescribe not only *what* should be written, but also *how* it should be written.

The Selections

This section begins with some pages from Marina **Tsvetaeva**'s *Moscow Notes*, describing a typical day of her hardship-ridden daily life in Moscow during the time of War Communism, which deprived her of her privileged social position, her economic security, her publication venues and her husband (he had joined the White Army). It "compensated" her with poverty, disrespect, and the daily battle to keep herself and her two children alive (one of them would eventually die). There remained Poetry, and Tsvetaeva, one of the most tragic figures of the period, did "feed" on it. Her subsequent life as an expatriate, first in Czechoslovakia and later in France, though it saw her reunited with her husband, brought many hardships. These were exacerbated when she returned in 1939 to the Soviet Union, where she committed suicide two years later. The first female commissar and soon also the first female ambassador in the world, Aleksandra **Kollontai**, in stark contrast, was making a meteoric career and had the satisfaction of seeing her cherished dreams come true—at least for a time, since criticism of her ideas was growing. She had been championing women's rights for decades, and believed that October would usher in what she called "winged Eros," i.e., freer and more equal sexual relations between the genders. She admonished young workers and revolutionaries of all ages to liberate women from domestic slavery and abuse, including the women themselves in her exhortations, feeling that they too must relearn their gender roles and above all not make love the sole focus of their lives. One way to liberate women would be to engage in communal living in large units, where cheap meals and child care would be provided. Such institutions did not appear, and what instead materialized in overcrowded cities, flooded by the hardship-ridden rural population, was a kind of parody—the communal apartment. The *kommunalka* was a large flat (once owned by a bourgeois family), inhabited by as many families as there were rooms. Kitchen and bathroom were shared by all. Dissident writer and (third-wave) émigré Andrei **Siniavskii**'s "The New Way of Life" presents the parodic reality of communal dreams in the description of life in a *kommunalka* which, with few exceptions, was everything but "communal." **Zamiatin**'s philosophical essay "On Literature, Revolution, Entropy, and Other Matters" brings out the contrast between dreams and reality once more as he sharply distinguishes between a genuine revolution, such as Nikolai Lobachevskii's overthrow of Euclidean mathematics, which really changed the world, and one that is a revolution in name only, wherefore it mass-produces slogans intended to hide its spiritual and material poverty.

    The literary criticism that follows begins with Kathleen *Lewis*'s and Harry *Weber*'s exploration of some of the targets of the satire found in Zamiatin's We (written in 1921, published in the writer's homeland in 1988). They find such targets in the poetry of the already mentioned **Proletkul't** movement, founded by the utopian philosopher and science fiction writer Aleksandr **Bogdanov**. This informative article is followed by Irene *Masing-Delic's* discussion of the ethics in Isaak **Babel**'s *Red Cavalry*, often seen as glorifying violence in the name of Revolution, an interpretation she does not share. Tracing the motif of physical versus moral blindness in the story-cycle, she instead discerns a clear condemnation of the stance that "everything is permitted," as long as it is done by the "brave young warriors" of the New World. "Dissatisfaction" with *Red Cavalry* was undoubtedly one of the reasons why Babel' was executed in 1940—powerful contemporaries sensed the distrust of the "new morality" in this work and in Babel's entire bearing. An increasing number of people felt compelled to embrace the morality of "the goal justifies any means," however, for a broad variety of reasons, ranging from ideological fanaticism to careerism, from fear to the wish to avenge themselves (their class) on the former masters.

Mikhail **Bulgakov's** most important work is *The Master and Margarita* (virtually completed in 1940 when he died, published in Russian in 1966 with many cuts), but his earlier novella, or short novel, *Heart of a Dog*, certainly also deserves full critical attention. In her "Bulgakov's Early Tragedy of the Scientist-Creator," Diane **Burgin** goes beyond seeing a satire on the current political situation in the tale, the target being the "dictatorship of the Proletariat," a proletariat which lacks the education and experience to rule. The critique of the uneducated and unskilled seeking power over the educated and skilled, compensating for ineptitude by smug arrogance, is no doubt there, but larger questions are also raised. To these belongs the issue of the validity of a science which is "science for science's sake," regardless of circumstances, means, and consequences. The demiurgical Professor Preobrazhenskii (Transfiguration), in her analysis, emerges as a Frankensteinian-Faustian creator of a "monster" for which he refuses to take responsibility, using a "perfectly good dog" and a much baser "human specimen" as some kind of scientific-experimental toys. Of course, he himself thinks he is furthering the evolution of humankind by creating his hybrid, and even his failure clearly will not deter him from continuing his dabbling in God's garden,

Nature. Serapion brother Mikhail **Zoshchenko**'s "heroes" are not monsters, but in some ways also the products of experimentation, social experimentation in this case. They are the "little men," often recently urbanized peasants, for whose sake, it is claimed, the Old World was toppled, but who do not quite know what to make of their new reality. Their confusion is expressed in many ways, most importantly through their grotesque language, which is a mixture of illiterate peasant speech, half-educated petty bourgeois language with political jargon, and propaganda slogans, with other "fancy" lexicon thrown in as well. *Victor Erlich's* article "The Masks of Mikhail Zoshchenko" discusses the relationship between the elusive author and the uneducated and confused heroes whom Zoshchenko lets speak for themselves in his miniature "*skaz*-stories," without "editing" them. Another "classical" article is Nils Åke *Nilsson*'s "Through the Wrong End of Binoculars," in which he analyzes the works of one of the most prominent fellow travelers of the period, Iurii **Olesha**, and his aesthetic imperative to make the world "strange" and thus palpable (as the Formalists wanted). Olesha imparts this ability to his protagonist, the social failure Kavalerov, who soon learns that the imagination is suspect in the "brave new world, which has such people in it" as "sausage-makers" in love with—sausage, machine-like soccer players, and young girls who do not dream of romance.

By the time Maiakovskii wrote his satirical play *The Bedbug*, the poet seemed to live in the world of technological marvels and triumphant socialism he had always dreamed of. True, he was concerned about the microbes of philistinism infecting the Soviet people, the main theme of his play, but as Edward J. Brown shows in his analysis of the text, matters are more complicated. The initially straightforward satire on the reemerging "Soviet bourgeois" ends on an oddly self-pitying and sad note—as if the alternative of triumphant socialism in a monolithic high-tech society held little charm for the poet. He even seems to sympathize more with the bourgeois vulgarian Prisypkin than with the impeccable and emotionally sterile people of the future. Two years later Maiakovskii would commit suicide, which deeply shocked his contemporaries and still invites speculation as to its causes.

Introduction

The first **Vignette** is Osip **Mandel'shtam**'s well-known poem from 1918, about the "twilight of freedom"—his apprehensive hopes, or still hopeful apprehensions, about the future which may turn out glorious but will exact its price. It did so, not least of the poet himself, who would die in a transit camp near **Vladivostok** in 1938. Two of Zoshchenko's famous *skaz*-stories paint the "new life" in the cramped hell of the communal flat and deflate the notion that Soviet citizens have acquired impeccable morals after their liberation from bourgeois exploitation. The fine translation by Jeremy Hicks succeeds in rendering the *skaz*-quality of the narrator's speech accurately. The last **Vignette** shows Maiakovskii in awe of the Brooklyn Bridge, to which he pays tribute in spite of his negative view of the United States of America. As already indicated, even admiration for man's technological might perhaps did not provide the poet with the answer to the meaning of human existence in the long run.

SUGGESTED FURTHER READINGS

Brougher, Valentina, and Mark Lipovetsky, eds. *Fifty Writers: An Anthology of 20th Century Russian Short Stories*. Introduction by Mark Lipovetsky and Valentina Brougher, translated by Valentina Brougher and Frank Miller. Boston: Academic Studies Press, 2011.

Boym, Svetlana. *Common Places, Mythologies of Everyday Life in Russia*. Cambridge, MA: Harvard University Press, 1994.

Brown, Clarence. *Mandelstam*. Cambridge: Cambridge University Press, 1973.

Brown, Edward J. "Prophets of a Brave New World." In his *Russian Literature of the Revolution*, 73-83. London: Collier Books, 1969.

Carden, Patricia. *The Art of Isaac Babel*. Ithaca: Cornell University Press, 1972.

Ciepela, Catherine. *The Same Solitude: Boris Pasternak and Marina Tsvetaeva*. Ithaca: Cornell University Press, 2006.

Falen, James E. *Isaac Babel: Russian Master of the Short Story*. Knoxville: University of Tennessee Press, 1974.

Freidin, Gregory, Ed. *The enigma of Isaac Babel: biography, history, context*. Stanford: Stanford University Press, 2009.

Mandel'shtam, Nadezhda. *Hope against Hope: A Memoir*. New York: Atheneum, 1970.

———. *Hope Abandoned*. New York: Atheneum, 1981.

Masing-Delic, Irene. *Abolishing Death: A Salvation Myth of Russian Twentieth-Century Literature*. Stanford: Stanford University Press, 1992.

Oulanoff, Hongor. *The Serapion Brothers: Theory and Practice*. The Hague: Mouton, 1966.

Schmemann, Alexander. *Introduction to Liturgical Theology*. Translated by Ashleigh E. Morehouse. Portland, ME: American Orthodox Publishing, 1966.

Tumarkin, Nina. *Lenin Lives!: The Lenin Cult in Soviet Russia*. Cambridge, MA: Harvard University Press, 1983.

Ware, Timothy. *The Orthodox Church*, second edition. New York: Penguin Books, 1993.

Everyday Life: Reality and Dreams

Attic Life

by Marina TSVETAEVA*

* From *Earthly Signs: Moscow Diaries, 1917-1922*. Edited, translated, and with an introduction by Jamey Gambrell. New Haven: Yale University Press, 2002. Pp. 75-77

I'm writing in my attic—I think it's the 10th of November—since everyone started living by the new calendar I don't know the dates any more.

I know nothing of S[ergei Efron, Tsvetaeva's husband] since the month of March, the last time I saw him was January 18, 1918, how and where—someday I'll say, right now I don't have the strength.

I live with Alia and Irina (Alia is six, Irina is two years and seven months) on Boris and Gleb Lane across from two trees, in an attic room which used to be Serezha's. There's no flour, no bread, under the desk there's about twelve pounds of potatoes, the leftovers of a bushel "loaned" by our neighbors—that's the entire pantry! The anarchist Charles took away Serezha's "élevé de Breguet" antique gold watch—I've gone to see him a hundred times. At first he promised to return the watch, then he said that he'd found a buyer for it but had lost the key, then that he'd found a key for it at Sukharevka [a market] but had lost the buyer, then that fearing a search he'd given it to someone else to keep, then that it had been stolen from the person he gave it to for safekeeping but that he was a rich man and wouldn't bicker over such trifles, then, turning nasty, he started to scream that he couldn't be expected to answer for other people's things. The upshot: no watch, no money. (That sort of watch goes for 12,000 now, i.e., fifty lbs. of flour.) The same thing happened with the baby scales. (Charles again.)

I live on donated meals (children's). Not long ago the wife of the shoemaker Granskii—a thin, dark-eyed woman with a pretty, long-suffering face—the mother of five children—sent me a lunch ticket and a little "dough-nut" for Alia through her oldest daughter (one of her girls had left for camp). Mrs. G-man, our neighbor on the floor below, sends the children soup from time to time and today forcibly "loaned" me a third thousand. She herself has three children. Small, gentle, worn down by life: by the nanny, by the children, by a powerful husband, by the routine—immutable as the movement of the spheres—of lunches and dinners. (In our home—a meal is always a comet!) She helps me secretly, hiding it from her husband, a Jew and a lucky man, whom I—in whose home everything but the soul has frozen and nothing save books has escaped destruction—naturally cannot help but irritate.

Occasionally, when they remember my existence—and I'm not blaming them, for we've known each other a short time—the actress Z-tseva and her husband help me, she, because she loves poetry, and her husband because he loves his wife. They brought potatoes, and several times the husband has torn down beams from the attic and sawed them up.

There's also R.S. T-kin, the brother of Mrs. Ts-lin, whose literary evenings I used to attend. He gives matches, bread. Kind, sympathetic. And that's it.

[The Symbolist poet] Konstantin Bal'mont would be glad to, but he himself is destitute. (If you drop by, he always gives you food and drink.) His words—"I keep feeling pangs of conscience, I feel I should help"—are already help. People don't know how immensely

I value words! (They're better than money, for I can pay with the same coin!)

My day: I get up—the upper window is barely gray—cold—puddles—sawdust—buckets—pitchers—rags—children's dresses and shirts everywhere. I split wood. Start the fire. In icy water I wash the potatoes, which I boil in the samovar. (For a long time I made soup in it, but once it got so clogged up with millet that for months I had to take the cover off and spoon water from the top—it's an antique samovar, with an ornate spigot that wouldn't unscrew, wouldn't yield to knitting needles or nails. Finally, someone—somehow—blew it out.) I stoke the samovar with hot coals I take right from the stove. I live and sleep in one and the same frightfully shrunken, brown flannel dress, sewn in Aleksandrov in the spring of 1917 when I wasn't there. It's all covered with burn holes from falling coals and cigarettes. The sleeves, once gathered with elastic, are rolled up and fastened with a safety pin.

Cleaning is next. "Alia, take out the basin!" A few words about the basin—it warrants them. This is the main protagonist in our life. The samovar stands in the basin because when the potatoes are boiling it splashes everything around. All the garbage is thrown into the basin. The basin is carried out during the day, and at night I rinse it out in the backyard. Without the basin—it would be impossible to live. Coals—sawdust—puddles... And the stubborn desire to keep the floor clean! I go for water to the G-mans by the back stairs: I'm afraid to run into the husband. I return happy: a whole bucketful of water and a tin can! (Both the bucket and the can belong to others, mine have all been stolen.) Then the wash, dishwashing: the dishpan and the primitive pitcher with no handles, "the play-school one" in short: "Alia, get the play-school ready for the washing!" Then the cleaning of the copper mess kit and the milk can for Prechistenka St. (an enriched meal from the patronage of that same Mrs. G-man)—a little basket containing the purse with the lunch tickets—a muff—fingerless mittens—the key to the back entrance around my neck—and I'm off. My watch doesn't work. I don't know what time it is. So, having mustered the courage, I ask a passerby: "Excuse me, could you please tell me approximately what time it is?" If it's two o'clock—I feel heartened. (Come to think of it, what is the present tense? Feel heartening? Doesn't sound right.)

The route: to the kindergarten (Molchanovka St. 34) to drop off the dishes—along Starokoniushennyi Lane to Prechistenka St. (for the enriched meal), from there to the Prague cafeteria (with the shoemaker's tickets), from Prague (the Soviet one) to the old Generalov store—to see if by chance there's bread on sale—from there back to the kindergarten to pick up the lunch—from there—along the back stairs, with pitchers, bowls and cans hanging from me—not a finger free! and fright in the bargain: has the purse with the lunch tickets fallen out of the basket?! Along the back stairs—homeward. Straight to the stove. The coals are still smoldering. I blow on them. Warm them up. All meals go into one pot: a soup that's more like *kasha*. We eat. (If Alia has been with me, the first order of business is to untie Irina from the chair. I started tying her up after the time she ate half a head of cabbage from the cabinet when Alia and I were out.) I feed Irina and put her down for a nap. She sleeps on a blue armchair. There's a bed, but it won't go through the door. I boil coffee. I drink. Smoke. Write. Alia writes me a letter or reads. About two hours of quiet. Then Irina wakes up. We heat up the remains of the mush. With Alia's help I fish out the potatoes stuck at the bottom of the samovar. We—either Alia or I—put Irina to bed. Then Alia goes to bed.

At 10 o'clock the day is over. Sometimes I chop and saw wood for tomorrow. At 11 or 12 I am also in bed. Happy with the lamp right next to my pillow, the silence, a notebook, a cigarette, and sometimes—bread.

I write badly, in a hurry. I didn't write down either the *ascensions* to the attic—there's no staircase (we burned it)—pulling myself up on a rope—for firewood, nor the *constant* burns from coals, which (impatience? embitteredness?) I grab with my bare hands, nor the running about to secondhand stores (has it been sold?) and cooperatives (are they selling anything?).

I didn't write down the most important thing: the gaiety, the keenness of thought, the bursts of joy at the slightest success, the passionate directedness of my entire being—all the walls are covered with lines of poems and NB! for notebooks. I didn't write down the trips at night to the terrible icy depths—to Alia's former playroom—for some book, which I suddenly have to have, I didn't write down Alia's and my abiding, guarded hope: wasn't that a knock at the door? Yes, someone must be knocking! (The bell hasn't worked since the beginning of the Revolution; instead of a bell—there's a hammer. We live at the top and through seven doors we hear everything: every scrape of someone else's saw, every stroke of someone else's ax, every slam of someone else's door, every sound in the yard, everything, except knocking at our door!) And—suddenly—someone's knocking! —either Alia, throwing on her blue coat, made for her when she was two years old, or I, not throwing on anything—head downstairs, groping, galloping, first past the staircase with no banister (we burned it), then down those stairs—to the chain on the front door. (Actually, you can get in without our help, but not everyone knows it.)

I didn't record my eternal, one and the same—in the same words!—prayer before sleep.

But the life of the soul—Alia's and mine—grows out of my verse—my plays—her notebooks.

I wanted to record *only the day*.

Make Way for Winged Eros:
A Letter to Working Youth
Love as a Socio-Psychological Factor

by Aleksandra KOLLONTAI*

* Alexandra Kollontai

** From *A Great Love: Selected Writings*. Translated with an introduction and commentaries by Alix Holt. London: Allison and Busby, 1977. Pp. 276-292.

You ask me, my young friend, what place proletarian ideology gives to love? You are concerned by the fact that at the present time young workers are occupied more with love and related questions than with the tremendous tasks of construction which face the workers' republic. It is difficult for me to judge events from a distance, but let us try to find an explanation for this situation, and then it will be easier to answer the first question about the place of love in proletarian ideology.

There can be no doubt that Soviet Russia has entered a new phase of the civil war. The main theater of struggle is now the front where the two ideologies, the two cultures—the bourgeois and the proletarian—do battle. The incompatibility of these two ideologies is becoming increasingly obvious, and the contradictions between these two fundamentally different cultures are growing more acute. Alongside the victory of communist principles and ideals in the sphere of politics and economics, a revolution in the outlook, emotions and the inner world of working people is inevitably taking place. A new attitude to life, society, work, art and to the rules of living (i. e. morality) can already be observed. The arrangement of sexual relationships is one aspect of these rules of living. Over the five years of the existence of our labor republic, the revolution on this non-military front has been accomplishing a great shift in the way men and women think. The fiercer the battle between the two ideologies, the greater the significance it assumes and the more inevitably it raises new "riddles of life" and new problems to which only the ideology of the working class can give a satisfactory answer.

The "riddle of love" that interests us here is one such problem. This question of the relationships between the sexes is a mystery as old as human society itself. At different levels of historical development mankind has approached the solution of this problem in different ways. The problem remains the same; the keys to its solution change. The keys are fashioned by the different epochs, by the classes in power and by the "spirit" of a particular age (in other words by its culture).

In Russia over the recent years of intense civil war and general dislocation there has been little interest in the nature of the riddle. The men and women of the working classes were in the grip of other emotions, passions and experiences. In those years everyone walked in the shadow of death, and it was being decided whether victory — would belong to the revolution and progress or to counter-revolution and reaction. In face of the revolutionary threat, tender-winged Eros fled from the surface of life. There was neither time nor a surplus of inner strength for love's "joys and pains". Such is the law of the preservation of humanity's social and psychological energy. As a whole, this energy is always directed to the most urgent aims of the historical moment. And in Russia, for a time, the biological instinct of reproduction, the natural voice of nature dominated the situation. Men and women came together and men and women parted much more easily and much more simply than before. They came together without great commitment and parted without tears or regret.

Prostitution disappeared, and the number of sexual relationships where the partners were under no obligation to each other and which were based on the instinct of reproduction unadorned by any emotions of love increased. This fact frightened some. But such a development was, in those years, inevitable. Either preexisting relationships continued to exist and unite men and women through comradeship and long-standing friendship, which was rendered more precious by the seriousness of the moment, or new relationships were begun for the satisfaction of purely biological needs, both partners treating the affair as incidental and avoiding any commitment that might hinder their work for the revolution.

The unadorned sexual drive is easily aroused but is soon spent; thus "wingless Eros" consumes less inner strength than "winged Eros", whose love is woven of delicate strands of every kind of emotion. "Wingless Eros" does not make one suffer from sleepless nights, does not sap one's will, and does not entangle the rational workings of the mind. The fighting class could not have fallen under the power of "winged Eros" at a time when the clarion call of revolution was sounding. It would not have been expedient at such a time to waste the inner strength of the members of the collective on experiences that did not directly serve the revolution. Individual sex love, which lies at the heart of the pair marriage, demands a great expenditure of inner energy. The working class was interested not only in economizing in terms of material wealth but also in preserving the intellectual and emotional energy of each person. For this reason, at a time of heightened revolutionary struggle, the undemanding instinct of reproduction spontaneously replaced the all-embracing "winged Eros".

But now the picture changes. The Soviet republic and the whole of toiling humanity are entering a period of temporary and comparative calm. The complex task of understanding and assimilating the achievements and gains that have been made is beginning. The proletariat, the creator of new forms of life, must be able to learn from all social and psychological phenomena, grasp the significance of these phenomena and fashion weapons from them for the self-defense of the class. Only when the proletariat has appropriated the laws not only of the creation of material wealth but also of inner, psychological life is it able to advance fully armed to fight the decaying bourgeois world. Only then will toiling humanity prove itself to be the victor, not only on the military and labor front but also on the psychological-cultural front.

Now that the revolution has proved victorious and is in a stronger position, and now that the atmosphere of revolutionary élan has ceased to absorb men and women completely, tender-winged Eros has emerged from the shadows and begun to demand his rightful place. "Wingless Eros" has ceased to satisfy psychological needs. Emotional energy has accumulated and men and women, even of the working class, have not yet learned to use it for the inner life of the collective. This extra energy seeks an outlet in the love-experience. The many-stringed lyre of the god of love drowns the monotonous voice of "wingless Eros". Men and women are now not only united by the momentary satisfaction of the sex instinct but are beginning to experience "love affairs" again, and to know all the sufferings and all the exaltations of love's happiness.

In the life of the Soviet republic an undoubted growth of intellectual and emotional needs, a desire for knowledge, an interest in scientific questions and in art and the theater can be observed. This movement towards transformation inevitably embraces the sphere of love experiences too. Interest is aroused in the question of the psychology of sex, the mystery of love. Everyone to some extent is having to face up to questions of personal life. One notes with surprise that party workers who in previous years had time only for *Pravda* editorials and minutes and reports are reading fiction books in which winged Eros is lauded.

What does this mean? Is this a reactionary step? A symptom of the beginning of the decline of revolutionary creativity? Nothing of the sort! It is time we separated ourselves from the hypocrisy of bourgeois thought. It is time to recognize openly that love is not only a powerful natural factor, a biological force, but also a social factor. Essentially love is a profoundly social emotion. At all stages of human development love has (in different forms, it is true) been an integral part of culture. Even the bourgeoisie, who saw love as a "private matter", was able to channel the expression of love in its class interests. The ideology of the working class must pay even greater attention to the significance of love as a factor which can, like any other psychological or social phenomenon, be channeled to the advantage of the collective. Love is not in the least a "private" matter concerning only the two loving persons: love possesses a uniting element which is valuable to the collective. This is clear from the fact that at all stages of historical development society has established norms defining when and under what conditions love is "legal" (i.e. corresponds to the interests of the given social collective), and when and under what conditions love is sinful and criminal (i.e. contradicts the tasks of the given society).

Love-comradeship

The new, communist society is being built on the principle of comradeship and solidarity. Solidarity is not only an awareness of common interests; it depends also on the intellectual and emotional ties linking the members of the collective. For a social system to be built on solidarity and co-operation it is essential that people should be capable of love and warm emotions. The proletarian ideology, therefore, attempts to educate and encourage every member of the working class to be capable of responding to the distress and needs of other members of the class, of a sensitive understanding of others and a penetrating consciousness of the individual's relationship to the collective. All these "warm emotions"—sensitivity, compassion, sympathy and responsiveness—derive from one source: they are aspects of love, not in the narrow, sexual sense but in the broad meaning of the word. Love is an emotion that unites and is consequently of an organizing character. The bourgeoisie was well aware of this, and in the attempt to create a stable family bourgeois ideology erected "married love" as a moral virtue; to be a "good family man" was, in the eyes of the bourgeoisie, an important and valuable quality. The proletariat should also take into account the psychological and social role that love, both in the broad sense and in the sense of relationships between the sexes, can and must play, not in strengthening family-marriage ties, but in the development of collective solidarity.

What is the proletariat's ideal of love? We have already sees that each epoch has its ideal; each class strives to fill the conception of love with a moral content that suits its own interests. Each stage of cultural development, with its richer intellectual and emotional experiences, redefines the image of Eros. With the successive stages in the development of the economy and social life, ideas of love have changed; shades of emotion have assumed greater significance or, on the other hand, have ceased to exist.

In the course of the thousand-year history of human society, love has developed from the simple biological instinct—the urge to reproduce which is inherent in all creatures from the highest to the lowest—into a most complex emotion that is constantly acquiring new intellectual and emotional aspects. Love has become a psychological and social factor. Under the impact of economic and social forces, the biological instinct for reproduction has been transformed in two diametrically opposed directions. On the one hand the healthy sexual instinct has been turned by monstrous social and economic relations, particularly those of capitalism, into unhealthy carnality. The sexual act has become an aim in itself--just another way of obtaining pleasure, through lust sharpened with excesses and through distorted, harmful titillations of the flesh. A man does not have sex in response to healthy instincts which have drawn him to a particular woman; a man approaches any woman, though he feels no sexual need for her in particular, with the aim of gaining his sexual satisfaction and pleasure through her. Prostitution is the organized expression of this distortion of the sex drive. If intercourse with a woman does not prompt the expected excitement, the man will turn to every kind of perversion.

This deviation towards unhealthy carnality takes relationships far from their source in the biological instinct. On the other hand, over the centuries and with the changes in human social life and culture, a web of emotional and intellectual experiences has come to surround the physical attraction of the sexes. Love in its present form is a complex state of mind and body; it has long been separated from its primary source, the biological instinct for reproduction, and in fact it is frequently in sharp contradiction with it. Love is intricately woven from friendship, passion, maternal tenderness, infatuation, mutual compatibility, sympathy, admiration, familiarity and many other shades of emotion. With a range of emotions involved, it becomes increasingly difficult to distinguish between the natural drive of "wingless Eros" and "winged Eros", where physical attraction and emotional warmth are fused. The existence of love-friendship where the element of physical attraction is absent, of love for one's work or for a cause, and of love for the collective, testify to the extent to which love has become "spiritualized" and separated from its biological base.

In modem society, sharp contradictions frequently arise and battles are waged between the various manifestations of emotion. A deep intellectual and emotional involvement in one's work may not be compatible with love for a particular man or woman; love for the collective might conflict with love for husband, wife or children. It may be difficult for love-friendship in one person to coexist with passion in another; in the one case love is predominantly based on intellectual compatibility, and in the other case on physical harmony. "Love" has many faces and aspects. The various shades of feeling that have developed over the ages and which are experienced by contemporary men and women cannot be covered by such a general and inexact term.

Under the rule of bourgeois ideology and the capitalist way of life, the complexity of love creates a series of complex and insoluble problems. By the end of the nineteenth century the many-sidedness of love had become a favorite theme for writers with a psychological bent. Love for two or even three has interested and perplexed many of the more thoughtful representatives of bourgeois culture. In the sixties of the last century our Russian thinker and writer Aleksandr Gertsen tried to uncover this complexity of the inner world and the duality of emotion in his novel *Who Is Guilty?* [*Kto vinovat?*], and Chernyshevskii tackled the same questions in his novel *What is to be Done?* [*Chto delat'?*] Poetic geniuses such as Goethe and Byron, and bold pioneers in the sphere of relations between the sexes such as [French woman writer] George Sand [her pseudonym], have tried to come to terms with these issues in their own lives; the author of

Who Is Guilty? also knew of the problems from his own experience, as did many other great thinkers, poets and public figures. And at this present moment many "small" people are weighed down by the difficulties of love and vainly seek for solutions within the framework of bourgeois thought. But the key to the solution is in the hands of the proletariat. Only the ideology and the life-style of the new, laboring humanity can unravel this complex problem of emotion.

We are talking here of the duality of love, of the complexities of "winged Eros"; this should not be confused with sexual relations "without Eros", where one man goes with many women or one woman with a number of men. Relations where no personal feelings, are involved can have unfortunate and harmful consequences (the early exhaustion of the organism, venereal diseases etc.), but however entangled they are, they do not give rise to "emotional dramas". These "dramas" and conflicts begin only where the various shades and manifestations of love are present. A woman feels close to a man whose ideas, hopes and. aspirations match her own; she is attracted physically to another. For one woman a man might feel sympathy and a protective tenderness, and in another he might find support and understanding for the strivings of his intellect. To which of the two must he give his love? And why must he tear himself apart and cripple his inner self, if only the possession of both types of inner bond affords the fullness of living?

Under the bourgeois system such a division of the inner emotional world involves inevitable suffering. For thousands of years human culture, which is based on the institution of property, has been teaching people that love is linked with the principles of property. Bourgeois ideology has insisted that love, mutual love, gives the right to the absolute and indivisible possession of the beloved person. Such exclusiveness was the natural consequence of the established form of pair marriage and of the ideal of "all-embracing love" between husband and wife. But can such an ideal correspond to the interests of the working class? Surely it is important and desirable from the proletariat's point of view that people's emotions should develop a wider and richer range? And surely the complexity of the human psyche and the many-sidedness of emotional experience should assist in the growth of the emotional and intellectual bonds between people which make the collective stronger? The more numerous these inner threads drawing people together, the firmer the sense of solidarity and the simpler the realization of the working-class ideal of comradeship and unity.

Proletarian ideology cannot accept exclusiveness and "all-embracing love". The proletariat is not filled with horror and moral indignation at the many forms and facets of "winged Eros" in the way that the hypocritical bourgeoisie is; on the contrary, it tries to direct these emotions, which it sees as the result of complex social circumstances, into channels which are advantageous to the class during the struggle for and the construction of communist society. The complexity of love is not in conflict with the interests of the proletariat. On the contrary, it facilitates the triumph of the ideal of love-comradeship which is already developing.

At the tribal stage love was seen as a kinship attachment (love between sisters and brothers, love for parents). The ancient culture of the pre-Christian period placed love-friendship above all else. The feudal world idealized platonic courtly love between members of the opposite sex outside marriage. The bourgeoisie took monogamous marital love as its ideal. The working class derives its ideal from the labor co-operation and inner solidarity that binds the men and women of the proletariat together; the form and content of this ideal naturally differs from the conception of love that existed in other cultural epochs. The advocacy of love-comradeship in no way implies that in the militant atmosphere of its struggle for the dictatorship of the proletariat the working class has adopted a strait-jacket ideology and is mercilessly trying to remove all traces of tender emotion from relations between the sexes. The ideology of the working class does not seek to destroy "winged Eros" but, on the contrary, to clear the way for the recognition of the value of love as a psychological and social force.

The hypocritical morality of bourgeois culture resolutely restricted the freedom of Eros, obliging him to visit only the "legally married couple". Outside marriage there was room only for the "wingless Eros" of momentary and joyless sexual relations which were bought (in the case of prostitution) or stolen (in the case of adultery). The morality of the working class, on the other hand, in so far as it has already been formulated, definitely rejects the external forms of sexual relations. The social aims of the working class are not affected one bit by whether love takes the form of a long and official union or is expressed in a temporary relationship. The ideology of the working class does not place any formal limits on love. But at the same time the ideology of the working class is already beginning to take a thoughtful attitude to the content of love and shades of emotional experience. In this sense the proletarian ideology will persecute "wingless Eros" in a much more strict and severe way than bourgeois morality. "Wingless Eros" contradicts the interests of the working class. In the first place it inevitably involves excesses and therefore physical exhaustion, which lower the resources of labor energy available to society. In the second place it impoverishes the soul, hindering the development and strengthening of inner bonds and positive emotions. And in the third place it usually rests on an inequality of rights in relationships between the sexes, on the dependence of the woman on the man and on male complacency and insensitivity, which undoubtedly hinder the development of comradely feelings. "Winged Eros" is quite different.

Obviously sexual attraction lies at the base of "winged Eros" too, but the difference is that the person experiencing love acquires the inner qualities necessary to the builders of a new culture—sensitivity, responsiveness and the desire to help others. Bourgeois ideology demanded that a person should only display such qualities in their relationship with one partner. The aim of proletarian ideology is that men and women should develop these qualities not only in relation to the chosen one but in relation to all the members of the collective. The proletarian class is not concerned as to which shades and nuances of feeling predominate in winged Eros. The only stipulation is that these emotions facilitate the development and strengthening of comradeship. The ideal of love-comradeship, which is being forged by proletarian ideology to replace the all-embracing and exclusive marital love of bourgeois culture, involves the recognition of the rights and integrity of the other's personality, a steadfast mutual support and sensitive sympathy, and responsiveness to the other's needs.

The ideal of love-comradeship is necessary to the proletariat in the important and difficult period of the struggle for and the consolidation of its dictatorship. But there is no doubt that with the realization of communist society love will acquire a transformed and unprecedented aspect. By that time the "sympathetic ties" between all the members of the new society will have grown and strengthened. Love potential will have increased, and love-solidarity will become the lever that competition and self-love were in the bourgeois system. Collectivism of spirit can then defeat individualist self-sufficiency and the "cold of inner loneliness", from which people in bourgeois culture have attempted to escape through love and marriage, will disappear. The many threads bringing men and women into close emotional and intellectual contact will develop, and feelings will emerge from the private into the public sphere. Inequality between the sexes and the dependence of women on men will disappear without trace, leaving only a fading memory of past ages.

In the new and collective society, where interpersonal relations develop against a background of joyful unity and comradeship, Eros will occupy an honorable place as an emotional experience multiplying human happiness. What will be the nature of this transformed Eros? Not even the boldest fantasy is capable of providing the answer to this question. But one thing is clear: the stronger the intellectual and emotional bonds of the new humanity, the less the room for love in the present sense of the word. Modern love always sins, because it absorbs the thoughts and feelings of "loving hearts" and isolates the loving pair from the collective. In the future society, such a separation will not only become superfluous but also psychologically inconceivable. In the new world the accepted norm of sexual relations will probably be based on free, healthy and natural attraction (without distortions and excesses) and on "transformed Eros".

But at the present moment we stand between two cultures. And at this turning-point, with the attendant struggles of the two worlds on all fronts, including the ideological one, the proletariat's interest is to do its best to ensure the quickest possible accumulation of "sympathetic feelings". In this period the moral ideal defining relationships is not the unadorned sexual instinct but the many-faceted love experience of love-comradeship. In order to answer the demands formulated by the new proletarian morality, these experiences must conform to three basic principles: 1. Equality in relationships (an end to masculine egoism and the slavish suppression of the female personality). 2. Mutual recognition of the rights of the other, of the fact that one does not own the heart and soul of the other (the sense of property, encouraged by bourgeois culture). 3. Comradely sensitivity, the ability to listen and understand the inner workings of the loved person (bourgeois culture demanded this only from the woman). But in proclaiming the rights of "winged Eros", the ideal of the working class at the same time subordinates this love to the more powerful emotion of love-duty to the collective.

However great the love between two members of the collective, the ties binding the two persons to the collective will always take precedence, will be firmer, more complex and organic. Bourgeois morality demanded all for the loved one. The morality of the proletariat demands all for the collective.

But I can hear you objecting, my young friend, that though it may be true that love-comradeship will become the ideal of the working class, will this new "moral measurement" of emotions not place new constraints on sexual relationships? Are we not liberating love from the fetters of bourgeois morality only to enslave it again? Yes, my young friend, you are right. The ideology of the proletariat rejects bourgeois "morality" in the sphere of love-marriage relations. Nevertheless, it inevitably develops its own class morality, its own rules of behavior, which correspond more closely to the tasks of the working class and educate the emotions in a certain direction. In this way it could be said that feelings are again in chains. The proletariat will undoubtedly clip the wings of bourgeois culture. But it would be short-sighted to regret this process, since the new class is capable of developing new facets of emotion which possess unprecedented beauty, strength and radiance. As the cultural and economic base of humanity changes, so will love be transformed.

The blind, all-embracing, demanding passions will weaken; the sense of property, the egoistical desire to bind the partner to one "forever", the complacency of the man and the self-renunciation of the woman will disappear. At the same time, the valuable aspects and elements of love will develop. Respect for the right of the other's personality will increase, and a mutual sensitivity will be learned; men and women will strive to express their love not only in kisses and embraces but in joint creativity and activity. The task of proletarian ideology is not to drive Eros from social life but to rearm him according to the new social formation, and to educate sexual relationships in the spirit of the great new psychological force of comradely solidarity.

I hope it is now clear to you that the interest among young workers in the question of love is not a symptom of "decline". I hope that you can now grasp the place love must occupy in the relationships between young workers.

THE NEW WAY OF LIFE

by Andrei SINIAVSKII*

* *Andrei Sinyavsky*
** From *Soviet Civilization: A Cultural History*. Translated from the Russian by Joanne Turnbull with the assistance of Nikolai Formozov. New York: Aracade Publishing, 1990. Pp. 164-169.

In the twenties and early thirties, attempts were made to create a new way of life based on the ideas of socialism. Particularly the planning and building of apartment blocs and mass housing designed for a collective way of life. According to socialist ideologies, one should live and be educated collectively. Living the old way was harmful, they claimed, because people lived isolated, in families or alone, in separate houses or apartments. This fostered disunity, individualism, and proprietary habits. Therefore this way of life had to be destroyed and replaced by one based on the principles of collectivism. Collective labor and collective ownership, cornerstones of the new society, demanded a new way of life: collective recreation, collective child-rearing, collective meals—at the factory as well as at home.

In the 1920s, then People's Commissar of Education Lunacharskii phrased it this way: "The revolution's goal is to make men brothers.... The revolution wants to build big houses where the kitchen, dining room, laundry, nursery, and club would be built according to the latest scientific methods and would serve all residents of the house-commune, who would live in comfortable, clean rooms with running water and electricity."

These projects had various names: House-commune, House-complex, NLH (New Life House), Proletarian housing. The big dining rooms were called "factory-kitchens" and meals there were meant to replace family meals.

A single person or couple was to be allotted the minimal amount of space, just enough to sleep in and change clothes. Life apart would be restricted in the name of life in the collective. Children were to be raised away from their parents, in their own collectives, guaranteeing them a purer socialist conscience. These projects also earmarked a lot of space for group activities: reading rooms, sports rooms, reception rooms, and so on.

The new way of life had other objectives as well, some of which initially seemed extremely appealing: for instance, to free women from the stove, the laundry, and daily housework, since they should work like men, and study and live collectively. But the key was that the individual and the family would now come second, behind the common cause and the idea of proletarian equality and brotherhood.

These plans never materialized. Some house-anthills were built, but they did not fulfill their function and so were rejected. The new way of life did not take hold for various reasons. The State, for one, was unable to provide for these gigantic projects and unable to supply such daily services as collective meals and laundries. Besides, the Soviet government had never regarded the people's material welfare as more than a distant priority compared with heavy industry and the military.

The utopian character of these projects, the fact that they were contrary to human nature, was one more strike against the new way of life. Even a person raised in the spirit of collectivism wants a corner of his own, his own saucepan, lunch at home with his family and, finally, his solitude. It is impossible, as we know, to live without society, but to be always surrounded by others is a heavy burden.

Ultimately, there was no new way of life. Just as there was no "new man" in the strict sense. Still, Soviet life possesses a number of distinctive aspects, including the fact that the Soviet man is obliged to lead a more collective life than he would like. The communal apartment, for example: this phenomenon is so characteristic that in the Soviet mind the expression "Soviet way of life" first conjures up visions of a communal apartment.

Communal apartments have remained a part of Soviet life like some inadvertent parody of the house-communes of the ideologues' dreams. In a communal apartment, every family lives unto itself and as best it can. But this sort of living arrangement is the result of a chronic housing shortage and an exponential increase in the urban population thanks to the growth of industry and the ruin of the countryside. Thus an apartment originally intended for a single family becomes home for half a dozen or more families, depending on the number of rooms, the largest of which may be subdivided. In the big cities, the so-called sanitary norm stipulates that an individual may not occupy more than nine square meters of living space, Plus an additional four square meters per family. It is in these forcibly close quarters that communal living was finally established, with its own laws and coloration.

This way of life, aside from being incredibly cramped, involves constant contact with total strangers. Each family, regardless of size, is confined as a rule to one room. People marry, have children, and continue to live in this one room with parents, brothers, sisters, and grandparents.

A friend of mine—from a fairly well off family of intellectuals— lived in the same small room with his parents and grandmother until he was middle-aged, sleeping on a folding bed that was stowed away during the day and set out each night, part of it tucked-under the table. So that my friend slept half under the table.

In a communal apartment, the corridor, the kitchen, and the toilet are "for general use." If there is a bath, it is also shared. As is the telephone, if there is one. These places for general use are the communal apartment's nerve center: small spaces where strangers are thrown together, forced to exchange words and insults in the eternal battle for some fraction of the common space. This accounts for its unusual, if not exotic look. In the corridor, you may see a trunk or a coat-rack, or a bicycle hanging on the wall: all can be sources of endless drama and conflict. Someone says he tripped over the trunk in the dark and demands that it be removed; someone else wants to put his own trunk in its place. The kitchen is stuffed with odd-size tables—one managing to take up more space than another—and cupboards, as many as there are families. The gas stove is communal, but there aren't enough burners for everyone at once. Before there was gas, every table had its own portable oil stove, filling the kitchen with soot and smoke. The kitchen is also the place where the laundry is washed and hung up to dry on clothes-lines running back and forth overhead. One line per person. But there is only one faucet for everyone—to take a sponge bath or wash the dishes, to fill the teakettle or a laundry tub. Lots of people and only one faucet ...

The word "neighbors" has a sinister connotation in the context of the communal apartment. Good relations are rare. More often one's neighbors are hostile, dangerous, alien, in one's way. Any molehill becomes a mountain, any trifle a catastrophe. The suspicion and hatred breed gossip, slander, scandals, fights, and denunciations. The Communist brotherhood is transformed into the most terrible civil strife. The crowding and the territorial wars aggravate the differences between people—not only materially, but socially and intellectually, in age and even taste. Someone likes to bathe at night, but someone else wants to rinse a child's diapers. One person gets up early and turns on the radio as loud as it will go, another person is always having guests over late at night. And yet another person spends too long in the john. The list of mutual grievances goes on and on. As one might suspect, intellectuals usually fare worst of all in these communal cesspools: they are both a minority and unlike the others by virtue of their education and habits.

Zoshchenko's "Summer Respite" (1929) centers around a prosaic communal dispute over who owes what on the electric bill: there's only one meter for the whole apartment, and everyone uses different amounts. Zoshchenko is mocking those ideologues who claimed that communal apartments would foster friendship and solidarity and thus become the cells of socialist society:

> Of course, to occupy one's own, separate apartment is philistinism. One must live all together, as one big family,

and not lock oneself away in one's castle home. One must live in a communal apartment. In the open. Where there's always someone to talk to. Someone to go to for advice. Someone to pick a fight with.

Of course, there are drawbacks. The electricity, for example, creates a problem. You don't know how to divide up the bill. How much to take from whom.

Of course, later on, when our industry has turned the corner and America is at our beck and call, every tenant in every corner can have two meters or more if he likes ... And then, of course, life in our apartments will shine like the sun.

But for now, indeed, we have nothing but problems.

For example, we have nine families and only one wire, only one meter. At the end of the month, one has to calculate the consumption. Which, of course, leads to serious misunderstandings, if not to blows.

So fine, you say: go by the light bulbs. So fine, we'll go by the light bulbs. But one conscientious tenant turns on his light for five minutes, the time it takes to undress or to kill a flea. And another tenant chews and chews on something till midnight with the light on. Refuses to turn it off....

There was one tenant, a loader, who literally went off his head because of this. He stopped sleeping and spent all his time ascertaining who was reading algebra at night and who was fixing himself something hot to eat....

He was an excellent controller. As I say, he literally did not sleep nights and ran inspections every minute. Ducking in here, ducking in there. Threatening to hack you up with an axe if he discovered any excesses.

Then the orgy begins: every tenant, suspecting the others of excess, tries to personally use up as much of the general electricity as he can. The bill goes up and up. "In a word, when the meter jumped to thirty-eight rubles, the electricity had to be turned off. No one would pay. A lone intellectual pleaded and clutched at the wire, but they ignored him. The electricity was cut."

This incident is neither invention nor hyperbole. I lived in a communal apartment for forty years and can confirm that the light bulb or the garbage pail or where to put the kettle on the stove made for real problems. To Zoshchenko's story, I can add this documentary vignette. We were, my family and I, the only intellectuals in our apartment. In the evenings I would read or write by the desk lamp, sometimes late into the night. The neighbors, naturally, noticed this and suggested I stop reading, turn out the light, and go to sleep earlier. So I began to pay double for my desk lamp. This didn't help. So I installed a separate electricity meter for my room. But then it was pointed out that at night I sometimes went into the corridor or into the kitchen or out-of-doors to walk the dog—at the expense of the communal electricity. So I installed my own hall light and connected it to a switch in my room so that it would register on my own electricity meter. At which point I thought the problem had finally been solved. But then it became a question of my dog. True, he never barked, never ran out of our room, and always sat quietly so not to provoke the neighbors' censure. Still, when I took him outside—twice a day—he did use the communal corridor, and his feet brought in more dirt than those of other tenants, meaning that we should wash the hall floor more often than they. I agreed. But then I was told that my dog, with his four feet as opposed to the usual tenant's two, tracked twice as much dirt inside, making it necessary to wash the floor twice as often. So I began carrying the dog—luckily a small one—through the corridor. In short, it was an unwinnable war. The more money and energy I invested in appeasing my neighbors, the more they hated me. Look at the barin (fine gentleman): he installed his own electricity meter, he has a dog, and whereas we wash the hall floor with our own hands, he hires a cleaning woman. Where did he get the money? And why does he stay up so late with the light on? I had a comfortable salary and a few Soviet privileges as a scholar and member of the Writers Union, but nothing would calm them. My way of life differed from theirs, arousing envy and suspicion: What was I really studying? Was I an American spy burning the midnight oil?

This is just one detail to do with the electricity. Others were worse. In the kitchen, every pot on the stove was under lock and key. To stir the soup or to taste it, one had to unlock the pot and then relock it, for fear a neighbor might filch a piece of meat—less from hunger than from spite—or slip something into it: extra salt, dirt from the floor, or just some spit...

This gives one a sense of the tension of life in a communal apartment. Socialism's ideologues and organizers hadn't anticipated that human nature could be so unbending or that cohabitation could breed such enmity. For years they blamed the scenes on the accursed capitalist past, on bourgeois vestiges which, they said, would disappear with time. But they did not disappear, they assumed these new forms that make Soviet life what it is.

On Literature, Revolution, Entropy, and Other Matters

by Evgenii ZAMIATIN*

* *Yevgeny Zamyatin*

** From *A Soviet Heretic: Essays by Yevgeny Zamyatin.* Edited and translated by Mirra Ginsburg. Chicago: University of Chicago Press, 1970. Pp. 108-112.

> *Name me the final number, the highest, the greatest. But that's absurd! If the number of numbers is infinite, how can there be a final number? Then how can you speak of a final revolution? There is no final one. Revolutions are infinite.*
>
> —Evgenii Zamiatin, We

Ask point blank: What is revolution?

Some people will answer, paraphrasing Louis XIV: We are the revolution. Others will answer by the calendar, naming the month and the day. Still others will give you an ABC answer. But if we are to go on from the ABC to syllables, the answer will be this:

Two dead, dark stars collide with an inaudible, deafening crash and light a new star: this is revolution. A molecule breaks away from its orbit and, bursting into a neighboring atomic universe, gives birth to a new chemical element: this is revolution. Lobachevskii[1] cracks the walls of the millenia-old Euclidean world with a single book, opening a path to innumerable non-Euclidean spaces: this is revolution.

Revolution is everywhere, in everything. It is infinite. There is no final revolution, no final number. The social revolution is only one of an infinite number of numbers: the law of revolution is not a social law, but an immeasurably greater one. It is a cosmic, universal law—like the laws of the conservation of energy and of the dissipation of energy (entropy). Some day, an exact formula for the law of revolution will be established. And in this formula, nations, classes, stars—and books—will be expressed as numerical quantities.

The law of revolution is red, fiery, deadly; but this death means the birth of new life, a new star. And the law of entropy is cold, ice blue, like the icy interplanetary infinities. The flame turns from red to an even, warm pink, no longer deadly, but comfortable. The sun ages into a planet, convenient for highways, stores, beds, prostitutes, prisons: this is the law. And if the planet is to be kindled into youth again, it must be set on fire, it must be thrown off the smooth highway of evolution: this is the law.

The flame will cool tomorrow, or the day after tomorrow (in the Book of Genesis days are equal to years, ages). But someone must see this already today, and speak heretically today about tomorrow. Heretics are the only (bitter) remedy against the entropy of human thought.

When the flaming, seething sphere (in science, religion, social life, art) cools, the fiery magma becomes coated with dogma—a rigid, ossified, motionless crust. Dogmatization in science, religion, social life, or art is the entropy of thought. What has become dogma no longer burns; it only gives off warmth—it is tepid, it is cool. Instead of the Sermon on the Mount, under the scorching sun, to up-raised arms and sobbing people, there is drowsy prayer in a magnificent abbey. Instead of Galileo's "But still, it turns!" there are dispassionate computations in a well-heated room in an observatory. On the Galileos, the epigones build their own structures, slowly, bit by bit, like corals. This is the path of evolution—until a new heresy explodes the crush of dogma and all the edifices of the most enduring stone which have been raised upon it.

Explosions are not very comfortable. And therefore the exploders, the heretics, are justly exterminated by fire, by axes, by words. To every today, to every evolution, to the laborious, slow, useful, most useful, creative, coral-building work, heretics are a threat. Stupidly, recklessly, they burst into today from tomorrow; they are romantics. Babeuf[2] was justly beheaded in 1797; he leaped into 1797 across 150 years. It is just to chop off the head of a heretical literature which challenges dogma; this literature is harmful.

But harmful literature is more useful than useful literature, for it is anti-entropic, it is a means of combating calcification, sclerosis, crust, moss, quiescence. It is utopian, absurd—like Babeuf in 1797. It is right 150 years later.

We know Darwin. We know what followed Darwin—mutations, Weismannism, neo-Lamarckism. But all of these are attics, balconies; the building itself is Darwin. And in this building there are not only tadpoles and fungi, but also man. Fangs are sharpened only when there is someone to gnaw on. Domestic hens have wings only for flapping. The same law is true for hens and for ideas: ideas nourished on chopped meat cutlets lose their teeth, like civilized, cutlet-eating man. Heretics are necessary to health; if there are no heretics, they should be invented.

A literature that is alive does not live by yesterday's clock, nor by today's but by tomorrow's. It is a sailor sent aloft: from the masthead he can see foundering ships, icebergs, and maelstroms still invisible from the deck. He can be dragged down from the mast and put to tending the boilers or working the capstan, but that will not change anything: the mast will remain, and the next man on the masthead will see what the first has seen.

In a storm, you must have a man aloft. We are in the midst of storm today, and SOS signals come from every side. Only yesterday a writer could calmly stroll along the deck, clicking his Kodak (genre); but who will want to look at landscapes and genre scenes when the world is listing, at a forty-five-degree angle, the green maws are gaping, the hull is creaking? Today we can look and think only as men do in the face of death: we are about to die—and what did it all mean? How have we lived? If we could start all over, from the beginning, what would we live by? And for what? What we need in literature today are vast philosophic horizons—horizons seen from mastheads, from airplanes; we need the most ultimate, the most fearsome, the most fearless "Why?" and "What next?"

This is what children ask. But then children are the boldest philosophers. They enter life naked, not covered by the smallest fig leaf of dogma, absolutes, creeds. This is why every question they ask is so absurdly naive and so frighteningly complex. The new men entering life today are as naked and fearless as children; and they, too, like children, like Schopenhauer, Dostoevskii, Nietzsche, ask "Why?" and "What next?" Philosophers of genius, children, and the people are equally wise—because they ask equally foolish questions. Foolish to a civilized man who has a well-furnished European apartment, with an excellent toilet, and a well-furnished dogma.

Organic chemistry has already obliterated the line between living and dead matter. It is an error to divide people into the living and the dead: there are people who are dead-alive, and people who are alive-alive. The dead-alive also write, walk, speak, act. But they make no mistakes; only machines make no mistakes, and they produce only dead things. The alive-alive are constantly in error, in search, in questions, in torment.

The same is true of what we write: it walks and it talks, but it can be dead-alive or alive-alive. What is truly alive stops before nothing and ceaselessly seeks answers to absurd, "childish" questions. Let the answers be wrong, let the philosophy be mistaken--errors are more valuable than truths: truth is of the machine, error is alive; truth reassures, error disturbs. And if answers be impossible of attainment, all the better! Dealing with answered questions is the privilege of brains constructed like a cow's stomach, which, as we know, is built to digest cud.

If there were anything fixed in nature, if there were truths, all of this would, of course, be wrong. But fortunately, all truths are erroneous. This is the very essence of the dialectical process: today's truths become errors tomorrow; there is no final number.

This truth (the only one) is for the strong alone. Weak-nerved minds insist on a finite universe, a last number; they need, in Nietzsche's words, "the crutches of certainty." The weak-nerved lack the strength to include themselves in the dialectic syllogism. True, this is difficult. But it is the very thing that Einstein succeeded in doing: he managed to remember that he, Einstein, observing motion with a watch in hand, was also moving; he succeeded in looking at the movement of the earth from outside.

This is precisely how a great literature, which knows no final numbers, looks at the movements of the earth.

The formal character of a living literature is the same as its inner character: it denies verities, it denies what everyone knows and what I have known until this moment. It departs from the canonical tracks, from the broad highway.

The broad highway of Russian literature, worn to a high gloss by the giant wheels of Tolstoi, Gor'kii, and Chekhov, is Realism, daily life; hence, we must turn away from daily life. The tracks canonized and sanctified by Blok, Sologub, and Belyi are the tracks of Symbolism, which renounced daily life; hence, we must turn toward daily life.

Absurd? Yes. The intersection of parallel lines is also absurd. But it is absurd only in the canonic, plane geometry of Euclid. In non-Euclidean geometry it is an axiom. All you need is to cease to be plane, to rise above the plane. To literature today the plane surface of daily life is what the earth is to an airplane—a mere runway from which to take off, in order to rise aloft, from daily life to the realities of being, to philosophy, to the fantastic. Let yesterday's cart creak along the well-paved highways. The living have strength enough to cut away their yesterday.

Whether you put a police inspector or a commissar into the cart, it still remains a cart. And literature will remain the literature of yesterday even if you drive "revolutionary life" along the well-traveled highway—and even if you drive it in a dashing troika with bells. What we need today are automobiles, airplanes, flickering, flight, dots, dashes, seconds.

The old, slow, creaking descriptions are a thing of the past; today the rule is brevity—but every word must be supercharged, high-voltage. We must compress into a single second what was held before in a sixty-second minute. And hence, syntax becomes elliptic, volatile; the complex pyramids of periods are dismantled stone by stone into independent sentences. When you are moving fast, the canonized, the customary eludes the eye: hence, the unusual, often startling, symbolism and vocabulary. The image is sharp, synthetic, with a single salient feature—the one feature you will glimpse from a speeding car. The custom-hallowed lexicon has been invaded by provincialisms, neologisms, science, mathematics, technology.

If this becomes the rule, the writer's talent consists in making the rule the exception. There are far more writers who turn the exception into the rule.

Science and art both project the world along certain coordinates. Differences in form are due only to differences in the coordinates. All realistic forms are projections along the fixed, plane coordinates of Euclid's world. These coordinates do not exist in nature. Nor does the finite, fixed world; this world is a convention, an abstraction, an unreality. And therefore Realism—be it "socialist" or "bourgeois"—is unreal. Far closer to reality is projection along speeding, curved surfaces—as in the new mathematics and the new art. Realism that is not primitive, not *realia* but *realiora*, consists in displacement, distortion, curvature, non-objectivity. Only the camera lens is objective.

A new form is not intelligible to everyone; many find it difficult. Perhaps. The ordinary, the banal is, of course, simpler, more pleasant, more comfortable. Euclid's world is very simple, and Einstein's world is very difficult—but it is no longer possible to return to Euclid. No revolution, no heresy is comfortable or easy. For it is a leap, it is a break in the smooth evolutionary curve, and a break is a wound, a pain. But the wound is necessary: most of mankind suffers from hereditary sleeping sickness, and victims of this sickness (entropy) must not be allowed to sleep, or it will be their final sleep, death.

The same disease often afflicts artists and writers: they sink into satiated slumber in forms once invented and twice perfected. And they lack the strength to wound themselves, to cease loving what they once loved, to leave their old, familiar apartments filled with the scent of laurel leaves and walk away into the open field, to start anew.

Of course, to wound oneself is difficult, even dangerous. But for those who are alive, living today as yesterday and yesterday as today is still more difficult.

1923

TRANSLATOR'S NOTES

[1] N.I. Lobachevskii (1793-1856), Russian mathematician who pioneered in non-Euclidean geometry.

[2] Frangois Babeuf (1760-97), French revolutionary who demanded economic, social and political equality; executed under the Directory for plotting to overthrow the government.

LITERARY CRITICISM

ZAMYATIN'S *WE*, THE PROLETARIAN POETS AND BOGDANOV'S *RED STAR*

by Kathleen LEWIS and Harry WEBER*

* From *The Ardis Anthology of Russian Futurism*, edited by Ellendea and Carl R. Proffer. Ann Arbor: Ardis, 1980. Pp. 263-278.

Zamiatin's brilliant novel *We* continues to exert a lasting fascination. There have been useful studies on the patterns of imagery in the novel, on the use of Dostoevskian themes, on Biblical myths, and on the work as political statement. Source studies have pointed to the works of [rocket scientist Konstantin] Tsiolkovskii, and H.G. Wells as antecedents. Jerome K. Jerome's "The New Utopia," in particular, has recently been cited as a direct source for certain details in the book. Soviet reactions to the novel are nearly non-existent; whatever commentary can be found deals with the book's political aspects. For example, Gor'kii is on record as saying that "*We* is hopelessly bad, a completely sterile thing." And [critic and journal editor Aleksandr] Voronskii's extensive essay terms the novel "a lampoon... not concerned with communism," adding that "Everything here is untrue." His opinion was essentially repeated... in *New World* in 1963.

This article addresses itself to one vital aspect of the novel which the authors believe has been neglected: the relationship of this novel to the literary milieu of the years immediately following the Revolution, specifically the proletarian poets and Bogdanov's novel *Red Star* (*Krasnaia Zvezda*). We believe that Zamiatin parodied the excesses of the proletarian poets through ridicule of their characteristic language and ubiquitous themes. Furthermore, Zamiatin underscores the parody by borrowing the hero and a number of key plot situations from *Red Star* (1908), written by A. A. Bogdanov, chief theoretician of the Proletkul't.

The most outspoken expression of Zamiatin's negative attitude toward the proletarian poets is to be found in his essay "Paradise" (1921),[1] in which he inveighs against their meaningless use of hyperbole, inhumane glorification of the instruments of war, intolerance and arrogance, and the urge toward "monophonism" in the new state. Many passages in the novel are identical in tone to verses quoted in Zamiatin's essay as exemplary of the bad taste or ineffective hyperbole of the new poets. Further, a close reading of the novel reveals clear echoes of specific themes, poetic clichés, and imagery then current in the endeavors of the proletarians.

I: We and the Proletarian Poets

The most important proletarian poets were V. D. Aleksandrovskii, M. P. Gerasimov, A. K. Gastev, V. T. Kirillov, V. V. Kniazev and S. A. Obradovich, who occupied a very prominent position in early Soviet cultural life. Their official organization, the Proletkul't, was founded by A. A. Bogdanov (Malinovskii), theoretician on art and the artist, in 1917, and was supported by [Anatolii] Lunacharskii, the People's Commissar of Education.

The Proletkul't saw as its task the creation and encouragement of new literary and cultural cadres from the ranks of the workers and founded its famous "litstudios" for that purpose. It developed a wide-spread net of "urban, provincial, district, regional, and factory proletkul'ts, which aimed at leadership, not only of literature, but of all branches of proletarian art. Special sections dealt with the theater, painting, music, workers' clubs, etc. ... in 1919 about 80,000 people took part in the work of the studios."

Directives and progress reports were given in nearly twenty Proletkul't journals, such as *The Forge* (*Gorn*), *The Smithy* (*Kuznitsa*), *Proletarian Culture* (*Proletarskaia Kul'tura*), *Factory Whistles* (*Gudki*), *Create!* (*Tvori!*), *The Coming Days* (*Griadushchee*) and the local proletarian organs. The works of the proletarian poets were frequently read at the meetings of the local Proletkul't groups. For example, a 1921 Petrograd Proletkul't review of its activities reports public readings from the works of Gastev and Kirillov on May 1, 1918; and the Moscow Proletkul't report for 1919-1921 speaks of performances by a speaking choir of Kirillov's "We" and the works of Aleksandrovskii.

The very title of Zamiatin's *We* is, as E. J. Brown notes, an ironic reference to the glorification of collectivism by the proletarian poets. Kirillov, Gerasimov, Aleksandrovskii, and Kraiskii wrote poems entitled "We," and the word occurs as part of the title in the verse of Malyshkin, Malakhov, Samobytnik, and Maznin, as well as in several of Gastev's poems—"We Grow from Iron," "We Are Together," "We Have Encroached," and "We Are Everywhere."[2] All of this accords with Bogdanov's view of the function of art as "the most powerful weapon for the organization of collective forces.... The former artist saw in his work the expression of his individuality; the new artist will understand and will feel that in him and through him a great whole is being created—the collective." And so in Record 1 of *We* D-503 promises to transcribe "only the things I see, the things I think, or, to be more exact, the things we think." Zoshchenko's remark about his own art comes to mind: "The fact is that I am a proletarian writer. Or rather, I am parodying with my things that imaginary, but genuine proletarian writer ... ." Zoshchenko's erstwhile teacher Zamiatin may well have invented this idea, embodying it in the figure of the mathematician-turned-writer composing paeans to the utopian future which sound suspiciously like the literary products appearing daily in the new Soviet state of 1917-1920. The overall tone of the novel is one of parody, and a closer look at language, themes, and imagery will bear out this view.

Zamiatin was extremely careful to use suitable diction and speech proper to the milieu which he was describing, as his essay "On Language" (1919-20) indicates. Propagandistic rhetoric is common in the works of the proletarian poets:

> Orchestras—louder, louder, banners—higher,
> Glorify the Great Workers' Union,
> Glorify the legions of world fighters,
> The army of blue soiled shirts.
>
> Long live the First of May!
> May the last ices vanish!!
> Let the whistle blow! Tell the whole world
> That we will all die or return with victory!
>
> "Get up, arise, working people!
> Your mortal enemy is at the gates!

This propagandistic and didactic language is echoed in *We*, in such lines as "Long live the Well-Doer!!!" (*We*, Record 1, 4), and the "poetry" of the State Poets. Demian Bednyi is perhaps the clearest representative of "agit-poetry" and, as [critic] V. L'vov-Rogachevskii says, "In 1920 it might seem that all literature had become Demian Bednyi-like." [Z. S.] Papernyi describes Bednyi's poetry as dealing with "the most everyday themes—a trait, as we shall see, which is particularly important for the literature of those years. [Art Historian] Camilla Gray indicates that artists during this period participated in public agit-displays on hygiene, or even on such topics as "how to breathe. This mundane, practical, and edifying subject matter is clearly mocked in *We*, especially in the titles of literary works: the versified "Mathematical Norms," "Thorns," "Daily Odes to the Well-Doer," "Flowers of Court Sentences," "the immortal tragedy 'Those Who Come Late to Work,'" and "the popular book, 'Stanzas on Sex Hygiene!'" (*We*, Record 12, 65).

Zamiatin also deals with the concept of poetic inspiration. Bogdanov himself had once written that "In the sphere of artistic creation the old culture is characterized by the vagueness and unconsciousness of its methods ("inspiration," etc.)." In *We*

(Record 4) the lecturer tells his listeners that their ancestors "could create only by bringing themselves to attacks of inspiration, an extinct form of epilepsy," and contrasts this condition with the superior method of cranking out three sonatas an hour on the newly-invented musicometer. One suspects that it was this mechanical quality which led Trotskii to complain: "But weak and, what is more, illiterate poems do not make up proletarian poetry, because they do not make up poetry at all. In Record 12, D-503 tells us that "in the same manner, we domesticated and harnessed the wild element of poetry. Now poetry is no longer the unpardonable whistling of nightingales, but a State Service! Poetry is a commodity." We know from Zamiatin's own article "I Am Afraid" (1921) that this idea is antithetical to his own that the poet must be a dreamer and a madman.

Zamiatin's article "Paradise" is useful here, too, because it displays a satirical tone which is also apparent in *We*. In the article Zamiatin speaks of a return to the state of paradise—lack of freedom—and says, "There shall be no more polyphony or dissonances. There shall be only majestic, monumental, all-encompassing unanimity... And so, it is clearly on this granite foundation of monophony that the new Russian literature and the new poetry are being created ... . After quoting examples from the proletarian poets he continues, ... hymns are the natural, logical, basic form of paradisiac poetry .... And the same label prevails as had once prevailed in relation to Ialdebaoth and the High Personages of earth: We, Ours, All-Blessed, All-Merciful." In *We*, R-13 takes up the same themes (Record 11): "The Well-Doer, the Machine, the Cube, the Gas Bell, the Guardians—all these are good. All this is magnificent, beautiful, noble, lofty, crystalline, pure... how about a little paradisiacal poem like that, eh?" The capitalized titles, the similar metaphors (Paradise, hymns), and similarity of diction ("majestic," "paradisiac") show the close relationship between the two passages. Another passage in *We*, the description of the Day of Unanimity—"Even if one supposes the impossible, i.e., some kind of dissonance amid our usual monophony ... "—also indicates the same satiric tone that is openly displayed in "Paradise" and directed specifically against the proletarian poets.

We deals in large part with four clusters of motifs: technology, the individual vs. the collective, the "mystery" of labor, and cosmism. Virtually all the proletarian poems of this period deal with these same motifs, and they vary primarily only in the proportion which each motif occupies in each poem. The most satisfying example of a nearly obsessive use of all of these themes is the work of Aleksei Gastev (1882-1941), a figure whom Lunacharskii called "perhaps the most outstandingly gifted proletarian poet"... Gastev's most popular work, "Shockwork Poetry," (1918) "was sold out in a short time, it was constantly quoted, referred to, republished." There were six editions in all by 1926 ... the popular "We Grow from Iron," "Factory," "Whistles," "Rails," and "Tower," were printed in 1918-19. {Prose writer] Viktor Nekrasov recalls that as a schoolboy in 1923, the literary studies for the fifth "group" consisted only of Radishchev's "Journey from Petersburg to Moscow" and Gastev's "Shockwork Poetry." What is most striking is not Gastev's poetry, however, it is his view of the world of the future, which is as bizarre as some of the elements of Zamiatin's *We*. In a statement on proletarian culture written in 1919, Gastev speaks of human psychology:

> The mechanization, not only of gestures, not only of production methods, but of everyday thinking, coupled with extreme rationality, normalizes to a striking degree the psychology of the proletariat. It is this very feature which gives the proletarian psychology a striking anonymity, which allows one to qualify the individual proletarian unit as A, B, C or as 325.075 and 0, etc ... The manifestations of such a mechanized collectivism are so alien to personality, so anonymous, that the movement of these collective-complexes approaches the movement of things so that it seems that there is no longer an individual human being, but even, normalized steps, faces without expression, a soul without lyricism, emotion measured not by a cry or a laugh, but my manometer and taxometer ... In this psychology, from one end of the world to the other, flow potent massive streams, creating one world head in place of millions of heads. This tendency will next imperceptibly render individual thinking impossible, and thought will become the objective psychic process of a whole class, with systems of psychological switches and locks.

Gastev's enthusiastic interest in production processes led him naturally to the works of Frederick W. Taylor, the American efficiency expert, and in the same article for *Proletarian Culture*, quoted above, the poet attempted a "taylorized" chart of four kinds of workers in the metal-working industry (...). Lunacharskii wrote that Gastev "is heralding the beginning of an epoch of pure technology and, following in Taylor's footsteps, is introducing the idea of subordinating people to mechanisms, of the mechanization of man." In the twenties, Gastev was made the director of the Central Institute of Labor (TsIT). [German writer] Ernst Toller's bemused account of his visit to Gastev's training workshops in 1926 is worthy of any scene in *We*, for Gastev literally practices the mechanization of human beings.

This mentality is reproduced by Zamiatin in *We*. D-503 expresses his admiration for Taylor early in the novel, and his thoughts are sometimes reminiscent of Gastev: "Up to now my brain was a chronometrically tested, sparkling mechanism..." (*We*, Record 7). Zamiatin develops the same idea in the parable of the Three Forgiven Ones: "for hours they repeated those motions which they had been used to making during certain hours of the day and were a requirement of their organism" (*We*, Record 34).

One of the clearest cases of parody of proletarian poetry in *We* involves the proletarians' cliché-ridden images of metal, factory, and forge. The motif is monotonously common:

We are of iron, or steel. . .	*My iz zheleza, iz stali...*
. . . The hammers sing:	*. . . . . . Molotki poiut:*
Here from morning to night	*Schast'e zdes' s utra do nochi*
The smiths forge happiness.	*Kuznetsy kuiut.*
Long ages forged	*Ego shagov stal'nuiu silu*
The steel strength of his steps.	*Kovali dolgie veka.*
Boldly in "The Smithy" we forge	*Smelo v "Kuznitse" kuem*
Our will, thoughts, feelings:	*Nashu voliu, mysli, chuvstva:*
Collectively we create	*Proletarskoe iskusstvo*
Proletarian art.	*Kollektivno sozdaem.*

Beside the forge, lit by
    a bright-shining fire
I forge with a hammer a piece
    of white-hot steel.
In this world, in this world,
    you alone created all,
Untiringly day and night you
    forged and forged and forged ...
	*Vozle gorna, osveshchennyi
	    iarkobleshchushchim ognem
	Ia kuiu otrezok stali
	    raskalennoi molotkom.
	V etom mire
	    ty odin vse sozdaval,
	Neustanno, dnem i noch'iu
	    vse koval, koval, koval . . .*

Kirillov apotheosized the "divine" mission of iron in his poem "Zheleznyi Messiia" ("Iron Messiah," 1918). But, even more than his fellow poets, it was Gastev who was drawn to metallic images. His poems speak of "iron" choirs, "forged" space, "iron" blood, the "steel" will of labor, and "steel, forged will." Gastev's overuse of such imagery was even parodied by a fellow proletarian poet, Kiselev, who accused him of weighing down his contemporaries with his "iron iambs" and ended, "Oh, how heavy are these iron days!"

Zamiatin wryly refers to this stock of images in his essay "New Russian Prose" (1923) by saying that in "The Smithy" and "Forge" several poets had been "hammered out" ("*vykovalos*'"). In *We*, D-503 hears just such an "iron" poem about Prometheus: "(he) harnessed fire to steel machine, / And enchained [*zakoval*] chaos with the Law." D-503 continues: "Everything is new, steel: a steel sun, steel trees, steel people... One could not have chosen more instructive and beautiful images" (*We*, Record 9). This is a clear case of parody of proletarian poetry. It is particularly reminiscent of Sadov'ev's "conquering dark chaos, / We rule the world collectively" and Gastev's "Boldly I called to battle dark once-terrible, evil elements: / I conquered, tamed, enchained [*zakoval*] them."

Two other favorite images of the proletarians were the railroad engine and the wheel. Gastev, for example, entitled one work "Express" and lines such as the following are common:

> The insatiable running of wheels is our banner...
> . . . our train rushes on . . .
> The express rushes on . . .
> . . . the train, bending its back rushing headlong . . .

In *We*, D-503 writes in Record 3: "The Tables transformed each one of us, actually, into a six-wheeled steel hero of a great poem." This is clarified by Zamiatin's remarks elsewhere. In a letter to [graphic artist] Iurii Annenkov in 1921, he told him in essence about *We*: "People are greased with machine grease." Again, in "I Am Afraid" he chided, "The proletarian writers and poets are diligently trying to be aviators astride a locomotive. The locomotive huffs and puffs sincerely and assiduously, but it does not look as if it can rise aloft." Thus the reference in *We* seems clearly related to the use of an engine as a major motif in proletarian poetry.

Gastev's "manifesto" of 1919 ... claim[s] the primacy of the collective over the individual, and the image of the one versus the "millions" constantly recurs: "Millions of voices sang these songs to me,/ Millions of blue-shirted, strong, bold smiths." These mass activities are particularly striking in Gastev's "Factory Whistles" ("*Gudki*"), one of his most popular works, cited in 1918 by Bogdanov as a superior example of proletarian art:

> When the morning factory whistles blow in the worker's districts,
> It is no call to bondage. It is the song of the future.
> Once we worked in miserable workshops and began
>   work in the morning at different times.
> But now, at eight in the morning, the whistles
>   sound for the whole million.
> Now minute for minute we begin together.
> The whole million takes the hammer at the very same instant.
> Our first blows sound together.
> Of what do the factory whistles sing?
> They are the morning hymn of unity.

This prose poem is closely paralleled by a passage in *We*, in which the ideas of the "million," or the "million-armed" body, and insistence on perfect simultaneity recur:

> Each morning, with six-wheeled precision, at the very same hour, at the very same minute, we, millions, arise as one. At the very same hour, millions as one, we begin work—millions as one we finish it. And merging into a single, million-armed body, at the very same second, designated by the Tables, we

raise the spoons to our mouths, and at the very same second we go out for a walk and go to the auditorium, to the hall of Taylor exercises, and go to sleep. (*We*, Record 3).

Gastev elevates labor to the status of a divine ritual—"But silence—a sacred moment: we put on our working shirts" ("Miracles of Labor")—and his "hymns" to labor find counterparts in the novel's "hymn of the United State" and the "solemn liturgy for the United State" (Record 9).

Proletarian poems are not only hymns, but also triumphal marches:

> In advance we rejoice and trumpet
> And we'll begin work with a march of victory ...
>
> With a victory march we'll drill into the clouds
> Of the dark day ...

Zamiatin makes much of this in *We*: "The pipes of the Music Factory thundered out harmoniously a March—the same daily March" (Record 7, 34). This March recurs frequently:

> As always, the music factory was playing the March of the United State with all its pipes. With measured steps, by fours, exaltedly keeping time, the numbers walked—hundreds, thousands of numbers, in light-blue unifs, with gold badges on the chest—the State number of each, male or female (Record 2).

This passage parodies the victory march, the anonymous masses, the sameness, and particularly the music of machinery which is omnipresent in the verse of the proletarian poets:

> iron scales, choirs of iron rumbling ...
> the steel round-song of machines ...
> by the machines singing songs ...
>
> From the Iron Mont Blanc there came to our working masses the poem raised by us... the exalted cry of the machine, the triumphant song of forged metal.

The concept of "cosmism," or conquering the universe and spreading the revolution to other planets and the stars was developed primarily by the proletarian poets of the Smithy group. Gastev had anticipated them with such lines as:

> Ever try to forge and forge, ever try to raise and push heavy steel rails into the endless, unknown, mute atmosphere to neighboring, still unknown, strange planets.

> ... they will enchain and girdle the universe with swift, strong rails of will.

> through the air came a burning poem of metal, a voice was heard, coming from earth through the beams past the clouds to the stars.

This theme is continued by the Smithy poets:

> We'll boldly fly up into the sky
> Like a thunder-roaring comet
> We'll slice through Milky Ways.
>
> Cosmic millions,
> We will plunge ourselves into the old world constellations.
> In the white star-clusters of Orion
> We'll light the fire of insurrection.
>   (Gerasimov, "We shall conquer, the power is simmering," 1918)

and

> And now we come out in orderly ranks,
> Victoriously greeting the heights.
> Participants in a great change...
> And with the songs of the proletariat
> The paths of the universe will be decked.
> Fellow-singers, make haste
> To shape the factory rumble into a hymn.
>   (Rodov, "Proletarian Poets," 1920)

Trotskii wrote sarcastically of the Smithy: "The idea here is that one should feel the entire world as a unity and oneself as an active part of that unity, with the prospect of commanding in the future not only the earth, but the entire cosmos. All this, of course, is very splendid, and terribly big. We came from Kursk and Kaluga, we have conquered all Russia recently, and now we are going on towards world revolution. But are we to stop at the boundaries of 'planetism'!"

The opening page of *We* is filled with the same theme: "One thousand years ago your heroic ancestors subjected the whole earth to the power of the United State. A still more glorious task is before you: the integration of the infinite equation of the Cosmos by the use of the glass, electric, fire-breathing Integral" (*We*, Record 1). This passage is surely nothing less than a parody of the proletarian's idea of cosmic revolution, given an "objective correlative" in *We* in the projected flight of an actual spacecraft.

Zamiatin draws still another parallel to the proletarian poetry in his depictions of the building of the Integral. There is great similarity between the Taylorized precision of Gastev's factories and the construction of the spacecraft:

Gastev:	*We:*
The factory... completely full of its steel, invincible pride, threatens the elements of earth... sky... universe and it is hard to understand, where machine is and where man. We have merged with our iron Comrades, we have reached an accord with them, together we have created a new spirit of movement	I saw how the people below bent, unbent, turned around according to the Taylor system evenly and swiftly, in time like the levers of one huge machine... I saw how the transparent-glass monster-cranes rolled slowly along the glass rails, and, just like the people, obediently turned, bent, thrust their loads inward, into the bowels of the Integral. And it was all one: humanized machines, mechanized people. It was the greatest most stirring beauty, harmony, music...
	(*We*, Record 15)

The "monster" machines appear both in Gastev and in *We*. Machines are humanized in both—the Integral "meditates" on its future (Record 15) and Gastev's "Express" "wants" to melt small souls to create one large one (...). Two other passages in *We* parallel those in "We Grow from Iron":

Gastev:	*We:*
... Girders and angle bars... Bend to the right and left. The rafters in the domes, like a giant's shoulders, hold the whole iron building.	Obviously, the balls of the regulators rotated, cranks, glittering, bent to the right and left: the beam proudly shook its shoulders ... (Record 2)
... *Balki i ugol'niki...* *Zagibaiutsia sprava i sleva.* *Soediniaiutsia stropilami v Kupolakh i, kak plechi velikana, Derzhat vsiu zheleznuiu postroiku.*	*samozabvenno kruzhilis' shary Reguliatorov, motyli, sverkaia, sgibalos'vpravo I vlevo; gordo pokachival plechami balansir...*
I merged with the iron of the building. I rose. I push my shoulders against the rafters, the upper beams, the roof. My feet are still on the earth, But my head is above the building... An iron echo covered my words The whole building trembles with Impatience ...	And it seemed to me that not past generations, but I myself had won a victory against the old god and the old life, that I myself had created all this. I felt like a tower: I was afraid to move my elbow, lest the walls, the cupola and the machines should fall to pieces. (Record 2)
Ia slilsia s zhelezom postroiki. Podnialsia. Vypiraiu plechami stropila, Verkhnie balki, kryshu. Nogi moi ehche na zemle, no Golova vyshe zdaniia. Zheleznoe eshcho pokrylo moi Slova, vsia postoika drozhit Neterpeniem ...	*Itak: budto ne tselye pokoleniia A ia—imenno ia—pobedil starogo Boga i staruiu zhizn', imenno ia Sozdal vse eto, i ia kak bashnia, ia boius' dvinut' loktem, chtoby ne Posypalis' steny, kupol, mashiny...*

Finally, one might also point to the ending of *We* and its note of assurance: "And I hope we shall prevail. More than that. I am sure we shall prevail. Because reason must prevail." Gastev is equally self-assured at the conclusion of "We Grow from Iron": "We shall prevail!"

In *We* Zamiatin holds up to ridicule an entire complex of ideas which are intimately connected with the poetry of the proletarians: its emphasis on collectivism, the mechanization of humans, cosmism, the apotheosis of labor and the glorification of the State. And the pages of *We* also resound with the incessant din of the motifs of metals, forges and locomotives. Zamiatin's essays show clearly that he was a close reader of the poems produced by this group of poets, and his re-creation of their religious tone and use of their industrial images point persuasively to the proletarians as the targets of some of the satirical shafts of the novel.

II: *We* and Bogdanov's *Red Star* (*Krasnaia Zvezda*)

There is no doubt that some of the urban setting and tone of the novel were surely suggested by Wells. The first part of this article has tried to show the many links between *We* and the language and themes of the proletarians. But evidence also suggests that both the hero D-503 and the overall parameters of the novel were inspired by another proletarian work, A. A. Bogdanov's utopian novel *Red Star* (1908). The details, themes and images common to both novels are too numerous to be accidental. Zamiatin mentions Bogdanov's novel in his 1922 article on H. G. Wells as one of the very few examples of science fiction in the Russian tradition.

Red Star, in brief, concerns the visit of an Earthling to the more advanced civilization of Mars. The hero, 27-year-old Leonid, is invited to join an "expedition" by a Martian working in disguise in the ranks of the Russian revolutionaries under the conspiratorial name of Menni. The purpose of Leonid's inclusion in the crew of the expedition is to serve as the liaison between the two worlds, to bring them closer together. The trip is marred by one event: an accident in the laboratory of the spacecraft during the journey to Mars pierces the skin of the craft, and a master chemist, Letta, sacrifices his life to save Leonid's. This incident earns Leonid the hatred of Sterni, Mars' leading mathematician, who deplores the loss of such a brilliantly-trained mind for the sake of an apparently inferior one. For in spite of his scientific training, Leonid finds himself unable to comprehend many of the technical achievements which the Martians have made. A series of scenes acquaint Leonid and the reader with the world of the future some 300 years hence: a tour of the *eteronef*, or spacecraft, Menni's Martian home, a factory, a children's home, an art museum, and a hospital.

....

Zamiatin seems to have transferred a number of details of Martian civilization to his utopian city. Two of the adjectives characterizing Martian life and nature, "clear" ("iasnyi") and "transparent" ("prozrachnyi"), are also used as D-503's leitmotifs. The material from which Martian clothing is made is transparent, at least until dyed; much of the body of the *eteronef* is glass; the Martian factory has a glass ceiling and networks of glass parquets supported by iron beams; Letta's casket is transparent. Martian houses all have a blue-tinted glass roof, which, as in *We*, gives their cities, when seen from an approaching spacecraft, the configuration of blue spots on the Martian topography. Martians in this fashion relax with their friends in bluish light, chosen specifically (like the dwellings in *We*) because of the tranquillizing effect of blue light on living organisms. We see that Zamiatin has taken many of these details and has made a much more consistent use of them in his anti-utopia than Bogdanov did. Some alterations are obvious. Menni, for example, lives in a small, individual, two-story house, while all the inhabitants of Zamiatin's city live in communal Crystal Palaces, whose transparent glass cages stretch in all directions. The light effect—filtered, quieting, even sunlight—is like that in Bogdanov's Martian parlors. The bird's eye view of Zamiatin's city buildings, the blocks of bluish ice, seems closely related to the Martian cities (Record 21) just described: "The icy blue relief map of the city" (Record 34). Zamiatin seems to have borrowed this detail, but has transformed its meaning by subordinating it to his pattern of images (including ice, blue, and squares) which signify entropy.

Zamiatin's utopians are feeding on petroleum food, a detail which may have been suggested by Bogdanov's novel. Since a food crisis impends, the Martians institute a crash program to produce a food substitute from albumen, and eventually they attempt to manufacture albumen from inorganic material.

The first section of this essay has pointed out the frequency with which the proletarian poets treated lyrically the theme of the machine. Bogdanov, too, informs Martian technology with aesthetic qualities: at the factory the machines "cut, sawed, planed, drilled the huge pieces of iron, aluminum, nickel, and copper. The levers, like gigantic steel hands, moved evenly and smoothly... The very sound of the machines, when the ear became somewhat used to it, began to seem almost melodic ...". Compare this with the beautiful passage in *We* which prefaces D-503's meditations on the beauty of the dance as "unfree movement." Like Bogdanov, Zamiatin personifies the various machines which are working "with closed eyes, in self-forgetfulness," "bending," "moving their shoulders," and "squatting" (*We*, Record 2).

As for the workers themselves, "In the expression of their faces was no tense concern, but only calm attention." We recall that in *We*, D-503 contentedly records that during the daily march, "our faces are unclouded by the insanity of thoughts" (Record 2). "More intangible and invisible from the side were those threads which connected the tender brain of people with the indestructible organs of the mechanism." Zamiatin also ties humans together with threads: based on his perception of "threads" D-503 suspects relations between I and S, between I and R-13. But then Zamiatin unexpectedly uses the metaphor to reveal a negative aspect of the political hierarchy in the City. He transforms the idea into the grotesque image of the spider web in which they all have been caught and are awaiting the arrival of the spider, the Well-Doer, on the Day of Unanimity (*We*, Record 24).

D-503 is the spokesman for the principle of rationality, a principle which the novel ultimately rejects. Bogdanov, however, makes it the basic axis of the Martian civilization. For example, suicide is permitted because there is no rational reason why it should not be permitted. And so a special room is provided for this purpose for those who have become incurably ill. Force, as a principle, is also permitted. Leonid asks for specifics, but the answer is given with only one example: "What rational being would reject violence, for example, for self-defense?"

Leonid finds these values further elucidated in the exhibits at the art museum, and he perceives that the aesthetic standards expressed there are part of the everyday life in the utopian future. Life and art become one. He sees that the early works of the past express harmony. Art works of the "transitional epochs" express plosion, passion, disturbing struggle; the art of the socialist epoch expresses "harmonious movement, the calm manifestation of strength, of movement alien to the morbidity of effort, striving free of worry, a lively activity permeated with the consciousness of its well-proportioned unity and its insuperable rationality."

Leonid also discovers that on Mars monuments are no longer erected in honor of people; rather they are commissioned to commemorate great events such as the first attempt to reach the Earth; the elimination of a fatal epidemic disease, or the discovery of the break-down and synthesis of all the chemical elements. This reminds us of the occasions on which poetry is composed and recited in *We*: R-13's poeticization of the Death Sentence (Record 8).

....

But what kind of "hero" did Zamiatin intend in D-503? We suggest that Zamiatin set himself the task of satirizing proletarian verse whose revolutionary lyricism lent itself to parody through its extremism, and the lyrical proletarian "I's" who strive to deprive themselves poetically of their individuality. He mocked the former with some bad doggerel (Record 12), and the latter by concocting the persona of a futuristic "proletarian" scientist and writer. Tonally, D-503 is as much an exponent of the United State as the lyrical "we" is of the proletarian poems of 1917-20. As [Dostoevskii scholar] Joseph Frank has convincingly shown, this device was practiced earlier by Dostoevskii in *Notes from the Underground*, where the Underground Man is the satirical representation of the "men of the sixties." Dostoevskii's satire is doubly devastating because the Underground Man is personally such a sick human being that his claiming that he shared the advanced views of the younger generation had to be insufferably insulting to the nihilists. Zamiatin has done the same thing in *We*. He has taken the ideas of the proletarians, including Bogdanov's, to their extreme, in order to dramatize their implications of dehumanization.

....

Zamiatin's satire is made particularly salient by the choice of Bogdanov's own hero Leonid as D-503's prototype. Zamiatin created D-503 out of the language, themes, and ideology made familiar by the proletarian poets and Bogdanov in the first years of the Soviet period. It seems that Zamiatin's particular targets in this work are Gastev and Bogdanov.

Some readings of *We* tend to dwell exclusively on its bleak, antiutopian vision of the future. But, although there is no doubt of the philosophical gravity of the work, this essay has tried to show the validity of another, generally neglected reading. *We* is a topical novel which grew consistently and naturally out of the literary models and practices predominating in the immediate post-Revolutionary period.

SELECTED NOTES

[1] Quotations from Zamiatin's critical articles are taken from Mirra Ginsburg's translation, *A Soviet Heretic* (Chicago, 1970). English quotations from the novel are taken from the Zilboorg translation.

[2] Other such poems ... are: B.D. Aleksandrovskii's "My" (We, 1921); "My umeem vse perenosit' ... " (We can overcome everything, 1921); M.P. Gerasimov's "My vse voz'mem, my vse poznaem ... " (We will take everything, we will know everything, 1917); A.P. Kraiskii's "My—odno" (We are One, 1918; I.S. Loginov's "My—pervye raskaty groma ..." (We Are the First Claps of Thunder, 1919); F.S. Shkulev's "My, Proletarskie poety" (We, Proletarian Poets, 1922). Many additional examples may be found in the proletarian journals *Kuznitsa* and *Gorn*.

Bright Hopes and Dark Insights

Vision and Blindness as Cognition Tropes in Babel's *Red Cavalry*

by Irene MASING-DELIC*

* From *For SK, In Celebration of the Life and Career of Simon Karlinsky*, edited by Michael S. Flier and Robert P. Hughes. Berkeley: Berkeley Slavic Specialties, 1994. Pp. 199-210.

It has been convincingly shown that correcting initial misconceptions is one of the main structuring principles in Isaak Babel's cycle of stories from the Polish Campaign of 1919-1921, entitled *Red Cavalry* (1923-1925). The transition from misconception to insight, as Jan van der Eng demonstrates, is often achieved by contrasting various types of "inner tales" with the narrative outer frames of the stories; their contrasting perspective may correct an initial impression presented in the framing narrative, as happens in "Crossing the River Zbruch," the first story of the cycle. Here the pregnant Jewess's account of her father's death at the hand of Polish soldiers forms the "inner" account of events that contradicts the narrator's preceding narrative, based on superficial first-hand impressions. The woman's story corrects the narrator: what he takes to be "Jewish sloth" and cowardice is, in fact, inflicted destruction and unobtrusive heroism. Conversely, "Italian Sun" (story six) shows two types of escapism: the first a genuine (creative) one into the world of the imagination that will yield art, in the narrator's frame tale; and the second false escape of a would-be Chekist into dreams of killing Italian royalty under the "sun of Italy," in the inner story. The poles of contrast are here reversed in regard to the "inner-outer" axis of the first tale.

Another critic, Wolf Schmid, speaks of the stories as "epiphany stories" where insight often results from having repressed knowledge rise to the surface involuntarily (e.g. in dreams), wherefore it often is repressed once again. The protagonist "forgets what he once knew," because he wants to. This critic thus sees not only an "effort to understand," as van der Eng does, but also an effort *not* to understand and to cling to comforting misconceptions. Schmid's brilliant analysis of "Crossing the River Zbruch" links genuine epiphanies to seeing without flinching, as when the narrator for the first time acknowledges his fear of slaughter and death by looking squarely at the dead man lying in the bed beside him: "The epiphany of death [acknowledged] makes the narrator into someone who knows. It opens his eyes, also to who he himself really is and leads to his inner retreat from previous positions. To retreat is however not permitted in the world of war. It is not by chance that in the dream he has, the shots fired at the brigade commander as punishment for his retreat are aimed at his head, at the eyes."

The aim of the present article is to add some observations on the epiphany theme in *Red Cavalry*, by examining the motifs of eyes which "see" and eyes which do not "see," in the Biblical sense of "understanding" and integrating what you perceive, or not doing so. The *Red Cavalry* cycle is a kind of educational novel, in which "seeing" and its opposite "blindness," specifically the oxymoron of the blind visionary and the "blinded" with good eyesight, constitute important motifs within the overall theme of the protagonist's gradual maturation. The protagonist's "education" is completed when he finally learns to look unflinchingly at that which he has avoided before and when he no longer reverts to suppressing epiphanies; it occurs when he learns to see, in other words to "face reality," instead of averting his glance, or allowing himself to be blinded and dazzled. It has been pointed out that "the colorful imagery and unusual metaphors" in the stories of the cycle "conceal a deep concern for morality," as well as "an ironic sense of history" (Efraim Sicher). I fully agree with this statement; it is my contention that the metaphors of light and darkness, illumination and (moral) blindness in *Red Cavalry* carry a significant burden of the cycle's ethical and historical-political stance. This message, contrary to much critical opinion, is, by the time we have read the last story, quite unambiguous in its rejection of violence and war and the ideologies inspiring these.

The chain of vision-linked images carrying the semantics of delusion and insight is set off in the already mentioned introductory story "Crossing the River Zbruch." There, as the critics mentioned above state, we find the narrator asleep and dreaming in the "messy" Jewish household he still perceives in purely negative terms. In his dream, he sees how the commander of the Sixth Division, the "captivating" Savitskii,[1] pursues his subordinate brigade commander shooting his eyes out of their sockets, as punishment for a retreat maneuver. They "fall to the ground." At this point, the narrator wakes up, because the Jewess is touching his face (opening his eyes), releasing him from his nightmare and telling him he has been shouting in his sleep. He then discovers that he has been sleeping next to her dead father whom he has mistaken for a fellow sleeper. She tells him of her father's murder by the Poles, who "hacked his face in two"; it becomes clear to the narrator who caused the "mess" in the household. He also learns of the dead man's heroism in his hour of death and his love for his daughter whom he wanted to spare the sight of his murder, begging to be taken outside for the execution. The soldiers did not heed his plea.

The prologue story, through the dream motif, thus conveys the narrator's subconscious knowledge of the fact that the leaders of the Revolution demand blind obedience to impossible demands ("never retreat!") and are ever ready to offer the most blinding of all insights: execution and death. The counter-revolutionary Poles are morally blinded also, in their case, by their anti-Semitism and therefore they are equally prepared to destroy and kill as their "red foes," while believing, like them, that they have the true insight into the situation at hand. The theme of "those with good eyesight who are morally blind," versus "those whose eyes have been ripped out, but not deprived of their inner illumination," is set. The old Jew whose face had been cut in two died physically blinded, but with his human dignity intact, when pleading with his killers to spare his pregnant daughter the sight of his slaughter. Of course, the killers who with their keen eye-sight knew exactly where to cut and how to rip apart a face, were not able to "see" the spiritual light of the old father pleading for his daughter at his hour of death.

Liutov, the narrator (with his "fierce" revolutionary pseudonym), at this stage is not yet ready to admit that killing is killing regardless of who perpetrates it. He still is—and for quite some time still will be—convinced that the Red Cavalry is entitled to kill, whereas the Poles are not. In his later conversation with the pious old Jew Gedali (in the eponymous story, number seven in the cycle), he praises the Revolution for ripping open closed eyes: "The sun cannot enter eyes that are squeezed shut..., but we shall rip open those closed eyes!," he announces to Gedali in the high-flown rhetoric of the romantic revolutionary discourse he is enthralled by. It is only in his dreams, when his eyes are closed but his conscience awake, that he is able to see the blindingly handsome commander Savitskii as the brute he is (he figures in Liutov's dream of the eyes shot out of their sockets). What Liutov as yet knows only subconsciously in his dreams, the implied author, of course, knows consciously at the time he is writing the *Red Cavalry* stories.

One of the things the implied author knows when writing about his still ideologically blinded protagonist Liutov (an alter ego figure) is that the New World is built on a graveyard just as much as the Old World was. The road from Brest to Warsaw was built on the bones of Nikolai the First's peasant laborers, Liutov tells his readers in the prologue story of "Crossing the River Zbruch," implying that his comrades from the Red Cavalry are fighting for a world in which no such sacrifices will ever be demanded again. The implied author knows, however, that during the Polish Campaign another layer of bones was added to the already existing one—the bones of slaughtered Cossacks, Poles and Jews.

This knowing author fully explores the ironies inherent in the encounters and dialogues that the blindly devoted Liutov (his own deluded former self), has with the piously Hasidic Jew Gedali. Gedali, in the eponymous story (story seven) had his eyes "closed" by the Polish counter-revolution, but physical blindness has only widened his cognitive competence; his insights do not rely on empirical channels and he can therefore see matters very clearly through his "smoky spectacles" and damaged eyes. In his dark world, he has learned to listen to "invisible voices" that tell him that there should be a "sweet Revolution" that can dispense with "gunpowder," "seasoned with the best blood." Gedali's wisdom is that of his Hasidism, which, according to him, has been "blinded," but still "stands at the crossroads of the winds of history." He may well be speaking for all the religions mentioned in the cycle: Catholicism, Judaism, and Orthodoxy have all, by the Revolution, been "blinded," i.e. robbed of their significance and power to "illumine" the world, but quite possibly they all, nevertheless, still stand "at the crossroads of the winds of history." Liutov, at this point, still the ardent revolutionary, does not share Gedali's view, believing religion to be dead; he does at this point not have the Biblical "eyes with which to see," but he will acquire them. At least, he will no longer be deceived by the romantic rhetoric of violence.

Still "blinded" by this rhetoric, he trusts his ideological spectacles more than those inner eyes that can never be ripped out, nor replaced by corrective optical instruments. Liutov's spectacles mark him not only as a defenseless Jewish intellectual among illiterate, violent and anti-Semitic Cossacks hating "four-eyed wimps," but also as one of the many deluded ideologues of the cycle. Like the would-be assassin of monarchs, the demented would-be Chekist Sidorov (in "Italian Sun"), he is one of those who have been ensnared by a merciless ideology that has reduced the complex patterns of reality to propagandistic catch phrases. Declaring Gedali's vision of the International of Good People to be "unattainable" and rejecting Rabbi Motale's Hasidic congregation as "the possessed, the liars and the unhinged," it is Liutov who is the deluded one. That this is so emerges from the blindness-insight imagery that closes the story "The Rabbi" (the ninth story of the cycle).

When he leaves the dark synagogue with its "unhinged" congregation, Liutov returns to the brightly illuminated railway station where his propaganda train awaits him (he is one of the journalists and propagandists who are in charge of the newspaper *Red Cavalryman* and the war propaganda material distributed by the train). There at the station, he is "greeted by the sparkle of hundreds of lights," and "the enchanted glitter of the radio transmitter." The epithet "enchanted" combined with "radio-transmitter" creates a slightly comical effect, but perhaps also has a sinister implication. It reveals the demonic essence of all this glaring light. As in Gogol's story "Nevskii Prospect," this is the kind of artificial light that—lit by the Evil One himself—shows "everything as it is not."[2] Particularly, when refracted by thick, ideological spectacles, the light of the propaganda train does not enlighten but rather "enchant" and, hence, deceive, making you see what you want to see and blinding you to other alternatives. In spite of Liutov's harsh judgment of the "liars" and "possessed" he met in Rabbi Motale's synagogue, it can be argued that it is the Rabbi who "sees" more than the dazzled Liutov. Judging by his motto "the sage shreds the veil of existence with laughter," the Rabbi is a man of insight, able to penetrate the veils of delusions by the kind of laughter that reduces the fake to its proper proportions. Liutov belongs to those to whom laughing wisdom does not come easily, however. It is true that he tells Motale that he is seeking "merriment," but it seems to be merriment *without* laughter. It is noteworthy that the blindingly handsome commander Savitskii's gray eyes "dance with merriment," when he signs orders about "the severest punitive measures," such as being gunned down "on the spot" for disobedience. It is this kind of "merriment" that impresses Liutov at this point when he still dreams futile dreams about being someone like the Cossack commanders, or at least their cavalry men.

Liutov is not only blinded by his brightly illuminated propaganda train, but also by the "splendor" of the charismatic Cossack Leaders he encounters—so unlike him with their "gigantic" bodies, splendid purple-crimson uniforms and unshakable and "merry" self-confidence. The epithets *oslepitel'nyi* (blinding) and *plenitel'nyi* (captivating) accompany Budennyi, Savitskii, and other leaders of the campaign almost like stock epithets. Budennyi's "dazzling grin," Akinf'ev's "dazzling teeth," and Savitskii's "captivating" bearing have, literally, dazzled Liutov and "enslaved" him. He is enchanted by their theatrical demeanor, such as the display of the "despotic indifference of a Tatar khan" when celebrating victory; he is dazzled by their circus rider tricks when half caressing, half whipping a dying horse into a last performance of lifelikeness, D'iakov demonstrates his power over the "trembling creatures" he masters.[3] He, the timid hero who cannot make himself kill a man or rape a woman, is in love with their glittering masculine beauty and cruel splendor. Love, as is well known, is often blind.

A scene of seduction opens the famous story "My First Goose" (story eight) where the sad Jew Liutov, hiding "autumn in his heart," cannot resist the "merriment" of splendid Savitskii's gray eyes. Enchanted by his gigantic body and beautifully curved legs, famously looking like "two girls wedged to their shoulders in riding boots," and infatuated with a vision of amoral heroism he covets for himself, Liutov notes the whip in the beloved Hero's hand. He himself is ready to act the mare who is galvanized into an unnatural semblance of life under D'iakov's whip, or in his case, to act out a false "heroism," to impress, against all odds, those he is infatuated with. Spurred on by the desire for "manliness," he kills an old blind woman's last asset, her goose. Just as the expiring horse, which, caressed and whipped by D'iakov's powerful hand, yet is enamored with her torturer, looking at him with her "dog-like, love-struck eyes," so Liutov looks at Savitskii, "bristling with envy at the steel and bloom of his youth." Recalling Savitskii's merry, gray eyes gives him the "courage" to ignore the plea of the old woman's "half-blind" eyes, the whites of which seem to trickle out of their sockets: the plea to spare her goose. It is "merriment" that the sad Jew Liutov is seeking, as he told Rabbi Motale. And he finds "merriment" in the "joke" he plays on the old woman, killing her pompous goose, "waddling through the yard." His reward is acceptance by the Cossacks, at least for the moment. Nevertheless, falling asleep, he is no longer merry. In his dreams, his eyes closed, he sees his true (and better) self and this is why his heart "crimson with murder, screeched and bled," or more literally "crunched and flowed" through the night. Schmid makes the fine observation that in Liutov's dream, his heart is "crunching and flowing"—an unusual expression for heart-ache—because, in his dream, he repeats the act of the goose's "murder." The bird's head "crunched" under his boot and the blood "flowed" out of it. Liutov is here definitely a parodic Raskol'nikov, reliving his crime in dreams and recollections, seeking in vain to cling to his comforting ideologies that justify murder.

In "My First Goose" we meet yet another "half-blind" elderly person then, in addition to Gedali. Why are so many of the victimized characters (half-)blind? Is the old woman's blindness metaphorical as well as "real," as in the case of Gedali whose vision was directed inward in order to see deeper layers of reality beyond the deceptive surface? If the old woman's blindness is also metaphorical as well as real, one aspect of her blindness could be that she has seen so much senseless cruelty that she does not care to "look" at the world any more. It is not only the loss of her goose that makes her want to "hang herself"—her wish is motivated by what she has seen and experienced and is forced to witness for the nth time in Liutov's wanton act. Naturally, the author does not imply that one goes physically blind when reality revolts one, but the impression here nevertheless is this: that the old woman has seen more than she cares for and that, as a result, she has "closed" her eyes to the world.

In any case, having committed the "murder," Liutov is beginning to doubt the value of flashy epiphanies, such as Savitskii rising up from his seat, clad in the splendor of his purple breeches and crimson cap, "splitting the hut in two like a banner splitting the sky." Possibly even the *sacred Word* of Lenin is beginning to lose some of its magic for him. Reading Lenin's latest article to the illiterate Cossacks who for the time being are his friends, he is "triumphant." Babel debunks jubilant Liutov, however, by making him read the article "like a triumphant deaf man." Like "blindness," "deafness" has its metaphorical side: the Party propagandists to whom Liutov belongs are deaf to all voices and opinions except their own. The admiring reaction of the Cossacks does nothing to elevate the occasion of the political reading either. Squadron commander Surovkov does praise Lenin's wisdom, but the image he uses is hardly flattering, even though it probably expresses sincere admiration on his part.

Saying that Lenin "wheedles out" the truth," like "a hen pecks up a grain of corn" from a pile of rubbish, may express "folksy" sentiments of admiration, but it is a "low" image. The notion of a hen picking grain out of rubbish (dung?), furthermore, recalls the proverb that even a "blind hen may find a grain of corn." Lenin's observation that "right now there is a shortage of everything" seems to belong to those insights that even a blind hen, her beak peeled to the ground, could find without too much intellectual effort. It could of course be argued that Liutov is adjusting the "curve" of Lenin's message into a perfectly "straight line" to suit his listeners' simple minds. Yet this curve is too easily straightened into a line to bespeak genuine complexities. If there is a "mysterious," or hidden, curve to Lenin's speech at all, it may be one perceived by Liutov alone, since he still wants to be the never-doubting ideologue of the new Leninist creed, seeing more in it than there is. Certainly the "impetuous rails" of Communist Party "statutes," hailed with much rhetorical panache in the story "Evening" (the twenty-second in the cycle) are straight, without hidden curves of complexity, as rails tend to be. The propaganda train rolls along the predetermined tracks of the Revolution that is taking all its devotees and their simplistic truths straight into the Future, while dumping all its enemies by the wayside, or so the propaganda claims.

In "Evening" we also learn that Liutov's colleagues at the *Red Cavalryman* are "pale and blind" Galin, consumptive Slinkin, and Sychev who has "withered intestines." This trio is as passionate as "Riazan' Jesuses" and they churn out "a rambunctious newspaper filled with courage and rough-and-ready mirth" (of the kind Savitskii loves). The contrast between their feeble physiques and the "rambunctious" and ever-cheerful newspaper they are concocting creates a strong impression of falseness. These rural (from the provincial city of Riazan') "preachers-propagandists" pretend to a forceful optimism which their puny and sick bodies hardly allow them to feel and which, therefore, they fake in their compensatory verbal outpourings. The imagery surrounding them emphasizes their impotence; even the sun shining on them is "cross-eyed" and soon "expires." Again, a character, Galin, is blind—again both in the sense of having poor eye-sight and in the sense of being ideologically blinded. One of the sources of his blindness is, as in the previous story "The Rabbi," the powerful "illumination" of the propaganda train.

In this story, however, the magic glitter of the train's artificial illumination seems diminished as the printing-press scatters lights "in all directions" and these burn "uncontrollably like the passion of a machine." Galin may be passionate about the Revolution, but his most genuine and much more focused passion is for Irina, the washerwoman. With his cataract-ridden eyes "twinkling" in the moonlight, he tries to entice her with endless stories about murdered and executed monarchs, but to no avail. She prefers the cook. Bespectacled Liutov himself offers a sorry sight with boils on his neck and bandaged feet. The story's last paragraph shows the disillusioned lover Galin "talking about the political education of the First Cavalry." He does so "in a dull voice, with complete clarity," his "eyelid flutter[ing] over his cataract." His talk seems to parody Liutov's own reading to the Cossacks in "My First Goose," as well as demented Sidorov's ravings (in "Italian Sun").

Even though the propaganda train seems to have lost its magic luster to Liutov who even confesses (in "Evening") that he is "tired of life in the Red Cavalry," it could be argued that it fulfills a useful educational function. Even if Galin's voice is "dull" when he speaks of the "political education of the First Cavalry"—he would rather be in bed with Irina—the *Red Cavalryman* perhaps plays a positive educational role in the life of the Cossacks?

Most likely it does not. Part of the Cossacks' primitive and merciless behavior could in fact be blamed on this "rambunctious" newspaper with its "rough-and-ready mirth" at the misfortunes of others and, undoubtedly, extremely simplistic presentation of ethical issues and black-and-white division of mankind into those who are for the "truth" and those who are not. It does not further the enlightenment of the minds of peasant lads and Cossack warriors whose ability to "see" is already limited by their upbringing in a crude warrior culture that had no room for any ethics beyond "defend your friends, kill those you are told are your enemies." It is an interesting detail that their ability to "see" seems limited when compared to that of their bayonets: these are described as "clairvoyant" (*zriachie*). Undoubtedly, it is the *Red Cavalryman* which endlessly speaks of the Revolution having to "rip open" eyes that are closed to the "truth" of the Revolution and the need to season the International with "gunpowder" and the "best blood." Liutov's high-flown rhetoric in "Gedali" seem to be taken straight out of the newspaper's pseudo-romantic and pseudo-heroic propaganda jargon. In short, the *Red Cavalryman*, with its editorial board of blind Galin and bedazzled Liutov presents a case of the blind leading the blind. In this newspaper a positive evaluation is guaranteed events such as these: an "evil" woman is shot to redeem the rapes of innocent girls ("Salt," the twenty-first story); a class enemy is trampled to death for hours on end ("The Life of Matvei Rodionovich Pavlichenko," the fifteenth of the cycle) and Polish prisoners of war are executed ("Squadron Commander Trunov," the twenty-fifth story of the cycle).

Regardless of whether the Cossacks return with, or without, limbs from the war, their minds and hearts have been mutilated without exception. It is quite possible that the Cossacks rip out eyes of old sages with their "clairvoyant" bayonets, and smash the "eyes" of synagogues, churches and castles, shoot at the eyes of statues and exterminate bees because they want to eliminate "witnesses" to their crimes. According to legend, the bees refused to sting Christ's eyes, although other insects that were blind and couldn't see where to sting, encouraged them to do so. It is the kind of legend the Cossacks would know and which would make them understand "deep down" that they are "closer to the blind gnats" than to the seeing and merciful bees. In any case, their obsessive "blinding" of objects and people alike would be the instinctive reaction of the dumb who are morally blinded by the war (and the past), the war propaganda and *agitprop*, but still aware in some dark corner of their conscience that they have stained themselves. This stain on their conscience they do not want Christ to "see." The fact that all bees have been killed in Volhynia should be considered in this context also. The honey of mercy certainly does not flow there any longer.

If the Cossacks move in the direction of increasing ideological blindness, Liutov does remove his distorting inner spectacles ever more often as the cycle progresses. In the end he even becomes perspicacious enough to see what others do not. He catches a glimpse of Christ himself, or at least a tall Galician dressed all in white.

In "Squadron Commander Trunov," a story replete with death-burial-resurrection symbolism, Liutov has made himself an enemy in commander Trunov, because he spoke up for sparing the lives of Polish officers taken prisoners. Trunov is shortly after their disagreement blown to pieces in an air raid, in which he displayed heroic behavior, engaging virtually single-handedly in a machine-gun fight with the airplanes. Strolling in the town of Sokal and mourning his enemy's death, Liutov suddenly glimpses a "Galician" (or is it a Galilean?).[4] There is something Christ-like about this man who is "sepulchral and gaunt as Don Quixote" and who wears white clothing reaching to his feet. He seems to be on his way to "a burial or ... the Eucharist." His small, snakelike, head looks as if "pierced" by nails (*probitaia*).[5] It is adorned by a straw hat of rural fashion, and he leads a "shaggy little cow" (*vzlokhmachennuiu korovenku*) by a rope; Christ was associated with the ass he would ride into Jerusalem on, another humble animal. Liutov sees this white-clad Galician peasant give a gypsy blacksmith some baked potatoes and then loses sight of him, verbally attacked by a friend of Trunov's who accuses him of having beaten up the squadron commander the same morning. Liutov merely reproached him for his inhumanity to his Polish prisoners.

This mysterious white apparition, on its way to either a funeral or the Eucharist, appears against a background of "ancient synagogues" and Jews "arguing about the Kabbala" and other religious differences [we are in a Polish town largely inhabited by Jews]. It is a scene which seems to recreate the atmosphere of Jerusalem at the time of Jesus Christ's crucifixion, when different religions and sects were vying with each other to be heard, especially at Passover time. And the tall gaunt man whose bony body reminds of gallows is surrounded by a mysterious aura.

Naturally Liutov's vision does not imply that he has become a Christian, or "seen God's Son," or is invoking Christianity as the true religion. Its elusive semantics suggest, however, that Christ in some sense is "not far away"; he is not the leader of the Red Cavalrymen as Christ is the leader of the twelve Red Guards in Blok's famous poem *The Twelve* (1918), but appears more as a manifestation of suffering and redemption, holding out the hope of more merciful times, however pale. In Andrei Belyi's novel *Petersburg* a pale, tall man appears at times, strangely comforting those who see him even though he cannot help them. Here the tall white apparition seems to point to some glimmer of hope in a world of blind violence. Perhaps it indicates to Liutov that Trunov redeemed his senseless cruelty to his Polish prisoners by his heroic death and terrible mutilation—he had his face shot to smithereens (was it *probitaia* by bullets, like the tall man's head seems pierced by nails?). The Quixotic Galician may symbolize forgiveness of the "brigand" Trunov who divided the clothes of his prisoners while they were still alive, perhaps because he "did not know what he was doing." Christ forgave the brigand next to him and presumably also the soldiers dividing his cloak, because these people acted without "knowing what they were doing." The Galician's small, snakelike head seems ambiguous— does it harbor deep wisdom, or is it possibly evil? Or does the snakelike head simply "go together" with the man's gallows-like (bony) figure, evoking all that which "Golgatha" stands for? The Galician's gesture of giving out baked potatoes to a gypsy could be in imitation of Christ's handing out bread and fish; perhaps he just shows generosity to a hungry fellow-being. In any case, it would seem to be a positive act. Or, is this Galician a "vegetative Christ" of rebirth, since Trunov was buried in a flower bed "in the public park" of Sokal, near the fence (*zabor*, *Izbrannoe*), while the Gothic cathedral bells rang out (they are *sobor*-nye). Does this bony Galician Christ-Don Quixote promise that there will be a return to life after the Golgatha of war and the apparent triumph of death, symbolized by the snake? Is the white "apparition" predicting a transfiguration that will make men out of beasts, as Blok's white Christ in his *The Twelve* seems to do? Or does it point to the ability of art to preserve and ennoble even the memory of "beasts" like Trunov who suffer like men?

Whatever the ultimate meaning of Liutov's vision, it points to the fact that his "sight" is improving and approaching that finely attuned eye of Gedali's, which sees even in the dark; perhaps his hearing is improving too and is now capable of listening to voices that are inaudible to others. As an artist-chronicler-writer, Liutov increasingly understands that he belongs to those who side with Pan Apolek (in the eponymous fifth story of the cycle) against the Sidorovs and Galins, Budennyis and Savitskiis. As has been shown in Babel'-scholarship, it is the encounter with the painter Pan Apolek's art—an art that endows the human flesh in all its frailties with a redeeming spirituality—which marks a turning-point in Liutov's ethics. Pan Apolek's use of peasants, prostitutes, and innkeepers as models for his virgins and saints in the church frescoes he comes across open Liutov's eyes to the "divinely human" in even the humblest representatives of mankind. Be it the naively wise paintings of Apolek, or the simple tunes of his blind friend Gottfried (whose name means "peace in/from God"), or the parable of a Christ who accepts the role of Bridegroom to Deborah, lying in the vomit of her terror, genuine art "renders justice."[6]

If this is the aesthetic and ethic stance taken in the cycle, it would imply that Il'ia in "The Rabbi's Son" (the thirty-fourth and last of the original cycle), dying amid the portraits of Maimonides and Lenin, the "Song of Songs" and revolver cartridges, made the wrong choice when he ultimately opted for Lenin and cartridges. This last of many Raskol'nikov figures in the cycle chooses the Revolution when he decides that a mother was but an "episode" in comparison with the Revolution. He should instead have heeded Gedali's notions of "only a mother [being] accorded eternal life" and of a mother's soul being "immortal." Abandoning his mother, he finds death. He betrays his mother not by leaving her, but by relegating her to the irrelevant status of an "episode," depriving her of her immortality. In this cycle all sons violating the sacred image of the Maternal Principle are doomed to blindness and death. Liutov, abandoning his memories of an old woman in a laced head-dress bent over the "Sabbath candle," for the glaring illusions of the propaganda-train, betrays this principle, just like his "brother" Il'ia. Death, herself a "woman," avenges the mothers by putting copper coins on the eyes of oblivious sons and closing them forever (in "Zamosc," the twenty-ninth story).

This fate befalls Liutov only in a dream, however—yet another "epiphany" dream showing him the true state of his inner being. Slowly learning from his dreams and from the laughter he encounters in the works of Hershele Ostropoler, a Jewish Tyll Eulenspiegel whom he is translating, he eventually removes the copper coins of blindness and death when he fully accepts himself. "Unmasked" by the Cossacks as a man wanting to live "without enemies" (in the story "Argamak," later added to the cycle)—in other words, as a "coward"—he accepts the verdict. Perhaps he remembers on this occasion how his own notions of courage and cowardice were once reversed in the Jewish household where he was told the truth by a future mother, the pregnant Jewess. The fact that squadron leader Baulin "sees through him" does not diminish Liutov's self-respect any more, as it would have done previously. He too can see Baulin for what he is, namely, an unforgiving Cain, as the "fiery spot" on his forehead indicates. The narrator himself belongs to the Abels of mankind. And though reconciliation between these two categories of men may not be possible, the non-acceptance by "Cains" no longer tortures Liutov. Self-acceptance leads, if not to the camaraderie with the Cossacks of which Liutov initially dreamed so fervently, then at least to inconspicuousness among them. Mimicry may be detrimental to heroes, but it gives an artist the best of all vantage points: that of the observer who empathizes with all and therefore is able to transmit the truth of many truths in aesthetically valid art.

Babel's *Red Cavalry* is often seen as part of literature about Cossacks, belonging to the tradition of Gogol's *Taras Bul'ba* (1835) and Tolstoi's *The Cossacks* (1863). It should also be viewed in the context of "Caucasus-literature," at least the Lermontovian tradition of a "hero's" quest for his true identity in a foreign milieu and in an extraordinary situation (war), which encourages such quests. Thus Pechorin in *A Hero of Our Times* (1840), like Liutov, is a complex quasi-hero, plagued by repressed envy for those whom he secretly deems to be more "manly," or more "ontologically secure," than he is. In this novel, which structurally is as much a "cohabitation of short stories" as *Red Cavalry*, the Chechen *dzhigit* Kazbich, the contra-bandit Ianko, the brave Serbian officer Vulich, and even the pathetically vulgar Grushnitskii, are men without self-consciousness, this blight that "makes cowards" out of would-be heroes. As non-reflexive people, they are carriers of a spontaneity and courage beyond Pechorin's reach. Naturally the Russian aristocrat Pechorin is in a better position to play the hero convincingly than the bespectacled Jew Liutov, and he dupes many—himself most of all. But the sense of inadequacy is there, nevertheless (as Ilan Buchman has pointed out). Pechorin plays the hero most convincingly before women, but even with them he may fail, as he does in "Taman'." Here his near-drowning by a woman offers a mock-heroic episode not entirely dissimilar in its essential semantics from the one found in "My First Goose." Certainly, there is a great deal of posturing in both stories where women are targeted as victims by "half-heroes."

In "Taman" we also find the oxymoronic imagery of the insightful blind. Facing the blind smuggler-boy in the beginning of the story "Taman'," Pechorin feels uneasy, since it seems to him that the boy "sees," in spite of his indisputable blindness, i. e. "sees through him," seeing him for who/what he is, even though he cannot see him physically. Pechorin himself does not learn to see himself and does not reach self-understanding, at least not at this point. He remains blinded by self-infatuation. In general, Pechorin remains a man who avoids looking unflinchingly at what he fears, playing Russian roulette with fate rather than deciding that he is free to take his fate in his own hands. Possibly he dies because, ultimately, he does understand the riddle of his fate and personality and having deciphered it, does not care to live any more.

Unlike Pechorin, Liutov learns to live with himself, reestablishing contact with human realities and abandoning romantic ideals of unrelenting manliness, i. e. "heroism à la Savitskii." From bright and alluring visions of false heroism (false for him at least), he transits, via dark insights, to "seeing" and genuine merriment. This merriment does not rely on human pain and suffering or unfeeling cruelty for its source. Liutov frees himself from the false self-image that he once pursued and is no longer "dazzled" by the blinding beauty of revolutionary heroism, nor deafened by its loud propaganda.

SELECTED NOTES

[1] Quoted in the translation of Peter Constantine (*The Complete Works of Isaac Babel*, edited by Nathalie Babel, Introduction by Cynthia Ozick, Norton Paperback, 2005).

[2] See the end of Gogol's story "Nevskii Prospekt" (from the *Petersburg Tales*).

[3] "Trembling creatures" is a quote from Pushkin's cycle of poems *Imitations of the Koran* (*Podrazhanie Koranu*).

[4] The Russian for Galician is *galichanin*, for Galilean *galileianin*.

[5] Constantine translates: ... led a bedraggled little cow tied to a rope. Over *its* wide back darted the tiny wriggling head of a snake. *On the snake's head* (*italics mine*) was a teetering wide-brimmed hat ..." Judging by the text of: I. Babel', *Izbrannoe*, Moscow: Izd. "Khudozhestvennaia literatura" (p. 112), this is incorrectly translated. The snake-like head belongs to the strange white-clad man and there is no actual snake wearing a hat around.

[6] Quoted from Patricia Carden, see *Suggested Readings* to "Introduction II."

Literary Criticism

BULGAKOV'S EARLY TRAGEDY OF THE SCIENTIST-CREATOR:
AN INTERPRETATION OF *THE HEART OF A DOG*

by Diana L. BURGIN*

* From *Slavic and East European Journal* 22:4 (1978). Pp. 494-508.

Because of the overwhelming critical interest in Bulgakov's *magnum opus*, *The Master and Margarita*, commentators have tended to overlook his other novels. This neglect is particularly unfortunate in the case of his early short novel, *Heart of a Dog* (*Sobach'e serdtse*, 1925). Those who have discussed the book have also overemphasized the obvious satirical meaning of the text while ignoring, or at best, merely hinting at its underlying tragic significance. This black-comic tale of a great creative scientist's ill-fated laboratory experiment that turns a likable dog into a hideous "human" creature, whose violent, sadistic nature is exploited by the Soviet state, has been read by one of its translators, Michael Glenny, as a political allegory of the Bolsheviks' disastrous attempt to force revolution on Russia prematurely. This anti-revolutionary interpretation is supported by the scientist-hero's comment to his loyal assistant, Bormental', that his experiment backfired because it was unnaturally hasty, that is, counter-evolutionary:

223

> And that's what happens, Doctor, when the investigator, instead of feeling his way and moving parallel to nature, forces the question and tries to raise the curtain... Tell me, please, why is it necessary to manufacture Spinozas artificially when any peasant woman can produce them at any time.

To interpret *Heart of a Dog* solely as a political parable is to oversimplify the novel in two important ways. First, by emphasizing the allegorical significance of the Professor's experiment at the expense of his highly individualistic personality and creativity this interpretation reduces a complex literary character—a potentially tragic hero—to a unidimensional allegorical symbol. Such an explanation of the text overlooks Bulgakov's multi-faceted attitude toward his hero, who serves as an autobiographical spokesman for his political and social satire and as a tragic, Romantic hero in the Frankenstein tradition. To reveal the monumental, tragic proportions of his hero, Bulgakov employs three different narrators to offer a broad assessment of the great man's character and work. Glenny's interpretation overlooks entirely the most striking characteristic of the novel: its narrative complexity. Second, the political message of the novel does not depend only on the allegorical meaning of the misfired experiment (as Glenny's interpretation suggests), but is conveyed explicitly through confrontation between the individualist Professor and House-Committee Head Shvonder—a self-proclaimed representative of the "revolutionary" collective way of life and, therefore, of the pervasive banality in Soviet society.

That the significance of the Professor's experiment transcends a narrow political explanation is strongly suggested by the novel's conclusion. If, having admitted and corrected his mistake, the Professor ceased experimentation in revolutionary science, the point of this political parable would have been made. Yet, for the Professor, the ending is not a resolution, but rather a frighteningly ambiguous continuation. The Professor does not cease experimenting. The last lines of the novel focus on the "stubborn, persistent, important man," driven to continue his search for a scientific method for "manufacturing Spinozas":

> I've been so lucky, so lucky, he thought, dozing off... True, they've slashed up my whole head for some strange reason, but... it's not worth mentioning ... And the gray-haired wizard sat, humming: 'Toward the sacred banks of the Nile.' The dog witnessed terrible doings. The important man plunged his hands dressed in slippery gloves into jars, pulled out brains, a stubborn man, a persistent one, searching for something all the time, cutting, examining, squinting and singing: 'Toward the sacred banks of — the Nile.'

This final view of the seeking, creative hero—ironically colored at the beginning by the dog-narrator's complacent estranged perception of his "benefactor"—invites us to speculate on the "important man's" motives and begs for serious consideration of the implications of his persistent experimentation. At the very least, this final image of the hero suggests there is more to the story of *Heart of a Dog* than a unidimensional, politico-allegorical interpretation provides.

The play on two narrative viewpoints (the dog's and the omniscient narrator's) in the final passages of *Heart of a Dog* is typical of the shifting perspectives offered throughout the novel. Indeed, by manipulating point of view Bulgakov lends this superficially unpretentious comic novel a deeply ironic and ultimately tragic dimension. The narrative structure thus deserves detailed examination.

Heart of a Dog is narrated from three distinctive points of view: two (the dog's, Bormental's) may be described as personal or subjective; the third (the omniscient narrator's) is impersonal, objective. Each has his own special voice, language, and mode of expression. The omniscient narrator's account provides the outer, frame narrative into which the two personal accounts are interpolated in sequential order. The dog begins the novel with his jaunty, sardonic, "slice-of-life" anecdote detailing how he came under the Professor's "protection."[1] Bormental's scientific notes on the experiment take over when the dog ceases to exist; and at the very end, the dog returns to offer his "rejuvenated" perspective. Both Sharik's and Bormental's narrations are thus framed narrations. These inner personal viewpoints are contrasted in terms of tone, but are similar in their naiveté. Neither personal narrator is fully aware of the implications of his story. The irony of the dog's tale is particularly acute since he thinks of himself, and is initially presented to us, as a shrewd, albeit estranged observer of humanity, yet his initial perspicacity is drastically at odds with his ultimate complacency. Similarly, Bormental's notes—although sincere and scientific—constitute, ironically enough, a nearly absurd point of view because his naive enthusiasm beclouds his comprehension. In his own way Bormental', like Sharik, is an eternal disciple and his judgments of his "god" must finally be corrected by the master himself. The irony in both personal viewpoints derives not so much from the perceivers' worship of the Professor (he seems to deserve it, after all) as from their naiveté. This irony is clarified through the omniscient narrator's subtle, persistent reevaluation of the disciples' points of view.

Bulgakov uses this triple perspective to reveal the complexity, ambiguity, and greatness of his hero's personality and scientific quest. The hero's ambiguousness, as well as the impossibility of defining him, is indicated by the apparent difficulty of the narrators to determine his identity; he is called at different times in the novel magician, enchanter, shaman, prophet, deity, priest, doctor, creator, "daddy," Faust, higher being and benefactor of dogs, and finally, "important man." This startling array of suggested names, some comic and some serious, shows the hero's central role as a personality of nearly confounding magnitude and the importance of point of view in deciphering his identity. This identity, it seems, depends on whom one asks; yet the use of an omniscient narrator to qualify the various personal opinions suggests that the hero's essence is greater than the sum of all opinions offered.

The elusive identity of this hero has been discussed in the critical literature on the novel. In comparing the heroes of "The Fatal Eggs" and *Heart of a Dog,* Ellendea and Carl Proffer comment that these "scientific heroes" illustrate "... the confident misuse of knowledge which, while promising human good, leads only to injustice and inhumanity." I would go further and say that the misuse of knowledge is not only confident, but supremely arrogant, and perhaps most important, ultimately tragic for the misuser. Very interesting in this respect is Glenny's comment that *Heart of a Dog* is a tale of a "modern Frankenstein." Yet Glenny, who sees the deeper meaning of the novel as its political allegory, fails to develop the tragic implications of the Frankenstein parallel. Like the Frankenstein story, *Heart of a Dog* pertains to creation—more specifically, to the relationship between creator and creature and the moral question of responsibility for the creative act. Its political message notwithstanding, *Heart of a Dog* is a tale of a creative personality whose essentially noble, yet arrogant creative effort ends if not in tragedy, then at least in moral ambiguity. As such, the novel represents an original contribution to Romantic "literature of the overreacher." The fact that the Professor is Bulgakov's most autobiographical hero suggests, moreover, that the tragic fate of the scientist constantly battling the unchanging banality of human nature and seeking at his own peril a way to overcome it parallels the similar fate of the creative artist in Soviet society. Such a parallel reveals a direct connection between this early novel and *The Master and Margarita*, a connection even more obvious when one realizes that Bulgakov synthesizes his tale of creation in *Heart of a Dog* from the same universal literary sources that he employs in the later, more monumental work. He draws on the Frankenstein story as well as the Christian and Faustian traditions, which is strikingly appropriate since the fundamental identity of his scientist-hero lies in his godlike (or "man-god-like") nature and the tragedy of his scientific creation resounds with Faustian overtones.

The crux of the Professor's tragedy is to be found in the Bulgakovian principle that creation necessarily implies its antithesis, anti-creation. The man who would be a god must suffer, understand, and transcend the power of the anti-creative forces that run amok in a chaotic world. Such transcendence alone is tantamount to deification. In the first half of *Heart of a Dog* (up through the creative act detailed in chapter five), Bulgakov uses his omniscient narrator to debunk the hero-worship attitudes of those who idolize the Professor through expediency or naiveté. The hero thus seems to fall from his high status; indeed, when he is compared by the omniscient narrator to a "sated vampire" (after the operation), he appears to be more demon than deity. If the Professor is to be a true creator, or even to aspire to that title, however, his creativity must be tested, even if this necessitates his knowing hell in order to attain to heaven. The Professor's spiritual journey through the depths—which he willfully undertakes when he "raises the curtain" and attempts to transform the image of humanity—is revealed by Bulgakov through irony and reverse parody.

Our first impressions of the Professor's practice and scientific interests are filtered through the estranged perceptions of Sharik, and the effusions of his patients—a microcosm of tasteless, crass humanity, whose major concern in life seems to be "eternal youth" and sexual potency. We overhear with Sharik, one of the Professor's sexually rejuvenated, grotesque patients praising his magical powers: "I am positively enchanted. You are a magician." An aging woman, desperately desiring to recover her youth, alludes to the devilish attractiveness of her young lover: "He is so fiendishly young." These testimonies to the Professor's magical powers and greatness are unworthy of him—they amount to little more than base flattery of a man who has satisfied the most banal of human desires. Whereas the Professor is certainly aware of the vulgarity of his patients, his powers of rejuvenation are nevertheless associated early in the novel with the devil. Sharik's speculation, "What the Devil did he need me for?" strikes an ironically ominous note, particularly in retrospect.

The irony intensifies as Sharik becomes increasingly spellbound by his benefactor's magnanimity, and the integrity of his judgments grows suspect. Having submitted to the seductive but cheap allure of comfort, Sharik predictably echoes the idolatrous sentiments of the others: "I know who he is. He is a wizard, a magician, and sorcerer out of a dog's fairy tale." Eventually, the dog comes to view the Professor as divine: "During those dinners, Filip Filippovich irrevocably earned the status of divinity (*zvanie bozhestva*)." Sharik illustrates all too well the power wielded by providers of food and shelter over living creatures' loyalties.

As the dog naively grows less suspicious of the Professor's motives, our skepticism intensifies. We come to depend increasingly on the less effusive, but far more serious and balanced perspective offered by the omniscient narrator. His view of Filip Filippovich is indeed objective: while essentially positive, it also makes us aware of the spiritual dangers and potential tragedy of the scientist's creative work. The narrator clearly agrees with the Professor's anti-Bolshevik speech against the ruinous decadence of the new Soviet society, and he supports the scientist's high opinion of himself by showing just how low everyone else is. Nevertheless, he notes the didactic tone of Filip Filippovich's speech. The great scientist does not merely converse at dinner, he seems to preach: "Reinforced by the hearty dinner (*sytnyi obed*), he thundered like an ancient prophet (*drevnii prorok*), and his head glittered with silver." The juxtaposition of "hearty dinner" to "ancient prophet" suggests rather ironically that this prophet's strength derives as much from a full stomach as from a fervent soul. Subsequently, the narrator establishes through Sharik's perception a connection between the source of the Professor's abundant gourmet meals, the kitchen, a veritable hell. To the dog the cook resembles a "furious executioner" as she hacks up "helpless hazel grouse." The oven door reveals a "terrible hell" (*strashnyi ad*) within. At night the frying pans gleam mysteriously, and Dar'ia Petrovna's amorous rendezvous are compared to trysts with the devil. She calls her lover a demon and connects his sexual prowess with the Professor's rejuvenations: "Pesters me like a demon.... Let go!... What's the matter with you, as though you'd been rejuvenated too?" We get the impression that hellish forces are fomenting just beneath the surface of the Professor's well-ordered home existence just as they are already running wild in the Soviet chaos outside.

After describing the cook's hellish domain, the narrator, again through Sharik, paints a rather ominous portrait of the "star of Prechistenka" alone in his dark study, cutting up human brains by the light of a green-shaded lamp:[2]

> Sharik lay in the shadow on the rug and looked, unblinking, at terrible doings. In a disgusting, caustic muddy liquid in glass containers lay human brains. The godhead's hands, bared to the elbow, were dressed in reddish rubber gloves, and the slippery, blunt fingers fumbled in the convolutions. From time to time, the godhead armed himself with a small gleaming knife and carefully cut into the firm yellow brains. 'To the sacred banks of the Nile,' the godhead sang quietly ...

This tableau, especially the musical phrase from "Aida," becomes a visual and aural leitmotif of the scientist's creative quest.³ His nocturnal experiments have more than a touch of horror, however, and the constant repetition of "godhead" sounds ironic in such a clearly undivine context.

The idea that the Professor's divinity (at least in the dog's facile conception) is more illusion than reality is reinforced in the narrator's ironic description of the scientist's appearance at the beginning of the fateful operation on Sharik:

> In the white blaze stood a priest who hummed through his teeth about the sacred banks of the Nile. Nothing but a vague smell indicated that this was Filip Filippovich. His cropped gray hair was hidden under a white cap, resembling a patriarch's cowl. The godhead was in white from head to foot.

In this passage, and throughout the operation, Filip Filippovich appears to be and is called a priest (*zhrets*), ironically in keeping with his humming from "Aida." His priestliness is not his essence, however, as Sharik's estranged perception makes clear; it is a costume and cannot ultimately hide his real human identity, for his smell gives him away. The Professor's garb (a costume) and humming (a piece of stage business) suggest his participation in an operatic, pagan rite, which contradicts the scientific seriousness of the occasion. Filip Filippovich is presented here not as a genuine godhead, but as an actor playing the role of high priest in an opera. Thus, the omniscient narrator uses the dog's estranged perception to undercut the godhead's significance at his moment of creation by suggesting he is no deity, but an actor singing a role in his own opera.

It is during and immediately after the operation that the tragic implications of the Professor's experiment are revealed. Both he and Bormental' are compared to murderers in their rush to finish the deed ("Then both became as frantic as hurrying murderers") and at the climactic point, when Filip Filippovich transplants the pituitary of Klim Chugunkin into Sharik, the doctor's face looks "positively terrifying"—he seems himself transformed by the violence of the transformation he is attempting on the dog. Almost as if he foresees that the defective material he is working with will somehow ruin his experiment, he starts to invoke the Devil, "He'll die anyway... ah, the dev...".

The omniscient narrator's ironic treatment of the Professor is counteracted momentarily by Bormental's unspoken admiration, "By God, he has no equal in Europe!," but his praise seems curiously at odds with the narrator's comparison (a paragraph later) of this "unequaled genius" to a "sated vampire" (*sytyi vampir*)—an epithet that recalls the earlier *sytyi obed* which gave the Professor strength to lash out against anti-progressive Soviet society. Far from breathing new life into his subject, the Professor seems to have sucked his life away, albeit without intending to do so.

Just as our initial impressions of the Professor come through the naive, overpraising eyes of Sharik, so our first impressions of the Professor's creature are formed through Bormental's equally naive, prematurely laudatory scientific notes. Again Bulgakov employs an estranged perceiver as an ironic foil, for Bormental' praises the Professor without reserve, but with no real understanding of the object of his praise. Bormental' is the first to bestow the title of "creator" (*tvorets*) on Filip Filippovich, but this highest praise is followed in his records by an inkblot, which no doubt the omniscient narrator causes him to note most dutifully and scrupulously: "The surgeon's scalpel has brought into being a new human entity. Professor Preobrazhenskii, you are a creator. (*Blot*)." Just as inkblots mar the written report of Sharikov's coming to life, so does some kind of existential blot darken the genesis of this creature, putting the flawlessness of his creation in doubt. Bormental's inkblots are the result of haste and over-excitement; and later, the Professor admits the whole creation of Sharikov was a too hasty mistake. In this admission the Professor seems to recognize his inability to change (*preobrazit'*) and to transcend the low human and animal material with which he was working. Just as the brain of the criminal spoiled Dr. Frankenstein's experiment, so the Lumpen-Proletariat nature of Klim Chugunkin is in part responsible for the Professor's failure. The impossibility of transforming so low a creature as Klim is implied by his last name, Chugunkin, based on the noun for "cast iron" and suggesting inflexibility, strength, and unyieldingness. Here is one base metal which apparently even the most talented alchemist cannot turn into gold. Initially, however—and here there is tragic irony—Bormental' considers his mentor's error to redound more surely to his glory by saying it produced not simple "rejuvenation,but complete humanization." The Professor's experiment, however, only produced humanization by accident, and hardly "complete" humanization at that. Sharikov is not a naturally born person, but an experimental abortion—half-dog, and worse, half-man—a creature for whom, as Bormental' says naively thinking he is bestowing praise, the Professor is alone responsible: "After all, he is your own creature, the product of your experiment."

The Professor's very own creature. Yes, and there's the rub, for, even if it is unintentional, creation implies responsibility, and the Professor is loathe to assume responsibility for this abortive non-entity (and in a sense, who can blame him?). He himself is befuddled by the creature's identity: "Only the Devil knows what it is!" he comments in exasperation. Shvonder, always eager for any dirt he can dig up about the Professor, starts the rumor that Sharikov is Filip Filippovich's natural son; later, Sharikov is disparagingly called his foster-child (*pitomets*), but the Professor resolutely disclaims his paternity, and regards his creation only as "an unexpected laboratory creature." In disclaiming his creation so vehemently Filip Filippovich is responding to the tragic ambiguity of his position as the sole person responsible for a creature it was never his intention to produce, a being who is, in fact, the very antithesis of his intention. Sharikov is an anti-creation composed of a soulless sexual "blueprint" grafted onto an animal's body (surely a demonic inheritance!), and he combines all the basest and most savage instincts of both the dog and the con-man, thief, and drunk, Klim. Although he sympathizes with the Professor's plight, Bulgakov nevertheless emphasizes the tragic moral dilemma that his scientific hero has unwittingly brought upon himself. The Professor's fate is certainly unjustly deserved, yet it also appears to be a confirmation of the risk he took in striving to improve on nature, a risk of which he might have been unaware while in the grip of his scientific enthusiasm. Bulgakov seems to ask whether the very unintentionality of this creative experiment, and the lack of moral purpose and awareness that accompanied it, do not in fact invalidate it as an act of genuine creation.

Bulgakov reveals the tragic difference between the god-like scientist's transformation experiment and a true deity's transcendent act of creation by suggesting that Filip Filippovich's relationship to Sharikov (the unintentional anti-creation) is a reverse parody of the Christian relationship between God and Christ. The existence of such a reverse parody is indicated in the text by several details concerning Sharikov's time of "birth," outward appearance, character, influence on the household and the outside world, and finally by the dual symbolic significance of the Professor's surname—Preobrazhenskii [Transfigurer]. Sharikov's birth can be construed as a parody of the Nativity. It coincides roughly with the Christmas season (23 December 1924—17 January 1925), and, according to Bormental's notes, the critical moment in determining the creature's future survival must have occurred on 25 December, since the next day brings the first "marked improvement" in his condition. Sharikov pronounces his first word, a sign that he may be a human being, not a dog, on 6 January (Epiphany). Furthermore, the creature's appearance comes at a time when Moscow is rife with apocalyptic rumors and predictions of the end of the world in the coming year. From the moment Sharikov comes to life, true to his demonic nature and birthright (his is a soulless inheritance of sex glands and animalism), he raises havoc in the Professor's well-ordered existence. Chaos and evil are always related in Bulgakov's works, and it is Sharikov alone (spurred on by the petty demon Shvonder) who is responsible for "turning life upside down" in the apartment on Prechistenka.[4] Characteristic of Sharikov's influence is the cat-chasing episode which ends with him stuck in the bathroom and causing a flood (a traditional apocalyptic symbol); this provokes Zina to call him a "damned devil." Later, his violent, sadistic nature is exploited by the State as he becomes the officially sanctioned murderer of stray cats.

That the morally ambiguous relationship between Filip Filippovich and Sharikov is a reverse parody of the Christian Creation is implied also in the symbolic significance of the Professor's surname, Preobrazenskii. As an emblem of the scientist's identity, it has a double meaning, like the verbal noun from which it is derived, *preobrazhenie* ("transformation"; figuratively, "Transfiguration" or *transcendent* transformation). Clearly worthy of the name "Transformer," the Professor demonstrates his shamanist powers in his scientific rejuvenations. As the more spiritual "Transfigurer," however, he fails to transcend the moral limitations of his material. He himself is unable to breathe soul into Sharik's animal body; rather he seems, like a vampire, to have drained his blood. Within the Biblical context of the Transfiguration story, the Professor's creature seems to be the antithesis of the Transfigured Christ both in appearance and in relationship to his "father." In Matthew 17:2 the Transfigured Christ is revealed in the blinding purity of his white robes as the Son of God: "And he was transfigured before them (*I preobrazilsia pred nimi*): and his face did shine as the sun, and his raiment was white as the light." The merely transformed Sharik appears before the household as Sharikov, wearing soiled, tasteless clothes, a magnificently glaring image of petty-demon *poshlost'*:

> Around his neck, the man wore a poisonously blue tie with a fake ruby pin. The color of the tie was so garish that, even when he closed his weary eyes from time to time, Filip Filippovich saw in the total dark, now on the wall and now on the ceiling, a flaming torch with a blue corona.

After the moment of Transfiguration, in Matthew 17:5, the voice of God proclaims Christ His Son: "… Behold, a voice out of the cloud, which said, This is my beloved Son, in whom I am well pleased; hear ye him." The non-familial relationship between "father" and "son" in *Heart of a Dog* is exactly antithetical to that in the Transfiguration story, for shortly after Sharikov's "appearance" in all his sham and vulgar glory, when he disrespectfully addresses his creator as "Dad" (*Papasha*),[5] the Professor, irate at this implication of paternity, renounces Sharikov as his son:

> "You're getting too hard on me, dad," the man suddenly blubbered …"Who's your dad here? What kind of familiarity? I never want to hear that word again!"

Thus has the Professor tragically produced in his unintentional creation not the revelation of God (the better side of man which he was striving for), but the vulgar mug of the petty demon. Sharikov is both a reverse parody of Christ and ironically, a parody of his maker. While the Professor is the very incarnation of good taste, refinement, and intellect, Sharikov exhibits shabbily ostentatious taste and aggressively stupid intellectual pretensions. While attempting to create something better than the low-grade humanity that surrounds (and threatens) him, the Professor has unwittingly given the "Soviet dogs" *entrée* into his private world of taste and intelligence. He has tragically and ironically unleashed the forces of chaos on himself.

The Professor renounces his creation often and angrily, but simple renunciation is not enough to stop this demon of destruction who, once let loose in the world of Shvonders, feeds on his own violent nature and is easily persuaded to turn against his creator. Filip Filippovich, by nature a peace-loving man who believes in influencing others with kindness, has no choice but to fight violence with violence. Yet his decision to murder Sharikov, understandable and necessary as it is, is fraught with moral ambiguity that ultimately remains unresolved and leaves us with that ominous final image of the scientist tragically in the grip of his possibly futile striving for human betterment.

The conclusion of *Heart of a Dog* is worked out through allusions to yet another of Bulgakov's favorite literary traditions, Faust. Filip Filippovich's decision to kill Sharikov is made after solitary deliberation about the cause of the events which turned life upside-down in his apartment. The cause, which the narrator remarks archly, "the very learned man very possibly understood," is the diabolical nature of his anti-creation. The narrator's comment indicates that the Professor recognizes the demonic nature of Sharikov. His understanding is also indicated in his response to the creature's request for identity papers and to his being correct that his odd name, Poligraf Poligrafovich,[6] is on the calendar. "It's the devil's work!" he swears in consternation at having to officially explain Sharikov's genesis.

Learned and pro-Western, the Professor expresses through his blunt slippery, probing fingers his scientific striving and commitment to human intelligence. From the beginning of the novel the hero has seemed an essentially Faustian personality, and we are therefore not surprised when the narrator compares him to Faust as he willfully makes the decision to solve the Sharikov dilemma:

> For a long time he burned a second cigar, chewing its end to a pulp, and finally, in total solitude, green, looking like an aged Faust (*sedoi Faust*), he exclaimed: "By God, I think I will."

It is interesting that earlier, Bormental' has already placed the Professor's experiment in the Faustian context of the creation of Homunculus while simultaneously differentiating it from that creative act: "A new realm is opening in science: a homunculus was created without any of Faust's retorts." These two references to Faust seem to add another dimension to the novel which serves Bulgakov as a unifying device, enabling him to integrate the novel's explicit political significance (failure of revolutionary science—failure of revolutionary politics) with its underlying moral theme (a purely scientific, yet unintentional act of creation portends the moral failure of the creative scientist).

Bulgakov's attitude to the Faustian scientific spirit in this novel seems to be ambivalent, and this too helps to explain the ambiguity (the mixture of sympathy and irony) of his hero's image. He lauds the striver, but is aware of the chaos that such a man can unwittingly unleash upon himself. He supports Filip Filippovich's political opinions and his dedication to science and individualism while revealing the dangers of his materialistic devotion to science as a means of bettering human nature. Ironically, it is the Professor himself who questions the rationale of his obsessive quest for the scientific method of transforming, even transfiguring, humanity. There is deep pessimism in the Professor's implicit admission that it may just be impossible to transform mankind, to transcend the pervasive and entrenched banality of the Chugunkins, and Shvonders; and there is moral tragedy in the benevolent Professor being forced to commit violence to restore peace. The denouement of *Heart of a Dog* reveals the tragedy of creative self-destruction as the scientist is forced to negate, by the violent means he deplores, the unexpected, devastatingly negative result of his experimental fervor. Like *Frankenstein*, *Heart of a Dog* is a story of the tragedy of after-birth which threatens the premises of the genuinely creative act and is in fact its very antithesis.

To save himself and others from "his own experimental creature" the Professor has no alternative but to destroy it. The necessity of this solution cannot hide the fact that it is a violent act which reduces the scientist, if only momentarily, to the level of the low, destructive humanity he disdains. The inherently evil nature of this murder is conveyed by the omniscient narrator through allusions to a demonic and evil presence that controls the doctors as they operate to change Sharikov back into a dog. Before he is in effect killed, Sharikov senses himself in the grip of an "impure spirit" (*kakoi-to nechistyi dukh*). Both doctors are diabolically transformed during the murderous deed; they lose all semblance of humanity. Violence in Bulgakov so often has precisely this dehumanizing effect. Bormental' works tensely with "not his own face" (*ne svoe litso*), and "neither was Filip Filippovich like his usual self that evening."

Ten days later our "graying Faust" seems to have regained his former self. He is again powerful and energetic, full of dignity and kingly pride. He dispenses so self-confidently with the investigator's questions, drily commenting that "science has not yet discovered methods of transforming animals into humans," and so clearly has the upper hand over the noisome Shvonder that we are amazed at the relative ease of his "salvation." But is this Faust really saved? In a materialistic sense, yes! The reader is actually grateful that Filip Filippovich has committed the perfect crime. Yet, the strikingly ominous final image of the great scientist (quoted at the beginning of this article) leaves us with grave doubts about the Professor's spiritual salubrity. Through the eyes of the grotesquely "rejuvenated" Sharik we see the "higher being and benefactor of dogs" totally absorbed in the same "horrible tasks" that brought him nearly to destruction. The Professor's intellectual curiosity and persistence seem more obsessive than ever, and there is the strong implication that he has become enslaved to his striving rather than expressing his will through it. No longer the "graying Faust" but now the "gray magician" Filip Filippovich himself seems to have been somewhat transformed; his human personality is submerged more than ever in his scientific search, and we are left to speculate on the ambiguous answer to the question of where his future experiments will lead him: to creation, or to destruction.

A careful exploration of all the literary and other allusions embedded in the complex narrative of *Heart of A Dog* reveals the novel to occupy a special place among Bulgakov's early works and in relation to his magnum opus, *The Master and Margarita*. Although it is similar to the science-fantasy satire "The Fatal Eggs," it differs from that work in the complexity and ambiguity with which the scientific hero is treated. Professor Persikov in "The Fatal Eggs" is also a genius who seems to have discovered a creative force that might well be used to improve the quality of human life. Persikov is victimized by the hasty misuse of his discovery by Rokk (like Chugunkin, a representative of the Lumpen-proletariat) who sets in motion the chaotic forces of evil which tragically ricochet and do modest Persikov in. It is true that Filip Filippovich, the hero of *Heart of a Dog*, is victimized in part by the defective nature of the man whose glands he transplanted into Sharik, but it is also true that as a much more willful and arrogant man than Persikov, he himself is responsible for undertaking his own experiment too hastily. Because of his willfulness and intense striving he is placed in a more morally ambiguous position by the miscalculated experiment than is Persikov. The endings of the two works reveal the difference in complexity and tragic stature of their respective heroes. At the end of "The Fatal Eggs" Persikov appears as a Christ figure, a great man tragically crucified by evil, stupid bureaucrats (with whom he lacked the strength to deal effectively). The denouement of *Heart of A Dog* is far more complicated. The great scientist triumphs over the petty demon bureaucrats. Yet his triumph is not without tragic implications for his moral self (it has forced him to commit the violence he deplores) and for the entire future of his dedicated experiments, as it is uncertain that they will ever achieve his progressive goals. If Filip Filippovich is in any sense a victim, he is a victim of his scientific self, of his stubborn quest to "manufacture Spinozas"—a quest that appears futile in the light of the evolutionary laws governing the appearance in the world of genius. The Professor himself admits that evolution is more dependable than his laboratory revolution, yet he continues the search.

....

Thus Filip Filippovich is eternally enslaved to the scientific spirit which he continues to believe will yield the key to the betterment of humanity. If Woland [in *The Master and Margarita*], like Mephistopheles, serves "that Power which wills forever evil / Yet does forever good," then does not Filip Filippovich, the great scientist, serve a power that wills forever good, yet, ironically, does forever evil?

SELECTED NOTES

1. The dog's perception is an excellent example of comic *ostranenie* which is often found in *skaz* narratives where irony is derived from the naiveté of the perceiver. The dog's viewpoint is limited not only by his canine intelligence (which is clearly above average!), but by his conviction that he has found a protector in the Professor. So sure is Sharik that the Professor is benevolent that he suppresses any urgings of the instincts that might mar his positive assessment of the Professor, preferring to remain blissfully ignorant so long as he is fed.

2. The motif of the green-shaded lamp runs through all of Bulgakov's works. It suggests hominess, tranquility, and intellectual calm, and it apparently has associations with Bulgakov's father.

3. The musical phrase from "Aida" in this tableau recurs throughout the novel in connection with the Professor and thus gives autobiographical significance to the image of the hero. According to Ellendea Proffer, Bulgakov had a great fondness for opera, particularly "Aida."

4. The Professor's apartment, like the Turbins' in *The White Guard*, represents a peaceful, intellectual haven from the chaos of Soviet life. As such it expresses Bulgakov's ideal world of peace, privacy, individualism, and intellectual values. Sharikov's incursion (like that of the House Committee earlier in the novel) symbolizes a kind of chaotic anti-life that makes peaceful co-existence impossible.

5. The word *Papasha* may also be interpreted as a Faustian reference. In the creation of Homunculus (*Faust*, Part II), to which Bormental' refers in connection with the creation of Sharikov, the Homunculus calls his creator *Väterchen*.

6. Sharikov's odd name and patronymic seems to satirize the Soviet penchant for obscure and absurd names that have a "modern" technological ring to them. As an emblem of the creature's identity it is also ironic since Lie Detector, Son of Lie Detector turns out to be essentially a metaphysical lie.

Literary Criticism

THE MASKS OF MIKHAIL ZOSHCHENKO

by Victor ERLICH*

* From *Literature, Culture and Society in the Modern Age*, In Honor of Joseph Frank: Stanford Slavic Studies. Volume 4:2, edited by Edward J. Brown, Lazar Fleishman, Gregory Freidin, Richard D. Schupbach, Part II, Stanford: Stanford University Press, 1992. Pp. 163-177.

In a letter to his brother Mikhail, written shortly after the appearance of his epistolary novel *Poor Folk*, Dostoevskii decried the proclivity of his readers for equating him with the novel's male protagonist, Makar Devushkin. "The public and the critics," he wrote, "are used to seeing everywhere the author's mug but I didn't show mine here. They cannot figure out that it is Devushkin talking and not I ..."

Dostoevskii's caveat comes to mind as one contemplates the troubled career of one of this century's finest comic writers, Mikhail Zoshchenko. In his most characteristic work, especially in his irresistibly funny sketches of Soviet everyday life, which earned him immense popularity both with the untutored reader and the connoisseur of literary stylization, his "mug" is hardly ever in evidence. He spoke throughout in someone else's voice. Though serious Zoshchenko scholars differ as to the precise location of this voice, they share the sense of a major cultural and moral gap between the implied author and the lowbrow, bumbling and notoriously unreliable narrator, and of the ubiquitousness of the latter. [Critic]

Sergei Bocharov hits the nail on the head when he speaks of what might be called the wall-to-wall quality of Zoshchenko's narrative manner: "His comic *skaz* fills the entire space of the story, its entire horizon, to the exclusion, let me add, of any other, more reliable perspective."

This absence of any direct clue to the underlying authorial stance has created something of a problem for Zoshchenko criticism even as it had frustrated and bemused the Soviet literary watchdogs.

Yet the difficulty in glimpsing the face beneath the mask, or, to put it differently, in pinning down the essential thrust of Zoshchenko's satire, is not the only perplexity that bedevils the interpreter of this deceptively easy writer. When in the early thirties Zoshchenko shifted gears from his comic short stories and blatantly parodistic novelettes to an ostensibly didactic genre, thoughtful commentators both at home and abroad disagreed profoundly about the nature of the enterprise, with some authorities confidently declaring it another Zoshchenkian spoof and other critics equally convinced of the master ironist's newly found seriousness.

It is not my intention to disentangle these ambiguities, to urge confident solutions to these quandaries. What I propose to do is rather to help define the rules of the elaborate game which Zoshchenko is playing with his reader as he stakes out a distinctive claim within the maelstrom of early Soviet artistic prose and to probe some of the salient uses of his successive masks.

Let me begin with a few more or less incontrovertible facts. Zoshchenko was born in 1895, into a fairly well-off intelligentsia family. His father, a Ukrainian squire with mildly radical leanings, was a reasonably successful realistic painter; his mother, a [...] Russian, was a former actress. He was barely twenty when he volunteered for military service during the First World War—a decision which, as he was to recall many years later, was impelled by restlessness rather than patriotism. ("I simply couldn't stay in one place because of my tendency toward hypochondria and melancholia." In any event, the act proved a fateful one—as a battalion commander on the German front, Zoshchenko was the victim of a gas attack which left him with permanent damage to his heart and liver. This did not prevent him from enlisting in the

Red Army in 1919. Once again, if we are to believe the already quoted retrospective account, his motives were predominantly negative: "I'm not a communist and I entered the Red Army to fight against nobility and landowners—a milieu which I knew only too well." Having been discharged because of his previous injuries, he "wandered around," trying his hand at "ten or twelve disparate occupations" ranging from a policeman to a telephone operator. In his remarkable if ill-fated attempt at introspection, *Before the Sunrise* (1943), Zoshchenko attributes this frantic "getting about" not to intellectual curiosity or a spirit of adventure but to his need to run away from himself and his depression.

By 1919, Zoshchenko stopped running: he was nearly ready for a literary career.

Recent research has shown that shortly before breaking into Soviet literature as a fiction writer Zoshchenko tried his hand at literary criticism. He was envisioning a collection of essays on early twentieth-century Russian literature, entitled *The Turning Point*. Judging by the extant fragments, as summarized by Marietta Chudakova in her invaluable study of Zoshchenko's poetics, the fact that the project was not brought to fruition is not necessarily cause for regret. Yet to a Zoshchenko scholar the material is of immense interest in that it reveals a consistently jaundiced and lopsided view of the Silver Age ethos, an impatience with the body of imaginative writing which had shaped the literary sensibility of many of Zoshchenko's contemporaries. The unfinished essays keep harping on such "unhealthy" characteristics of the "doomed" era as Nietzschean individualism, over-refinement, hermeticism, morbid fascination with death. Nor was Aleksandr Blok exempt from this acerbic diagnosis. "Though examined with love and respect," writes Chudakova, "Blok's ocuvre is reduced quite simplistically to such motives as boredom and taedium vitae." Blok's work in toto is adjudged "obsolete discourse" (otzvuchavshee slovo). Significantly, the would-be critic makes an exception for "The Twelve." "In this heroic poem," he says, "everything is new, from the idea to the words." As we examine the context, it becomes evident that what matters most to Zoshchenko is "the words." Zoshchenko hails Blok's profoundly innovative poem because "it made him suspect that there is such a thing as proletarian poetry," a notion which, in his view, accredited proletarian verse, where ultra-revolutionary content was so often embodied in a stale and derivative rhetoric, did little to validate. What entranced Zoshchenko about "The Twelve" is that, for the first time in the history of Russian poetry, the "language of the street" has invaded, indeed inundated, the precincts of high literature. As Chudakova aptly puts it, "it is not the mere fact of introducing colloquial, 'vulgar' speech into the structure of the poem, but the substitution of this speech for the poet's own voice that impressed Zoshchenko most."

The young Zoshchenko's reaction to "The Twelve" provides a significant clue to his emerging literary stance. His fascination with the demotic aspect of the poem foreshadows the verbal thrust of his own fictions: the budding writer's admiration for Blok's "heroic" act of lyrical self-effacement points towards the dominance of what Mikhail Bakhtin calls "alien discourse" (*chuzhoe slovo*) that was to become his own trademark.

These two strains in Zoshchenko's incipient poetics converged in the deftly contrived *patois* [non-standard language] of *Nazar Il'ich, Gospodin Sinebriukhov* (Mr. Bluebellied), "a semi-literate ex-noncom in the tsarist army, spinning loquacious yarns about his misadventures during the First World War and its aftermath. As Chudakova correctly notes, the salient fact about Zoshchenko's early *skaz* is that it is couched, not in authentic, pungent, down-to-earth folk speech, but in its adulterated, corrupted version. A peasant who has been around and has had fitful exposure to urban culture, Sinebriukhov speaks substandard language overlaid with ill-digested bits of journalese and bureaucratese. ("This little boy of hers, he is merely a sucking mammal" ... "What are you up to? Are you disturbing disorder?").

....

The Sinebriukhov tales can be seen as a gateway to the quintessential Zoshchenko narrative which took shape by the mid-twenties and survived well into the thirties—a short short story cast in the form of a monologue of a sub-literate city bumpkin and featuring such unprepossessing settings as the communal kitchen, the public bathhouse and the crowded street car. In contradistinction to the Sinebriukhov cycle, it fails to project a coherent image of an individualized narrator. Such pseudo-identifications as occur here—"Grigorii Ivanovich sighed loudly and began"—are essentially spurious. What we confront in these stories instead is a recognizable cast of mind or of mindlessness, and above all, an inimitable language whose brilliantly contrived inanities largely account for the unique and often nearly untranslatable effectiveness of these slender anecdotes. This language—a virtual orgy of the "mangled word," or better, the mangled cliché—is a major comic achievement. Whether it is also, as was claimed by some Zoshchenko watchers and by the writer himself, an accurate mimicry of the "language of the street" is quite another matter. In his perceptive discussion of Zoshchenko's art, Edward J. Brown argues vigorously against this notion. He calls the language of Zoshchenko's heroes "totally invented" and insists that "no one has ever spoken" it."

Professor Brown clearly has a point. No single individual or, specifically, no conceivable Soviet man-in-the-street, could be expected to perpetrate within the compass of relatively few sentences such a gaudy plethora of semantic monstrosities as fairly leap from the pages of a typical Zoshchenko story. Unquestionably, we are dealing here with intricate stylization, with an artful literary concoction, or, if you will, an artistic intensification of the actual.

But if the consistency of what Edward Brown calls "a weird linguistic brew" can be credited to Zoshchenko alone, its ingredients are all too real. So is the predicament of the confused but resilient "little man," caught in the coils of social dislocation, buffeted by stringent exhortations and barely intelligible slogans, but pathetically eager to make an adjustment, however precarious, to the new realities and phraseologies. In fact, it could be argued that such strenuous attempts at adaptation are at once mocked and enacted by the narrator's inept yet insistent manipulation of Soviet shibboleths.

Let us take a brief look at three salient instances of this procedure. "Aristokratka" (Lady Aristocrat) features the speaker's aborted attempt to play the man-of-the-world by taking a ludicrously misnamed "fancy dame" out to the theater. The escapade proves a minor disaster, due presumably to the lady's retrograde stance. "It was in the theater that it all happened. There in the theater she deployed her ideology to its full extent." What actually happens is that during the intermission the lady embarrasses her escort by showing a more active interest in the refreshments than he thinks he can afford to subsidize, a contingency which provokes an unseemly scene at the bar, followed by an acrimonious parting of ways: "And at home she says to me in this bourgeois tone of hers: 'It's pretty swinish on your part. Those who have no money don't go out with ladies'." And I say, 'Happiness doesn't lie in money, citizeness, excuse the expression.' And that's how we parted." And the speaker concludes firmly: "I don't care for lady aristocrats."

The tendency to overideologize the trivial is writ large in another old-time favorite, "Nervous People": "Not long ago a fight occurred in our communal apartment. The main reason is folks are very nervous. They get upset over mere trifles. They get real worked up and because of this they fight crudely, as if in a fog." This time the "trifle" which triggers the brawl is a squabble over a scouring pad of which Maria Vasil'evna availed herself even though it presumably belonged to Dar'ia Petrovna. An altercation between two housewives escalates into a free-for-all capped by the appearance of a militiaman who announces calmly: "Get ahold of coffins real quick. I'm going to shoot." At the trial which follows, a people's judge, who also happens to be a nervous person, scolds those who fought: "You're not Soviet people but relics of a collapsed empire. But revolutionary legality will not allow you to engage in your debauchery on the ruins of past life." The speaker ends sententiously: "This is just, brothers. Nerves are one thing, but fighting is another."

In "The Grimace of the NEP" the habit of invoking the Soviet code is placed in a context not merely incongruous but unmistakably ironic. A group of passengers on a suburban train are incensed by the high-handed behavior of a dandyish young man who makes an old woman accompanying him carry his luggage and rudely orders her around. The protests are sharp and principled:

"This is an exploitation of excesses! This is a mockery of a free personality! This is a regular grimace of the NEP!" However, the indignation promptly subsides when it appears that the drudge is not an exploited domestic as has been assumed but the dandy's old mother: "Now wait," he remonstrates, "maybe there is no grimace of the NEP here at all? Maybe I'm just going to Leningrad with my mom?" Most of the accusers beat a hasty retreat with the young man now acting the injured party. "'I have a doctor's certificate that I'm a nervous person. Please don't tell me whom I should yell at and whom I should load with my bags.' The other passengers fell silent and carefully avoided the injured man's eyes."

Interestingly enough, this time the narrator dispenses with an explicit summation. Is it because the invisible author comes into his own, however obliquely? The satiric intent of the story can scarcely be missed.

We are back to our starting point—the tantalizing problem of the under-lying authorial stance, or, to put it simply, of what Zoshchenko is up to. As already indicated, official Soviet criticism was less than happy about having to deal with this conundrum. [American slavist] Hugh McLean is essentially right that "a combination of irony, ambiguity and camouflage" served Zoshchenko reasonably well by keeping him out of trouble, until, that is, Zhdanov's obscene attack in 1946." Yet even at the peak of his popularity this strategy could not prevent occasional harassment. By filling his stories to the brim with philistine chit-chat, by refusing to offer the reader positive guidance as to how the events narrated ought to be viewed, Zoshchenko ran afoul of the era's essential requirement: he failed to provide edification. No wonder the age-old fallacy deplored by Dostoevskii back in 1846, the tendency to confuse the hero or narrator with the author, exacerbated now by suspiciousness, the professional disease of the heresy-hunter, produced some invidious and wrong-headed assessments. Suffice it to cite the Zoshchenko entry in the *Soviet Literary Encyclopedia* (1930): "The anecdotal brittleness and a lack of a social perspective lend to Zoshchenko's work a petty-bourgeois and philistine flavor."

In his vivid and affectionate memoir, Kornei Chukovskii dubs the above "utter nonsense." The truth, he argues forcefully, is just the reverse. A writer with a deeply troubled conscience, Zoshchenko used his considerable satiric gifts to expose and deride insensitivity, acquisitiveness and selfishness which he saw all around him. Rather than casting his aspersions on Soviet reality, he was unmasking the opportunistic adjustments made by petty manipulators and time-servers "who have mastered (?) the noble terminology of Soviet society in order to use it as a camouflage for their lowly designs."

To applaud Chukovskii's scorn is not necessarily to endorse fully his view of Zoshchenko's satire. The eminent critic was absolutely right in positing the distance, indeed a chasm, between Zoshchenko and his neo-philistine narrator. He was on equally safe ground in insisting—a notion which incidentally was strongly seconded by Nadezhda Mandel'shtam in her appreciative but not uncritical assessment of Zoshchenko the man—that rather than being a purveyor of carefree mirth, Zoshchenko was a deeply serious and anguished moralist, dismayed and often appalled by the unseemly antics which were the stuff of his vignettes. Granted, too, that the moral universe of *Esteemed Citizens*, with its triviality, small-mindedness and grubbiness, is not a pretty spectacle. And yet I find Chukovskii's strenuously high-minded vindication of Zoshchenko slightly off-key. It seems to me that the matter was stated more accurately by a contemporary no less astute, if less honorable, than K. Chukovskii, A. N. Tolstoi, when he wrote in a retrospective, essay "Twenty-Five Years of Russian literature": "It was in the ambiguity-ridden atmosphere of the NEP that was born the sly, wise, delightful prose of M. Zoshchenko, with its ironically deflated hero, whom he both mocks and pities."

I would suggest that "sly" is the operative word here for it points toward the main reason why the view of Zoshchenko's satire as a ruthless indictment of Philistinism might be adjudged a bit simplistic or lopsided. I am speaking of the thinly disguised polemic with, or a subtle debunking of, the official critics and their standard expectations. To put it differently, though "Philistinism" is very much at issue here, it is not the only, and at times not the prime, target of Zoshchenko's irony. For to read closely Zoshchenko's writings of the twenties and the early thirties is to begin to wonder whether the joke is mainly on the crass, small-minded, "opportunistic," neo-Philistine, or rather, on the unprofessional ideologues and cheerleaders who, intoxicated by their own grandiose rhetoric, have lost sight of the recalcitrance of human nature, of the tenacity of "the old Adam."

One of the leitmotifs in Zoshchenko's half-serious, half-facetious programmatic pronouncements, in his tongue-in-cheek authorial or quasi-authorial asides, is the insistence on his right to eschew heroics and bombast and to focus on the mundane, the insignificant and the unprepossessing realities which, whether we like it or not, are still very much with us. Thus, in the appendix to *Youth Restored* (1933), Zoshchenko openly confronts the critics who wonder why he persists in writing about the *petite-bourgeoisie* that no longer exist as a class: "No, this is no mistake. I do write about the *petits-bourgeois*, and I suppose *I'll have enough material to last me the rest of my life*" (my italics, V. E.).

A few years later, in referring to a cluster of novellas entitled *Sentimental Tales*, Zoshchenko averred: "This book ... is written at the height of NEP and the revolution and the reader, to be sure, has the right to expect from the author revolutionary content, large themes, global projects and the like—in a word, full-fledged and lofty ideology. So as to save the reader of modest means unnecessary expense, the author hastens to announce with genuine anguish that the book will not contain much that is heroic. This book is written about the little man, about the philistine in all his unpresentability." Some of us will recall that when Zoshchenko fired his first shot in a low-key campaign against cant, in his contribution to the much-quoted 1922 symposium "The Serapion Brothers about Themselves," he derided the demand that "a writer have a precise ideology." He made then a frank admission: "In their general swing, the Bolsheviks are closer to me than any other party and I'm willing to bolshevik around (*bol'shevichit'*) along with them. But I'm not a Communist, or rather, not a Marxist, and I don't think I'll ever become one."

Were it not for its facetious manner, this latter passage could have been authored by many a "fellow-traveler," including, say, Boris Pil'niak. Yet the larger context of Zoshchenko's whimsical credo is a far cry from Pil'niak's literary position. If the author of *The Bare Year* shared Zoshchenko's eschewal of "precise ideology," he proved only too susceptible to "large themes and global projects." Early on Zoshchenko chooses the "low road"—the road of mundane actualities, rather than that of sweeping abstractions or vast canvases: "There is a view that what is needed today is a red Lev Tolstoi. Now this order must have been placed by some careless publishing house. If we are to talk about what is ordered, it is a small-scale type of work which was previously associated with rather dubious literary traditions. I have opted for this sort of thing and I don't think I've made a mistake. I have no intention of climbing into high literature. There are plenty of writers there as it is."

Clearly, what is at issue here is not simply opting for the "small form," a short narrative rather than for the full-fledged novel or the epic, but a recoil from the pre-revolutionary elite genres, a vindication of what V. Shklovskii called "the junior branch of literature," in recognition of the sea-change which brought into Russian culture millions of untutored, half-literate, "mass" readers. Zoshchenko claimed, perhaps tongue-in-cheek, that he had contrived "a shorn sentence, accessible to the poor." "Accessibility" is proclaimed here as a strategic objective, indeed, as an organizing principle: "I've changed a bit and simplified both the syntax and the composition of the story." One might say that seeking quite self-consciously a way out of the crisis of Russian artistic prose Zoshchenko chose to mobilize the resources of substandard speech and of the "dubious," sub-literary genres to fit, enact or parody the temporary cultural limitations of the new reader. This is how he put it himself in his already quoted 1928 credo: "Let me make a confession which may appear strange and unexpected. The fact of the matter is that I'm a proletarian writer. More exactly, I parody in my works an imaginary but genuine proletarian writer who might exist under the present conditions and in the present environment."

Now, "parody" is the literary strategy that dominates the cluster of novelettes which Zoshchenko was producing toward the end of the twenties under the deliberately misleading title *Sentimental Tales*. However, what is parodied here is not the still nonexistent proletarian writer or a "naive" mass reader but an equally imaginary "petit-bourgeois" *intelligent* writer, nurtured on pre-Revolutionary literary models yet trying hard to "reorient himself"—to get in step with the new realities and expectations. The narrator in "Apollon and Tamara," "A Terrible Night," "What the Nightingale Sang" or "The Lilacs are Blooming" is no longer semi-literate; he is quasi- or pseudo-literate, indeed, painstakingly if often clumsily literary, an aspiring, half-baked *litterateur*. Yet like his predecessor he is emphatically *not* M. M. Zoshchenko. In fact, one of the salient characteristics of this cycle is persistent toying with the discrepancy between the narrative voice and the "real" author, a discrepancy pointed up by attributing the tales to one I. V. Kolenkorov, allegedly "a right-wing fellow-traveler"[1] and repeatedly laid bare in facetious prefaces to four presumably successive editions of *Sentimental Tales*. The fundamental difference between I. V. Kolenkorov and M. Zoshchenko is driven home in the preface to the putative fourth edition: "Neurasthenia, ideological wavering, gross contra-dictions and melancholia—those are the traits with which we are forced to endow our self-made man I. V. Kolenkorov. As for the author, the writer M. M. Zoshchenko, the son or brother of such unhealthy people, he has left all this far behind and at the moment has no contradictions whatsoever. In his soul there is complete clarity and roses unfold. And if at times these roses fade and his heart is not at peace, this is due to entirely different reasons which the author will tell about some other time ... At this point, this is a mere literary device."

This elaborate tomfoolery is an appropriate prelude to what is probably the most blatant exercise in literary self-consciousness to be found within the Zoshchenko literary canon. In the tales themselves, the parodistic impulse is at work on several different levels and in several different modes. Let me mention in haste two indubitable subtexts. In "Apollon and Tamara," a story of a dashing tap dancer gone to seed, the mock-lyrical description of the hero's good looks is strongly reminiscent of the narrator's inane raptures over Ivan Ivanovich's astrakhan in Gogol's "The Two Ivans": "And his flowing hair! And the velvet blouse! And the splendid dark-green tie!" (The Gogol' connection, incidentally, is signaled by the chief protagonist's comically Ukrainian name, Perepenchuk.)

Equally Gogolian are the sheepish non-sequiturs such as the following: "Seventeen years ago a regiment of some kind of hussars was stationed here. And it was such a magnificent regiment—these hussars were such dashing characters and they had such a strong influence on the natives from the aesthetic standpoint that all the female infants born during this time were named, through the good offices of the governor's wife, Tamaras and Irinas."

In "The Lilacs are Blooming," rather than echoing a congenial nineteenth-century mode of parody, Zoshchenko takes time out to caricature and slyly mock a contemporary literary trend, notably the Futurist "trans-sense language." (It is fair to assume that this master whose incessant search for a new departure in Russian artistic prose was appreciated by V. Shklovskii and acclaimed by O. Mandel'shtam, saw avant-garde experimentation as but another aspect of high literature which he abjured). Here is the aspiring author, protesting his inadequacy as he attempts to sketch out a backdrop for a lover's tryst: "Just the same, the author will attempt to take a plunge into high artistic literature ... The sea gurgled. Suddenly there was a curling, scurrying and prickling. It was a young man uncinching his shoulders and cinching his hand into his side pocket." After this facetious digression, the author returns with some reluctance to the 'young couple,' mutters once more "The sea gurgled" and gives up his attempt to be "with it": "Oh, the hell with it!"

Yet the main thrust of parody in *Sentimental Tales* lies in consistent deflation of sentimental clichés of pulp fiction: "They fell in love with each other passionately and dreamily"; "They couldn't see each other without tears and quivers." At times the romantic spell, such as it is, is wantonly broken. As the lovers listen (in "What the Nightingale Sang") to the singing of the nightingale in the suburban woods, "Lizochka would inquire time and again, wringing her hands: 'Vasia, what do you think the nightingale sings about?' Belinkin would answer with restraint: 'He wants grub, that's why he sings.'"[2] It is not altogether surprising that so ardent a courtship fails to usher in marital bliss, the more so since at the last moment Belinkin's prospective mother-in-law staunchly refuses to surrender a chest-of-drawers which he considers absolutely essential to his happiness.

I.V. Kolenkorov's prose, astutely described by Chukovskii as cliché-ridden literary language with an occasional Smerdiakovian tinge, serves as a fit medium for half-comic, half-pathetic tales about the gradual deterioration of the ineffectual holdovers from the margins of prerevolutionary intelligentsia who, not unlike Kolenkorov, reached adulthood on the eve of the First World War and warily entered the post-Revolutionary era only to see their dreams of personal happiness and worldly success gradually dissolve. Some, like Volodin, in "The Lilacs are Blooming," though dislodged by the Revolution, manage to make marginal adjustment. ("He looked around to see what was what and what made the wheels go round. And he saw that the Revolution did change a great deal but not so much as to justify panic.")

....

The intricate narrative frame of *Sentimental Tales* served several interlocking purposes. Zoshchenko used it a) to escalate his "sly" polemic with official critics, b) to distance himself further from high literature, whether of traditional or experimental variety, and c) to expose the shallowness and fatuousness of what he was to call in an autobiographical note "the milieu he knew only too well."

The thirties had little patience with literary games: "Our time does not tolerate ambiguity," opined the influential literary zealot L. Averbakh in his attack on a heterodox writer, A. Platonov. Almost miraculously, Zoshchenko managed to publish during this grim decade a number of his comic vignettes featuring disparities between official ideology and stubborn facts of ordinary life. To be sure, he found it necessary to strike some unequivocally positive notes. Whether the relentlessly orthodox "The Story of One Reforging" (Zoshchenko's contribution to the deplorable collected volume [on the construction of the Belomor Canal] masterminded by Maksim Gor'kii) and a rather crude hatchet job on the hapless head of the Provisional Government, "Kerenskii," were, as has been surmised, merely "bones thrown to the critics" (Mclean) is a matter of conjecture. What is certain is that neither story required or reflected Zoshchenko's distinctive gifts.

....

I had better signalize, in a hasty attempt at summation, some of the salient ironies of the master ironist's ambiguity-ridden career: 1) Though Zoshchenko's avowed objective was "to be accessible to the poor," he could be fully appreciated as an artist only by a sophisticated, form-conscious reader. 2) While Zoshchenko's existential literary choice partook of the innovative impulse of Russian modernism, it was dictated in part by a strong populist bias, which was quite pronounced already in his aborted critical project. 3) A writer with a born satirist's eye for the ineradicable human folly, for the ludicrous, the absurd and the trivial, slyly subversive of Bolshevik triumphalism, was also a man who in his indiscriminate recoil from the culture that had nurtured him, seemed to be reaching desperately toward the new society and its extravagant claims, and craving to make a "constructive" contribution to it. Much has been said, and with some justice, of Zoshchenko's open insouciance vis-à-vis the Marxist doctrine. But it is at least arguable that he was less immune to some other strains in Soviet culture, e. g., its tawdry mythology of Progress, its naive cult of Reason and Science that promised to do away, once and for all, with human misery.

Need I suggest that for a master caught in this kind of predicament, a mask or a succession of masks may have been a useful device not only for keeping the literary watchdogs at bay, but also for distancing one's own unresolved inner contradictions?

SELECTED NOTES

[1] "At the present time, D. V. Kolenkorov, who belongs to the right wing of the 'fellow-travelers,' undergoes a reconstruction (*perestraivaetsia*) and, probably, will occupy within the near future one of the prominent places among the writers of the Natural School."

[2] Incidentally, this deconstruction of the romance is promptly followed by a "sly" manipulation of a Soviet shibboleth: "But later, having familiarized himself a bit with the young lady's psychology, Belinkin would answer more vaguely and in greater detail. He would assume that the bird sang about some kind of splendiferous future life. The author too thinks that it must have sung about an excellent future life which would exist, say, in three hundred years or maybe even earlier. Yes, my reader, I wish these three hundred years would pass like a dream and then we would really live. But if there too things turn out to be rough, why then the author will consent with an empty and cold heart to deem himself a superfluous figure against the backdrop of rising life."

Through the Wrong End of Binoculars: An Introduction to Iurii Olesha

by Nils Åke NILSSON*

1. Iurii Olesha's novel *Envy* opens with an amusing picture of one of the main characters, creator of the salami trust "The Quarter." We are present when he gets out of bed in the morning; we hear him singing in the lavatory; we see him doing his gymnastics. For the last operation he is stripped except for jersey drawers, done up in the middle of his stomach by a single button. This turns out to be not just an ordinary button; it has another function too: "The pale blue and pink world of the room is spinning around in the mother-of-pearl objective of the button."

This magic button introduces at the very beginning a highly characteristic device Olesha uses throughout the whole novel when describing people, objects, settings. He seldom gives us a direct and straightforward description, a simple full-face view of an object or a person. Instead we usually see his world of objects and people reflected in buttons, mirrors and metallic surfaces; we catch distorted glimpses of them through glass windows and bars; they appear enlarged or diminished through

* From *Scando-Slavica*, tomus XI. Copenhagen: Munksgaard, 1965. Pp. 40-68.

binoculars, telescopes or microscopes. Light and shadow may suddenly change their proportions and inter-relationships and make us see things we had never suspected before. Rain and wind may make them depart from their everyday course and reveal them from a new and unexpected side. And, if we only know the trick, if we are only shown how, our eye is ever eager to accept the most unexpected optical illusions, of which our world is full.

The morning sun is rising. We learn about it from Andrei Babichev's suspenders: "In the metal clips of his suspenders there are two burning clusters of the sun's rays." The sun is setting, and, to tell us this, Olesha introduces a gypsy with a brass bowl: "The day was closing shop. A gypsy in a blue waistcoat was carrying a clean brass bowl on his shoulders. The day was moving off, riding on the gypsy's shoulder. The disc of the bowl was bright and blind. The gypsy walked slowly, the bowl swayed gently, and the day wheeled inside the disc."

These are just two examples chosen at random. Let us now take a closer look at the many devices Olesha uses in *Envy* and in his short stories. Let us see how they function in their contexts and try to find a background to and a common explanation for them.

We can start with the window. It may seem difficult for an author to have achieved any special effects by presenting an object or a person through an ordinary window. But Olesha knows how to do it: a glass pane is not always reliable from a strictly realistic point of view. When Andrei Babichev drives off to his work "his laughing face swayed through the window of his limousine like a pinkish disc." Looking at the clouds reflected in a window something strange can happen: "Clouds were moving across the sky and the windowpanes, and in the windows their paths were getting entangled." At the end of *Envy* Ivan Babichev and Kavalerov enter a glass gallery, where several panes have been broken; and it is here that they obtain a peculiar picture of the heavens: "The sky was broken up into sections of varying blueness and varying remoteness from the observer." Later, Andrei Babichev passes through the same gallery but now the author regards him from the outside; a cubist effect is created: "Somebody was walking along the porch, and the windows were dismembering him as he went. Different parts of his body moved independently. It was an optical illusion. The head ran off ahead of the rest of the body."

Turning from windows to the mirror, we might well expect this to be one of Olesha's favorite devices. To be sure, the looking-glass is our most common means of reflecting things, of giving us an indirect picture both of ourselves and of the reality around us. On the other hand, it has already been used so frequently in fiction to give, for instance, a description of an interior; by this means, authors could dispense with a long enumeration of furniture and objects, bound to impede the flow of narration, and just give rapid glimpses of a few accessories necessary to the context. Further, the well-known trope of holding up a mirror to nature, the idea of the novel as "a mirror carried along a roadway," has given this image definite connotations: it has become a symbol of literary realism. Thus the mirror could hardly interest Olesha very much; his sparing use of this device shows, however, that he knows that even an ordinary mirror is sometimes able to disclose unusual things. When Kavalerov wakes up the morning after he had come home drunk "he saw an uncommon sight in the mirror—the soles of his feet in close-up." When Anna Prokopovich and her husband won the magnificent bed in a lottery, they drove it away on a cart: "The blue sky appeared and disappeared, reflected in the swaying mirror-arcs, as if lids of a pair of beautiful eyes were opening and then slowly drooping again."[1]

But there is a variety of mirrors that Olesha actually does like. When Kavalerov and Ivan Babichev meet for the first time it is in front of a street-mirror. Here the author makes a pause to tell us how fond he is of such mirrors. They possess a quality quite lacking in ordinary mirrors. When a pedestrian spots a street-mirror, he says, the world around him suddenly changes: "The rules of optics, of geometry have been shattered. The very motive force behind you is shattered, that which made you move and go precisely where you did go . . . The streetcar that just disappeared from your sight is again rambling past you, cutting off the edge of the avenue like a knife chopping off a slice of cake. A straw hat hanging on a blue ribbon over somebody's wrist (you saw it; it attracted your attention but you did not have time to turn toward it) is back, sailing across your field of vision. There is an open space in front of you. You are certain that it is a house, a wall. But thanks to your gift you know that it is not a house. You have broken a mystery. It is not a wall; there is a mysterious world here where everything you have just seen is repeated with the stereoscopic clarity and neatness of outline that one gets from looking through the wrong end of binoculars."

Here Olesha mentions another of his favorite means of obtaining a different view of reality. One passage in *Envy* does express his fondness of this instrument in a way similar to his praise of the street-mirror. But it is, as we notice, not the common use of binoculars that Olesha is interested in, just as he does not care for ordinary mirrors: "I find," he says, "that a landscape viewed through the wrong end of binoculars gains in brightness, clarity and stereoscopy. The colors and contours seem somehow more precise. An object is still familiar but becomes at the same time suddenly small and strange."

The next step from the binoculars would be the microscope. In fact, we meet this transformation in one of Olesha's short stories, *Our World* (*V mire*). One day, as he is sitting on a bench somewhere on the coast in the south, his eye fastens on a little flower on the edge of a cliff. It stands out clearly against the blue skies: "I concentrate my vision, then suddenly something happens in my brain: somebody turns the screw of an imaginary pair of binoculars, trying to bring the picture into focus. And now the focus is sharp: the flower stands before me translucent as a section under the microscope. It has become gigantic. My sight has been given microscopic strength. I am become a Gulliver in the land of the giants. The tiny little flower, not bigger than a straw, frightens me. It is terrible. It looms before me: a construction of some unknown grandiose technique. I see giant bowls, pipes, joints, levers. And the reflection of the sun on the stalk of the vanished flower I see as a blinding metallic glare."

After the microscope, the next step will be to look for the telescope. Although the word is mentioned a few times in *Envy*, Olesha has in fact devoted a special little sketch to it, entitled *In Summer* (*Letom*). When one night he happens to look at the stars through a telescope, he experiences a surprise similar to those given him by the street-mirror, the binoculars and the microscope. The telescope transforms his earlier idea of the sky: "Now you know that this is Sagittarius, this is Cassiopeia, this is Perseus, these are the Pleiades, and this is Andromeda. The sky is no longer just a display of fireworks. It has, so it seems, stopped before your eyes. You experience a stunning feeling which cannot be compared with anything else."

But there are still other things, not necessarily instruments, which can produce similar effects. One is the play of light and shadow which Olesha uses in *Envy* with the skill of a stage director. One evening Andrei Babichev is talking to his brother from a balcony: "Babichev turned abruptly and came back into the room. His shadow leaped diagonally across the street and almost caused a storm in the foliage of the garden opposite." And a moment later, when he rushes out on to the balcony once more: "Now there is indeed a storm in the trees. His shadow, like a Buddha, falls over the city." Another time a huge cloud "with the outline of South America" is moving towards the town. "The cloud gleamed in the sun, but its shadow looked threatening. The shadow, with astronomical slowness, was creeping over Babichev's street. All those who had already entered the mouth of the street and were moving against the current saw the approach of the shadow and felt things darkening before their eyes. The shadow was sweeping the soil from under their feet. They were walking as if on the top of a revolving sphere."

One Sunday morning Ivan Babichev and Kavalerov are walking through the holiday-deserted city. There is a fascinating display of light and shadow: "The light, broken by traffic, remained all in one piece, as though the sun had only just risen. They were walking across geometrical patterns of shadow and light, or rather through a three-dimensional field, since the light and shadow intersected each other not only on the flat but also in the air. Before they reached the Moscow City Soviet they found themselves completely immersed in shadow. However, in the gap between two buildings there was a large block of light. It was very thick and dense, and it was no longer possible to doubt that light was made of matter: the dust tearing around inside it could easily pass for waves in the ether."

In *The Tale of the Meeting of Two Brothers* we get the opposite picture, the play of light and shadow at night: "The evening was black. The lanterns were white and circular, the tarpaulins glowed redly, and the abysses below the wooden gangways were deathly black. The lanterns swung back and forth on their humming wires. It was as though the darkness was raising and lowering its eyebrows. Around the lanterns, insects were fluttering and dying. As they swung upward, the lanterns made the windows on their way blink, and then, as they descended again, tore out the outline of some far-off house and hurled it at the construction site. And then (until the swinging lantern came to rest) the scaffolding came to life, everything was in motion and the building set sail straight at the crowd like a high-decked galleon."

In this passage the wind, as we notice, plays an important part. In fact, the wind is also able to disorder things, to play tricks on our eyes and reveal objects from a new angle. Gusts of wind fan a flamingo vase into a flame, setting the curtains alight. A draft gives Kavalerov "a wing" and anesthetizes half his face. When he sits down to drink a beer in an open-air restaurant he watches "the wind trace delicate shapes out of the corners of the tablecloth." In the soccer game at the end of *Envy* we find a particularly good example of the wind at work: "Then the wind butted in. A striped awning collapsed. All the treetops swung far to the right. The ring of idlers dissolved. The whole picture disintegrated. People were running to find shelter from the dust. Valia took the full force of the blast. The light dress, pink as a shell, flew up and Kavalerov saw how transparent it was. The wind blew the dress over Valia's face and Kavalerov saw it outlined in the pink, fanned-out material."

There is a similar episode in the story *Love*; here the wind is part of the transformation of the world through the love besetting Shuvalov: "They took leave of each other standing in the draft, which in this world seemed to be very active and many-voiced. It opened the doors downstairs. It sang like a charwoman. It ruffled Lola's hair, picked up Lola's hat, released the wasp and blew it into the salad. It was whistling. It picked up Lola's nightdress and stood it on end."

Rain too has the same faculty of letting us suddenly see a landscape or a well-known object in a new, fresh light: "After rain the city acquires brilliance and stereoscopic relief. Anyone can see it: the streetcar is carmine; the paving stones are far from being all the same color, some of them are even green; a house-painter who was sheltering from the rain like a pigeon has come out of his niche and is now moving against the background of his brick canvas in a window." In another passage Olesha tells us how after a shower "the city sparkled as if hewed out of Cardiff coal."

But there are still other means of getting something new out of the world around us. We do not always need some kind of instrument. We can simply use our eyes. The world is full of wonders if we only have time to discover them. At the beginning of *Envy* Kavalerov says that he spends his time in Andrei Babichev's apartment observing things, astonished by all the mysteries of our everyday life: "Have you ever noticed that salt falls off the edge of a knife without leaving a trace—the knife shines as though nothing had been on it; that a pince-nez sits on the bridge of a nose like a bicycle; that a human being is surrounded by tiny letters like a scattered army of ants: on forks, spoons, plates, on a pince-nez frame, on buttons, on pencils?"

We can also choose a special angle; if, for instance, you look at something from above you will get an often surprising impression. Kavalerov stands on a bridge and looks down on a boat: "From my bird's-eye view, a tugboat slid swiftly by. From this height, I saw, instead of a tugboat, something looking like a huge almond cut in half lengthwise. The almond vanished under the bridge." Later in the novel, Kavalerov looks down on the town from the roof window of a huge building: "From this vantage point, it seemed to him that the little yard was groping for breathing space. All the surrounding stone hulks were pressing in on the little yard. The yard lay like a doormat in an over-furnished room. Strange roofs revealed their secrets to Kavalerov. He saw weather vanes full size and skylights whose existence nobody down below suspected; he caught a glimpse of a child's ball irretrievably lost when it had rolled into the gutter. Among the antenna-spiked buildings beyond the yard, the cupola of a church, freshly painted with red lead, filled an empty spot in the sky, and it seemed as if it had been wafted along on the breeze until Kavalerov's eye had caught it. He saw a trolley in the terribly remote street, looking like Siamese-twin question marks facing each other, and also another observer, leaning out of a faraway window and either eating something or sniffing at it, who in his obedience to perspective was almost leaning on the trolley."

Kavalerov has similar experiences when he is looking at something from below. When Andrei Babichev finds him in the gutter, he is driven away in a car: "Coming to my senses, I saw a pale sky, growing lighter and rushing like water from the soles of my feet to somewhere behind my head." Later, at a construction site, he is searching for Andrei Babichev, but gets only a sudden glimpse of him as he passes above him on an iron girder: "He flew by above me. Yes, he literally rushed past through the air. In an absurd foreshortening, I saw his rigid flying figure—not his face, only his nostrils. I saw two holes, as if I were looking at a statue from underneath."

Still another thing able to cause interesting optical illusions is distance. Things look different at different ranges. If an observer lets his imagination run away with him, the most exciting transformations can take place. At the airfield Kavalerov watches a plane take off and notices "how with the changing distance, the plane kept changing into various objects. Now it was a gun-lock, now a pocket-knife, now a trodden lilac blossom." The same thing happens when he stands on a street corner for a good hour, watching the inside of a bell tower where the ringer is working with his twenty bells. Because of the distance he cannot see him or his bells very clearly, and so he lets his imagination work along a metaphorical line.

There exists, however, yet another way of observing and describing things. One can put oneself—deliberately or not—into a special emotional state, where things present themselves in a new light. One can, for instance, imagine that one is still a child among grown-up people, a Lilliputian in the world of giants. And this is just what Kavalerov does when he wants to tell us about Anichka Prokopovich's fantastic bed, made of expensive wood, varnished with dark-cherry lacquer and with inset mirror-arcs on the inside of its ends. The strange architecture of this bed could, as it seems to him, be described best of all from the perspective of a Lilliputian or a child. If he were, for instance, Anichka's own little son, "then neither distance nor scale nor time nor weight nor gravity had to be taken into consideration, and I could have crawled inside the narrow passages between the frame of the bedspring and the edge of the bed; I could have hidden behind the columns which today seem to me no thicker than a broomstick; I could have set up imaginary catapults on its barricades and opened fire on the enemy who would beat a hasty retreat over the soft boggy ground of the quilt, leaving behind the dead and the wounded; I could have held receptions for foreign envoys under the mirror-arcs, exactly like the king in the novel I had just read; I could have gone off on fantastic journeys along the fretwork—higher and higher, up the legs and buttocks of the cupids, climbing over them like climbing on a gigantic statue of Buddha, seeing only one bit of the huge details at a time; and then, from the last arch, from a dizzying height, I would have slithered down the terrifying precipice, into the icy abyss of the pillows."

There is another state, also connected with childhood, which Olesha is particularly fond of. This is how Kavalerov describes it: "On this sofa, I fly back into my childhood. It's blissful. Like a child, I have at my disposal the tiny time interval between the first heaviness felt in the eyelids, the first melting away of things, and the beginning of real sleep. Once again, I know how to prolong this interval, enjoy it, fill it with the thoughts I want and, before sinking into sleep, still in control of my conscious mind, observe how my thoughts acquire a body of dream substance, how the ringing bubbles from the submerged depths become rolling grapes, how a heavy bunch of grapes is formed, a whole vineyard thick with bunches, and then there is a sunny road beside the vineyard, and the warmth. . . ."

It is not a dream—although dreams also play a certain role in *Envy*—but the particular state between dream and wakefulness, a state in which everything is real and unreal at the same time, in which all objects by the power of his imagination are interchangeable, and can be transformed into something else: a world of fairytale and wonderful metamorphosis, the world of a poet.

To a poet or a child such fantastic transformations seem quite natural. But such a state is characteristic not only of a child but also of a man in love: he too lives in a world of unexpected analogies and metaphors. We find an illuminating example of this in *Love*. Before Shuvalov falls asleep he follows the pattern on the wallpaper:

"He realized that that part of the pattern on the wallpaper, that section of the wall under which he was falling asleep, had a double existence—the usual one, the daytime one, ordinary coronets with nothing remarkable about them, and another existence, a nighttime one which only opened itself up to him five minutes before he dived into sleep. Suddenly, a part of the pattern came close enough to touch his eyeballs, was magnified, revealed previously unseen details, changed its appearance. On the threshold of sleep, close to childhood's sensations, he did not resist the transformation of familiar and lawful forms, especially as the transformation was touching: instead of the rings and spirals he discerned a she-goat and a chef in his white cap...

—And that is a violin key, Lola said, understanding him.

—And the chameleon ... he said, already asleep."

Thus we get a peculiar triumvirate in Olesha's works: the child, the lover, the poet. They are all related to each other; they share the same source of happiness. They all have that special sight which unfolds to them an "invisible world," a world unseen by other people. To those so gifted all things in the universe are wonderfully connected with each other. This makes it so easy for their imaginations to work along metaphorical lines. Olesha's world is not only a world of unusual perspectives and optical illusions but also—and for the most part just because of them—a world of startling metaphors. An object loses its firm contours, becomes material pliable to the will of the imagination, which starts to form new things out of it. But this is not all; there is a further stage. As sometimes happens with the imaginations of children, the metaphor itself comes true, is materialized. It is not just a simple comparison, made in passing. We witness a fantastic metamorphosis.

When Kavalerov stands on a bridge looking down on the tugboat gliding under him he compares it to an almond. But in the next second the metaphor is materialized. What passes under the bridge is not any more a tugboat which looks like an almond. It is an almond. When the narrator in the story *The Cherry-Stone* stands at a streetcar stop waiting for Natasha, people for some reason start asking him which car they should take. Soon he feels like a policeman who must have a ready answer to all questioners. After a while it is no longer a comparison. The metamorphosis takes place: he is already a policeman, with a truncheon and everything.

A good example of how the imagination works is to be found in the scene just mentioned, where Kavalerov is listening to the church bells. A bell ringer is working with his twenty bells of various sizes. Kavalerov watches him at a certain distance, and the distance starts to distort the proportions and evoke fantastic associations. It is, as it seems, not the ringer who pulls the ropes, but the contrary: "twenty bells were tearing him apart." The ropes are transformed into cobwebs; the ringer becomes a mysterious musician—black, ugly, a Quasimodo. And then, by a sudden shift of associations, the ringer is now a laborer manhandling different-sized pieces of hardware.

And the sound itself also starts a play of imagination. First he hears the noises in a restaurant or a railway station. But after a while the sounds arrange themselves into a little tune: "Tom-vee-ree-lee." These words carry the associations further. They remind him of a name, and suddenly "there was some Tom Vereley floating around in the air." Kavalerov sees him now clearly before him, a handsome young man with a rucksack, on his way to the town, to Andrei Babichev's house, where he already hears him walking up the stairs, knocking on the door. Dream and reality now cross each other (as in the first act of Ibsen's *The Master Builder*). In fact, somebody knocks on the door, waking Kavalerov up from his metaphorical play, and a real Tom Vereley appears: it is Volodia Makarov, Andrei Babichev's protégé, a swarthy young man holding a bag.

The most amusing examples are to be found in *Love*. Right at the very beginning, where Shuvalov is waiting for Lola in the park, he notices how his thoughts all the time take an unpredictable, metaphorical course, and how he, against his own will, makes strange observations about the trees and flowers, observations which he would never have made before. And when he wakes up the next day after a night spent together with his beloved "the transformation of the world that had started the day they met had been completed." He has achieved the power to materialize his thoughts. The old metaphor of a lover, for instance, comes true. It does not surprise anybody. "'Flying on the wings of love,' somebody said behind a window as he passed."

What we learn from Olesha's stories is that there exist two worlds—the world we ordinarily live and act in, and an "invisible world." This "invisible world" is part of our common, everyday reality, only we do not usually notice it. One has to know the trick. Window-panes, street-mirrors, binoculars, rain, wind, unusual angles, optical illusions—all these things are keys with the magic power of opening the closed door to this fantastic world, a world which to Olesha is as real and important as the "visible" one. Some know how to manipulate them without instruction: the poet, the child, the lover. But nobody is locked out from the enchanted garden of poetry. Olesha extends a generous invitation to everybody. He is always willing to give the necessary instruction and encouragement. Anyone can see it, he says about the town renewed and refreshed, gleaming in bright colors after a sudden shower. Everyone who pays attention can do likewise, are his encouraging words about the optical illusions with the flower on the cliff.

2. The existence of an "invisible world" will provide us with an answer to the natural questions arising after we have acquainted ourselves with the list of Olesha's devices: why is he so fond of them? why does he, wherever possible, avoid any direct presentation of characters, objects or landscapes? So as not to leave us in any doubt, he has, moreover, given a simple and clear answer in his story *Our World*. Having recounted his experience with the eye as a microscope, he concludes: "You have to look on the world from a new point of view"... adding: "It is extremely useful for an author to occupy himself with such fantastic photography. And furthermore—this is no distortion of reality, no expressionism. On the contrary: this is pure, sound realism."

Such a statement seems to imply an indirect address to the RAPP critics: when it was written, the word "fantastic" was not in high esteem, and Olesha's way of linking it with "realism" must certainly have smacked of "formalism" to those critics. But there is also another meaning behind this statement, and a very important one. The use of the word "fantastic" could be understood to mean that Olesha was interested in mystic or metaphysical speculation. Apparently he wants to defend himself against such an interpretation. His "invisible world" has no metaphysical or mystical connotations; it is, as I just mentioned, quite simply part of our reality. In fact, it is our world, only seen from a different angle. By his term "fantastic photography" he has in mind, above all, a wider-angled view of the field of realism, a discovery of new things around us, things which are always there, although we do not usually notice them. It is true that he recommends his readers and fellow writers to look at the world through the wrong end of a pair of binoculars, but the reason for this is not any desire to obtain a distorted picture ("no expressionism"). On the contrary: as he points out, in this way you will in fact get a clearer, sharper, more distinct picture of reality.

If we now should try to outline the background to Olesha's favorite devices and his concept of fantastic photography, we have to start with a writer to whom Olesha, in fact, makes a direct allusion in *Envy*, without, however, mentioning his name. When Ivan Babichev takes Kavalerov to show him his "Ophelia," they cross an empty lot. Ivan points out various discarded objects just to convince Kavalerov that this is not a dream. Suddenly he spots a bottle: "There is a bottle. Wait, it is still whole, but tomorrow the wheel of a cart will smash it, and if, soon after us, some dreamer follows our path, he will have the pleasure of contemplating the famous bottle-glass, celebrated by writers for its ability to reflect light, to glint amidst garbage in a waste land and create mirages for lonely travelers."

This "famous bottle" is, of course, that mentioned by Chekhov in a letter from 1886, when he tells his brother Aleksandr how to achieve the effect of a moonlight night "by simply writing that the glow is like a light from a star flashed from a broken bottle on the milldam." As we know, Chekhov himself used this image in the story *The Wolf* written the same year; later, in *The Seagull*, he lets Trigorin repeat the same recommendation. This bottle has become a kind of symbol for Chekhov's impressionism: opposing a too painstaking realism, Chekhov gave a call for more economy and concreteness in all kinds of description.

It is true that the following prose generation did learn a great deal from Chekhov; his call for economy, especially, was taken up by many writers. Olesha was certainly one of them; further Chekhov had something more to give him: the device of indirect description. Now, as we have already seen, Olesha makes much more out of it than Chekhov ever tried to do. In Chekhov it is mostly a means of avoiding the long, tedious descriptions of earlier realism; by mentioning the church and the sunset at one and the same time he could save at least one sentence in the indispensable presentation of the setting. To Olesha the indirect description is, as we have seen, an important part not only of his poetics but also of his view of the world.

... When Olesha brings together words like "realism" and "fantastic," we are, of course, reminded of Dostoevskii; in fact, he does the same thing in some of his letters, pointing out that what most critics consider fantastic and exceptional is to him the very essence of reality. Now Olesha and Dostoevskii are certainly very different as writers, and a closer comparison will not lead us far. Nevertheless, Olesha's "fantastic photography" points, without any doubt, in the direction of Dostoevskii, Dostoevskii the writer, struggling with the concept of realism, asking himself if "the fantastic has or has not the right to exist in art."[2] Here Olesha felt a certain kinship with Dostoevskii; he was, as Dostoevskii, ready to answer the question in the affirmative, and even, as also Dostoevskii did, to state that this was in fact "pure, sound realism."

For the same reason Olesha interested himself in another writer, a writer who also explored the fantastic element in our everyday life, namely Edgar Allan Poe. When discussing his "fantastic photography" he is, in fact, making direct reference to Poe. What he has in mind is *The Sphinx*. It is characteristic for Olesha that this is a story in which the fantastic element is given a very natural explanation at the end. Poe relates here how one day, while sitting at an open window overlooking some river bank and a distant hill, he suddenly catches sight of "a living monster of hideous conformation, which very rapidly made its way from the summit to the bottom, disappearing finally in the dense forest below."[3] As it later turns out, the monster is simply an insect, wriggling its way up a thread, which some spider had wrought along the window sash; the hill in the background and the author's position in the window had caused an optical illusion.

....

However, we do not have to go so far back in time, for there is a contemporary writer who, I think, has been the most inspiring model for Olesha in the field of fantastic photography. This is Evgenii Zamiatin. In fact, the now very familiar passage from *Our World*, the one about the flower, comes very close to a passage in a lecture by Evgenii Zamiatin on contemporary Russian literature. If we look at our own skin through a microscope, he says, we will doubtless be frightened at first. "Instead of your pink, smooth, soft skin you will see kinds of clefts, enormous hillocks, pits; from a pit rises something of the same girth as a young lime-tree—it is a hair; beside it there is a big clod of earth—this a speck of dust. What you see will have very little in common with the usual kind of skin: it seems to you improbable, nightmarish. Now ask yourself this question: which is the truer, which is the more real—the pink, smooth skin, or this one with the clefts and hillocks? Having given it a thought we have to answer: it is this improbable skin, which we see through the microscope that is true and real."

It may not come as a surprise to us that Zamiatin in the same context makes an allusion to Dostoevskii and his fantastic realism. At this time Zamiatin believed he had found a concept which could explain the new trend in Russian prose after 1910. He called it, as we know, "Neo-Realism." This was a synthesis of realism and symbolism, an opposition to and yet a continuation of the sweeping trends which had dominated Russian literature in the 19th and the beginning of the 20th century. This meant a realism of a new kind, a realism unafraid of symbolic planes and fantastic implications. The writers had to try new devices and uncommon angles to get something new out of the old theme of "byt." And, as the example with the skin under the microscope tells us, Zamiatin saw a truth more real than that of ordinary realism in such fantastic close-ups of reality.

3. An important aspect of this trend [the new realism] was a belief that the poet is a man who breaks the spell of automatization, a spell which permanently threatens our perception of the world. This was usually based on the philosophy of Henri Bergson, so popular at that time. Again and again in his works Bergson presents the same image of the poet: *For centuries there have appeared people whose function has been none other than make us see what we do not perceive by ourselves. Those are the artists... We others do barely look at an object; it suffices us to know what category they belong to. But every now and then, thanks to fortunate circumstances personalities surface whose senses, or consciousness, are less dependent on the manifestations of ordinary life. Nature has neglected to link their perceptions to the need to act upon them. When those persons observe an object, they look at it for its own sake, and not for their practical needs. They do not perceive a thing in order to act on their perception with nothing else on their mind; they perceive in order to perceive ...* [translated from the French by IMD].

Very similar ideas were expressed in a Russian booklet, *The Resurrection of the Word* (*Voskreshenie slova*), published in 1914 by Viktor Shklovskii. In it he stresses that "we do not experience the usual things; we do not see them, we merely recognize them. We do not see the walls of our room. It is so difficult for us to notice a mistake in a proof, because we cannot make ourselves see and read the common words: instead we merely "recognize" them. An epithet may at first sound fresh and give new lease of life to a noun, but if it is repeated sufficiently often we will not experience its freshness anymore: it will have already become commonplace. And not only single words or expressions can be fossilized in this way but sentences and even whole books as well.

It is easy to quote from almost any of [the Soviet literary critic Aleksandr Voronskii's] articles to prove [similarity of views between him and Olesha]. To limit ourselves to just one example, let me choose a passage from an article, published in *Krasnaia Nov'* [*Red Virgin Soil*] in 1923, entitled *Art as a Means of Knowing Life* (*Iskusstvo kak poznanie zhizni*). Here it is easy to recognize his attempts to bring his ideas of art as discovery and revelation into harmony with the new literary situation. Still more interesting is it to note his use of the "microscope image," giving it the same sense as Zamiatin and Olesha did: by enlarging objects the artist gives us a new view of them, a view which is truer than "the most real reality" (cf. Olesha's defense of the microscope and fantastic photography):

> A true work of art is always astonishing in its novelty, always draws you in and always is an epiphany. Life around us follows its well-known familiar course from day to day. And even when the pattern of that life is disrupted, even when its most solid foundations have been undermined, our consciousness and our feelings inevitably lag behind; our perceptions do not keep pace with the new events happening in life; we remain enslaved to the past; our eye is incapable of catching, of making out that which is being borne in the midst of the roar of historical change, and its accompanying floods and catastrophes. But in the very midst of dizzying storms a genuine artist—having an eye, an ear, and an "inward sense" capable of perceiving—is capable of grasping things that we pass by without noticing, things that still make no impression on us. Out of tiny details he creates in his imagination something great and significant. He magnifies people and objects in his artistic microscope, ignoring what is established and known. He raises life to the level of a "pearl of creation." He gathers up and brings together details and features that are scattered around us, and singles out what is typical. In this way he creates in his imagination a life that is condensed and purified, a life better than reality, and closer to truth than the "most real reality." And we ourselves begin to see, with the artist's help, things we passed by without noticing but which are present around us, or are taking form in prophetic anticipation of the future [translated from the Russian by IMD].

There are many other passages in Voronskii's criticism which could be quoted as parallels to Olesha. When Voronskii says in one of his other articles that right from our childhood years prejudices, the pressure of the environment and society, illness and overwork will result in the fact that "the most important and the most beautiful things in life and the Universe become invisible to us," he comes close to Olesha's idea of the "invisible country." And when he says that the special ability of "seeing the world as it is in itself" is something we may attain "only in childhood, in our early years and at exceptional moments of our life," we are reminded of the special triumvirate of the child, the poet and the lover in Olesha's world. Voronskii too makes a division, similar to that of Bergson, between artists and "ordinary people," and the title of one of his books, *The Art of Seeing the World* (*Iskusstvo videt' mir*), could, in fact, fit very well as a general characterization of Olesha's works.

....

To give one more variation of the idea of "novelty and freshness with old and familiar objects" in contemporary literature I should like to mention James Joyce's well-known "epiphany." In *Stephen Hero*, Stephen Dedalus tells Cranby about the clock of the Ballast office in Dublin: "I will pass it time after time, allude to it, refer to it, catch a glimpse of it. It is only an item in the catalogue of Dublin's street furniture. Then all at once I see it and I know at once what it is: epiphany.

....

There was a certain general idea about the aims and methods of poetry, topical in Europe at this time. It is reflected in various ways in different writers and different countries, but we can easily recognize the common traits, sometimes even find very similar expressions for the same experience. The above discussion has, I think, clearly demonstrated how well Olesha fits into this trend.

4. At first glance it appears as if Kavalerov and Andrei Babichev were perfect illustrations of the two types Bergson suggests in his aesthetic works: the man of action and the artist, the people who perceive for the purpose of action, who think in standardized categories, and, on the other hand, the people who perceive for the pure pleasure of perceiving, who "see the table where others see just a table." Such a division seems to suggest a solution to the old conflict of the artist contra society. The artist has his special tasks in society, which are as important as those of the bureaucrat or the scientist. It is his job to discover aspects of reality that we are too busy to notice, aspects which are beyond the reach of the special tools and methods of science. This should, it would seem, give him a certain satisfaction of performing a useful mission in modern society, and balance the inferiority complex which has become one of the artist's obsessions since the rapid advance of science and technology during the past hundred years.

But it is not quite that simple. Those of Olesha's heroes who have been given the faculty of apprehending the invisible country soon find that this is a double-edged gift. There are very definitely moments when Kavalerov feels it a burden and a torment. "I do not want to speak in images. I want to express myself simply," he exclaims in despair. And in his letter to Andrei Babichev, he is anxious to explain that he is able not only to describe Valia in metaphorical language—which Andrei cannot understand—but "in ordinary terms" as well.

....

This dilemma is, in fact, the main theme of *Envy* and of most of Olesha's short stories. It is not the usual romantic conflict between dream and reality. Kavalerov is not the successor of, let us say, Piskarev in Gogol's *Nevskii Prospect*. Our world is not simply a detestable world to be avoided at any price. In many respects it is a most exciting place. Kavalerov may take his refuge in bed, in dreams or in his favorite state between sleep and wakefulness, just as Piskarev desperately reaches for his opium in order to escape from reality and revive his dreams of pure beauty. Nevertheless, this world attracts him again and again. It is, among other things, an excellent field for visual revelations and sudden discoveries. But this is still not enough for Kavalerov. There is in him at the same time an explicit desire to experience reality in the same simple, self-evident way that most people do. This is one important explanation of the envy the title tells us about: envy of Andrei Babichev, of Volodia and Valia, of people for whom life is simple and straightforward, for whom the adjustment to a new society does not involve any problems.

Kavalerov may despise and even hate Andrei, his way of eating, his whole appearance, his materialistic approach to life. But he cannot also help feeling a certain envy of him. Andrei moves around freely in the new world; he is accepted everywhere; in his way he is a famous man. If Kavalerov had been a man like Piskarev he could have parted from Andrei with a smile of contempt and contented himself with a "he has his world, I have mine." Instead he is now both repulsed and attracted at the same time. In the presence of Andrei he feels a permanent need to assert himself. He has to convince himself that he is no more inferior a representative of his age than this "sausage-maker." His letter to Andrei expresses it very clearly: "But does that make me an unworthy son of our century, and you a good one? Does that make me nothing and you something great?" Characteristic is the scene in which Kavalerov tries to get in to the airfield but is stopped by a soldier at the gate. He has to produce some kind of invitation card and he does not have one. "'Comrade, I am no ordinary citizen,' I began excitedly, unable to find anything better to say. 'What do you think I am? Just a bystander? Kindly let me through. I belong over there."

It is a symbolic scene. It is true that Kavalerov has just noticed that aviation has changed since the days of [pioneer aviator] Lilienthal, when an aircraft with its light, transparent wings resembled most of all a beautiful bird. Now it looks more like a ponderous fish. "How quickly aviation has succumbed to commerce." It is the same thing that frightens him in Andrei Babichev — the development of modern man into something materialistic and commercial. Nevertheless he claims that "I belong over there." He is also "a son of his age." What he is most of all afraid of is to be taken for a nonentity, for a petty bourgeois. In fact, he feels superior to Andrei, because he stands above the reduction of life to a materialistic, petty-bourgeois happiness which is symbolized in Andrei's sausage (the end of the story thus involves his second and decisive capitulation to Andrei because here he surrenders to the same limited materialistic "happiness" he has fought against in the person of Andrei). What makes him say "I belong over there" is a feeling that there is no way back and that people like Andrei after all are only temporary phenomena. His hope for the future is embodied in Valia. Before her his envy is changed into a painful, nostalgic yearning for this other world, to which, as it seems, he does not have the right invitation card:

> Sunlight slipped down her shoulder, and her collar-bones gleamed like two daggers. They remained like that for five seconds, and Kavalerov grew cold as he realized what an incurable nostalgia would remain in him forever. He knew he was watching a creature from a different world, alien and puzzling, while at the same time he felt how hopelessly charming she looked, how oppressively unattainable she was—because she was a little girl and because she loved Volodia. He felt how unslakable was the temptation.

When he approaches her with the words: "I have waited for you all my life. Take pity on me," his words do not reach her, she does not hear him and she passes him without an answer. "She ran, leaning against the wind."

It is obvious that the conflict between Kavalerov and Andrei as well as Kavalerov's inner conflict, his attraction to the new world and his repulsion by it, has its specific Russian explanation, that they are closely connected with the political and social situation in the Soviet Union after 1917. I do not need to take up this question here, especially since this is the very aspect of the novel which has been most widely discussed since its appearance. It is instead, I think, more important to stress another part of the background, one which has attracted less attention.

On one occasion Kavalerov tries in vain to convince Andrei that he too belongs to the new world. He does it with words he thinks should be sufficient as an introduction card: "My youth coincides with the youth of the century." But Andrei is too busy to listen. In one of Olesha's short stories, in which he looks back on his childhood, he says almost the same thing about himself as a high-school-boy: "You were of the same age as the century." This is not the only parallel which could be drawn between *Envy* and the short stories. As a matter of fact, they offer good explanations for many things in the novel. The hero of these stories could often be taken for Kavalerov as a young boy.

This high-school-boy has an open mind to the modern development of science and technology. In his family he stands out, in his own words, as "a European, a journalist, a technician" against the general stuffy petty-bourgeois atmosphere. He knows all the heroes of the new century by name: Latham, Farman, Wilbur and Orville Wright, Lilienthal and the Voisin brothers. He tries to acquaint his parents with the sensational news that "Bleriot has flown across the Channel"; he tries to convince them of the beauty of a word like Issy-les- Molineaux, the Paris airport. But they do not understand the magic of words like these, nor does Orlov, his sister's student boy-friend. Thus he meets with the same fate as poor Kavalerov when he tries to convince Andrei about his solidarity with the new century: nobody pays any attention to him.

....

The conflict of Olesha's hero thus has its psychological as well as its specific sociological and political background. But it is at the same time a conflict well known to writers outside Soviet Russia as well; it is a conflict of our century. Such non-Soviet examples may have other implications, but a parallel to Olesha, will sometimes be interesting enough in itself. Let us take Guillaume Apollinaire's *Le Poète Assassiné* [The Assassinated Poet] from 1916. With this, Apollinaire wanted to demonstrate the dilemma of poetry at the beginning of our century. The hero is no longer set against the philistine, the bourgeois, as was usually the case in the preceding century, but against the scientist—the scientist who considers poetry an unnecessary luxury in modern society and states that in our days "true glory has forsaken poetry for science, philosophy, acrobatics, philanthropy, sociology, etc." (cf. Kavalerov's yearning for glory and his complaint that there is no more glory for people like him in the Soviet Union). And this scientist demands that the poet shall no longer be afforded a place in society, a verdict which results in a general persecution all over the world. Further, the hero is killed, although he claims to be the greatest living poet. Later, however, Apollinaire tried to resolve this pessimistic note by seeking "conciliation between the work of the scientist and the modern artist."

We meet many variations of the same fear in Russian and European literature at this time, a fear of what modern technology may mean for the poet and poetry as well as for mankind and the human heritage in general. That this fear is part of the literary background to Olesha's *Envy* is obvious; in the same category are Zamiatin's *We* (in spite of the fact that the book was not published in the Soviet Union) as well as Chaplin's *Modern Times* (which was released after the appearance of *Envy*; cf. Olesha's interest in Chaplin and his hero). Olesha's place in this marked trend will, I think, stand out more clearly only when studies will be made not only of the utopian theme in Russian literature of the 1920's but also of the topical discussion on the art and science of the same period.

....

I think we could stop here. What I have tried to do in this brief introduction to Olesha's works (his later period is not treated here) is to outline some important features and suggest their background. In his view on art and life Olesha is, as we have seen, connected with some well-known Russian masters of "fantastic photography," but he also stands out as an interesting representative for a general trend in Western literature as well.

SELECTED NOTES

[1] Cf. in Vladimir Nabokov's *The Gift* a more elaborate use of this device: "As he crossed toward the pharmacy at the corner he involuntarily turned his head because of a burst of light that had ricocheted from his temple, and saw, with that quick smile with which we greet a rainbow or a rose, a blindingly white parallelogram of sky being unloaded from the van—a dresser with mirror across which, as across a cinema screen, passed a flawlessly clear reflection of boughs, sliding and swaying not arboreally, but with a human vacillation, produced by the nature of those who were carrying this sky, these boughs, this gliding façade." (Nabokov, V., *The Gift*, New York 1963).

[2] See, for instance, his letter to [the poet] Apollon Maikov, dated December 23, 1868 (with its passage which comes close to Olesha's: Mezhdu tem eto iskonnyi, nastoiashchii realism! [But its genuine, real realism!—IMD].... Of course, Gleb Struve is right when he points out the parallel between Kavalerov and Dostoevskii's *Man from the Underground* as well as certain other parallels with Dostoevskii's works.

[3] Poe, E. A., *The Complete Poems and Stories*. Vol. II, A. A. Knopf, 1946.

Two Plays

by Edward J. BROWN*

The plays written by Maiakovskii in 1928 and 1929 constitute a two-part dramatic satire directed against old enemies whom we have already met under the generic name *byt* and who appear now in the form of *bourgeoisis vulgaris*, a species closely allied with *bedbugus normalis*, and "the Soviet bureaucrat." Both plays are satiric utopias in the sense that they present a vision of a future in which the world will be purified of such specimens. *The Bedbug* is a two-part drama in which the action of the first part takes place in the year 1928 and of the second part fifty years later in a well-ordered communist state. The principal character is one Prisypkin, a successful Soviet "promoted worker," for whom proletarian blood, callused palms, and the trade union card have become symbols of privilege and power. As the play opens, he has jilted his working-class girl-friend for a beauty-shop operator and manicurist, Elzevira Renaissance, and is shopping in a huge department store in preparation for the wedding. Various street salesmen are promoting their wares—buttons, dolls, whetstones, lampshades, glue, perfumes, fur-lined brassieres, and the like—in jingles that parody Maiakovskii's own commercial poetry. Prisypkin, as

*From *Mayakovsky: A Poet in the Revolution*. Princeton: Princeton University Press, 1973. Pp. 325-335.

acquisitive as any bourgeois, purchases a variety of such wares, announcing that his house must be filled with such things "like a horn of plenty." Prisypkin is accompanied by a poet named Oleg Baian, whose function is to educate this working-class person in an appreciation of the "finer" things, such as poetry, the fox-trot, and the tango. Oleg Baian is a barely disguised portrait of an actual poet, Vladimir Ivanovich Sidorov, who had adopted a pseudonym redolent of Russia and poetry, "Vadim Baian." [Baian is a bard mentioned in the medieval epic *The Lay of Igor's Campaign*.] He had taken part with Maiakovskii in the futurist tour of the provinces in 1914, presenting his verses in competition with [the Futurist poets] Burliuk, Severianin, and Maiakovskii himself. After the revolution Sidorov had indeed occupied himself with the literary education of young workers and he had composed communist wedding songs, as well as politically oriented games (*igry*) and dances to be performed by peasants. This activity Maiakovskii satirizes directly and without mercy, and when Sidorov-Baian complained of it in an open letter published in the *Literary Gazette*, Maiakovskii answered briefly and scornfully, suggesting that if he objected to the character in the play he should change his own name.

Prisypkin's rejection of his working-class girl-friend, Zoia Berezkina, who tries to commit suicide, revives in dramatic form two recent polemical episodes, his answer to Molchanov,[1] and his poem "Marusia Has Poisoned Herself" (*Marusia otravilas'*), concerning a girl who committed suicide in desperation over her abandonment by such a one as Molchanov. Both these poems, as well as the main plot of the scenario *Forget about the Hearth*, are closely connected with Maiakovskii's work on the newspaper *Young Communist Truth*, and with the campaign against decadence and backsliding sponsored during those years by its editor, Taras Kostrov, who was deeply troubled about the tendency of young people, often under the influence of foreign movies, to adopt bourgeois dress and manners. The basic idea of *The Bedbug* and much of the material in the play, it would seem, grew out of Maiakovskii's work as a newspaper propagandist. Yet the play itself deviated strangely from its announced and initial direction, as we shall presently see.

Prisypkin's wedding ceremony takes place in the "Renaissance" beauty-shop amid the odor of hair-tonic, curling tongs, and perfumes. The beauty shop serves as a mighty symbol of resurgent philistinism and is actually prophetic of the revival under Stalin of make-up, manicures, and brilliantine. Oleg Baian's production of this "red wedding," moreover, suggests the flowery sentimental ceremonies, with bride and groom bedecked and attended, that developed much later as an appendix to simple registration of the marriage as a vital statistic at a government office. Prisypkin, whose speech is cluttered with clichés mechanically transferred from Party and trade-union life to other spheres, declares the wedding "open." The guests, soon drunk in the traditional fashion, repeatedly shout the traditional Russian wedding toast "Bitter!" (*Gor'ko!*) whereupon the bride and bridegroom must kiss (Prisypkin kissing "with a sense of his worth as a member of the proletariat") and the guests again drain their glasses. Oleg Baian (Sidorov, we remember) recites speeches and poetry on the subject of the good life and the elegant luxuries (vodka and herring, for example) now at the disposal of the working class, lines certainly intended as a parody of the ego-futurist [Igor'] Severianin. A drunken "best man" serves as a kind of self-appointed policeman enforcing order and propriety, and when Baian intones "Beauty is the mother..." the "best man" thinks he's heard a "mother-oath": "Who said 'mother'...? Don't talk like that in front of the newlyweds."

The directions for stage business call for an ignorant mixture of attempted elegance and vulgarity. Someone calls for "Beethoven and the Kamarinskii," the latter a peasant dance. The "best man" understands Elzevira's French affectations in his own way:

> ELZEVIRA: Ah, that's so *charmant*, oh, it's simply a *petite histoire*....
> BEST MAN: Who said *pissoir*!? Please! In front of the newlyweds....

The "red" wedding of the petty bourgeois Elzevira and the proletarian Prisypkin (who has changed his name to Pierre Skripkin) symbolizes the continued debasement of revolutionary ideas in the Soviet Union. The color red, which belonged properly to the Soviet flag and the blood of the working class, is now bestowed on ham, wine-bottles and painted lips.

At last the drunken guests set fire to the house, which burns to the ground destroying the inmates and all their neo-bourgeois trappings. In Scene IV the firemen report to one another on the burnt-out remains, and incidentally offer a Maiakovskian rhymed homily on the dangers of vodka when mixed with fireplaces and primus stoves.

Each of Maiakovskii's plays, beginning with the *Tragedy* [1913], divides more or less evenly into two parts, one concerned with the present, the other with the future. *The Bedbug* is closely reminiscent of the *Tragedy* in its structure in that the second part shows us a future world that has come about as the result of a revolution and a reordering of life. Fifty years after the fire the bridegroom Prisypkin, together with his close companion, a bedbug, is found, by workmen excavating for a new structure, perfectly preserved in a block of ice, and both are brought to life by scientists of the "Bureau for the Resurrection of the Dead." Prisypkin's "unfreezing," though a scientific success, is not an unmixed blessing to the inhabitants of the future, for he is found to contain a petty-bourgeois infection called "love," along with a fondness for strong drink and sentimental songs. Moreover, the citizens of the socialist future are not immune to these infections, which they pick up much too easily, and it is necessary to isolate Prisypkin and encompass him with disinfectants. Otherwise he will spread by contagion that ancient disease called love, "a state in which a person's sexual energy, instead of being rationally distributed over the whole of his life, was compressed into a single week and concentrated in one hectic process. This made him commit the most absurd and impossible acts."

The authorities of the State of the future place Prisypkin in a cage in the municipal zoo, where he is displayed in all his natural filth for the education and edification of the citizens. These people of utopia have, supposedly, forgotten a way of life that called for the use of poison (vodka), the disorderly and unhealthy consumption of tobacco, the use of foul language, the strumming of guitars, and idle talk about one's "heartstrings." And when the director of the zoo lets Prisypkin out of his cage to see the spectators and to address a few words to them in order to prove that he has mastered human speech, Prisypkin, suddenly looking out at the theater audience, is overjoyed at seeing so many people like himself: "Citizens! Brothers! My own people! Darlings! How did you get here? So many of you! When were you unfrozen? Why am I alone in the cage? Darlings, friends, come and join me! Why should I alone suffer? Citizens!"

This pathetic appeal of the caged Prisypkin has been interpreted in recent times as a veiled attack on the police state, but of course it is nothing of the sort. Prisypkin's apostrophe to the Soviet audience of 1928 is reminiscent of a very similar scene in Gogol's *Inspector General*, when the dishonest and foolish mayor turns to the audience to ask them whether they are not laughing at themselves rather than at him. You all have a bit of Prisypkin in you, Maiakovskii is saying in this scene, you are all attached to vulgar bourgeois values. Like Prisypkin you smoke, drink, and use intemperate language. Like him you want your houses to be "horns of plenty," crammed with buttons, brassieres, and bathos, and like him you have debased the humanitarian ideals of the revolution to the pursuit of comfort and power. Worst of all, you still preserve the infections of individualism and sexual love.

This is Maiakovskii's ostensible and consciously devised message in the play, yet something went wrong with the images in which he presents it. In the first place, there crept into the figure of Prisypkin a measure of identification with the poet himself, and this resulted in sudden, unexpected, and discordant notes of pathos throughout the second part, and especially at the end of the play.

Maiakovskii's satire in *The Bedbug* is clearly directed at himself as well as at his contemporaries. We have already noted that the ditties recited by the peddlers in the first scene are a parody of his own verse written for the Moscow Food Stores. Maiakovskii's most accomplished work is a poetic expression of that "disease of the brain" known as sexual love. It has been pointed out that Maiakovskii, in satirizing Prisypkin's yearning for "roses" and "visions," may be lecturing himself: "Only books on horticulture have anything about roses, and visions are mentioned only in the medical books, in the section on dreaming." And the ugly caricature of a "bourgeoisified" proletarian Prisypkin in search of conventional marital bliss may be that alter ego of the poet with whom he disputed in the poem *About That* [1923]:

> Have you greased your way
>   into that caste of theirs?
> Will you kiss?
>   Feed yourself?
>   Grow fat?
> Do you intend
>   yourself
> to dig yourself into their way of life
> and practice that family happiness of theirs?

The identification of Prisypkin-Skripkin with the poet himself is borne out in a curious reminiscence of the actor who played the part, Igor Il'inskii, in which he tells us, almost inadvertently, of this identification:

> In his author's interpretation Maiakovskii did not endow Prisypkin with any characteristic traits or moral attributes. He read the part in his usual manner of monumental authoritativeness and with a solemn, even noble . . . pathos, peculiar to himself.
> . . . I built Prisypkin's part as a "monumental" flunkey and boor . . . Though it may seem paradoxical, I adopted for Prisypkin, even externally . . . Maiakovskii's manner.

Other evidence tends to support Il'inskii's interpretation of the part. Prisypkin is brought back from death by a chemist of the future (possibly "broad-domed") very like the one to whom Maiakovskii himself applied for resurrection in the poem *About That*; but Prisypkin's experience in the brave new world represents later and gloomier thoughts on the rationalized future society: "Comrades, I protest. I didn't get unfrozen just so you could dry me out!"

The zoo itself and Prisypkin's cage in it suggest Maiakovskii's own identification with animals, and the sympathy both he and Khlebnikov felt for the beast, who offers the poet both moral analogies and metaphors. Maiakovskii's menagerie of animal-selves would serve as a very respectable small public zoo: it included, ..., dog, elephant, giraffe, bear, and ostrich; he signed most of his letters to [his great Love] Lili Brik "Puppy" (*Shchen*), and in some of them the pathetic puppy is shown behind bars; in *About That* he says the zoo is where he would prefer to work in the future world, and "she herself" would come there, because "she loved animals, too."

"She herself" wrote a delightful character sketch of Maiakovskii, entitled "Puppy" (*Shchen*), in the disguise of a delicate vignette about a stray dog adopted by the Briks and Maiakovskii. Her sketch is not only a humorous and sensitive treatment of a dog by a woman who knows and understands the character, quality, and life style of dogs, but it is also an extended metonymy for the proper name Maiakovskii: "They were very like one another. They were both huge and had huge heads. They both carried their tails high. They both whined pathetically when they wanted something and wouldn't give up until they got it. Sometimes they barked for no good reason at anybody who came along, just to have something to say."

The caged clown and cretin Prisypkin suddenly turns pathetic when we realize that this is Maiakovskii himself caught in the cage of the futurist world that he and his comrades were so busily building. The petty-bourgeois ambiance in the first part of the play smells of hair-tonic, as [Italian Slavist] Ripellino has pointed out, but the principal odor of Maiakovskii's world of the future is that of disinfectant. It is a painfully disinfected world, clean not only of emotion, but of germs. We recall in this connection Maiakovskii's own neurotic fear of germs, his compulsive hand-washing, and his habit of drinking coffee through a straw to avoid contact with dubious cups. The second part of *The Bedbug* is a nightmarish realization of his deep fear of contagion. *The Bedbug* is, therefore, an extremely complex satiric system, so complex that at times it does not hold together. Voices from the crowd in the last scene break in upon the action and the mood with a sudden plea that mercy be shown the caged beast, Prisypkin-Skripkin:

> "Don't, don't! Don't torment the poor animal...."
> "Oh how awful!"
> "Professor, stop!"
> "Oh, please don't shoot!"

Prisypkin himself in his apostrophe to the audience asks pathetically, "Why am I suffering?" The philistine symbolized by Prisypkin-Skripkin is the normal Soviet man of the late twenties who has deserted the "trenches" of revolution for the sake of middle-class happiness. He is also Maiakovskii himself, the unreconstructed poet of his own all-important self, who no matter how hard he tried never quite succeeded in choking off the love lyric. With his barbarous ways, Prisypkin seems no better than an animal to the citizens of the rationalized world of the future. That world itself is presented in satiric images by the Maiakovskii who is himself part Prisypkin: the world-wide mechanical voting-apparatus; the organized mass dances which are the only kind that survived; the comical search among old books for something on "love"; and the steel, concrete, and glass backdrop against which the man of the future lives—a construction worthy of [avant-garde artist] Tatlin—are hardly offered as a happy prospect.

Maiakovskii in this play is caught in a dilemma that is both historical and personal: he abhors the philistine individualism of Prisypkin and the tawdry values that survive in him, but he does not really believe either in the hardening scientific utopia that threatens to crush Prisypkin—and Maiakovskii. The future world he shows is something like the Single State of Zamiatin's *We*, where human beings are simply numbers, each one specialized for a certain job, and where love "has long since been forgotten." In that state there could be no surprises and no unforeseen events; similarly in Maiakovskii's future: "External events are rare ...," though "Our years are full of deep experiences and disturbances of an internal nature." That statement might have been made of Zamiatin's D-503, who, though he lives in a perfectly organized state, suddenly experiences inward conflicts due to the re-assertion of his individual self. Indeed it is most likely that Maiakovskii when he wrote the second part of *The Bedbug* was responding in his own way to *We* (1921), and even engaging Zamiatin in dispute over the importance of values that, both thought, would probably disappear in a fully rational world. Ostensibly, Maiakovskii despised Prisypkin's "heart strings," his individualism, and his dirty indulgence in cigarettes and vodka. For Zamiatin in *We* those very things are symbols of rebellion against social regimentation. But Maiakovskii throws a perverse doubt on his own argument by making his prehistoric bourgeois animal into a pathetic creature imprisoned in a world he never made and can't understand. Into a play that was planned as a simple propaganda exercise Maiakovskii, characteristically, injected a moment of his own pain, and a muffled cry for help.

Flawed though it is as a play and uncertain in its final effect, *The Bedbug* is nevertheless a valid record of human experience. *The Bathhouse*, on the other hand, is derivative in its plot, deficient in action, devoid of dramatic suspense or interest, and, what is worst of all, Maiakovskii himself is not present in it. The play is stiff and schematic, without feeling or conviction, and even as spectacle it is uninteresting. *The Bathhouse*, like *The Bedbug*, was cut to a propaganda pattern. It is simply and pointedly directed against the Stalinist bureaucracy that was taking form at the time...

....

Perhaps part of the reason for Maiakovskii's failure as a dramatist [in the *Bathhouse*]—and there is now no question that he did fail—was that the lyricist Maiakovskii could not refrain from injecting himself and his own personal concerns into the plays, thereby abandoning disciplined development of character and conflict. The central, even at times the sole, character in those plays, is Maiakovskii himself and the cast of characters is at least partly illusory. We recall that his earliest play, *Vladimir Maiakovskii, A Tragedy*, features the poet himself as author, director, and hero, and the other characters, the mutilated men, the women with tears, and so forth, are fragments of Maiakovskii himself. The characters in *Mystery-Bouffe* are conventional puppets whom Maiakovskii manipulates, and though it may have been successful as spectacle, it had little dramatic quality. *The Bedbug* ends on a note of emotional confusion when Prisypkin, suddenly and without any preparation, speaks for Maiakovskii. *The Bathhouse* was a puppet-show rather than a play.

....

In spite of the occasional flashes of genius that are in it, *The Bathhouse* is now quite dead, and probably could not be revived.

SELECTED NOTES
[1] Ivan Molchanov, a young proletarian poet, wrote a poem ("Rendezvous") in which he bids farewell to his buxom and plainly dressed working-class girl friend, preferring a more "delicate" and "rich" girlfriend to her.

BROTHERS, LET'S GLORIFY THE TWILIGHT OF FREEDOM

by Osip MANDEL'SHTAM*

Brothers, let's glorify the twilight of freedom,
The great crepuscular year.
A heavy forest of nets has been dropped
Into the seething waters of the night.
You are rising during gloomy years,
O sun and judge, O people.

Let's glorify the destined burden
Which the people's leader tearfully assumes.
Let's glorify the somber burden of power,
Its unbearable yoke.
He who has a heart, O time,
Must hear your ship sinking to the depths.

We have bound swallows
Into fighting legions, and now
We cannot see the sun; this entire element
Is chirping, stirring, living;
Through the mesh, the thick twilight,
We cannot see the sun and the land floats away.

Well then, let's try: an enormous, clumsy,
Creaking turn of the rudder.
The land floats away. Courage, men.
Cleaving the ocean as with a plow,
We shall remember even in Lethe's cold
That Earth cost us as much as ten heavens.

May 1918, Moscow

* Osip Mandel'stamm

** 1891-1938. Printed in *Modern Russian Poetry: An Anthology with verse translations.* Edited and with an Introduction by Vladimir Markov and Merrill Sparks. Macgibbon & Kee, Printed in Great Britain, 1966 P. 297.

A Dogged Sense of Smell

by Mikhail ZOSHCHENKO*

* From *The Galosh and Other Stories*. Translated from the Russian with an introduction by Jeremy Hicks. New York: Overlook Press, 2006. Pp. 95-97.

Comrades, you know they can do amazing things with science these days, incredible! A dog for example. Take a simple dog: four legs, a tail, ears and so on. They can even get a simple dog to grab a criminal by the trousers and unmask him there and then.

I used to take a skeptical attitude towards the abilities of dogs. But not now, now I fear and respect dogs. There really is something amazing about a dog's sense of smell. Or maybe that wasn't it after all. Anyway, this is what happened.

The merchant Eremei Babkin had his coonskin-coat swiped.

The merchant Eremei Babkin started howling. It broke his heart to lose that coat.

"That coat," he said, "was so good it hurts me to lose it, citizens. It's a crying shame. I'll spare no expense to find the criminal. Then I'll spit in his face."

And so Eremei Babkin called for the militia sniffer-dog. This man in a peaked cap and puttees [leggings] appeared, and with him this dog. A brown dog with a sharp snout and it didn't look too friendly.

This man pushed his dog towards the footprints near the door, said *tsst* and stood back. The dog sniffed the air, eyed the crowd (some people had gathered of course) and suddenly went up to Old

Fekla, a woman from number five, and started sniffing her skirt. The woman tried to hide in the crowd. The dog took hold of her hem. The old woman moved away—and the dog went after her. It clamped onto the old woman by the skirt and wouldn't let go.

The old woman fell to her knees before the officer.

"Yes, she said, 'you've caught me. There's no denying it," she said. "The five buckets of yeast—it's true. And a vodka-still—it's all true. Everything's in the bathroom," she said. "Take me to the militia."

Well, of course the crowd all went "ooh!" and "ah!"

"What about the coat?" they asked.

"I don't know anything about the coat," she said, "and I don't care, but the rest is just as I said. Take me away and punish me."

So they led the old woman away.

The officer took hold of his dog again and rubbed its nose in the footprints, said *tsst* and stood back.

The dog looked up, sniffed the empty air and suddenly went up to Citizen Chairman of the House Committee.

The Chairman of the House Committee went white as a sheet and fell flat on his back.

"Kind people, class-conscious citizens!" he said. "Tie me up. I," he said, "collected money for the water, but I spent that money on myself."

Well, need I say, the tenants jumped upon the Chairman of the House Committee and started to tie him up. Meanwhile the dog went up to a citizen from number seven. It started tugging at his trousers.

The citizen turned pale and fell to the ground before the people.

"I'm guilty," he said, "I'm guilty. It's true," he said, "I wiped a year off my work-record. A young stallion like me ought to be serving in the army, defending the Motherland, but I'm living in number seven and benefiting from electricity and other communal services. Grab me!"

People didn't know what to do.

"Just what," they thought, "is this amazing dog?"

So the merchant Eremei Babkin blinked his eyes, looked around him, took out some money and gave it to the militiaman.

"Take your mangy dog," he said, "back to its pig-sty of a kennel. Let's forget about the coonskin-coat," he said. "It's gone. Ah well, never mind ..."

But the dog was already onto him. It was standing in front of the merchant with its tail twitching.

The merchant Eremei Babkin didn't know what to do, he moved away and the dog followed. It came up to him and sniffed his galoshes.

The merchant started babbling and turned pale.

"Well," he said, "if that's the way it is then God sees the truth. I," he said, "am a son of a bitch and a swindler. And that coat," he said, "comrades, it wasn't mine. I borrowed it off my brother and didn't give it back. I could weep for shame!"

People fled whereever they could. The dog didn't even have time to sniff the air, it just grabbed two or three people at random and held onto them.

They confessed. One had lost state funds at cards, the other had taken a swipe at his wife with an iron, what the third admitted is too embarrassing even to mention.

People ran off in all directions. The yard emptied. There was only the dog and the militiaman left.

And then suddenly the dog went up to the militiaman with its tail wagging.

The militiaman turned pale, and fell before the dog.

"Bite me," he said, "citizen dog. I," he said, "receive three ten-ruble notes for your dog food and take two for myself ..."

What happened next I'm not sure. I locked myself in my room. The dog didn't grab me by the leg. It probably didn't quite manage to. And what would I have done if it had? I would have fallen on my knees before the crowd:

"Comrades," I would have said, "I am the worst criminal of all: though I didn't touch the fur-coat, I take advances from magazines, publish the same story twice, and all the rest of it. Beat me, wretch that I am."

1924

Nervous People

by Mikhail ZOSHCHENKO*

* From *The Galosh and Other Stories*. Translated from the Russian with an introduction by Jeremy Hicks. New York: Overlook Press, 2006. Pp. 95-97.

The other day there was a fight in our communal apartment. Not so much a fight as a full-scale battle. On the corner of Glazovaia and Borovaia.

Of course, they were really putting everything into the fight. Gavrilov, the invalid, nearly got his head—all he had left—chopped off.

The main reason for it all is that people are very nervous. They get upset about minor trivialities. Tempers flare. And that makes them lash out like blind things.

Of course, they say that nerves are always shaken after a civil war. Maybe that's true, but all the same, this ideology won't make the invalid Gavrilov's head heal up any sooner.

So one of the tenants, Mar'ia Vasil'evna Shchiptsova, went into the kitchen at nine o'clock in the evening, and lit the primus. She always, you see, lights the primus around this time. She drinks tea and applies a compress.

So she went into the kitchen. Stood the primus in front of her and lit it. But it wouldn't light, the stupid damned thing.

She thought:

"Why the hell's it not lighting? The stupid damned thing's not gone and got clogged up with soot has it?"

So she took a scourer in her left hand and was about to clean it.

She was about to clean it and took the scourer in her left hand, but another tenant, Daria Petrovna Kobylina, whose scourer it was, saw what had been taken and answered:

"By the way, most esteemed Mar'ia Vasil'evna, would you mind putting that scourer back."

Shchiptsova, of course, lost her temper at these words and answered:

"There you are Daria Petrovna, go and choke on your scourer. I can't even bear to touch it," she said, "let alone pick it up."

So then of course, Daria Petrovna Kobylina lost her temper at these words. They started conversing. Then the noise started: crashing and banging.

The husband, Ivan Stepanych Kobylin, whose scourer it was, appeared on hearing all this noise. A healthy sort of man, even got a big paunch, but he too suffers from nerves.

So Ivan Stepanych appeared and said:

"I," he said, "work like an elephant for thirty-two rubles and a few kopecks in a cooperative, I smile to the customers," he said, "and weigh out their sausage for them, and out of this," he said, "with my hard-earned kopecks, I buy myself scourers, and there's no way I'm going to allow some passing personnel I hardly know to make use of these scourers."

Then noise and discussions started up again on the subject of the scourer. So of course all the tenants came barging into the kitchen. Making a fuss. Even the invalid Gavrilov appeared.

"What's all the noise for," they said, "and where's the fight?"

Then straight after these words the fight was realized. It started.

But our kitchen's narrow, you see. Not suited to fighting. No room. Saucepans and primuses all over the place. Not even space to turn round. And now there were twelve people who'd shoved their way in. You want to smash some bastard in the face, say, and get three instead. And of course you bump into everything and fall over. An invalid with no legs hasn't a chance, even with three legs you haven't a hope in hell of staying standing.

But this invalid, the bloody dodderer, despite this pushed his way right into the thick of it. Ivan Stepanych, whose scourer it was, shouted at him:

"Get out of the way, Gavrilov. Look out or your other leg will get torn off."

Gavrilov said:

"Then my leg's had it," he said. "But I can't get out now. My facial ambition's been beaten to a pulp," he said.

And that moment someone really did give him one in the mouth. So he didn't get out, but kept on throwing himself about. Then someone hit the invalid across the skull with a saucepan.

The invalid just flopped onto the floor and lay there. Looking depressed.

Then some parasite ran off to get the militia.

The copper appeared. He shouted:

"Get the coffins ready you bastards, I'm going to shoot!"

Only after these fateful words did people come to a bit. They ran off to their rooms.

"Well, that's a strange thing," they thought, "however did we get into a fight, esteemed comrades?"

People ran off to their rooms, only Gavrilov the invalid didn't run off. He just lay there, looking depressed. And blood was trickling from his crown.

Two weeks after this incident the trial took place.

The People's Judge was a nervous sort of man too: he booked everyone.

1925

BROOKLYN BRIDGE

by Vladimir MAIAKOVSKII*

Hey, Coolidge boy,
make a shout of joy!
When a thing is good
            then it's good.
Blush from compliments
            like our flag's calico,
even though you're
            the most super-united states
                        of
America.
Like the crazy nut
            who goes
                        to his church
or retreats
            to a monastery
                        simple and rigid—
So I
   in the gray haze
            of evening
humbly
      approach
            the Brooklyn Bridge.
Like a conqueror
            on cannons with muzzles
                        as high as a giraffe
jabbing into a broken
            city besieged,

---

* *Vladimir Mayakovsky*

** 1893-1930. Printed in *Modern Russian Poetry: An Anthology with verse translations.* Edited and with an Introduction by Vladimir Markov and Merrill Sparks. Macgibbon & Kee, Printed in Great Britain, 1966. P. 297.

so, drunk with glory,
              alive to the hilt,
I clamber
       proudly
              upon Brooklyn Bridge.
Like a stupid painter
                 whose enamored eyes pierce
a museum Madonna
            like a wedge.
So from this sky,
            sowed into the stars,
I look at New York
              through Brooklyn Bridge.
New York,
       heavy and stifling
                 till night,
has forgotten
         what makes it dizzy
                and a hindrance,
and only
        the souls of houses
rise in the transparent
             sheen of windows.
Here the itching hum
         of the 'el'
             is hardly heard,
and only by this
        hum,
            soft but stubborn,
can you feel the trains
            crawl
                with a rattle
as when dishes
          are jammed into a cupboard.
And when from
          below the started river
a merchant
        transports sugar
               from the factory bins—

then
    the masts passing under the bridge
are no bigger
        in size
            than pins.
I'm proud
   of this
      mile of steel.
In it my visions
         are alive and real—
a fight
   for structure
       instead of arty "style",
the harsh calculation
       of bolts
          and steel.
If the end
      of the world
          comes—
and chaos
      wipes out
          this earth
and if only this
       bridge
         remains
rearing over the dust of death,
then
   as little bones,
         thinner than needles,
clad with flesh,
      standing in museums,
           are dinosaurs,—
so from this
     bridge
       future geologists
will be able
      to reconstruct
         our present course.

They will say:
>   —this
>   paw of steel
joined seas,
>   prairies and deserts,
from here,
>   Europe
>   rushed to the West,
scattering
>   to the wind
>   Indian feathers.
This rib here
>   reminds us
>   of a machine—
imagine,
>   enough hands, enough grip
while standing,
>   with one steel leg
>   in Manhattan
to drag
>   toward yourself
>   Brooklyn by the lip!
By the wires
>   of electric yarn
I know this
>   is
>   the Post-Steam Era.
Here people
>   already
>   yelled on the radio,
here people
>   already
>   flew by air.
For some
>   here was life
>   carefree,
>   unalloyed.
For others
>   a prolonged
>   howl of hunger.

From here
          the unemployed
jumped headfirst
               into
                      the Hudson.
And finally
          with clinging stars
                      along the strings of cables
my dream comes back
          without any trouble
and I see—
        here
        stood Maiakovskii,
here he stood
        putting
              syllable to syllable.
I look,
    as an Eskimo looks at a train,
I dig into you,
        like a tick into an ear.
Brooklyn Bridge.
Yes,
    you've got something here.

1925

Section Three

The Stalinist Period and World War II

- Introduction
- Memoirs
- Cultural Contexts
- Socialist Realism
- War Diary
- Vignettes

Introduction

> *The 1930s was a decade of enormous privation and hardship for the Soviet people, much worse than the 1920s.*
> —Sheila Fitzpatrick

> *We create kulaks as we see fit.*
> —Soviet Village Chairman in 1930, as quoted by Robert Conquest

> *We will lead humanity to happiness with an iron fist.*
> —Political slogan

What made the 1930s a tougher decade than the 1920s? There were many factors that made it so. The privations of daily life increased for large sectors of the population in both the cities and rural areas. NEP had brought some goods to at least some sectors of society: not least, the peasant population benefited from the (limited) market economy that allowed them to sell their surplus grain once more. In 1927, Stalin eliminated NEP, however, focusing on his utopian and inhumane **collectivization** and **forced industrialization** programs, which resulted in a catastrophic dearth of essential goods, such as bread and clothing. Living space in the cities grew ever scarcer because of the rural population's flight to the cities, leading to a desperate situation for many. In Bulgakov's novel *The Master and Margarita*, Satan pays a visit to Moscow to have a look at the changes that, he has heard, have taken place there, and at the "new" Soviet people living there now. During his visit, he arrives at the conclusion that the Muscovites have actually not changed much, and that they are very much like they used to be and like people are almost everywhere else. There is, however, one issue that he feels has impacted them negatively: the "living space problem." Many were prepared to do literally *anything*, including writing denunciations with fatal consequences for the denounced, in order to escape living, for example, in one room together with not only wife and children, but also her, or his own, parents and perhaps some grandparents as well. Quite often divorced couples had to go on living together, as well as with members of the divorced spouse's family, since there was no other living space available. Having a spacious flat and/or *dacha* was the most coveted privileges Soviet society could offer. Those who were considered "of value to the country," coveted perhaps three more rooms in addition to their allotted five—the range of socially conditioned desire was broad, but certainly desperate in overcrowded communal apartments.

In the countryside, collectivization took a heavy toll on living standards and lives themselves, as the campaign for "liquidating the *kulaks* as a class" went ahead. According to some historians, there were in fact no "real" kulaks to be found in the countryside anymore, i.e., there were no wealthy peasants "exploiting" destitute hired labor. They had been eliminated by 1918. There were, at best, peasants who had recovered to a certain extent after the ruthless requisitions of war communism and who now owned perhaps two cows and hired some labor help occasionally, e.g. at harvest time. In the years 1930-1931, millions of such "kulaks" nevertheless were deported from their homes, exiled to distant regions (such as Siberia) where nothing in the way of housing or nourishment was available to them, and sent to the labor camps of the **GULAG** (acronym for *Chief Administration of Corrective Labor Camps and Colonies*), as well as executed on the slightest pretexts. Total general chaos reigned as the last remnants of private property—the right to own some land and cattle—were abolished with terror methods. To take land from the gentry and give it to the peasantry had been one of the main goals of the Revolution in the early days, but this was clearly the case no longer as expropriation reached the peasantry itself.

As a result of agriculture becoming more like industry, famines broke out all over the Soviet Union, with the most terrible one taking place in Ukraine in the early thirties. It can be qualified as the most terrible both in terms of the millions of lives it took and also because it was a man-made, engineered, and willed catastrophe. The purpose of creating and maintaining this famine was to break the strong Ukrainian resistance to collectivization, especially since this resistance was linked to Ukrainian aspirations for greater national independence in general. Stalin could not allow a showdown between individually-run agriculture and collectivized agriculture—the former undoubtedly would prove much more successful, particularly in view of the overall better soil quality Ukraine could boast. Nor could Stalin allow a "happy fraternal nation" to prefer its own vision of how to run itself to the one he had staked out for its people and all other peoples of the Union. His path was the best and only one. In all, the death toll of executions, deportations, hard labor in the camps, and the "terror-famine" was somewhere around 14 to 15 million people.

The number of lives which the "peaceful" 1930s took was larger than the number killed during the Civil War decade of the 1920s, and there were some terrible famines in the 1920s, too. This increase in the number of lost lives was caused by this difference: in the 1920s, the famines were acknowledged and help, even from abroad, was allowed to reach the stricken but in the 1930s Stalin's government denied that any famines existed. Also, **dekulakization** was presented as a highly beneficial measure for the peasantry and entire country in spite of its egregious cruelty and obvious failure to bring about rural abundance. **Forced collectivization**, it was claimed, brought not only prosperity and technology (such as tractors) to the countryside, but "culture" as well. Literacy did in fact increase widely in that decade.

In 1936 Stalin presented his **Constitution**, a very democratic and humane one. It was greeted with enthusiasm and relief, since most people did not understand that it was a constitution on paper only. Duped by its humaneness, many hoped that terror was finally done and over with. The "terror-famines," after a brief respite, were followed by "terror-purges," however. Known as **The Great Terror**, the purges reached their peak in 1937-1938. The unpredictable or perhaps cleverly calculating Stalin this

Introduction

time focused not only on "liquidating class enemies." Instead, he set about destroying military, administrative, and intellectual communist elites, very possibly in order to have scapegoats to put the blame on for failures and "excesses" in the collectivization and industrialization processes. Another reason for their persecution—apart from psycho-pathological factors—that is often brought forward is that these elites were made up of the old Leninist guard, and that Stalin wished to "purge" the Party of them. Establishing his own cadres, with no memories of the past, he would surround himself with people who were absolutely loyal to him. Perhaps it was the inner logic of the system itself that made the "revolution eat its own children." One astonishing aspect of the Terror is that virtually no one refused complicity, i.e., refused to denounce others and themselves. Of course, torture, false promises and threats to "liquidate" spouses and children were part of the interrogation methods.

The pretext for the purges was the December 1934 murder, quite possibly staged by Stalin himself, of the head of the Leningrad Party Organization, Sergei **Kirov,** who some at the time were suggesting should replace Stalin. Thus "prophylactics,"—i.e., getting rid of potential future rivals and their backers—were also a likely motivation for the purges. The planning of this assassination (the actual deed was done by a certain Leonid **Nikolaev**) was attributed to the former oppositionists and friends of Lenin Grigorii **Zinov'ev,** Lev **Kamenev**, Nikolai **Bukharin,** and above all the "satanic mastermind" Lev **Trotskii.** The period of the great **show trials** began, during which all the accused (except for Trotskii, who had been expelled from the country and was not available) confessed not only to being behind the Kirov murder, but also to being involved with a long string of fantastic plots aimed at wrecking and destroying the entire Soviet Union with the help of various categories of evil traitors, collaborating with foreigners—alleged fascists, foreign agents and spies. They, and thousands more from other "undesirable categories" of the population, were executed. Initially **NKVD** boss Genrikh **Iagoda** was in charge of the terror, but he too was executed by his successor Nikolai **Ezhov.** Ezhov, in his turn, was executed in 1940 by his successor Lavrentii **Beria**—

who would himself be executed after Stalin's death. After Ezhov's rule of terror, and the total elimination of the old Party cadres, a short period of calm set in. Stalin even had time to assassinate Trotskii.

Cultural Developments

In August 1934 (a few months before the Kirov assassination), the First Congress of the **Union of Soviet Writers** met under the leadership of Maksim **Gor'kii** to lay down the rules for the new aesthetic program that all the arts from then on would have to adhere to: **Socialist Realism**. As the term makes plain, Realism was revived after the avant-garde experiments of the Silver Age and the 1920s, but it was not the Realism of the previous century. The qualification "socialist" implied that the depiction of reality should be optimistic and foster complete trust in the Party, its leaders and its policies. It should also show the indescribably glorious future already illuminating the wonderful present. Although obligatory for all who did not want to write for "the drawer," become an "inner émigré," or risk execution, it was greeted (like the Stalin Constitution later) with relief and hope. Many fellow travelers and even fervent communists (with an avant-garde past) had in the late 1920s been hounded by **RAPP** (the *Russian Association of Proletarian Writers*) and other literary vigilante organizations, and were now hoping for more creative freedom. In fact, many of the relentless "hounders" were now in their turn demoted and even executed, such as, for example, their leader Leopold **Averbakh**. Joyful relief soon dwindled, however, as a campaign against "formalism," i.e. any avant-garde experimentation, was launched in 1936. Its most famous victims were world-renowned composers Sergei **Prokof'ev** and Dmitrii **Shostakovich**, who were told their art was "muddled" and unsuited for the popular masses. Their lives were spared, but others fell victim to the campaign. Thus prose writer Leonid **Dobychin**, knowing he was "targeted," committed suicide. Still others, tainted by the fact that they either had been "formalists," or still were trying to present avant-garde art, were made to feel the "ultimate consequence" of not serving the People well enough. Prose writer Boris **Pil'niak,** for example, was accused of Trotskyism and espionage and was executed, as was Isaak **Babel'** on similar charges. Theater director Vsevolod **Meierkhol'd** was yet another great artist accused of absurd crimes and shot. His wife, the famous actress Zinaida **Raikh**, was stabbed to death by "bandits" when she protested her husband's arrest. Almost the entire group of surrealist-absurdist poets which called itself "The **Oberiuts**" died an unnatural death—their leader Daniil **Kharms,** for example, died of hunger in prison, and Nikolai **Oleinikov,** a former member of the group, was shot, whereas Nikolai **Zabolotskii** "got away" with arrest, torture, and eight years of hard labor and exile in Siberia, but at least could return to his family and home in 1946. Just as the last remnants of private property were liquidated in the dekulakization campaign, and the Leninist old guard was eliminated, so the last representatives of the "alien" avant-garde were done away with. Also eliminated were loyal literary critics, historians, and journalists, as were patriotic generals, devoted party officials, and members of Stalin's inner circle and family.

Nevertheless, many were hoping for a restoration of law and order and peaceful times in the later 1930s. Some were encouraged in their hopes by the fact that so many communists were "removed" in the purges, assuming that this would mean a return to normality. They rejoiced when NKVD leaders like Iagoda and Ezhov were executed, believing Stalin was distancing himself from their reign of terror. They rejoiced when the "traitors" Nikolai **Bukharin** and Komintern secretary Karl **Radek,** to mention but two victims, were shot, hoping that soon all evil enemies of the Soviet Union would be exterminated. They also found comfort in the fact that Stalin took on ever more strongly the paternal role of "Red Tsar," reintroducing, for example, pre-revolutionary markers of military rank. The new uniforms, too, looked remarkably like tsarist ones. Stalin's historical role model was Tsar Ivan "the Terrible," or more correctly translated, "the Awe-Inspiring One" (*Groznyi*). The famous film director Sergei **Eisenstein**'s *Ivan the Terrible* (Part I, 1944) was conceived if not as a eulogy to, then as a justification of, both the titular tsar and Stalin. It did win the Stalin Prize, but the experimental and politically incorrect sequel (*Ivan the Terrible*, Part II) was not shown. In 2009, France-based Pavel **Lungin** made another film on Tsar Ivan which clearly alludes to Stalin, titled *Tsar*. It presents a very different perception of Ivan and Stalin from the one Eisenstein had to project.

To return to the optimism that permeated many aspects of Soviet life in the 1930s, for some "comrades" the quality of life had indeed improved in many ways—it was "more joyous" (*veselee*) for the new "upper classes." In diurnal reality there was a great deal to be proud of and enjoy under the rule of the "just red Tsar," implacable with his enemies but good to his people, who was building up the country's international importance and freeing it from traitors and wreckers. There were athletes' parades, military parades, international successes in aviation, heroic labor performances (including the **Stakhanovite** workers' movement); there were even Hollywood-style musicals in the movies, such as "Happy-Go-Lucky Guys" (*Veselye rebiata*) or "Circus" (*Tsirk*). Ethnic relations in the heterogeneous Union were fraternal, at least on the surface. All non-Russian groups were content to be the "younger brothers" of the first nation to realize the Revolution, Russia, and to be guided by her wisdom and experience. In other words, any strivings for cultural autonomy were strongly discouraged and political autonomy was unthinkable. Daylight reality was bright. Nocturnal reality was invisible. Arrests were made at night, executions were performed in cellars, cars transporting victims were disguised as "Bread Delivery," or "Meat Products." This perhaps was the most characteristic feature of the 1930s—the stark division of life into an optimistic daylight-reality in which one "triumph" after another was celebrated and a nocturnal reality of atrocities and tragedies. As Berthold Brecht said (in another context): "Some live in the shadow./ Others live in the lime-light. / Those in the light you can see easily,/ The ones in the darkness you can't see." It also helped to close one's eyes, or to see very selectively. The ideology of the times emphasized that one should focus on the grand perspectives and not pay attention to "details," or the "small errors" which inevitably had to occur. You can't make an omelet without breaking eggs, as the saying goes.

Introduction

The War and the 1940s

> *All that had been false demagoguery and fake artifice in the prewar period now acquired authenticity.*
> —Efim Etkind

Many of those executed in the Great Purges had been accused of running the errands of fascist powers. It therefore came as something of a surprise to the general public that in 1939 Nazi Germany and Soviet Russia signed a non-aggression pact and pledged neutrality in the case that either of the two would become engaged in war. The "deal" behind the pact was to divide Europe into spheres of interest. Thus the Soviet Union (increasingly striving to become like and outdo the old tsarist empire under the leadership of the **Red Tsar**) retook the Baltic States, a part of eastern Finland (after a war with that country that proved hard for the Soviets to win), and parts of eastern Poland. Germany acquired western Poland and counted on adding many further territories in western Europe and the Balkans to its already considerable winnings. Nevertheless, in 1941, without warning, Nazi Germany attacked the Soviet Union, desiring its spacious location and resources and planning to settle Germans there. The German nation, it was claimed, was in need of *Lebensraum* (space to live). Some historians believe that Stalin was surprised by the moment of attack, but not by the attack itself. He had hardly envisioned that the pact of the two rivals competing for world hegemony would be a lasting one. Initially, the war was disastrous for the Soviet Union. The destruction wreaked by the victorious German army and its surprise tactics (*Blitzkrieg*) was immense, and its ruthless extermination of the civilian Slavic and Jewish populations, considered racially inferior to the Germans, was inhuman—and, eventually, counter-productive, inspiring fierce resistance. After the decisive battle of **Stalingrad** (now **Volgograd**) in 1943, fortunes turned, and the Soviet Union emerged in 1945 as the great victor of WWII, extending its territorial gains and spheres of influence to the middle of Europe. The taking of

Berlin marked a peak in the demonstration of "invincible" Soviet might.

WWII brought unspeakable suffering and devastation to the country, but there is a consensus at least in the Russian intelligentsia circles that it was also a time of spiritual liberation. National solidarity triumphed over class tensions in the face of ruthless aggression and an ideology based on racist theories that included the "inferiority" of the Slavs. It was, however, disconcerting that even during the war there was a strong tendency not to "acknowledge the contributions made to the war effort by Jews, Uzbeks, Azeris, Tadzhiks, and other minorities," but to promote a Russo-centric "national Bolshevism," even though "anti-Semitism and belittling of the non-Russian peoples did not explicitly figure into the party's agenda between 1941 and 1945" (Brandenberger). The open "belittling" would come later. The Russian majority profited from the ideological relaxation, however. Thus being an Orthodox believer was no longer frowned upon, the concept of the Beloved Mother-Land was reintroduced, and old-fashioned patriotism was rehabilitated. Gone were the theatrical show trials, the fantastical heinous crimes allegedly committed by people who had "faked" their devotion to socialism for decades, the groundless hatred of the "kulak-peasantry" that was fanned in order to pit the destitute against the somewhat better off—all of these disappeared like bad dreams. In the *Epilogue* to Pasternak's *Doctor Zhivago*, the protagonist's two friends—one back from camp, the other back from war—agree that "compared to everything in the thirties … the war came as a breath of fresh air." The reality of war, the massacre of civilians, war atrocities, and huge material losses were "real" issues to cope with, as opposed to the political "aburdist theater" of Stalin's invention. Facing this reality, religious, ideological, ethnic, and class enmities were forgotten, at least within the nation that was the "first among equals," Russia. Even the émigrés were largely happy for Soviet victories. There was a hope shared by very many that finally the tribulations of founding the first socialist-communist state in the world would soon be over, that victory would restore normality, and that national harmony, at least within the **RSFSR** (Russian Soviet Federative Socialist Republic], would continue. Zhivago's aforementioned friends from the novel *Doctor Zhivago*, speaking of the future, also express the hope that the non-socialist-realist poetry of their dead friend, Zhivago, would again be published and appreciated.

Unfortunately, these hopes were not fulfilled. Both politically and culturally Stalinism returned with full force after 1945, together with an "unabashed sense of Russian exceptionalism" (Brandenberger) and its corollary, the campaign against "cosmopolitans" (read: Jews). With Stalin's full approval, Andrei **Zhdanov**, who had been active in the First Congress of Soviet Writers and who had replaced the murdered Kirov in Leningrad and participated in the Great Terror before becoming the ideologue of post-war Soviet culture, was making sure no offenses were committed against the principles of Socialist Realism. He "improved" on its doctrines by stating that in the "all-good" Soviet Union only the struggle between "good and better" could be depicted in the arts. The struggle between "bad and worse" was left to the evil West, with which **Cold War** relations soon replaced the international friendship forged during the war with Nazi Germany. Zhdanov was the logical choice to lead the new witch-hunts in this culture of slander and persecution, and he became a master of the genre of denunciations. Especially well known are his crude attacks on Anna **Akhmatova** and Mikhail **Zoshchenko**. In the political sphere, Lavrentii **Beria**, who replaced Ezhov as Chief of the NKVD (*The People's Commissariat for Internal Affairs*), reintroduced terror and used the GULAG prison population in gigantic projects of the type started in the early 1930s with the **Belomor** (White Sea) Canal construction. Slave labor continued to be part of the economic system. Specifically, Beria used the GULAG prisoners for the extraction of uranium as the Soviet Union began building its own atom bomb. During the war, Beria had been responsible for the massacre of 22,000 Polish officers and members of the intelligentsia in the **Katyn** forest near Smolensk. (This massacre was blamed on the Germans for a long time, but eventually the truth became known.) He was likewise responsible for the deportations of whole nationalities, such as the Crimean Tatars, Chechens, Volga Germans, and other minorities suspected of seeking collaboration with the German invaders.

Although Stalin was wary of him, during the aging Leader's last years Beria was entrusted with his last big project, the prelude to which was the so-called **Doctors' Plot.** Jewish doctors were accused of willfully poisoning high-ranking leaders of the Soviet Union, and some doctors were executed, others deported, and the fortunate ones merely dismissed from their jobs. Show trials were planned and mass deportations of Jews were to take place—to a special **Jewish Autonomous Region**, in the Far East, the capital of which was to be the town of **Birobidzhan**. It is surmised that the plan was to start a large-scale anti-Semitic campaign in which, following the traditional patterns, hundreds of thousands would be executed and deported. Stalin died in March of 1953, before the plan could be implemented, however, and perhaps it was seen as unfeasible even before he died (or, possibly, was helped to die by the delaying of medical assistance). In early April, a few weeks after Stalin's death, the Doctors' Plot was officially declared a hoax. Beria (from Caucasian **Mingrelia**), who saw himself as Stalin's heir, apparently planned to tone down official Russo-centrism, but he was executed when his bid for power failed. It was Nikita **Khrushchev** who emerged as the victor in the struggle for power and who, at the **Twentieth Party Congress** in 1956, would reveal some of Stalin's crimes and release groundlessly arrested GULAG prisoners. Rapid **de-Stalinization** (the **Thaw**) followed, even though the Leader's death had initially led to shock-waves throughout the entire land—the Soviet Union had become "orphaned," as many mourners and the newspapers put it.

Selected Texts

Section III starts with three arrest stories. The first is written by Iurii **Olesha,** author of the classical Soviet novel *Envy* (*Zavist'*, 1927), who himself escaped arrest, but remembered the arrests of his close friends **Meierkhol'd** and his wife Zinaida **Raich**. In his memoir, *A Book of Farewell* (*Kniga proshchaniia*), he does not record the actual arrest—which he did not witness—but his strange presentiment that it would occur, even at a time when nobody would have predicted such an end to the famous stage director's successful life. **Ivanov-**

Introduction

Razumnik's memoirs of his arrest are unusual in the sense that they report the event in a humorous vein. This sociologist and literary critic, who once befriended **Blok, Belyi, Meierkhol'd**, and many more of the most outstanding artists and poets of the Silver Age, had been close to the Socialist Revolutionaries, and thus had already experienced tsarist prisons prior to his arrests by Soviet authorities. Perhaps it was his sense of humor which enabled him to survive his *Prisons and Deportations,* as the title of his *Memoirs* would be if literally translated. Babel's second wife, Antonina **Pirozhkova** (who eventually would move to the United States), gives an eyewitness account of her husband's arrest. She also relates the authorities' strange desire to hide the actual execution date of her husband from her. Presumably the impression to be taken away from their denials of the fact that their prisoner was long dead was that he had not been executed, but had died of natural causes in the camps many years after his arrest. This camouflage of facts applied to many more cases than Babel's alone, and explains why for a long time in literary histories of the Soviet period death dates for executed writers would vary.

Andrei **Siniavskii**, who was imprisoned and sent to the GULAG in 1966—as one of the last dissidents treated in this way—had published his works abroad (under the pseudonym of Abram **Tertz**). Here, he discusses the specifics of the Stalin, or so-called "Personality," Cult. What was the Leader's secret? How did he manipulate his people? Was it solely through terror? One strategy was perhaps his appeal to Biblical texts. A former student of a theological seminary (in **Tbilisi**, Georgia), was Stalin perhaps posing as the "earthly god" who had superseded the Biblical one? Daniel *Collins*, in his "The Tower of Babel Undone in a Soviet Pentecost," demonstrates how the success of the multi-ethnic and multi-national labor force engaged in the giant construction projects of the times was shown in Soviet novels to be the result of a total reciprocal understanding between all the workers involved. The ability to successfully communicate transcended all linguistic barriers in the fiction of the five-year plans. In the Stalinist travesty of the Pentecost, the "Holy Spirit" was the enthusiasm experienced by all who were "burning" for the Soviet New World, which was building a tower of Babel that *would* reach the "heavens." Even Americans and other foreigners with no inkling of Russian were part of this "Pentecost," if they believed in the cause of Socialism and Stalin's "divinity."

Alexander *Poznansky*'s article on "Tchaikovsky as Communist Icon" illustrates a very common problem encountered by Soviet culture policy makers: what do you do with geniuses whom the Soviet Union wants to claim for its cultural heritage but whose biography "contradicted" its puritanical morality? What was to be done with **Chaikovskii (Tchaikovsky),** for example, whose homosexuality was unacceptable to the Soviets (homosexuality was criminalized from 1933 to 1989). Do you reject him as a representative of a corrupt class and not play his music? Not if his popularity proves to withstand all such attempts and remains in high demand. Instead, the "reprehensible" fact is concealed. "Reprehensible" facts included religiosity, "wrong" social background, committing suicide, being a skirt-chaser or alcoholic, and many, many more. The consequences of such concealments impacted editions of *Collected Letters*, memoirs and biographies. Biographies became hagiography, collections of letters shrank in size because of all the excisions, and memoir writers remembered very little.

The Soviet Union proclaimed full gender equality in theory, but in practice soon reverted to viewing women as best suited for the roles of caregiver and guardian of the domestic hearth—while also being fully employed in the labor force, usually in secondary positions. Being relegated to this kind of "inferior" status (as well as the double load of work) had some advantages, such as being relatively inconspicuous. Women clearly were not repressed to the same extent as men during the various terror campaigns and purges, even though they were far from exempt from harsh punitive measures. As Beth *Holmgren* discusses, this relative safety from repression enabled some widows and relatives of famous men to preserve the artistic heritage of their repressed, deported, and/or executed husbands/fathers/sons, often becoming writers themselves in the process. Anna Akhmatova's cycle of poems *Requiem*, voicing women's experience of the victimization of loved ones—famous, or not—was an important model text in this process of voicing the suffering of the "secondary sex." Holmgren's discussion includes some paradoxical results of official gender equality policies that resulted in secondary status, and of maintaining some traditional gender roles based on inequality that gave women primary status. Certainly in literature Soviet heroines were relegated to the background as the "positive hero" towered over them, whereas traditional heroines in novels such as Bulgakov's *The Master and Margarita* and Pasternak's *Doctor Zhivago* dominate the plot. These "romantic" novels also allow men to redefine official "masculinity."

The GULAG, or the system of labor camps, which Aleksandr **Solzhenitsyn** metaphorized as a cancer, producing ever more "metastases," i.e., ever more camps spread over the vast continent or "sea," emerged directly after Lenin's Red Terror and became a "regular" part of the Soviet state's "labor market" in the 1930s. Leona *Toker*'s "Introduction" to *Return from the Archipelago* tells the history of the infamous prison system and discusses its double function: to provide an endless supply of cheap labor and to eliminate political, religious, and ideological dissidence. Writer Vasilii **Grossman** was not sent to the GULAG, but his WWII novel *Life and Fate* was confiscated and even "arrested" in 1961 (this latter meaning that it was carried off to NKVD's book "depots"). Grossman, whose mother was murdered in her hometown of Berdichev together with twenty thousand fellow Jews by the invading Germans, was a successful war correspondent who wrote about the crucial **Stalingrad battle** (for the *Red Star*) and later also witnessed the fall of **Berlin**. His account of what he saw in Berlin is "strangely" free of hatred, but this circumstance is certainly not based on indifference to the fate of Jews. Together with Russian-Jewish writer Il'ia **Erenburg**, Grossman was trying to compile a *Black Book* of the atrocities of the Holocaust, but met with resistance from the Soviet State, increasingly bent on its anti-cosmopolitan (anti-Jewish) campaigns, as already discussed. The **Jewish Anti-Fascist Committee** involved in the project was dismantled, and one of its members, the actor and director of the **Yiddish Theater** in Moscow, Solomon **Michoels**, was murdered by the NKVD in 1948 in a staged accident. Grossman never saw his novel in print—two manuscript copies were rescued, however, and *Life and Fate* was eventually published in Gorbachev's

glasnost' Russia (in 1988, after its 1980 publication in the West). One reason it could not have been published before in the Soviet Union was "its tacit parallelism between the Nazi and Soviet regimes" (Sacks).

Socialist Realism, as already stated, was the obligatory aesthetics of all Soviet art in all media. The next two items are dedicated to elucidating its principles and goals. Maksim **Gor'kii**, who had become a cult figure as the "progenitor" of this aesthetic doctrine, outlined his vision of what it should accomplish at the 1934 **First Congress of Soviet Writers**. In his view, art originates in labor processes and folklore, the People's art. Folk art expresses the people's aspirations for a better material life and inspires humankind to strive for it—for example, the fairytale motif of the flying carpet inspired the creation of airplanes. Soviet literature should glorify labor as the force moving progress. Doing this, it would become a literature far superior to the decadent and escapist entertainment literature of the West. Katerina *Clark* in her analysis of Socialist Realism presents the taboos and musts that the "method" prescribes, focusing on the general "master plot" that novels were supposed to both follow and create variations of. The outline of this plot focuses on the maturation of an impetuous and enthusiastic young man into a fully "conscious" positive hero, who not only is enthusiastic about the Soviet cause but also knows how to control his inner self, thus becoming ready to pick up the "baton" that the "fathers" of the previous generation are handing over to him. She also discusses the loopholes the method left for new signals, not always the ones that "party-mindedness" (*partiinost'*) demanded. Her article here offers a synthesis of ideas expounded in greater detail in her classic book *The Soviet Novel, History as Ritual*. Boris *Groys* in his much-debated *The Total Art of Stalinism* presents socialist realist art as the inheritor of the Russian avant-garde legacy, which demanded "that art move from representing to transforming the world." Naturally, he does not claim that it continues its formal-aesthetic quests, but it does continue the avant-garde's aspiration for aesthetic control over all spheres of life, not least political life and everyday life (*byt*), its intolerance of competing aesthetics, and its project to "transform" human nature and the world it inhabits. The section chosen here demonstrates that the "realism" of socialist realism hardly qualifies as such, since it is not mimetic realism [which was decried as "naturalism"], but the detailed, pseudo-realistic depiction of a "reality" created by Stalin's and Stalinists' "dreaming" about reality—what it would be when totally in line with their vision of what reality should be. In case someone wonders why Groys speaks of socialist realist paintings being hidden away in cellars in the last paragraph of the excerpt, this comment refers to the fact that, at the peak of **perestroika** (in the late 1980s, when his book was conceived), socialist realist art was being removed from displays by perestroika enthusiasts and hidden away by the "faithful," apparently in the hope they would some day be "totally displayable" again.

The **Vignettes** begin with the poem that very much contributed to Osip Mandel'shtam's arrest—it may not belong to his greatest works, but it testifies to his moral courage, later to be repeated by his widow Nadezhda **Mandel'shtam** in her writing and publishing of her "blunt" memoirs. Georgii **Ivanov** is an outstanding émigré poet of the Parisian emigration who—somewhat like Vladimir **Nabokov** (with whom he did not get along)—found his theme and voice in writing "nihilistically" about the loss of his cultural heritage and homeland. Marina **Tsvetaeva** is another émigré poet who was not impressed by Soviet "achievements" and knew she was a stranger everywhere, abroad and in her new Soviet homeland. Nevertheless, she could not "wipe out" the memories of Russia, at least not Russian nature, here represented by the rowan tree with its glowing red berries with which she feels a "kinship" (as she states in other poems). Her return to the Soviet Union would end in suicide—her husband, who had become a Soviet agent in France, had returned before her—he would soon be executed. Nabokov undoubtedly was happy about the Soviet victory in WWII, but this fact did not sway him in his negative evaluation of everything the Soviet Union stood for, as he states in his poem about the "Soviet tinsel." Of course, Nabokov is better known as a prose writer than as a poet, not least for his American novels, especially *Lolita*. Vasilii **Lebedev-Kumach** and Mikhail **Isakovskii** represent the kind of Soviet poetry that glorified "achievements that had not been achieved" and exalted the image of the Infallible Leader. As Efim

Etkind, a third-wave dissident Russian scholar, points out, however (see the epigraph above), Lebedev-Kumach's song of the Beloved Motherland acquired "authenticity" during the war. Even the lines about Soviet Russia being the freest country in the world rang truer than before. It came closer to being believed as the country fought desperately for its liberation from German subjugation. And there was the hope that it would also liberate itself after the victory. These hopes were not realized, as already discussed.

Introduction

SUGGESTED FURTHER READINGS

Brandenberger, David. *National Bolshevism: Stalinist Mass Culture and the Formation of Modern Russian National Identity, 1931-1956*. Cambridge: Harvard University Press, 2002.

Brown, Edward J. *The Proletarian Episode in Russian Literature, 1928-1932*. New York: Columbia University Press, 1953.

Clark, Katerina. *The Soviet Novel: History as Ritual*. Bloomington: Indiana University Press, 2000.

Conquest, Robert. *The Harvest of Sorrow, Soviet Collectivization and the Terror-Famine*. Oxford: Oxford University Press, 1986.

———. *The Great Terror: A Reassessment*. Oxford: Oxford University Press, 1990.

Dobrenko, Evgeny. *The Making of the State Reader: Social and Aesthetic Contexts of the Reception of Soviet Literature*. Translated by Jesse M. Savage. Stanford: Stanford University Press, 1997.

Engel, Barbara Alpern. *Mothers and Daughters: Women of the Intelligentsia in Nineteenth-Century Russia*. Cambridge: Cambridge University Press, 1983.

Fitzpatrick, Sheila. *Everyday Stalinism: Ordinary Life in Extraordinary Times, Soviet Russia in the 1930s*. Oxford: Oxford University Press, 1999.

Geller, Mikhail, and Aleksandr Nekrich. *Utopia in Power: The History of the Soviet Union from 1917 to the Present*. Translated by Phyllis B. Carlos. New York: Summit Books, 1986.

Gutkin, Irina. *The Cultural Origins of the Socialist Realist Aesthetic, 1890-1934*. Evanston, IL: Northwestern University Press, 1999.

Stites, Richard. *Revolutionary Dreams: Utopian Vision and Experimental Life in the Russian Revolution*. New York: Oxford University Press, 1989.

———. *The Women's Liberation Movement in Russia: Feminism, Nihilism, and Bolshevism, 1860-1930*. Princeton: Princeton University Press, 1978.

Tertz, Abram [Andrei Siniavsky]. *On Socialist Realism*. Translated by George Dennis. New York: Pantheon, 1961; with *The Trial Begins*: New York: Vintage, 1965; Berkeley: University of California Press, 1982.

Zbarsky, Ilya & Samuel Hutchinson. *Lenin's Embalmers*, translated from the French by Barbara Bray. London: The Harvill Press, 1998.

Memoirs

1930: How Meierkhol'd Put on My Play

by Iurii OLESHA*

Moscow, October 4, 1954, Diary

Why didn't I write this diary [then]?

Now this inscription (written in ink of course) is 20 years old. "List" was staged in 1931.[1] That means it has been 23 years... But I remember perfectly how, on the day after the premiere, with the stale taste of alcohol still on my breath, I stood on that dreary day among the gray hues where Briusov Lane meets Gor'kii Street...

Soon after they killed Raikh. They say they gouged out her eyes—this rumor, in all likelihood, did not come from nowhere. The lovely black eyes of Zinaida Raikh—who, for all her demonism, still looked at the world with the obedient, earnest gaze of a little girl. [The poet] Perets Markish, who it seems has also died, informed me at some sorry banquet at the Gertsen House, where

* From *A Book of Farewell* (*Kniga proshchaniia*). Moscow: Vagrius, 2006. Pp. 223-225. Translated from the Russian by Justin A. Wilmes of the Ohio State University.

I sat drunk, unhappy, arguing with everyone, lonely, ruined—that they had definitely killed Raikh (for some say she was only badly beaten)... Markish relayed the words of his doctor friend who... But perhaps it didn't happen that way, I already don't remember.

They killed her in 1938.

I remember her all in white—bare shoulders with a transparent *peignoir* thrown over them, powdered—in front of a mirror in her dressing room in the theater—while the bells on the ceiling rang out and a blinking red light bulb called her out onto the stage.

They loved me, the Meierkhol'ds.

I fled from their overzealous love.

During the period of his greatest renown and recognition, by precisely the government, he would often lean towards me and—apropos of nothing—whisper:

They are going to execute me.

Anxiety lived in their home—alongside them, of its own accord. When I lived in this house in their absence, I saw, heard, felt this anxiety. It stood in the next room, suddenly moved over to the wallpaper; it forced me, when I came home in the evening, to inspect every room—could there be someone there who had sneaked in while I was out—to look under the beds, behind the doors, in the closets. What could imaginably have been threatening this home then—at the very peak of its owner's glory? Nothing was threatening it—quite the contrary, recognition came from all sides in the form of bouquets, money, praise, trips abroad. And yet the anxiety was so powerfully present in this empty home that sometimes I simply took to running—away from nothing: from the wallpaper, from the portrait of the lady of the house with her big black eyes that all of a sudden seemed to me to be crying.

She was stabbed to death in this home. Before the killers appeared I had already heard them, almost seen them—for several years.

Its owner was executed, shot—just as he anticipated.

Her murder is shrouded in mystery. The killers entered from the street climbing over the balcony. She struggled. They say they gouged out her eyes. She was brought in an ambulance to the hospital where she died from loss of blood. They buried her police-fashion, so to speak,[2] but the ballerina Gel'tser dressed her for the display in the coffin.

Before they were murdered they said good-bye to me in a dream. They came up to some sort of window, from the outside, from the street, and stopping at the window that was dark but that I could see through, they bowed to me.

Vsevolod Meierkhol'd and Iurii Olehsa

TRANSLATOR'S NOTES

[1] I.e. Olesha's play *List of Blessings* (*Spisok blagodeianii*).
[2] In a detached, sober fashion.

IVANOV-RAZUMNIK
(RAZUMNIK V. IVANOV)*

II

I had spent the whole of February the second in my study engrossed in my work—first, on the proofs of Volume VIII of the works of Blok and then ("a rest is a change of occupation"), on material for Volume VIII of the works of Saltykov [Mikhail Saltykov-Shchedrin, a Russian satirist, writing in the second half of the nineteenth century]. At about nine p.m., satisfied with the day's work, I laid down my pen and prepared to end the day's celebration of our mutual jubilee over a glass of tea with V. N. [Ivanov-Razumnik's wife] in quiet comfort.

Just then guests arrived—the veteran writer Viacheslav Shishkov and his young wife—"only for five minutes," to tell us of some minor occurrence. They were on the point of leaving when I said:

"Although you're in a hurry to get home, you'll have to stay with us a little longer when you learn what day it is for V. N. and me."

And after exchanging a glance with V. N. I told them, half jokingly, about our double jubilee.

Our guests exclaimed with pleasure. Being a "newly wedded couple," they

* From *The Memoirs of Ivanov-Razumnik*. Introduction by G. Jankovsky, translated and annotated by P. S. Squire. London: Oxford University Press, 1965. Pp. 62-67.

could scarcely credit the fact that we had been married for thirty years; and thirty years of literary work also struck them as an "impressive" figure. We sat down round the samovar and a bottle of wine, clinked our glasses—and spent our jubilee evening very cosily. Viacheslav Shishkov asked, incidentally, why we had kept this jubilee of ours secret and not said anything about it to our friends and acquaintances?

Properly, he said, a real celebration should have been organized with lots of people present and plenty of fuss.

"Well, you be patient," I said, "a celebration may yet be held. After you've gone home and we've retired to bed, who knows but what Auntie may not come round to congratulate us!"

"Auntie" was the name we used to give in our small circle of writers to the GPU [*State Political Directorate*, or Secret Police, 1922-1934]. It had its origins in two lines of the poem "Komsomoliia" by that remarkable Russian poet, [Aleksandr] Bezymenskii:

> The Comsomol's my daddy,
> The VKP's [Communist Party] my mummy...

This memorable distich, which delightfully parodies (without the author's knowledge) Gleb Uspenskii's parody—"the one who was my daddy, the one who was my mummy..."—had led me on a certain occasion in the past to point out that, although we did not all have a three-letter mummy, each of us possessed, in the GPU, a three-letter auntie. Even Famusov [a character in A. Griboedov's classical comedy *Woe from Wit*] knew of her when he threatened to banish his daughter from the capital—"To the country with you, to Auntie, to that far distant hole, Saratov!"

I had not been favored with a visit from this Auntie since 1919, but during recent nights she had been calling on my close and distant acquaintances with renewed fervor. D. M. Pines ... had been arrested at the beginning of January, much to the detriment of our edition of Blok's prose works and its bibliography. Two or three other acquaintances of mine had also been arrested—in every case former SRs of Left or Right persuasions [SR—Socialist Revolutionaries]. But at the same time there had been further arrests in Tsarskoe Selo among people I knew who were not in any way connected with political parties. One of them, G. M. Kotliarov, the Librarian of the Academy of Sciences, was a dear friend of mine who, being a keen amateur chess player, often came round to play a couple of games with me; another, the writer A. D. Skaldin (the author of the satirical novel *The Wanderings and Adventures of Nicodemus Senior*), I had not seen since his last visit to me which had occurred two years before. I could hardly believe my ears when I learned soon afterwards (in Auntie's lodgings, in fact) that both had been arrested on the charge of having been members of my "circle." And although no such circle really existed, they were both exiled to Alma-Ata. All this, however, lay in the future.

Viacheslav Shishkov laughed at my idea and said that such coincidences never happened in real life.

"Even supposing that Auntie should pay you a visit (which I don't believe), in any case, you can sleep peacefully tonight. A jubilee coincidence like that is too improbable; you wouldn't even come across it in a bad novel by an unskillful writer. Life is more intelligent."

"My dear friend, it is more daring," I replied; "literature is life, but life is not literature."

....

About midnight we saw our friends to the door, after that we sat talking for a little longer, and at half-past twelve, I put the light out in my study and prepared for bed. Just then we heard the sudden sound of Sulkhan barking in the garden (he was a setter thoroughbred, a real friend of the family), then the trampling of numerous feet on the stairs and after that a knock on the door. It was laughable. Although I had only just maintained that "life" was stranger than "literature," I had no idea, to tell the truth, that I should prove so brilliant a prophet and that Auntie would really arrive with her congratulations that very night.

I hastily dressed — and came out into the hall where I met V. N. emerging from her room.

"She's come all the same!" she said.

I asked "Who?" as a matter of form and, receiving the expected answer, opened the door. I was amazed to see how many admirers had turned up to congratulate me on my jubilee. They were commanded by a young GPU man whom I discovered to be one Buznikov, a "special plenipotentiary" of the GPU's Secret Political Section.

There could be no doubt that my secret political crime (secret from me, I mean) was one of some magnitude if a whole army should have been thought necessary for the purpose first of conducting a search and secondly of acting as my escort. Some of them, headed by Buznikov, occupied my study, others took possession of V. N.'s room and a third detachment set off into the garden to search the wood-shed. What might I have kept there? Machine-guns? Bombs? A printing press? I have no idea, and in any case I know nothing of the details of their search because Buznikov requested me to remain in my study, where he seated himself at my desk, opened its drawers and began reading the letters and papers he found there.

I lit a pipe, took a chair and remained seated throughout the whole noisy search which went on till five in the morning. I sat there in silence, smoking and thinking. One finds a good deal to think about when one's apartment is searched at night.

The first thought that occurred to me was of a humorous nature: what if Auntie had known of my double jubilee—would she have put in an appearance on this identical night, or would she have arranged her visit several nights before or after? I reflected that consideration for my jubilee would not discourage her from paying me a call. Indeed, the reverse was more likely: "Ah-ha, so you're celebrating two thirty-year jubilees? Well, I'll come and congratulate you too the very same night, thus creating an aesthetically perfect background for your subsequent jubilee celebrations."

Meanwhile the search was taking its normal course. Auntie's various aides-de-camp [subordinates] came in and went out again, eying my huge bookcases and their several thousand volumes with a somewhat rueful air of dismay—"What a lot of work there's going to be for someone!" They asked questions. Where's the attic? Where's the wood-shed? They went down into the basement; they went all over the garden. They were also highly active in V. N.'s room: they pulled out all the drawers in the chest-of-drawers, they rummaged around among her clothes and overturned mattresses. In a word, everything went on according to the old classic form of such proceedings. How familiar it all was!

Indeed it was only too familiar and hence of little interest. I found it much more interesting to observe the behavior not of the human beings concerned, who merely stirred me to feelings of pity, but of the animals, the silent witnesses of this nocturnal search. I refer to Sulkhan the dog and Mishka the cat.

It has often struck me as surprising that memoir-writers have devoted so little space in their autobiographies to the part played in their lives by man's four-legged friends. And, generally speaking, literature has dealt sparingly with them. Of our writers only Mikhail Prishvin has attempted a serious and sympathetic study of "canine psychology." Perhaps those who lack the necessary skill are better advised to leave the subject alone. But nevertheless I found the behavior of our dear Sulkhan on this jubilee night so profoundly striking and so moving that I cannot refrain from mentioning it here.

Benvenuto Cellini [1500-1571] tells us in his colorful biography how, during his imprisonment in St. Angelo at Rome, his dog shared the solitude of his cell. One night the jailer and hangmen came to take Benvenuto to his execution, whereupon his dog, usually a good-natured creature, attacked them furiously and it was only with difficulty that they finally beat off his onslaught.

Sulkhan's behavior was entirely different. He was the most even-tempered animal, although always extremely vigilant and inclined to be hostile towards strangers (as was right and proper for a self-respecting watchdog who was always let off the chain at night). The instant he heard our jubilee visitors coming to congratulate us he rushed out at them barking wildly; but after sniffing at a neighbor of ours, a resident in the house whom he knew and who had been roped in as witness, he stopped barking and hurried into our rooms along with our visitors. He ran straight up to me and spent the whole five hours of the search (to my amazement!) beside my chair, which he did not leave for a second, with his muzzle buried in my lap and his tail between his legs. People came in and out, doors banged, there was a lot of talking—and he paid not the slightest attention to anything; and this was in striking contrast to his usual behavior. With what higher canine intuition did he sense that a jubilee celebration had befallen his master?

But having told the story of this moving interlude with our dog I should at the same time not omit to tell of the humorous interlude with our cat which took place on the same occasion. The more so because we have nothing in our literature on "feline psychology" and a cat is a far more complex creature than a dog ...

It is with no idea of filling in this gap, but simply because it is relevant here, that I must include some details of our beautiful black Mishka. He was loving and affectionate with all of us but, like any self-respecting cat, proud and quick to take offense. He was asleep on the little sofa in my study and paid no heed to either the noisy entrance of our visitors or his friend and companion, Sulkhan. The night was drawing to an end when one of the GPU men threw a packet of papers on to the sofa. It just touched him. Mishka slowly got up, arched his back, surveyed all those present with a look of intense scorn and then, with his tail erect, made for the corner by the stove. There this most well-behaved and well-educated cat, who in all the four years of his life had always asked to be let into the garden, proceeded—and far from silently—to commit the *crimen lesae majestatis* [the crime of offending authority, a crime of high treason], after which he stalked with all solemnity toward the door and requested to be let out.

Naturally I feel remiss for having introduced these passages into my story—the slightly sentimental interlude of the dog and the quite unseemly interlude of the cat—but a song must have all its words, and these were some of the notes in our jubilee *nocturne*. Besides, I am committing to paper now what I thought then and these were some of my thoughts at the time, some serious and others—not so serious.

Antonina PIROZHKOVA*

In the year 1936, Moscow saw the trials of the so-called "enemies of the people," and every night friends and acquaintances of ours were arrested.

Babel' was acquainted with many people, among them important politicians, military personnel, journalists, and writers. He used to say to me: "I am not afraid of arrest as long as they let me keep writing." And even before that, after the death of Gor'kii, he had once said: "Now they are not going to let me live."

It seemed as if the door to our house never closed. Not only did the wives of Babel's comrades come by, but also the wives and parents of prisoners unknown to him. These visitors cried as they begged Babel' to intervene on behalf of their loved ones. Babel' would get dressed up and, literally bent down by it all, would head off to see some of his former comrades in arms who had, as yet, survived and still held influential positions. Babel' would turn to them either for help or for information. He would come back looking extremely grim, but he tried to find words to comfort the people who had turned to him.

Babel' was suffering terribly during this ordeal, and I actually used to picture

* From *At His Side: The Last Years of Isaac Babel*. Translated by Anne Frydman and Robert L. Busch. South Royalton, VT: Steerforth Press, 1996. Pp. 103-105; 111-125.

his heart as large, wounded, and bleeding. It was apparent that Babel' did not want me to suffer, for he tried to avoid talking about the whole issue. Still, I asked, "Why is it that during the trials they all confess and heap shame on themselves? Really, there's never been anything like this. If they are political opponents, why don't they use the opportunity to tell the whole world about their views and their principles?"

"I myself don't understand it," Babel' replied. "They are all intelligent and brave. Perhaps it's that they are influenced by their Party training and by a desire to save the Party overall?"

I knew that he didn't believe the accusations but I also knew that he didn't understand why everybody was confessing to such fantastically crazy accusations. There were many of us then who didn't understand this. In those years none of us could allow even into our minds the possibility of torture in Soviet prisons. In the tsarist period, yes—that was possible; but in the Soviet state? It was simply unthinkable. Hypnotized by this kind of belief, there were even those among us who refused to acknowledge anything that was happening or accept the evidence before them.

When Iakov Livshits, the Director of National Transportation, was arrested, Babel' could not contain himself and said, "They expect me to believe that Livshits wanted to restore capitalism to our land! He comes from a working-class family, and believe me, nobody was worse off under tsarism than working-class Jews. And during the Revolution, you had to restrain Iakov from summarily executing the bourgeois every chance he got. That's how much he hated them. And now I'm supposed to believe that he wanted the restoration of capitalism. How monstrous!"

In January of 1939 [Nikolai] Ezhov was removed from his position as head of State Security. Babel' had long known Ezhov's wife, Evgeniia Solomonovna, and he used to visit their home. Having married Ezhov and become part of the official elite, she then wanted to have her own literary salon. For this reason Babel' was invited to Ezhov's home on days when they were having company. Ezhov himself rarely took part in these gatherings, most often arriving toward the end.

[Solomon] Mikhoels [Director and Actor of the Moscow Yiddish Theater], [jazz singer] Leonid Utesov, and other representatives of the arts were also invited since they were known to be lively and witty people to spend an evening with. And if you invited people "for Babel'," they all came.

Babel' had his own purely professional interest in Ezhov. It was through this man that Babel was trying to understand the things that were happening "at the very top."

By the winter of 1938 Ezhov's wife had poisoned herself. Babel' thought the reason for her suicide to have been the arrest of someone close to her who often came to their home. But that may have only been the final straw. "Stalin can't understand her death," Babel' told me. "His own nerves are made of steel, so he just can't understand how, in other people, they give out."

....

We made plans for all of us to move out to the dacha at the end of May [1939] when the weather got warm. Work on the film scenario for *My Universities* [based on Gor'kii's memoirs] was almost over, and shooting had already begun. "I feel I owe it to Gor'kii," Babel' said. He had been involved to some degree or other with all the filming of Gor'kii's [memoir] works—*Childhood*, *In the World*, and finally, *My Universities*. He told me, "I have my mind on other things right now, but Ekaterina Pavlovna [Gor'kii's first wife] asked me to keep an eye on these filmmakers to be sure they don't distort his work or do something in bad taste."

As he left for Peredelkino Babel' said good-bye cheerfully, remarking: "I won't be returning to this house soon."

He asked me to bring Mark Donskoi and his assistants out to see him on May 15th, as it was Donskoi who was directing *My Universities*. We arranged for them to pick me up at Metroproject after work.

At the time, the only ones home besides me were our housekeeper, Shura, and Ester Grigor'evna Makotinskaia, who took care of little Lida.

On May 15, 1939, at five o'clock in the morning, I was awakened by a knock on the door of my room. When I opened it, two men in army uniforms entered and said that they were searching for someone and that they needed access to the attic.

It turned out that four men had entered. Two climbed up to the attic and two stayed downstairs. One of them announced that they needed to see Babel', who could tell them where this person was, and that I should drive out to the *dacha* in Peredelkino with them. I got dressed and we set off. I was accompanied by two men in addition to the driver, who knew the way perfectly and did not once ask me for directions.

When we arrived at the dacha, I woke up the watchman and entered through the kitchen with the two men behind me. Hesitant, I stopped in front of the door to Babel's room. With a gesture one of the men ordered me to knock. I did so and heard Babel' say, "Who's there?"

"Me."

Then he got dressed and opened the door. Pushing me away from the door, the two men walked right up to Babel' and commanded, "Hands up!" Then they felt his pockets, frisking him for weapons. Babel' kept silent.

We were ordered into another room—mine. There we sat down, huddling close together and holding each other by the hands. Talking was beyond us.

When the search of Babel's room was completed, they put all his manuscripts into folders and ordered us to put on our coats and go to the car. Babel' said to me: "They didn't let me finish." I understood that he was speaking of his book "New Stories." Then, very low, he said: "Inform André." He meant André Malraux [French writer and political figure who was sympathetic to the communists at the time].

In the car, one of the men sat in back with Babel', and me while the other one sat in front with the driver. "The worst part of this is that my mother won't be getting my letters," Babel' said, and then he was silent for a long time.

I could not say a single word. Babel' asked the secret policeman sitting next to him, "So, I guess you don't get much sleep, do you?"

And he even laughed.

As we approached Moscow, I said to Babel', "I'll be waiting for you, it will be as if you've gone to Odessa... only there won't be any letters..."

He answered, "I ask you to see that the child not be made miserable."

"But I don't know what my destiny will be..."

At this point, the man sitting beside Babel' said to me: "We have no claims whatsoever against you."

We drove up to the Lubianka prison and through the gates. The car stopped before the massive, closed door where two sentries stood guard.

Babel' kissed me hard and said: "Someday we'll see each other..." And without looking back, he got out of the car and went through that door.

I turned to stone, and I could not even cry. For some reason I kept thinking, "Will they at least give him a glass of hot tea? He can't start the day without it."

They drove me to our home on Nikolo-Vorobinskii where the search was still going on. One of the men who had gone out to Peredelkino made a telephone call to report that Babel' had been brought in. It was apparent that he was asked the question; "Did he crack jokes?" To which he answered, "He tried."

I asked for permission to leave so as not to be late for work. Permission was given, so I changed and left. Ester Grigor'evna, who lived with us, managed to whisper to me that she had been able to move a few pieces of Babel's clothing into my closet to keep for him should he need them. Before I left, one of the NKVD men made a telephone call to ask how many rooms to leave me, one or two. Then, addressing his partner, he said: "The instructions are to leave her two."

Actually, this was rather remarkable for the times: I was being allowed to keep two separate rooms out of the three-room Moscow apartment for my little daughter and myself. At the time, however, I did not pay the slightest attention to this. Besides this information, I was given a telephone number for the NKVD's First Section where, if necessary, I could call.

They sealed Babel's room, took away his manuscripts, diaries, and pages with signed dedications that had been torn from his books.

Now, remembering the telephone conversations, turning over in my mind all the details of the search and arrest, I conclude that Babel' even then, *beforehand*, had already been convicted.

Summoning all my strength, I worked at the Metro project all day long [Pirozhkova was an engineer involved in the construction of the Moscow metro]. I had to consult with project organizers at the Palace of Soviets to request DC-grade steel for the construction of the Paveletskaia-radial Station, which I was in charge of at the time.

Mark Donskoi and his associates, whom I was supposed to take to the dacha to see Babel that day, never came to Metro-project to call for me. Obviously, they already knew that Babel' had been arrested.

When the working day was over, I made my way home and only then broke down. What had happened was terrible, though I could not imagine a bad outcome to it all. I knew that Babel' could not possibly be guilty of anything, and my hope was that this was all a mistake, that *there* everything would be cleared up. But the very experienced Ester Grigor'evna, who had already been through not just a husband's arrest but also a daughter's, made no effort to console me.

Later, I was to learn that Meierkhol'd and [journalist] Mikhail Kol'tsov had been arrested at almost the same time as Babel'.

....

It was the feeling of being helpless that was the most awful part of the whole experience. Imagine the person you care about most being in trouble, and you can do nothing! I wanted to run to the Lubianka and tell them what I know about Babel' that they couldn't know. Again, it was the veteran, Ester Grigor'evna, who saved me from that step.

It was a good thing I had my work and that I had Lida. I would come home, take her in my arms and, for hours on end, pace the room from corner to corner. Ester Grigor'evna had to go home to do translations so that she could earn money for parcels to send to her own prisoners. That meant I had no adult companionship.

I wrote to my mother in Tomsk about everything and asked her to come and stay with me. When she arrived and began to take care of Lida, I started to work like someone possessed. I also took driving lessons just to keep from having any spare time on my hands.

Prisoners were not allowed visitors. All I could do was go once a month to drop off 75 rubles for Babel' at a small window in a courtyard off the Kuznetskii Bridge. One stood in line to give the money, for which there was no receipt. The lines were long, stretching from the window to the street entrance and even beyond. I was always so downcast that I never noticed particular people. I did notice that the people came from the intelligentsia and that, although there were some men, most of those standing in line were women.

After Babel's arrest, no one telephoned me any longer—with one exception, Valentina Aronovna Mil'man, who was [Soviet writer] Il'ia Erenburg's private secretary, and who called within a few days of Babel's arrest. She was afraid to see me at home, so we arranged to meet near the Bol'shoi Theater, and she offered me money. I refused the money since I was still working, but this action of hers, so rare for its time, I have never forgotten. From that time on, and for many years after, she became one of my closest friends. It was only sometime later that I guessed that the money was being offered by Erenburg, since his secretary, who probably earned a modest wage, could never have offered me such a sum.

Babel' had introduced me to Erenburg back in 1934. One evening Il'ia Grigorevich had come to see Babel', whom he usually met not at our house but either at his own or in a café.

Neither during supper, nor afterwards, did Erenburg pay the slightest bit of attention to me. He smoked a cigar, dropped the ashes on his jacket, talked with Babel' exclusively, and never looked in my direction. I was not accustomed to such treatment.

Usually, everyone that Babel' introduced me to spoke with me, asked me questions, showed some kind of interest in me. This was attributable to my being a construction engineer involved with the building of the Moscow subway. For a woman to be an engineer at that time was something rare, and the construction of the subway was of interest to everyone.

But only with Erenburg was it different, and as hard as Babel' tried to get him interested in me, telling him, for example, that I had worked in the construction of the Kuznetsk Metallurgical Factory, which Erenburg had written about in *The Second Day*, nothing worked. He simply ignored me. Needless to say, I immediately conceived an intense dislike for Erenburg and, at future meetings, when he arrived, I excused myself after supper or lunch and went to my room.

At the time of Babel's arrest in May 1939, Erenburg had been abroad and only returned to Moscow in 1940. Valentina Aronovna told me that when Erenburg unpacked his suitcase, the first thing he pulled out was a book by Babel', lying right on top.

When I learned this I understood how much Erenburg cared for Babel' and that caused me to change my feelings about him. At the time, Babel's books were being withdrawn from all the libraries, and even keeping them at home was risky.

Some two months after Babel's arrest, I began to be harassed by court officials. Babel' had signed agreements with some publishing houses from whom he had received advances. In order to recover the advances, these publishers had decided to take legal action against me. One after another the court officials turned up not only to inventory the furniture that was left in the two remaining rooms but even my dresses. I had no idea what to do, so I decided to seek advice from our "very good friend," Lev Romanovich Sheinin, who was then working in the Prosecutor's office.

When he spotted me, he became very upset, even turning pale. Was this the same man who had spent so many evenings with us, often staying until daybreak? Was it the same man who had been so lavish in the compliments he paid to our home and to me, particularly? Once he had regained his composure, Sheinin asked me to wait in an adjoining room. A little later he entered the room accompanied by a man in uniform. He clearly felt that, for his own safety, he had better talk to me in front of a witness.

As he heard me out, Sheinin appeared to calm down when he saw that I had not come to ask him to intercede on Babel's behalf. Still, it was not Sheinin, but his companion, who advised me to telephone the First Section of the NKVD. When I got up to go, Sheinin suddenly asked me, "Why was Babel' arrested?" I responded with an "I don't know," and left.

When I got home I decided I would finally use the NKVD telephone number that one of the agents had given me during the search for the first time. I called and reported on the inventory being made. The party on the other end of the line said, "Don't worry, they won't be coming any more." And, indeed, I never saw them again.

There would be another time that I had to telephone the NKVD. I had received a call from the local police in the Peredelkino area informing me of the theft of rugs in the dacha—one that had been in my room and another smaller one from Babel's room. It turned out that they had been stolen by the watch-man's brother, who had come from Ukraine. He had been apprehended after he had sold the rugs, so they confiscated the 2,000 rubles he was carrying. The local police said that I should get this money. When I phoned the First Division of the NKVD, I was told, "Go and get the money."

I did not go right away, but waited perhaps a month. When I finally went, I learned that the local comptroller had been convicted of embezzling the money, for which he received a five-year sentence.

....

Just prior to the celebration of the Anniversary of the October Revolution a young NKVD officer came by—I can't remember whether he phoned ahead or not. He asked me to give him trousers, socks, and handkerchiefs for Babel'.

How fortunate we were that Ester Grigor'evna had managed to transfer trousers to my room. There were also handkerchiefs and socks for him in my dresser. The handkerchiefs I scented heavily with my perfume and then gave everything to the officer. I so much wanted to send Babel' a greeting from home, even if it was just a familiar scent.

My mother and I wondered what the possible significance of the officer's visit could be. It seemed to us that it was a good sign, a sign that conditions were improving for Babel'.

I was able to get money to Babel' from June until November, when I was told he had been transferred to the Butyrskaia Prison, where in the future I would have to take the money from now on. There, they accepted the money for November and December of 1939, but in January 1940 I was informed that Babel' had been convicted and sentenced by the Military Tribunal.

A lawyer I knew arranged for me to meet with a procurator for the Military Tribunal, a gaunt, ascetic-looking general. After he had looked through some papers, he told me that Babel' had been sentenced to ten years without the right to correspond and with the confiscation of all his possessions.

Before meeting with the general I had heard someone say that "ten years without the right to correspond" was a euphemism intended for relatives that actually meant the person had been executed. I asked the general about this, assuring him that the truth would not cause me to faint. He said: "That does not apply to Babel'."

After this visit with the Procurator for the Military Tribunal, I went to the NKVD reception office. I remember this as being on the second floor of a most unprepossessing two- or three-story building that used to stand where the Children's World department store was later built on Dzerzhinskaia Square. The general reception area was somber and led into a corner room where a card catalog stood. I was met by a young and unpleasant snub-nosed man who dug through the card catalog and then told me officially what I had already heard. And then he added, "A heavy sentence—you need to get your life in order." This angered me, so I said to him: "I have a job, how else am I supposed to put my life in order?"

He had bluntly hinted that Babel' had been shot, but I was not about to accept it.

During the summer of 1939 I stayed with little Lida in Moscow the entire time. I could not leave on vacation to take her to a dacha; every day I was hopeful I might receive news of Babel'. Rumors about his situation constantly surfaced in Moscow: someone had supposedly shared a cell with him, another person asserted that the state's case against Babel' wasn't worth the paper it was written on, etc., etc. I tried to meet with these people but each time something prevented it. It would always turn out that the sources of the rumors had not themselves been in prison with Babel', but rather they knew people who had either left Moscow or were afraid to meet with me.

....

The anguish of loss never leaves me, and the thought that for eight months in an NKVD prison he had to endure a mass of insults, humiliation and torture, and that his last day on earth was lived with the knowledge of his impending execution—all of this tears at my heart.

Cultural Contexts

The Mystery and the Magic of Stalin's Power

by Andrei SINIAVSKII*

* Andrei Sinyavsky

** From *Soviet Civilization: A Cultural Historyl*. Translated from the Russian by Joanne Turnbull with the assistance of Nikolai Formozov. New York: Arcade Publishing, 1990. Pp. 103-113

Though corrupted by power, Stalin understood its nature perfectly and made secrecy its mainspring. Stalin wasn't just a ruthless dictator, he was a kind of hypnotist who managed to convince the people that he was their god by shrouding his cult in the mystery he knew power required. Witness the unpredictability of his decisions (when he had both friends and enemies killed), his black humor—and even his laconic speech. Stalin spoke very slowly between long pauses, creating an illusion of enormous import, no matter how flat the phrase, and superhuman wisdom. Though Stalin didn't say or write anything wise, the sheer inscrutability of his words and acts signified his "wisdom," his ability to see and know all, his divine powers, his omniscience. Stalin's ubiquitous secret police penetrated every pore of Soviet society and, repressive functions aside-added to the aura of supreme mystery around the workings of the omniscient almighty.

In a similar vein, Stalin tried to pass himself off as a leading light in all branches of science. Though not a scholar, he affected a universal erudition. This explains, in particular, his contributions to linguistics, a field which would seem far removed from his own.

By setting forth his authoritative views here, Stalin showed everyone that his intellect extended to everything, that nothing escaped him. Some claimed that Stalin had a photographic memory allowing him to read a thousand pages a day: rather than having to scan every line, a glance at the page was enough for it to be imprinted in his memory.

When Stalin died, many people thought that everything had died, even those who weren't politically attached to the regime or worshipers of Stalin. It's just that Stalin had become a synonym for the entire State, for life on earth. "Stalin's name is life!" wrote the poet Aleksandr Tvardovskii. It's no accident that during the war soldiers mounted an assault with this one motto: "For the Motherland! For Stalin!" Stalin was the Motherland. He was often deferentially referred to as "the Proprietor." Everyone knew that the Proprietor was Stalin.

Stalin's posthumous "reappearances" were legend. This "mysticism" matters to us here only as an example of the magical power Stalin possessed in the minds of Soviet people, including those who didn't love him. Stalin's ghost appeared as a kind of demon. The noted writer Leonid Leonov recounted this curious incident in a private conversation. This happened after the Twentieth Party Congress (1956), where Khrushchev had denounced Stalin, and the latter's name was being crossed out everywhere. Leonov and his secretary had just spent an evening removing every reference to Stalin in a book of his due to be reissued. She then left—only to fall on the stairs and break her arm. In superstitious horror, Leonov seriously insisted that this was Stalin taking revenge and added that he too had felt poorly ever since. So Stalin, like an evil spirit, put hexes on everyone who crossed him.

Of interest to us here is this dark fascination that Stalin exercised in death as in life, a fascination which is explained by the profound mystery in which he cloaked his power and his own person.

Schematically, Stalin's magic has two faces: the light and the dark. One half of Stalin's personality belongs to the bright light of day, when the people rejoice, when buildings are built and parades parade, when the art of Socialist Realism thrives. But the principal business is done at night: arrests, executions, political intrigues, and governmental sessions associated with binges of black humor and sinister buffoonery. This nocturnal style of life corresponds to the mystery with which Stalin invested the very notion of power. Which is why it's so interesting to read about Stalin. The mystery sucks you in, swallows you up. Aleksandr Orlov's book is called *The Secret History of Stalin's Crimes*; this sounds like music or an absorbing novel à la *Mysteries of Paris*, *The Mysterious Island*, *Mystery of Two Oceans*. Stalin, you might say, was able to transform the history of Soviet society into the secret history of his own crimes.

....

In the secrecy of his rule, Stalin undoubtedly leaned on the old Russian tradition of autocracy, even if his power surpassed that of all the tsars. Interestingly, soon after Lenin's death, Stalin once let the cat out of the bag, declaring that Russia needed a tsar. At a dinner the conversation had turned to the pressing question of how to run the Party without Lenin. Suddenly Stalin said: "Don't forget that we are living in Russia, in the land of the tsars. The Russian people like to see one man alone at the head of the State." No one noticed the remark, nor did it occur to anyone that Stalin had himself in mind for the role of emperor. But this proposal materialized, and on a prodigious scale. If Lenin laid the foundations of one-man rule, Stalin was able to imbue it with a religious, even mystical quality. From Russian traditions, he had gleaned that the tsar must be terrible, even terrifying, while offering the people his smile as the supreme kindness. Stalin's oriental nature may also have influenced his monarchistic style, evoking the ancient despots of the Orient. But at the same time it expressed Stalin's feel for the strictly Russian national character.

In his Russo-centrism, Stalin sometimes resorted to pre-revolutionary arguments. In 1945, for example, in honor of the victory over Japan, Stalin made the following speech:

> The defeat of the Russian forces in 1904 during the Russo-Japanese War left painful memories in the people's consciousness. It left a black stain on our country. Our people knew that the day would come when Japan would be beaten and the stain liquidated. We, the older generation, waited forty years for this day. And now this day has come.

Surprising rhetoric, given that at the time of the Russo-Japanese War, the unpatriotic Bolsheviks were rooting for Russia's defeat in the belief that this would benefit the revolution. And of course by 1945, everyone had forgotten about the score to be settled with Japan. But not Stalin.

Stalin's monarchism also showed in the revival of pre-revolutionary practices. So that, while the word "officer" had long been considered an insult, epaulets, ranks, and titles were reintroduced in the army. If this touched and pleased some older émigrés, it could shock people brought up on Soviet norms and Leninist traditions. This was the logic of the new, Stalinist epoch, with its attempts to restore certain monarchistic forms and customs. Stalin was feathering himself a tsarist nest.

It's funny that Stalin imposed one-man rule everywhere when he alone was ruling the entire country. Even literature had its hierarchy, the pillar of Socialist Realism being Gor'kii, with Maiakovskii for poetry. The top theater director was Konstantin Stanislavskii. The government had its Jew: Lazar Kaganovich.

But one has to admit that Stalin's personality cult found popular support; it wasn't only imposed by force. The mysticism of his power appealed to people. They were impressed by his grandeur, his inaccessibility, his mystery. This speaks, in my view, not just of the Russian people's attachment to its tsars but also of its affinity for power stamped with the seal of an irrational mystery. One might even suppose that herein lies a sign of the religiousness of the Russian soul, distorted in the deification of Stalin, a tsar invested with quasi-divine powers. This explains how the Russians could prefer a dictator to a parliament. Most reacted with astounding indifference to the dispersal of the Constituent Assembly—their parliament-treated by the Bolsheviks with a contempt that communicated itself to the people. Because parliamentary power utterly lacked the mystery that surrounded the tsar.

Even today, many in Russia still equate Stalin with a time of order that disappeared with him. Because Stalin was all-knowing and all-powerful. I once tried long and hard—and without success—to dissuade a worker who assured me that the simple people lived much better under Stalin, since the bosses feared him, while he periodically—every ten years—had them shot: this was the only way to run the country. According to this logic, the bosses became slack after ten years and had to be eliminated and replaced by new bosses who hadn't had time to let themselves go; thus Stalin was only thinking of the common good in systematically liquidating the ruling cadres, the executions bespoke his kindness to the simple people. And if you point out that simple people were also shot, you're told: "That's how you have to treat us. That's why there was real order under Stalin." Such was the magic of his power.

This power and its magic cost Stalin. He was very alone and trusted no one; hence his gloominess, which then turned into a persecution complex. There was one anecdote that went around while he was still alive in which, by analogy to cog*nac*, he was called "ma*niac* three stars"—an allusion to the three gold stars given to a Hero of the Soviet Union, an award he had bestowed upon himself.

Stalin's suspiciousness was a function of his having killed so many people that it always seemed to him that someone wanted to settle the score; so he had to go on endlessly killing new friends who had become suspect.

His persecution complex was especially aggravated toward the end of his life which, consequently, was not easy. They say that at the dachas where Stalin lived there were generally several bedrooms and he moved from one to the next. Fresh linen was laid out in each room, and Stalin made his own bed. Before going to sleep, he looked under the bed with a special lamp. It seems that he rarely worked at his desk, preferring to move around the room with his chair, dodging would-be snipers. He also seems to have had several doubles. Not to mention the permanent guard and ubiquitous surveillance that shadowed everyone, the government and Politburo included.

There are those who claim that Stalin was killed. This strikes me as unlikely. No one in his entourage could have contemplated such a thing, while all the daredevils who would have been capable had been destroyed long since. Retribution caught up with Stalin only after his death, which elicited unseemly jubilation in many people. Reportedly the first to rejoice that the tyrant was dead was his most faithful and terrifying servant, Lavrentii Beria; possibly this was calculated to absolve himself of responsibility for many crimes of power. But there were also simple people who exulted openly.

"Personality cult" is a rather narrow term and somewhat absurd insofar as it reduces the content of the Stalin era to Stalin's personal mistakes and failings. But these so-called mistakes diverted the entire country and its history from the path prescribed by the original doctrine. Even so, the concept of a personality cult conveys an important aspect of Soviet civilization. The word "cult" implies a religion, religious worship, religious rites. But in this case, it's a religion without God, who is replaced by the State power and its flesh-and-blood representative: Stalin. Thus the deification of Stalin is a manifestation of the Soviet State's ecclesiastical nature. The State of scholars under Lenin gave way to a Church-State under Stalin, though the necessary conditions for such a transformation existed much earlier: the religious worship of an omnipotent power that enjoys the right to resort to any means of violence, covert or overt. Marxist ideology itself, as we have seen, has something in common with religion, only without God, and with communism in place of the Heavenly Kingdom and historical necessity replacing divine Providence. And even before Marxism, Russian socialism possessed its own religious potential.

Stalin's cult evolved naturally from all of this, except that early socialism deified man in general, whereas Stalin deified himself as the personification of State power. And the State turned Church embraced everyone—their soul and their consciousness. To disavow the Party doctrine was subversive, tantamount to a crime against the State. All this began with Lenin, who ordered comrades shot for "bourgeois propaganda," but Stalin completed this unification of the country, of social groups and people's own thoughts. Soviet writers bragged, not without reason, about the harmony of the

Soviet world: the past was dominated by discord and people lived in enmity; but we are happy because we are living in the century of great unanimity, which will never end, which will gather up all of humanity.

Dostoevskii claimed that Catholicism had transformed the church into a state, whereas our Orthodoxy, he said, would ideally like the State to transform itself into the church. Dostoevskii's dream came true, but topsy-turvy; the Godless State transformed itself into a Godless Church with unlimited claims on the human soul. Thus Stalin doesn't just speak, he officiates, and every one of his adversaries, real or imagined, must confess his sins before being shot.

Hence the enormous importance of uniformity. There is one science: Marxism; one eminent Marxist: Stalin; one "creative method" in art and literature: Socialist Realism; one basic history book; and so on. All originality is dangerous and suspect. Conspicuous stylistic deviations are forbidden. The fight against "formalism" [literary and artistic experimentation] is a fight for the Party standard, for a strict, ecclesiastical form in art and literature. This extends to everyday life: beards and long hair on men are seen as a sign of nonconformity; men shouldn't wear narrow pants; women shouldn't wear pants period, or miniskirts...

If Lenin required of Marxism a concrete analysis of the historical situation, Stalin wanted exact prescriptions: all speeches had to conform to strict criteria, including set quotes from Lenin and Stalin, and God forbid one should misquote. The form constricts and congeals; here again it resembles the religious devotion to the holy letter. In the 1930s and later they even imprisoned people for misprints in a newspaper or a book, since these were interpreted as hostile attacks. True, there was one benefit: Soviet publications contained precious few misprints. Stalin's lessons stuck in people's minds.

The cult of the leader clearly began with Lenin, who enjoyed unquestioned authority. Curiously, this cult gained a religious dimension when Lenin died and his body was embalmed and placed in a mausoleum—perhaps the most graphic display of the Soviet State's ecclesiastical nature. An especially macabre display, since Lenin in his mausoleum implies the worship of a corpse.

Initially, the Soviet State fought Orthodox religion, removing holy relics from the churches, desecrating and destroying them. Then it turned Lenin into an artificial relic. Holy relics assume faith in God, in the immortality of the soul, and in the resurrection of the dead; here, in the absence of genuine faith, they preserve the dust. Krupskaia reportedly objected to the mausoleum, but they ignored her and mummified Lenin for the sake of the State. Their prototype was probably the mummies of the pharaohs. But in ancient Egypt, this rite relied on faith in God and in a kingdom beyond the grave; and the pharaoh, to himself and to the people, was a truly deified monarch, not just the head dictator.

Lenin's mausoleum, in the heart of Red Square—regarded as the symbolic center of the country and the entire world—functions as a kind of cathedral. The successive Leaders file out onto its rostrum to show themselves to the people during parades and demonstrations. It's a cathedral built for a corpse, without faith in God, with faith only in the idea and the legitimacy of one's own cause, faith in one's own deified power.

Many years ago, when I was still a student, I learned that in our country they tortured political prisoners to extract confessions of guilt. I relayed this fact to a friend of mine who was much older and already a Party member. Fortunately, he wasn't an informer. But his utterly sincere response, not prompted by fear, was this: "Don't talk to me about any torture. Even if this is true, I don't want to know about it. Because I want to believe, I have to have faith." At the time, I was taken aback that someone would wittingly, in the name of faith, close his eyes to the reality.

All this speaks of Soviet civilization's religious foundation. Since then, many things have changed in the country and the faith in communism has been badly eroded, though the State continues to maintain its ecclesiastical exterior. The faith is gone but the dead shell remains, strong and solid like a petrified coat of mail, nostalgic for the Stalin era, which precluded change. Because then, order prevailed, and the power was not a soulless mechanism but a mystery.

The Tower of Babel Undone in a Soviet Pentecost
A Linguistic Myth of the First Five-Year Plan

by Daniel E. COLLINS*

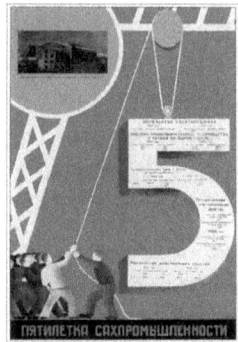

* From *Slavic and East European Journal*, Vol. 42, No. 3 (1998): pp. 423-443.

The vision of a Holy Spirit that would unify humanity was prominent in Russian thought prior to the Revolution, particularly in the "Third-Testament Christianity" of the God-seekers and in the rival programs of the god-builders, who sought to adapt Christian doctrines—in this case, Orthodox pneumatology—to Marxism. Whereas the God-seekers believed that the pre-existing Word would become incarnate in mankind in the kingdom of the Holy Spirit, the god-builders argued that the only god was the collective will of the folk (or proletariat), which, triumphing, would fuse humanity into an immortal, eternal spirit and turn the earth into a New Jerusalem. Like other god-building doctrines, the image of the Holy Spirit as the collective will of the laboring classes was appropriated by the mythopoeic Soviet culture of the 1920s and 1930s, despite Lenin's anathemization of god-building itself (see Clark; Masing-Delic). This transfer belonged to the general tendency of Soviet culture to emulate Christianity, seen, for example, in the cult of Lenin, who from the early 1920s was portrayed in images derived from the veneration of saints and latria [supreme worship] of Christ (see Tumarkin).

One of the aspects of the god-building vision that came to the fore in Soviet culture of the 1920s and early 1930s was the advent of the Holy Spirit and the founding of the Church of the collective will. Whereas the God-seekers and god-builders had to project their kingdoms of the Holy Spirit into a desired future, the Soviet heirs of the god-builders could look for their Pentecost in actual events such as the beginning of the First Five-Year Plan, the putative groundbreaking for a classless society. In this Soviet version of the myth, party workers were the apostles (a pattern seen already in Blok's *Dvenadtsat'* [*The Twelve*]), who, filled with the Holy Spirit, were building a society of god-men to fulfill the Great Commission of their departed but still immanent messiah.[1] As the antihero of *Den' vtoroi* (*The Second Day*, Erenburg 1932-33) observes with unintended accuracy, the Komsomol are "builders of a new life, apostles called to prophesy'."

As will be shown below, an important component of the Pentecost model that was co-opted by Soviet culture during the First Five-Year Plan was the image of the Spirit overcoming communicative barriers and divisions. According to this myth, enthusiastic communists are able to achieve mutual understanding regardless of differences in linguistic form; conversely, unbelievers in the Spirit of collective labor are, in effect, deprived of their ability to communicate even with speakers of their native languages and lapse into frustrated silence. This double-sided picture of ideologically driven communicative success can be found... in the highly mythopoeic production novels of the First Five-Year Plan, which pay considerable attention to details of language. The presentation of linguistic heterogeneity in these and other works of the period may be interpreted as a manifestation of a linguistic myth—the emergence of a pan-proletarian language, which would eventually embrace all humanity in the classless society of the triumphant collective spirit.

The Pentecost of the First Five-Year Plan

Pentecost, one of the twelve Great Feasts, is prominent in Orthodox thought as the commemoration of the beginning of the New Testament—that of the Holy Spirit (hence *Dukhov Den'* "Day of the Spirit")—and the founding of the church. The holiday's liturgy emphasizes unity and shared life in the Holy Spirit. Among the readings are prophecies about how believers will gather from all nations, perform miracles, and be shown wonders in the earth (see *Triod' tsvetnaia*)—events also promised by the spirit of collective labor in the mythopoeic thought of the First Five-Year Plan.

In production novels of that era, the tongues of flame that manifest the Spirit's presence appear in the zeal for labor, which unites party workers and proletarians regardless of their origin.[2] The most usual term for this is enthusiasm (*entuziazm*)—a usage that goes back at least to the god-builders.... In the prototype production novel, Gladkov's *Tsement*, enthusiasm is the faith that moves mountains.... Enthusiasm is the new religion, meant to supplant the signs of Orthodoxy, as the unbeliever Safonov in *Den' vtoroi* recognizes in spite of himself: "Volodia laughed: what, then, had changed? They said "enthusiasm"; previously it was called faith. It was born in the same year in which icons were burned and relics were disemboweled" (Erenburg). In the same novel, a passionate old Bolshevik justifies the unavailability of German machine parts to a foreign engineer by referring to this faith and the transformed life of its believers: "We have a different economy and different nerves. But mainly we have—how can I explain it to you? Officially it's called enthusiasm."

In this milieu, any true understanding, any successful act of communication depends on shared belief; enthusiasm is a religious mystery only the faithful can understand. Thus the term enthusiasm is depicted in novels of the First Five-Year Plan as "an arena of the class struggle," a sign whose meaning is contested. Unbelievers misunderstand the concept and give the word connotations of naiveté and excess, like the scoffers at Pentecost who think the apostles are drunk. In [The River] *Sot'*, a skeptic dismisses the factory planner Potemkin as a dreamer: " 'You are an enthusiast, a well-known enthusiast,'... he knew in advance that Potemkin had nowhere to get the money" (Leonov). In Il'enkov's *Vedushchaia os'* (*Leading axle*, 1932), a bourgeois engineer sees enthusiasm as a journalistic cliché: "The masses, of course, have enthusiasm and all that, as Iuzov [a reporter] writes in his leading articles." The Bolshevik Vartan'ian recognizes this as blasphemy against the Holy Spirit and retorts, "Pardon me—the enthusiasm of the masses is the greatest power. Why the sarcasm?"

The Soviet version of Pentecost confronts its Orthodox archetype explicitly in Leonov's *Sot'* (1930), which depicts party workers as apostles to the northern peasantry. In one of the central incidents in the novel, Komsomol members disrupt a Pentecost religious procession and drown out the chanting of a sottish priest by playing popular songs on concertinas (new signs for old). In the course of the holiday they win many peasants to the cause of collective labor—a vital event in a novel focusing on proletarianization. Among the converts is a young worker who has been carrying an ecclesiastical banner in the procession; he later becomes the leader of another kind of religious body, the *volost'* [district] soviet. On the evening of Pentecost (a traditional day for baptizing converts) the positive hero converts the alienated young monk Gelasii; he washes him of his monastic filth with the words, "There, the lad's baptized into the new faith."

....

Pentecost as Anti-Babel

As mentioned above, one of the ways in which the unifying power of the Holy Spirit was manifested in the pentecostal mythopoeia of the First Five-Year Plan was in overcoming problems posed by linguistic heterogeneity, which had traditionally been taken as a sign of disunity. As recounted in *Acts* 2: 1-47, the descent of the Holy Spirit at Pentecost miraculously enabled the followers of Christ to speak in foreign languages, so that everyone in the polyglot crowd of "Parthians, and Medes, and Elamites," etc., visiting Jerusalem "heard them speak in his own language." In Orthodox theology (part of the cultural background of early Soviet thought), these events have generally been interpreted as a nullification of the Confusion of Tongues, which had been visited on humanity as punishment for building the Tower of Babel (Genesis 11: 1, 4-9) e.g., in one of [Church Father] John Chrysostom's Pentecost sermons, "Just as in antiquity people, fallen into madness, aspired to build a tower that would reach into Heaven, and God destroyed their evil union by confusing their tongues, so now the Holy Spirit descends on the apostles as tongues of fire to unite the divided world... As in antiquity tongues divided the world and disrupted an evil union, so now tongues have united the world and brought the former division into unanimity."

....

The pentecostal vision of language is evident in production novels of the First Five-Year Plan, which present a world where zeal for labor overcomes all obstacles to cross-linguistic understanding (at least in essentials) and where the apostles of the collective can speak, as it were, in other tongues (see below). In *Leading Axle*, Il'enkov exults that "the class energy of the [working] class... builds, creates, conquers, charging millions of people with its creative current... and explodes the age-old obstacle of language differences [*raznoiazychiia*] with its current." Production novels characteristically depict motley crowds that are or will be unified by the collective spirit—e. g., the "Englishmen, Germans, Americans, Chinese, Blacks" that arrive for the Comintern in *Leading Axle*. Il'in's *Bol'shoi konveer* (*The Big Conveyor*) begins with a Soviet May 1 parade met with jubilation by a crowd of Germans, Blacks, and other foreigners, including one who turns to a Russian and says "loudly and happily in English, "'Hello [Khelou]! Moscow is still Moscow!'," obviously expecting to be understood. Representative groupings of this kind, in which people of different countries, nationalities, regions, or classes mix and fuse together, recall the "Parthians, and Medes, and Elamites," etc., who come together at the first Pentecost. The Babel of voices is united into a single chorus by the workings of the sovietized Holy Spirit.

The image of Pentecost was especially potent because Babel loomed large in the cultural context. The Tower had been invoked as a symbol of futile human efforts in the polemics between the God-seekers and the god-builders (e. g., in [Vladimir] Bazarov's article "Christians of the Third Testament and builders of the Tower of Babel"). After the Revolution, Soviet culture initially appropriated the Babel image in a positive value, as a metaphor for conquest of the natural order. [Vladimir] Tatlin's design for the Third Communist International building (1920) recalls Brueghel's paintings of the Tower. In "Bashnia" ("Tower," 1918), Gastev offered the Babel-like image of millions of workers constructing a skyscraper that conquers the heavens: "It has long since torn [and] scattered the clouds, it accompanies the moon through the nights..., it extinguishes it with its light, it quarrels with the sun... the steel spire soars above the world by triumph, labor, achievement." In this tower, the workers of the world are fused into a single soul—an echo of god-building dreams. In "Kran" ("Crane"), the proletariat prepares a crane so huge that it can haul loads across the ocean, move mountains, and shift the earth; Gastev invokes Babel as a precedent whose failure will not be repeated: "We shout to the Babylonian builders over a hundred centuries: again your impulses breathe in fire and smoke, the iron sacrifice is raised beyond Heaven, the proud idol of work again rages." Likewise, the futurist Khlebnikov in "Ladomir" ("GoodWorld," 1920) compares the new order approvingly to the building of a tower into the heavens ("Build your tower of values, Worker... /And, clinking glasses with the constellation Virgo,/ It will recall the wise tunes/ And voice of ancient strongmen."

....

The ecumenical vision that "class energy" could enable communication in spite of previous language barriers was reflected not only in mythopoetic literature but also in the speculations of Soviet linguistic theories. In particular, it was a ramification of N. Ia. Marr's belief that languages evolved from plurality to unity (not vice versa, a la "bourgeois" comparative-historical linguistics) in defined stages and that "glottogonic" shifts from one stage to another were caused by "new modes of thinking" resulting from revolutionary changes in material life, technology, or social structure. For Marr, all language was class-based; the languages spoken by a given class in different countries were more closely related than were those of different classes in the same country, formal similarity notwithstanding. This implied that the world proletariat spoke, if not yet in a common tongue, at least in tongues that were transcendentally linked and, by inference, mutually comprehensible to some extent on the level of meaning.

....

In the 1920s, Marr predicted that a single world language would be created by social engineering as humanity was transformed under true communism—"a root restructuring, a shift... onto the path of revolutionary creativity and the creation of a new language."

"Every man ... in his own language"

One of the primary tasks of production novels of the First Five-Year Plan was to depict how the zeal for labor—the Soviet Holy Spirit—would prevail over the divisive individualism that lingered from the pre-Revolutionary and NEP eras. The unanimity achieved by workers in the course of a novel was to prefigure the concord of the communist New Jerusalem. This harmony could only be attained through the transformation of the workers, who abandoned self-interest for enthusiasm or else found themselves mute and alienated.

....

Philosophical unanimity is not reflected in unity of linguistic form, as might be expected. This was not mere realism; the novels describe not what is but what *should be*. What should be, in the mythopoeia of the First Five-Year Plan, was a sweeping away of linguistic barriers, which were made irrelevant by the unifying enthusiasm of collective labor (or would be so in the next stage of "glottogonic development"). This could be conveyed most effectively not by eliminating linguistic differences but by making them trivial—by showing believers achieving communicative success in the midst of a Babel of tongues, like the apostles at Pentecost.

Models for this anti-Babel can be found in earlier Soviet literature in depictions of apostolic endeavors. In Ivanov's *Bronepoezd 14-69* [*Armored Train 14-69*], Red partisans (speaking in a hubbub of Siberian dialect and Sino-Russian pidgin) are frustrated in their attempts to establish contact with a captured American soldier, whom they wish to convert; finally one of their leaders finds the proper password—"Lenin!" The American replies joyously in English, "There's a chap!" (given without gloss in Roman letters). To "Sovetska [sic] respublika" he shouts, "That is pretty in deed [sic]"...; subsequently he reacts to the Russian's evangelism with "Pro-le-ta-ri-at ... We!" and "Imperializm, awy [sic]!".... The partisans are elated that "he understands" and say of their leader, "Petia speaks American"; they release their prisoner, who has proven to be their spiritual brother.

Communist watchwords are also enough to establish meaningful contact in an encounter between Soviet and English sailors in Gladkov's *Tsement*. When the hero Gleb Chumalov identifies himself with a mixture of words and gestures as a Bolshevik, the seamen lustily shout, "Bolshevik... orra... proletariia." Noting "For the time being we understand one another successfully," Chumalov asks them what their most important word is; one sailor, obviously comprehending, replies, "Kom-in-tern!," which his comrades echo: "Kom-in-tern... ollrait..." At that Chumalov observes, "Correct, Englishmen! That's in our language... No need to expand on that; everything's understood."

....

Conclusion

Production novels and other works of the First Five-Year Plan appropriated the cultural model of Pentecost to convey a myth of the emergence of a proletarian language. In this myth, the Holy Spirit of enthusiastic collective labor—itself a motif inherited from the god-builders—undid the Babel of the pre-revolutionary and NEP periods by facilitating communication among communists, regardless of origin or linguistic differences; it thereby unified believers in the teachings of Lenin into a single community. By contrast, individualists who scorned the enthusiasm of proletarian labor were befuddled and silenced, since there could be no communication or even identity outside of the ideology of the collective. Led by the apostles of the Party, enthusiastic proletarians were laboring to build a Church Universal by overcoming social, regional, and national boundaries; a new form of humanity was in the making and with it, à la Marr, a future language that would be shared by all the workers of the world. Infused with the spirit of collective labor and communicating without difficulty in many languages, the united workers of the sovietized Pentecost myth were given the power to carry out their Great Commission—to evangelize their country and the world at large with the values of the proletariat, to lay the foundation for the New Jerusalem of universal communism, where all would speak in a single tongue.

SELECTED NOTES

[1] On belief in the posthumous immanence of Lenin, see Tumarkin [more data in SUGGESTED FURTHER READINGS].

[2] Enthusiasm is often presented as energy (as in the title of Gladkov's *Energiia*), fire, heat, or fever.

Tchaikovsky as Communist Icon

by Alexander POZNANSKY*

In a letter of 16 April 1883, Petr Il'ich Chaikovskii shared his thoughts on the doctrine of Communism with his benefactress and patroness, Nadezhda von Meck:

> It is impossible to find any utopia more absurd, anything more discordant with the natural tendencies of man. And how dull and unbearably colorless life will surely be when this equality of wealth reigns supreme (if it ever does). Life is the struggle, and if there were no struggle—then neither would there be life, merely senseless vegetating. But it seems to me that any serious implementation of these doctrines is still far off.

In this last opinion at least Chaikovskii proved to be a poor prophet. It was in fact less than thirty-five years later that the October Revolution would usher in the reign of Communism in Russia and, with it, the "unbearably colorless life" and "senseless vegetating" for her inhabitants that Chaikovskii had predicted.

A strange twist marked the perception of Chaikovskii's music and his personality within the Soviet Union. For some two decades following the Bolshevik *coup d'état* of 1917, the composer was

* From *For SK, In Celebration of the Life and Career of Simon Karlinsky*. Edited by Michael S. Flier and Robert P. Hughes. Berkeley: Berkeley Slavic Specialities, 1994. Pp. 233-246.

systematically condemned by the official press as a phenomenon altogether alien to the proletarian consciousness. But Chaikovskii's music stubbornly continued to reach all levels of Russian society.

The prevailing view saw Chaikovskii's music as decadent and melancholic, fraught with pessimism and ennui, and therefore incompatible with the goals of world revolution. The enlightened Bolshevik Anatolii Lunacharskii, who in 1917 was appointed People's Commissar for Education, considered anyone who loved Chaikovskii's music a "sick person" and a "biologically inferior human being." Yet the available evidence demonstrates, however ironically, that amid the collapse of the Russian Empire, the civil war, and widespread hunger, people felt an increasing need for this very kind of music. A new phenomenon emerged—the rally-concert, at which speeches on revolutionary themes were followed by performances of classical music. Among regular theaters, Moscow's *Aquarium* opened its first season of symphonic concerts in the spring of 1918 with a program of Chaikovskii's works. His operas *Eugene Onegin, Iolanta, Mazepa* and *Queen of Spades* were performed during the years that followed, and the Bol'shoi Theater presented his ballets *The Nutcracker* and *Swan Lake*. Chaikovskii was on his way to becoming "a bard of the working intelligentsia."

Considerable attention was also paid to the Chaikovskii Museum in Klin, near Moscow, where the composer's archives had been preserved by his brother Modest who, after his death in 1916, left the house to the *Russian Musical Society*. In June 1918 the Museum was granted a charter of immunity by the Soviet authorities, and on 26 August 1921 Vladimir Lenin signed a decree that nationalized the museum at Klin, declaring it to be "a national and cultural monument whose preservation intact is of importance for the entire country."

....

[Still] ... Anatolii Lunacharskii, while recognizing that Chaikovskii's music was perhaps "very attractive," nevertheless called it "poisonous." Only music in a major key, declared the People's Commissar, could correspond to Bolshevik ideology, whereas music in a minor key was, by its very nature, Men'shevik."

....

During this period of the supremacy of the Russian Proletarian Writers' Association and the *Proletkul't*, a radical organization aimed at the creation of a so-called proletarian culture, Chaikovskii's work was ordered uprooted from Soviet musical culture and proclaimed—together with "bourgeois" culture in general, that is, the entire artistic legacy of the past—to be no longer relevant. At the same time, his music continued to win increasing numbers of listeners. Lenin himself had a weakness for his "Barcarole" and even for the "pessimistic" Sixth Symphony.

By 1928, from a poll conducted among ordinary citizens visiting the *Narva Palace of Culture* in Leningrad, there was a pronounced preference for Chaikovskii's music "among laborers, office workers, and students, but especially among the former." The working-class listener felt little concern for the "corrupting influence" that so worried the Party critics: "We are in no danger of falling prey to ennui, and therefore we are able to appreciate Chaikovskii." [From R. Gruber's interviews with workers.]

The obvious fact that the proletariat itself somehow both failed to recognize the dangerous effects of Chaikovskii's music and continued to hold him dear was much deplored. An editorial in the journal *Muzyka i revoliutsiia* (Music and Revolution) in November 1928 waxed indignant that "the entire musical season proceeds under the banner of Chaikovskii," going on to complain: "Chaikovskii is being presented unchecked in enormous doses.... And all this with no attempt on our part to place any limits on this infatuation, with no critical effort at interpreting the class significance and orientation of the work of Chaikovskii, who is largely alien to the revolutionary consciousness of the present time."

....

But the continuing vilification went unheeded by the masses. Despite the fact that the composer's "hysterical pessimism" and "petty-bourgeois elegiacism" were declared thoroughly incompatible with the goals of the Revolution, ecstatic crowds and enthusiastic applause continued to greet performances of his music. Eventually the authorities realized the dilemma they faced. Either Chaikovskii would have to be banned from the concert halls once and for all, or he would have to be acknowledged a national treasure. Even in the pompous "brave new world" of the Soviet Union in the 1930s the first solution was ridiculous and unthinkable. Thus the authorities capitulated.

....

Finally, in the wake of the far-reaching decree of 23 April 1932 whereby the Communist Party dissolved all existing literary associations, replacing them with the single *Union of Soviet Writers*, similar measures were taken in regard to all other forms of artistic activity, including music. The last remnants of free discussion on cultural themes disappeared. The radical approach of rejecting wholesale the cultural legacy of the past was condemned as "oversimplified" and "vulgar-sociological." From now on, all more or less significant literary and artistic figures of the past were to be classed as "realists." Thus, in the end, the "decadent" and "reactionary-romantic" Chaikovskii triumphed "realistically," as did also Pushkin and Dostoevskii and all the others who had been ordered thrown overboard from the ship of modernity.

....

The period from 1932 to 1940 was the most fruitful in Soviet Chaikovskii studies and probably the most favorable for exploring his biography and music. These years saw the publication of the only edition of the composer's personal (rather than professional) correspondence fully conforming to academic standards, the three-volume publication of his exchange of letters with [his patroness]

Mrs. von Meck. Their correspondence, edited by Vladimir Zhdanov, a Tolstoi specialist, and Nikolai Zhegin, director of the Klin Museum, appeared between 1934 and 1936—that is, before the imposition by Soviet authorities of a strict ban on homosexual themes. Male homosexuality was made a crime by Stalin toward the end of 1933, but it took some time for this law to affect literary censorship. In fact, the subject did not become absolutely taboo until about 1940. Zhdanov and Zhegin's edition of the correspondence with Mrs. von Meck contains extensive commentary with numerous excerpts from hitherto unpublished documents.

It is in this commentary that we encounter what seems to be the only direct confirmation in a Soviet publication of Chaikovskii's homosexuality. "Chaikovskii belongs to history," the editors reasonably state. "His life is a subject of serious study, and we are obliged to lay bare to scholarship all the facts, without fearing the morbid curiosity of the chance reader." They then go on to explain, in the spirit of the positivist psychiatric attitudes of the thirties: "Chaikovskii was homosexual, and in this, subjectively and objectively, his great tragedy lay... Chaikovsky was obviously homosexual by nature, therefore his attempt to change the character of his sexual life [through his disastrous marriage] proved ineffectual." Ill-informed in this matter, Zhdanov and Zhegin were unable to give a thorough account of the complexity of this phenomenon through the full span of Chaikovskii's life and were too quick to conclude that Chaikovskii was continually "tormented by his separateness." Recent scholarship, based on the publication of Chaikovskii's complete correspondence, has shown this view to be superficial and, in the final analysis, unfounded.[1]

But in his foreword to this edition, Boleslaw Przybyszewski, onetime head of the Moscow Conservatory, tried to present Chaikovskii as a symbol of the dying nineteenth-century Russian nobility in the face of inevitable revolution. He saw in the composer's life "traces of the tragic doom" of his class and described his symphonies as "wordless musical tragedies." "His fundamental world-view was not epic, but tragic," declared Przybyszewski, who contended that the Sixth Symphony was in fact a funeral march for the dying aristocracy and bourgeoisie.

The publication of Chaikovskii's correspondence with Mrs. von Meck, especially the editorial commentary, became definitive in Soviet musicology for many years to come. The linking of an image of Chaikovskii tormented by his homosexuality and the "doom of the ruling classes" was long fixed in the minds of Soviet scholars of the thirties....

....

The hundredth anniversary of Chaikovskii's birth in 1940 was celebrated with unbelievable pomp and ceremony. The Moscow Conservatory, founded by Nikolai Rubinshtein, was named after Chaikovskii, as were streets in both Moscow and Leningrad. But the culmination of the festivities was a special decree of the Council of People's Commissars "on perpetuating the memory of the great Russian composer," which called for the erection of a statue in his honor and the publication of a complete edition of his musical compositions and his literary and epistolary legacy. The resolution marked the official canonization of Chaikovskii in the Soviet Union, and only the paradoxical nature of the Soviet system was to blame for the fact that this hard-won recognition had the worst consequences for biographers of the composer.

Chaikovskii became an object of worship in the eyes of the Soviet authorities. From then on, not a single negative word could appear about Chaikovskii in print. From an "alien class element" he was transformed overnight into a "standard-bearer of human progress." Official musicology barely blinked at the transformation or even at the monumental obstacles that now loomed, among them not only the composer's unmentionable homosexuality but also his unswerving monarchism and reactionary politics and his hatred of socialist doctrines. The new ideological interpretation of Chaikovskii's music as expressing "progressive" ideals—that is, ideals compatible with Communist doctrine—became pervasive in all subsequent Chaikovskii scholarship: the man and his creation became indivisible. Falsification was henceforth prerequisite and was pursued with thorough efficiency.

The masses had won a victory over professional music criticism, but in terms of genuine cultural interests it was a pyrrhic one. Everything written about Chaikovskii was now subjected to strict censorship and revision. His biography and political views were made to conform to officially acceptable, often idiotic, standards. His writings, particularly his letters, were published with ruthless cuts, while access to the fuller published versions was made difficult. Chaikovskii's archives were closed to all but a few ideologically trained "specialists." Any sort of exchange of materials with the West ceased for a long time.

....

Indeed, it can be argued that hardly any other figure in the entire history of Russian culture (with the possible exception of Lenin) has been the object of such a complex strategy of accumulated silences and falsifications. One result of this suppression has been a vast number of works about Chaikovskii published in the Soviet Union in the decades following the World War II that totally ignore his important personal characteristics. The standard Soviet biography of Chaikovskii fails even to hint at the true circumstances behind his catastrophic marriage or his unique epistolary friendship with Mrs. von Meck, not to mention his relations with his brothers or his passion for his nephew Bob Davydov.

The other side of the coin has been the mythmaking, though in unwritten form, that existed side by side with official scholarship and that affected popular imagination. Where censorship and restraints on free research created a virtual information vacuum, word of mouth became the chief source of information. Those inquiring about Chaikovskii in musical and artistic circles in the former Soviet Union were treated to a gamut of contradictory notions and fanciful rumor. Some people believed that Chaikovskii had been erotically happy all his life and that his music was in fact a meticulous record of his homosexual experience. Others (among them many serious musicologists) implied that, on the contrary, his sexual inclinations and his incapacity to love women had driven him to such misery and torment that he had even contemplated (and, according to some, had indeed committed) suicide.[2]

Rumors, by definition, cannot serve as factual sources. They reflect not what really happened, but only what people wish to have happened or feel should have happened. Yet in the autumn of 1980, in the pages of the Russian émigré newspaper *Novyi amerikanets* (New American), the least believable version of Chaikovskii's alleged suicide was revived and proclaimed as truth. The article, "Taina zhizni i smerti Chaikovskogo" (The Mystery of Tchaikovsky's Life and Death), by Aleksandra Orlova, a former Soviet writer on music, not only announced as all-but-established fact the notion that Chaikovskii had taken his life, but also claimed, on no other basis than unsubstantiated gossip, that he had been blackmailed into doing so by a cabal of his former classmates from the School of Jurisprudence with the purpose of saving the "honor" of their alma mater from some supposed homosexual scandal. This was a singularly implausible story, so bizarre and extraordinary that one would not expect any person acquainted with nineteenth-century Russian society and social history, let alone a specialist, to give it credence.

....

The absurdity of this theory was quickly demonstrated in the West in a rebuttal to Orlova's allegations by three distinguished Slavicists, Nina Berberova, Malcolm H. Brown, and Simon Karlinsky. Soviet scholars were slower to respond to Orlova's article, but it was Chaikovskii's homosexuality, not his alleged suicide, that made them uncomfortable. Nikolai Blinov prepared a detailed account of Chaikovskii's last days that excludes any possibility of violent death, but he did not live to see it in print. Not until 1986 did the journalist Ol'ga Chaikovskaia venture to bring the suicide allegation to the pages of the popular literary monthly *Novyi mir* (New World). Chaikovskaia, obeying the puritanical Soviet views on sexuality, was emphatic in her insistence that any penetration into Chaikovskii's private life was morally inadmissible, which of course precluded any real clarification of the matter. Readers of her article were left ignorant even of the gender of the person with whom the composer was alleged to have been romantically involved.

The new Soviet policy of *glasnost'* finally brought talk of Chaikovskii's sexual preferences back into the open in Russia, in various publications of Russian gay organizations (among them, the Chaikovskii Fund) and in the mass media. The result, however, was ambiguous: what was made public, after decades of suppression, was not the scholarly verified material about Chaikovskii's personal life, but by and large the same sort of folk mythology about him.

An attempt, however hesitant, to break the taboo on the part of Soviet scholars was finally made in 1990, the one hundred and fiftieth anniversary of Chaikovskii's birth, when Boris Nikitin, in his book *Chaikovskii: Staroe i novoe* (Chaikovskii: Old and New), acknowledged the composer's sexual orientation, calling it an "anomaly." Such anachronistic vocabulary notwithstanding, his book was the first to offer some biographical information hitherto unavailable in Russia.

The present moment is critical as it concerns the vicissitudes of the image of Chaikovskii in Russia—not in terms of another re-evaluation of his artistic achievement, but owing to the newly revealed aspects of his life. Given a lack of sexual education in today's Russian audience, the authorities are understandably hesitant to make public all available information about Chaikovskii and fully open his archives. They fear that this may result in a popular perception of Tchaikovsky as primarily a homosexual, a characteristic that is still largely associated by many with criminal offence, and consequently impair his status within Russian culture.

....

While in the former Soviet Union Chaikovskii as Communist icon is no longer in vogue, it does not mean that his human dimension is already restored to the public. The only way to arrive at the true Chaikovskii is to steep oneself in his own voluminous writings, primarily his letters and diaries, and in the testimony of reliable witnesses unaffected by later prejudice or censorship. It seems, however, that the time for this has not yet come to Russia.

SELECTED NOTES

[1] Alexander Poznansky, *Tchaikovsky: The Quest for the Inner Man* (New York, 1991).

[2] Among the verbal dramatic "disclosures," told variously with horror or even with gusto, were claims that the adolescent Petia was raped during his first night at the School of Jurisprudence by a gang of his classmates led by the future poet Aleksei Apukhtin and as a result of this experience was turned inevitably and forever into a homosexual; that at the end of his life, exposed in an affair with an unspecified teenage member of the Imperial family, Chaikovskii was confronted by Emperor Alexander III himself (who was known to be a particular admirer of his music) with the ultimatum, "Siberia or suicide!"; or, depending on the version, the same ultimatum might have come not from the tsar but from Chaikovskii's own brother Modest in an attempt to save the family honor; cf. Baker's *Biographical Dictionary of Musicians*, 7th edition.

Cultural Contexts

POWER RELATIONSHIPS AND AUTHORSHIP

by Beth HOLMGREN*

Lidiia Chukovskaia

Nadezhda Mandelstam

* From *Women's Works in Stalin's Time: On Lidiia Chukovskaia and Nadezhda Mandelstam.* Indianapolis: Indiana University Press, 1993. Pp. 5-25.

After a decade of diverse experiments in political and economic programs, social legislation, and artistic trends, Soviet society underwent a colossal transformation in the first few years of Stalin's rule (1929-33). According to most observers, Stalin built his dictatorship on the bedrock of enforced and rewarded conformity, mass entertainment, and pervasive government control. The Soviet state became seemingly monolithic; in the words of one historian, "it substituted itself for society, to become the sole initiator of action and controller of all important spheres of life" (Moshe Lewin). Whatever his strategies for gaining power (and these have been well debated elsewhere), Stalin took strong measures to ensure the state's dependence on his personal rule and vision.[1] He performed drastic surgery on his party elite, purging potentially "hostile" elements and recruiting personnel who were, above all, demonstrably loyal to him. He implemented a command economy that operated according to a vertical hierarchy and entailed forced collectivization of agriculture, the use of forced labor, and the imposition of unrealistic work quotas in agriculture and industry. He encouraged loyalty and patriotism, on the one hand, by awarding material privileges to his new elite and engaging the rank and file with an uplifting, accessible popular culture. On the extreme other hand, he extorted compliance from Soviet society by expanding his secret police force and unleashing waves of political terror against "suspect" segments of the population—first violent collectivization and the "terror-famine" against the peasantry (1929-33) and then successive purges conducted against various groups (party and army personnel, the cultural and technical intelligentsia, different nationalities). Historians may never be able to determine the exact number of victims, but it is estimated that at least twenty million died as a result of Stalinist repressions and about forty million were victimized.[2]

....

This cult, atmosphere, and supporting fictions have led several literary critics to comment on the peculiar aesthetic properties of Stalin's dictatorship. Boris Grois [Groys in other texts] argues that Stalinist culture represented the culmination of the avant-garde movement, for it succeeded in aestheticizing all of Soviet life, transforming the population into "extras" and "stagehands" and Stalin himself into its "single author and spectator" (B. Grois). The writer Abram Tertz (the provocative alter ego of the critic Andrei Siniavskii) has pondered Stalin's "artistry" for most of his career. In his very first essay *What Is Socialist Realism?* he identifies the "magical night" of Stalin's dictatorship and ironically laments the Leader's fall from magnificent hyperbole into mortality. In a later essay he characterizes the Stalinist period as a time when art

> was totally replaced by the games of a single Magician, who for a lengthy period was able to lend history itself the power and appearance of fairy-tale fantasy. Art vanished and rotted away so that for a while life (if one looks at it from a standpoint that is detached and tolerant of evil) might acquire the aesthetic savor of nightmarish and bloody farce played out according to theatrical and literary rules. One only has to consider the detective-novel conception of history

which the leader managed to inculcate in millions of people, or his love of realizing metaphors...The pathos of 1937 lay not only in the extent to which the country was gripped by a Bacchic frenzy, nor in the fact that the purges destroyed the most loyal party zealots, but also in the extraordinarily vivid, novelistic way in which metaphors came to life—when the whole country was suddenly crawling with all kinds of invisible (and therefore especially dangerous) reptiles, snakes and scorpions with such terrible names as "Trotskyite" or "wrecker"... Stalin had brought into play (without possibly suspecting it) the magic powers contained in the language and Russian society, ever susceptible to a graphic perception of words and the miraculous transformation of life into the plot of a novel (from which, incidentally, stem the beauty and grandeur of Russian literature), submitted to this terrifying illusion of living in a world of miracles, sorcery, and artifice. These elements were visibly in control of reality and produced a certain intense theatrical pleasure, even as they sent shivers down everybody's spine.

Whether or not Stalin was the artist Siniavskii/ Tertz senses him to be, it is clear that the ruler conceded art extraordinary power—at least according to his own value system; he seemed ever wary of the danger of uncontrolled words and images. Under his general direction, fiction writers and journalists carefully determined and recycled plots, characters, and metaphors that would legitimize state power and rationalize the irrational atrocity of the state's actions. An artist who wrote otherwise would be subverting an ontology thoroughly inscribed by the regime, committing an act of political sabotage and so incurring the punishment of oblivion (being written out) or obliteration (the link between literary and literal in Stalinist "aesthetics").

....

Writers who would not abide by the terms of this contract could not simply turn their backs on the literary establishment, for it was their single source of employment. Yet their official status as author clearly eroded as they worked out forms of partial dependence. Not wishing to write according to the dictates of socialist realism, they tried to earn money by translation or, in some cases, scholarship focused on pre-revolutionary subjects and thus were sidetracked from the high position of the artist in Russian culture. If their works were denied publication in the most visible (and therefore most closely censored) forums, then they were forced to resurface in the margins (e.g., the provincial press) or adjunct spheres (film, radio) of this vast centralized network. In sum, if a writer refused to harness his or her power to the state's machinery, then he or she was deprived of the means to exert it in any other service and effaced as a cultural presence. Under Stalin there could be no public recurrence of writerly authorities like Lev Tolstoi or, for that matter, the political philosopher-turned-novelist Nikolai Chernyshevskii. In nineteenth-century Russia such authors had functioned as spiritual and moral leaders beyond government control. In the Stalinist state writers were always suspected of harboring this ambition, and once "proven guilty," they were demoted further to the status of criminal (Siniavskii/ Tertz). In these cases, the state ruthlessly maintained its pronounced ontology: It expelled such writers from Soviet society, concealed them in the invisible underworld of the prisons and camps, and rewrote their images and life stories to conform to the official fictions about "enemies of the people."

In spite of these dangers, a number of writers continued to produce work they knew was unpublishable and "criminal" and consequently improvised their own means of production, preservation, and (very restricted) circulation. In place of professional editors, proofreaders, and printers, they had to rely on the volunteered service of family and friends and all these enlisted parties had somehow to cope with the risks of the material text. During the 1930s, the decade of Stalin's most virulent purges, Soviet citizens learned to evaluate written documents and private archives according to government practice. In the assessment of Marietta Chudakova, a renowned Soviet archivist and literary critic, "documents were no longer potential or actual monuments of culture—they were perceived in large part as potential material evidence incriminating their owner." With very few exceptions, writers could not hope to save their work from state impoundments by depositing it in state-controlled archives. Nor could the participants in unofficial literary production venture to "publish" a manuscript—even on a very limited scale. At best, writers and readers struggled to preserve a text without alerting the authorities to its existence and endangering the lives of all those contaminated by their contact with it. These pieces of "material evidence," then, were cautiously dispersed, concealed, and even de-materialized. Several copies of a poem might be distributed among trusted friends for safekeeping and manuscripts were secreted in the homeliest places—stuck in saucepans, carted around in old suitcases and trunks and baskets, even buried in jars in the garden. In other instances, texts were committed to memory rather than paper. The text was thus preserved as a domestic or oral artifact and the archive transposed from physical plant to private household or human body.

These desperate, ingenious modes of production and preservation complicated and intensified the relationship between writer and reader. Given the terrible penalties involved, their interaction resembled nothing so much as a conspiracy. The writer put the reader at the same risk he or she had assumed in creating; both had to rely on mutual trust and maintain a fervent belief in the high value of uncensored art. Yet because responsibility for the text was shared, the reader was empowered as well as endangered. He or she became, in effect, a joint owner of a manuscript, even a joint archive for memorized texts... Thus, the reader of unofficial literature was invested with a tremendous privilege—the authority to re-create and interpret the writer's text as well as the writer's image and life story.

The Domestic Sphere and the Situation of Women

If Stalinist society was so well-controlled and policed, where could this unofficial production and maintenance take place? What space existed outside the institutions and organizations in and through which the government exercised its power? The "total" notion of "totalitarian" would seem to preclude a discrete part in the whole, an overlooked underground. Yet, as a result of Bolshevik and then Stalinist policy (as well as traditional Russian attitudes toward women), the state never fully colonized the domestic sphere. It was never subject to the same degree of scrutiny and control applied to the workplace and spaces for public use. The writing, reading, and hiding of unofficial literature, therefore, was chiefly managed in the not altogether private Soviet home.

As in so many other cultures, this sphere was recognized as the domain of women, but it was not conceded the special significance it projected in Western European capitalist societies. Scholars like Nancy Armstrong, Gillian Brown, and Anita Levy have argued that English and American literatures, in tandem with the emergence of capitalism, privileged the domestic sphere and the domestic woman as a means of legitimizing and universalizing middle-class authority and concepts of selfhood and individualism. Under Stalin, the domestic sphere and its official literary depiction were certainly manipulated to support state policies, but never moved into the foreground; the workplace held that position. Indeed, the Bolsheviks had instituted this ranking from the very outset. The new Soviet state granted absolute legal equality to women and initially recognized women's double burden of work and home. Its remedy, however, was to elevate professional labor over domestic work and, at least in its early dreams of a communist utopia, to replace this sphere with collective services—day-care centers, communal kitchens and households.[3] To a great extent, this program mirrored the party's general policy on women: It lobbied to recruit women for the work force and involve them politically in establishing the new Soviet state. A special organization, the *Zhenotdel* (Women's Section), had been created to address their specific developmental needs—particularly as workers and public citizens. Their domestic roles did not hold the party's attention.

These somewhat limited organizations and projects were then discarded in the Stalinist period because, as the press kept insisting, Soviet women had already achieved full equality. In order to ensure a stable work force, the government legislated a retreat to more conservative social policies; in public discourse "[d]omestic labor, self-determination, and sexuality became non-issues" (Buckley). That is, while the state restored the ideal of the nuclear family and urged women to become Heroine Mothers (as well as shock workers in industry and agriculture), it simply ignored their domestic burden and made no pragmatic investment in the domestic sphere. Unlike the explicitly conservative programs of fascist Germany and Italy, the Stalinist system emphasized labor over all. It agitated to retain and recruit female workers—especially after the devastation wrought by collectivization and the purges. Therefore, although Stalinism "assigned a set of functions and roles to women that in some respects intensified the sexual division of labor," it never exclusively vaunted the domain of the family hearth and the image of the female homemaker. This limited focus on the home resulted in material neglect but also a kind of political reprieve. Because women were treated (if not acknowledged) as secondary in society—the rank and file in industry and politics and the invisible homemakers—they were less targeted for party approval or censure.[4]

I argue, then, that despite significant restrictions and deprivations, the domestic sphere under Stalin benefited from this political neglect, and women acquired a valuable low profile along with their secondary status. The neglected domain of women furnished the most likely site for venting difference and creating other-than-official works of testimony or art. In a variation on Western European practice, the domestic sphere and its creative possibilities under Stalin could be conflated as readily with an alternative society as with the status quo. Here lay both the symbolic potential for opposition (...) and a real arena for dissident acts. And this sort of conflation had long been exploited in Russian society. In the nineteenth century, the exclusionary structure of the tsarist government relegated any opposition to the domestic sphere (reading circles and study groups), a developing underground, and the lone public forum of literature, through which different philosophical and political views could be coded (e.g., by Aesopian language), if not openly stated, for the Russian audience. Hence writers and readers in the Stalinist period were historically trained to activate this link between private life, political resistance, and the written word. In their more controlled context, however, writing and reading had to be more closely guarded and the domestic sphere had to serve as shelter, a place of furtive rather than open exchange.

This historic conflation of the domestic sphere and political dissent also established patterns of women's involvement in the opposition. Of course, during the tsarist period women were more confined than liberated within the domestic sphere; for much of the nineteenth century they were largely prevented from entering public life and the skilled labor force. Yet because women were exposed to radical and liberal ideologies mainly through reading and discussion in the home, the domestic sphere furnished them an inadvertent connection with the political underground. While they could not leave home for an assured university education or government service, they could run away from home to join makeshift households of the underground—its fictitious marriages and actual communes. The reform agenda emerging in the wake of the Crimean war (1855) already included the cause of women's emancipation, and very early on, women of the gentry and the intelligentsia enlisted in the service of this and other more subversive causes. In fact, these other causes diverted many women from what they perceived to be the narrow interests and middle-class privileges of feminism. They seemed more readily attracted to the movements (nihilist, populist, socialist) which at least claimed to serve the whole of society, or, more urgently, the oppressed masses of peasants and workers. It seemed, too, that when women managed to escape the strict confines of home and surmount the educational and professional restrictions placed on them, they were propelled further in their dedication and self-sacrifice. Their participation became noteworthy: By the second half of the nineteenth century, "women constituted a substantial and influential minority in the Russian radical intelligentsia" (Engel).

Their evident altruism often led women to disregard their specific needs in favor of "generic" (i.e., tacitly male-oriented) goals, but it garnered them a special prestige among their male cohorts. Assessing women's involvement in the populist movement, one historian observes:

> The women's moral fervor, their "spiritual beauty," earned populists the sympathy of a sector of the educated public …
> (These qualities)also contributed to the creation of a sort of mythology, which defined the revolutionary woman as

limitlessly devoted and endlessly self-sacrificing, a martyr heroine. A myth with enormous appeal to women as well as men of the left, it would remain alive in every subsequent revolutionary movement and war (Engel).

....

By the Stalinist period many of these revolutionary women had been appropriated as official heroines and their successors welcomed into public life and government service. Nevertheless, their model of response, divested of any terrorist elements, proved useful under rather different oppositional circumstances. In the Stalinist state there could be no active underground—certainly not the sweep of nineteenth-century reading and study circles. The secret police apparatus was too well-invested and empowered to miss such "loopholes." But there were vast numbers of people—and of these more women than men—who had been victimized by the regime and left at large in society. In a small, exceedingly brave group of this mass of victims the traditions of literary protest and certain aspects of female-ascribed political resistance coalesced and produced new scenarios of heroism and opposition. For at this point even personal and textual survival were construed as forms of political dissidence; the virtues of self-sacrifice and care-taking could therefore be reapplied to the preservation of these "criminal" lives, texts, and biographies. After Stalin's death, these survivor-caretakers and their new brand of heroism would help to shape a far more comprehensive mode of political dissidence against the totalitarian state.

The Gender Scripts of Socialist Realism

....

Socialist realist literature... developed certain gender constructs in a rigid hierarchy, projecting a reductive and powerful standard that laid down the terms of debate for both official and unofficial writers. As sanctioned expression of the state, these works necessarily took their cue from Stalin himself, who symbolized military and industrial strength and embraced the martial, elitist, and authoritarian in his governing and self-display. The combined elements of physical might, technical and industrial prowess, and military style were promoted in all aspects of public life and suggested a cult of stereotyped, hyperbolized masculinity, although they did not interfere with official rhetoric about equality between the sexes.[5] Rather, these properties—along with an all-consuming work ethic and loyalty to the state—were to be inculcated in men and women alike. This generated very interesting effects in official literature. Especially in the period of "high Stalinism" (the pre-war decade), socialist realist works staged the most important action in the public world or the workplace—in the factory or at a construction project or on the collective farm—and featured heroes of great physical courage and generally martial bearing. In her analysis of the socialist realist novel, Katerina Clark provides an implicit catalog of these "masculine" heroes and their plots. As culled from real life (i.e., for newspaper portraits) and created for fiction, the socialist realist hero echoed the figure of the *bogatyr'*, the mighty warrior in Russian folklore, and was "all s̀truggle,' vigilance,' heroic achievement, energy and another cluster of qualities rather like the 'true grit' of the American frontier: 'stickability' (*vyderzhka*), 'hard as flint' (*kremen'*), and 'will' (*volia*)."

Plots, too, were built around conventionally masculine images and themes that fictionalized political lessons. By the early 1930s, "Soviet society's leaders became 'fathers' (with Stalin as the patriarch); the national heroes, 'sons'; the state, a 'family' or 'tribe'" (Clark). The state was figured as master patriarchy, extending lines of qualified patrilineal inheritance and inspiring the "sons" to the quests and trials that comprised both essential service to the state and a prerequisite rite of passage [from "spontaneous" to "conscious" commitment; see Clark's contribution to this *Reader*].

....

With this predominance of male heroes, male lines of authority, and conventionally male professions and plots, female characters blended into the foreground; their difference was lost or dismissed. At least in the first edition of Fedor Gladkov's *Cement* (1925), a prototype for the socialist realist novel, the figure of Dasha occasionally steals the limelight from her hero-husband, Gleb Chumalov. A product of the less hierarchical 1920S, she had earned a peculiar sort of hero status along with her separate-but-equal leadership in *Zhenotdel*: Her work as a Party activist is accorded special attention in the text, and she is depicted besting her warrior husband in terms of discipline and Party literacy. Yet Dasha's model did not become productive. While women did write socialist realist fiction and female characters did appear as protagonists, these heroines wore the straitjacket of male role models. They, too, had to subordinate the personal to the political, invest themselves wholly in their professional labors, and perform Herculean physical feats in service to the state. In effect, they won equality through conformity, playing surrogate "sons" to unchanged "fathers."

Any display of presumed "feminine" traits and duties shunted them into the role of supporting player. In her study of female characters in official Stalinist literature, Xenia Gasiorowska, reiterates that "the introduction of proper femininity into the characterization of the woman comrade may be responsible for her having never developed leadership, the distinguished quality of the hero." What most often obtained in female characters was a mélange of Stalinist masculine ideals and careful signals of a conventional wholesome femininity—"modesty" and "a sweet naiveté" (for girls), marital fidelity, and abiding maternal instincts. Whatever her marital state or class background (Gasiorowska itemizes peasant, worker, and intelligentsia categories), the female character usually and willingly ceded place of importance to the male. She equaled the average male, but was "seldom allowed to be anything more than average." If married, she almost invariably worked and also served as her husband's helpmate and faithful follower; if single, she could attain the position of esteemed worker (even "Stakhanovite"), but never that of innovator or leader. And although female characters were lauded as mothers in socialist realist fiction, their more or less exclusive domain of childrearing and homemaking remained conveniently out of focus.

Erected in the 1930s, these rigid hierarchies of setting, plot, and characterization set a standard of public conduct that endorsed the features and behaviors of an outsized masculinity and projected the domain and "feminine" traits of women as subordinate; women appeared as leaders neither in Stalinist society nor in Stalinist fiction. It is important to recognize, however, that even official writers began to dismantle some of these hierarchies in response to postwar conditions. By the end of World War II, Soviet military and industrial might had been proved, and accordingly, authors could transform their heroes from warriors to white-collar workers and transfer them from building sites to the family circle. Love and family relations were more fully integrated into the hero's development; indeed, the role of hero was often conferred on a wife or mother who struggled to keep her family intact. While these changed emphases did not fundamentally alter the secondary status of women, they forecast certain preoccupations central to the post-Stalin era and indirectly productive of women's greater role in unofficial Soviet society.

Just as these texts cautiously anticipated the concerns and values of the thaw period—for example, a call for greater "sincerity" and a focus on emotional development and family life—they faintly echoed a much stronger, earlier backlash in unofficial literature against the warrior ethos. The domestic world they began to claim for the state was already in the process of being staked out and interpreted—much more boldly and eloquently—by unofficial writers. We cannot gauge the scope of this prior exploration, for we never will know how many manuscripts were lost or destroyed. But I propose to consider this phenomenon on the evidence of several important writers and their texts—specifically, the works of Osip Mandel'shtam, Mikhail Bulgakov, Boris Pasternak, and Anna Akhmatova. Composed and preserved in the Soviet Union during the Stalinist years, their texts generated significantly different plots and heroes and posited alternative constructs of gender.

Alternative Scripts

In a richly complex way, the poetry and essays of Osip Mandel'shtam (1891-1938) prepared this different focus; as we shall see, the roles he devised for men and women encouraged his wife in part to become one sort of writer. Mandel'shtam already sensed and meditated on the cataclysmic effects of revolution in *Tristia*, his second collection of poems (1916–20), and this "eschatological vision" [Isenberg] consequently informed much of his life work. Enacting his self-styled role as the "preserver of cultural continuity," he countered the revolution's disruption of culture with the evocation of a composite underworld—one that interspersed classical imagery of the afterlife with the utensils and artifacts of a multicultural domesticity.[6] Stocked with images of honey, wine, clay jugs, a loaf of bread, yarn, and spinning wheels, this underworld seemed to incarnate the "domestic Hellenism" that Mandel'shtam subsequently prescribed for Russian poetry in his 1922 essay "On the Nature of the Word":

> Hellenism is the conscious surrounding of man with domestic utensils instead of impersonal objects; the transformation of impersonal objects into domestic utensils; and the humanizing and warming of the surrounding world with the most delicate teleological warmth. Hellenism is any kind of stove near which a man sits, treasuring its heat as something akin to his own internal body heat. And finally, Hellenism is the Egyptian funerary ship in which the dead are carried, into which everything required of man's earthly wanderings is put, down to perfume phials, mirrors, and combs.

Already in the first years of the Soviet state, Mandel'shtam had defined a set of important, connected oppositions: the revolution's disruption of culture versus cultural continuity maintained in a domestic underworld; a culture in which words are enslaved for "liturgical use" (at this point he is attacking the Russian Symbolists) versus a "man-centered" culture that cherishes the crafts and materials of its own home (that is, the ideal of his own poetic group, the Acmeists). It was as if he were prophesying his response to the disruptive violence and restriction of Stalinism; in both oppositions, he privileged his own peculiar, elastic vision of the domestic sphere. In this early period, however, Mandel'shtam still hoped that his views could be incorporated into the new social order. A decade later, when he reasserted his "organic poetics" and the "sacralization of everyday life" in the travel essay "Journey to Armenia" (1933), he had become a pariah in the literary establishment and was having great difficulty publishing his work. It would seem that Mandel'shtam's "man-centered" values and poetics inexorably cast him as an opponent in the Stalinist system. (Indeed, the exceptional appearance of "Journey to Armenia" in the magazine *Zvezda* cost its editor, Tsezar' Vol'pe, his position.) His defamatory poem about Stalin then made him a palpable criminal, and he was arrested, exiled, and officially repressed as a writer.

Although Mandel'shtam's complex assignations of gender (particularly to the formation of the poet) developed throughout his writing life, I would argue that they are also essentially connected to the vision of *Tristia*. While Mandel'shtam wished to inculcate "a perfect manliness" in Russian poetry by way of responding to a new "heroic age," his *Tristia* poems had already imaged this "manliness" in a series of noble, doomed gestures. The manly hero of socialist realist fiction was inadequate for Mandel'shtam's purpose; he anticipated and displaced the victorious warrior with portraits of a courageous, vanquished, dying brotherhood who "shall remember even in the Lethean cold/ That the cost of this earth was ten heavens" ("Twilight of Freedom"). In coping with the tragic defeat he first evoked in *Tristia*, Mandel'shtam located, among many other mythologies, a model of the kenotic Christ which could embody the tragic and the manly along with a capacity for transcendence. In his book, *A Coat of Many Colors: Osip Mandelstam and His Mythologies of Self-Presentation*, Gregory Freidin analyzes this and other mythologies in Mandel'shtam's work with great perspicacity and erudition; what I want to consider here, therefore, is not the specific application of the model, but the androgynous possibilities it contains. According to Christian scriptures, Christ was incarnated as a man and called only men to be his disciples. But, as interpreted by Mandel'shtam and several other Russian writers, he eschewed a martial ideal for a martyrdom/ heroism permeated with the traditional "feminine" traits of gentleness, compassion, and utter self-sacrifice. By appropriating this model for his own self-image as a poet, Mandel'shtam was extending, perhaps, his own very early definition of the lyric poet as a "two-sexed creature" (*"dvupoloe sushchestvo"*). Most certainly he posed the figure of the suffering, redemptive poet—particularly the poet Mandel'shtam— as the true hero of his age.

In the tradition of many poets, Mandel'shtam developed an androgynous model of the creator which nonetheless was to be assumed by himself and other men. Yet, among the various images he ascribed to female subjects and addressees, he reiterated one important role for women that engendered its own heroism and, in some cases, creative personae. Once again, his *Tristia* poems set the pattern: They project enduring images of women as the "blessed wives" (*"blazhennye zheny"*) who can divine the future and "will gather the light ashes" of the dead ("In Petersburg We Shall Meet Anew"). In his vision, women were not magnified as surrogate "sons," but valued and symbolized in the more traditionally female vocations of mourner and seer. The final lines of the poem *Tristia* make this assignation: "Not for us conjectures about Greek Erebus,/ wax is for women what bronze is for a man,/ Only in battles do we learn our lot,/ but they are granted death in the act of divination." And once again, Mandel'shtam's vision functioned as a sort of prophecy. Foretold in *Tristia*, this role, in a sense, was commemorated in his last poem "Toward the empty earth" ("K pustoi zemle nevol'no pripadaia"). As Jane Gary Harris notes in her biography of Mandel'shtam, this poem was begun as a tribute to Natasha Evgen'evna Shtempel', a young schoolteacher who befriended the Mandel'shtams in their Voronezh exile and helped Nadezhda Mandel'shtam in the dangerous, difficult task of preserving Osip's work. Mandel'shtam's poem beautifully defines and generalizes her heroism:

> There are women kin to the damp earth
> And their every step is a resonant sobbing.
> To escort the resurrected and be first
> To greet the dead is their calling.

> To demand caresses from them is criminal,
> And to part with them is unendurable.
> Today—an angel; tomorrow—a graveyard worm,
> And the day after that—only an outline.
> What had been her step will become unrecognizable.
> Flowers are immortal. Heaven is whole.
> And what will be is only a promise.

Mandel'shtam's prescience was distinctive, but his basic views on the domestic sphere and male and female roles coincided to a remarkable extent with the visions of other writers forced to work unofficially. In particular, I have in mind the two major fictions of Mikhail Bulgakov and Boris Pasternak—*The Master and Margarita* and *Doctor Zhivago*. While these texts are set in different historical periods (only Bulgakov's novel takes place in a carefully manipulated version of Stalinist times), their portraits of the Soviet artist resemble each other in their response to and deviance from the Stalinist model.

Both texts stem from their authors' own experience, although neither Bulgakov nor Pasternak suffered the extreme persecution of Mandel'shtam. Despite bans put on his plays, Bulgakov (1891—1940) managed to keep working as a playwright and a librettist in various theaters for most of his life; in one of the most curious episodes in Soviet literary history, Stalin himself interceded to return Bulgakov to his post. Pasternak (1890-1960) was not severely attacked in the Stalinist years, but he had to take refuge in translation during the waves of pre- and postwar purges. Nevertheless, both men were aware that their novels would be deemed criminal by the regime.[7] They worked (more or less) in secret on their texts, shared them only with friends and close associates, and did not try to publish them while Stalin lived. Within that sustaining network of friends and family, both writers especially relied on the support of the women they loved—Pasternak on his second wife, Zinaida Neigauz, and his mistress, Ol'ga Ivinskaia, who maintained a separate household for him and suffered imprisonment largely on his account; Bulgakov on his third wife, Elena Shilovskaia, who preserved his novel after his death and eventually saw to its publication in the 1960s. Perhaps in consequence, their novels—whatever their historical setting—highlight the conditions and parties involved in the unofficial literary process.

Both novels focus on the experience and reception of an independent artist. The literary establishment plays little or no part in their protagonists' creative development. It is simply absent in *Zhivago*. In *The Master and Margarita* it is the object of extravagant satire: The Union of Soviet Writers (renamed MASSOLIT) is exposed as an organization of hacks and bureaucrats who scramble for the material privileges of official writers—special villas, paid vacations, entrance to the "best restaurant in Moscow." The artist-heroes in these works therefore rely on other, nonliterary means of support and the creative workspace of home. The poet Zhivago, for example, earns his living as a doctor and writes poems in catch breaths from his work and the onrush of history—especially when he finds himself in the right domestic environment. When his family flees Moscow for the remote Ural town of Varykino, Zhivago keeps a journal in the winter evenings when everyone relaxes around a warm stove, the women sewing or knitting and the men reading aloud. Later, when he returns to Varykino to make a temporary home with his mistress, Lara, he is once again inspired to write by "the warm, well-lit room," the writing utensils on his desk, the clean linen on the beds, and the pure faces of the sleeping Lara and her daughter. He christens his last lodging, a studio specially provided him for work, a "banqueting room of the spirit, a cupboard of mad dreams, a storeroom of revelations."[8] And as he savors his first home in Varykino, Zhivago articulates a definition of art which spurns the "high-flown rhetoric" of revolutionary literature and echoes, on a purely Russian scale, Mandel'shtam's ideal of "domestic Hellenism":

> Only the familiar, touched by the hand of genius, is truly marvelous. The best object lesson in this is Pushkin. What a hymn to honest labor, duty, the customs of everyday life! Today "bourgeois" and "petty bourgeois" have become terms of abuse. Pushkin anticipated this criticism in his "Family Tree":
>
> "I am middle-class, I am middle-class."

Bulgakov's Master, on the other hand, is a professional historian who wins one hundred thousand rubles in a lottery, quits his job, and devotes himself to writing a novel about Pontius Pilate. The prize money furnishes him with income and, much more important, two basement rooms in a small house with a garden—"an altogether private apartment with a foyer, and a sink in it" and "small windows just above the pathway leading to the gate."[9] This is the sanctum in which he and his mistress, Margarita, become completely absorbed in the creation of his novel. After many fantastic events, when the Master and Margarita have been spirited away into the afterlife by a peculiarly beneficent Satan, they are granted the final refuge of a secluded country home with a Venetian window, a "vine climbing to the very roof," and a babbling brook nearby.

Thus, Pasternak and Bulgakov figure the domestic sphere as the birthplace (and perhaps guiding spirit) of art and the artist's ideal workplace. Their heroes feel most comfortable in this sphere and seem both reluctant and ill-equipped to assert themselves in a public role; they contrast with the socialist realist hero in body as well as spirit. Zhivago possesses a snub nose and an "unremarkable face," while the Master appears dressed in shabby hospital garb. They do not metamorphose into warriors or important bureaucrats or even official authors. Zhivago is esteemed as a doctor and an artist, but he effectively shuns professional glory and material status. Bulgakov's hero has renounced his job, his past, and even his name in order to be identified, in a half-ironic homely way, as a "master"; the only emblem of his lofty vocation is a greasy skullcap Margarita has embroidered with the letter "M." Neither achieves public fame as a writer. Zhivago's works are published through the good graces of friends and are highly valued by friends and "collectors." The Master does submit his novel for official publication, but the resulting wave of vicious condemnation (directed at a text that is never published) terrorizes him into burning his manuscript and committing himself to a mental hospital.

Unimposing by socialist realist standards, Zhivago and the Master instead reiterate certain features of Mandel'shtam's heroism, evincing comparisons with the figure of Christ. Curiously enough, the parallels in the Master's case apply to his frail humanity as well as his conception of himself as an artist—that is, his commitment to express his intuition of the truth. The Yeshua (Christ) he depicts in his novel is no powerful deity, but an itinerant, well-meaning young man who seeks to elicit the good in people through his own "good words." Yeshua explicitly discounts the myths that are being ascribed to him, and when he seems to demonstrate a superhuman power (divining the physical suffering of Pilate), he explains his ability as a simple process of human deduction. Wise and compassionate, this version of Christ is nonetheless earth-bound and physically unheroic. He is eager to avoid torture and in no way seems prepared for the meaningful self-sacrifice of a kenotic Christ.

For Zhivago the association is more self-conscious and self-styled, a fundamental theme in the narrative and the poems carefully displayed at the novel's end. Zhivago's Christ, connected to the figure of Hamlet in his first poem, is the epitome of self-renunciation, receptivity, and inner freedom or, in the words of his philosopher uncle, the ideas of the "free personality" and "life as sacrifice." Zhivago, in turn, manifests these qualities in his capacious nature— his unwillingness to commit to a partisan cause or a public persona, his great sensitivity toward others and his love of life (his surname derives from the Russian root *zhiv* or "live"), his aversion to mortal combat and what one critic identifies as "an almost complete lack of male aggressiveness" (Hingley). Moreover, Zhivago's model of a non-aggressive, receptive, self-sacrificing Christ clearly joins the dissident and the domestic. The Christ theorized in the narrative of *Doctor Zhivago* overturns the beastliness and corruption of all previous empires with his "emphatically human, deliberately provincial" image, his birth to a simple girl, his truths taken from everyday life. Both Pasternak and Bulgakov, then, use the figure of Christ to develop a heroism which is oppositional and "emphatically human-if not an implicit synthesis of masculine and feminine traits, then a non-aggressive, self-sacrificing model of masculinity.

Of course, this "emphatically human" Christ and the heroes he inspires are all men; as in so many Russian novels, only male characters seem endowed with the gift of artistic creativity. But, perhaps more than ever before, the male creators are depicted here as dependent, frail creatures whose creations inevitably overshadow and transcend them.

....

As one might guess from her absence in the title of *Zhivago*, Lara emerges as the more conventional man-made character. Raised in a petty bourgeois family, she works as a governess and then a teacher, serves as a nurse in the first world war, and becomes the most beloved and influential of Zhivago's three "wives." All three share the "common denominator of domesticity," but Lara especially incarnates and articulates it as an ideal. Lara's beauty most enthralls Zhivago when she is "busy at her domestic chores"—cooking, washing, cleaning, ironing. Although she is initially sympathetic to the revolution, she expresses primary allegiance to her home and daughter. Her first household—with her husband Pavel Antipov—had been destroyed by the sloganizing and conformist ethos of the times; this artificial atmosphere misled Antipov into military service, first in the tsarist army and then in the Red Army. For Lara, Antipov's feats of military valor are beside the point, an obstacle to her real goal: "If by some miracle, I could see the window of our house shining, the lamplight on Pasha's desk and his books, even if it were at the end of the earth—I would crawl to it on my knees."

Therefore, while Lara reiterates the stereotype of the domesticated woman, her domesticity may also be read as a source of alternative power in a regimented, politically invasive society. It is important that her equally stereotyped feminine capacities for attracting, nursing, coping, and facilitating are idealized in the novel, not demoted to a secondary plot. While it might seem that Pasternak is simply resurrecting the traditional nineteenth-century Russian plot of the superfluous man and the beautiful woman who symbolizes a "higher Purpose," he has filled both Purpose and symbol with material, human content. The ideals he opposes to the status quo are not visions of a new social order, but the tangible Lara and the domestic refuge she creates—in short, Pushkin's "housewife" and "bowl of cabbage soup." And unlike the superfluous antihero, who always proved incapable of appreciating and committing himself to his beloved, Zhivago avidly pursues a relationship with Lara until political circumstances force them to separate.

....

Compared with Lara, the figure of Margarita is much more devoted to her supportive literary role. But she, too, embodies yet another variant of conventional femininity. Whereas Lara actively keeps house and mothers her daughter, Margarita is a childless lady of leisure—a woman married into the Soviet equivalent of the upper middle class ... Her privileged status frees her from the duties of wife, mother, and working woman; her intermittent life with the Master constitutes a further rarefaction, a secret (even underground) household that conspires in romantic love and artistic creation. For the Master and Margarita both, domestic bliss rests on the convenient juncture of financial security, illicit love, and idealistic desires.

But when this secret home is lost and the Master languishes in an asylum, Margarita finds she cannot return to the world of material comfort. Instead, she charts a new, actively heroic, wholly fantastic course for her character. Margarita emerges as the stronger partner in their relationship, avenging the Master's persecution and displaying extraordinary courage and determination in her attempts to recover him. Of all the residents of Moscow, she alone eagerly cooperates with the Devil—on blind faith that he will lead her to the Master. In a striking departure from Goethe's Faust (to which this novel frequently and playfully alludes), Margarita navigates between Gretchen's passive suffering and Faust's overweening ambition as she strikes her own deal with the Devil. Her pact results not in the acquisition of creative power, but in a kind of quest-romance with the gender roles reversed. Here Margarita is the bold hero who braves fantastic adventures in order to rescue her beloved (the "bride-figure" in traditional romances). The female helper thus plays the role of active hero and undergoes both metamorphosis and death to achieve her goal. In yet another reversal, the demonic figures she meets in her quest are not her enemies; rather, she invokes their supernatural aid (and standards) against the evils of Stalinist society. We saw in Zhivago how the artist and the domestic sphere were allied with and sanctified by the figure of Christ. In *The Master and Margarita* the home and persons of writer and reader are guaranteed by Satan—albeit beyond the limits of Stalinist reality. As in Mandel'shtam's vision, the locus of unofficial culture is once again figured in a benevolent underworld.

In Bulgakov's version of the underworld, then, Margarita considerably exceeds the figure of "blessed wife." Rather than enduring as mourner or seer, she is transformed into a witch, a woman possessed by supernatural powers and outcast because she reverses "normal and socially accepted behavior." She enjoys the most fantastic sights and adventures in the novel as she flies over Moscow, attends a witches' Sabbath, and presides over Satan's ball; just as the Master is named for his work, so she earns the underworld title of Queen. Although her powers derive from Satan, she—like her mentor—intends evil and works good within the inherently immoral system of Stalinism. In effect, Margarita embraces and wields the criminality assigned her and the Master by Stalinist society. Transformed into a fantastic criminal, she finds that she has real power to act—to break with the corrupted world, to wreak vengeance on the literary establishment (she destroys the home of the Master's chief persecutor), and to rescue her beloved and their treasure.

Nevertheless, the impulse of the "blessed wife" lies at the heart of her witchery. Margarita's thrilling metamorphosis does not alter her fundamental concerns with the writer and the text. She does not plead to remain a witch (as does her capricious maid, Natasha). Before, during, and after her bewitchment, Margarita remains uniformly devoted to the Master and, more particularly, to his manuscript. It is Margarita who eagerly reads and rereads the text as it is composed, who rakes out the remains of the burned manuscript with her bare hands, who cherishes and keeps these charred pages as one of her most treasured possessions. (In this story, the blessed wife literally tends the ashes of the destroyed manuscript.) Her avid interest, reverence and devotion suggest that she perceives the novel as common property, even a collective divination.

....

In life Mandel'shtam, Pasternak, and Bulgakov all depended on the ministrations of the women closest to them to produce and maintain their work. The autobiographical texts of real-life "blessed wives" like Nadezhda Mandel'shtam then tell this story from the other side and with the supposedly greater authenticity and lesser imagination of nonfiction.

In telling their story, however, these "wives" confront a culturally imposed gender gap between preserving and creating; men have already scripted their noble images, acts, thoughts, and speech in the roles of helpmate and reader, not writer. As I will explore on their individual examples, Chukovskaia and Mandel'shtam came to write out of a complexity of influences and sanctions, but it is important to note here that they were specifically empowered by one unofficial female artist — that is, the poet Anna Akhmatova (1889-1966). Under Stalin, Akhmatova earned a martyrdom similar to that of Mandel'shtam: Although she did not die in the camps, her third husband and only son were imprisoned, her first husband was executed, and she herself was expelled from the Union of Soviet Writers after World War II. She lived in poverty and fear for most of her life. Yet throughout the Stalinist years she produced unofficial poems that reflected on and generalized from her terrible experience — most often through a female persona. Akhmatova, therefore, demonstrated the possibility of a woman writing about these times from her own perspective.

More specifically, Akhmatova does not rewrite the scenario of the unofficial male creator; rather, she explores the special capacity and experience of those left in charge of the domestic sphere and shows how a woman writer can achieve the status of an unofficial bard, a true heroine of her age. In striking contrast to her male associates, she does not idealize the domestic sphere but uses it as resonating place of torment—a private space where women agonize over their victimized loved ones and cope with the dual reality of Stalinist life. Akhmatova, unlike Bulgakov and Pasternak, addresses the horrors of Stalinism as they occur In her famous poetic cycle "Requiem" (written from 1938 to 1940) she chronicles the anguish of a female "I" (what seems to be an autobiographical persona), whose son has been arrested. Alone in her room, the woman endures waves of illness, alienation, guilt, madness, and a longing for death. Her home provides no comfort, only a place for confronting the truth. When the woman receives word of her son's sentence, she registers its impact in chilling domestic terms—in the incongruity of "that bright day and deserted house."

Furthermore, Akhmatova connects this anguished domestic sphere with yet another kind of underworld—the silent and silenced world of prison queues where petitioners wait to receive word about their imprisoned loved ones and to send them packages, letters, and money. Women largely people both of these spheres; the poetic "I" bears witness to the different women who stand there and quotes one beautiful girl who comes to the queue "as if it were home." With its cast of women and alternating settings of prison line and domestic interior Akhmatova's text suggests that the prison queues comprise an inevitable extension of the domestic sphere. Charged to maintain the home and family, women are compelled there—to the very threshold of the prisons and camps—out of concern for their missing family members and friends. Given the impossibility of a political underground, this threshold world ventures the one collective site where the bereaved and victimized can gather together and observe among themselves "how faces fall apart,/ How fear looks out from under the eyelids, How deep are the hieroglyphics/ Cut by suffering on people's cheeks."[10]

Thus, while Mandel'shtam, Pasternak, and Bulgakov posit an idealized or, metaphysical refuge and opposition, Akhmatova chooses to focus on this real space and potential community of women's experience. She even binds her image as artist to the prison queues. In the prose foreword to "Requiem" (...) she consoles a woman with her promise to write this experience; in the "Epilogue" she directs future generations to erect the monument before the prison gates "where I stood for three hundred hours: And where they never, never opened the doors for me." Through the sequence of "Requiem" Akhmatova projects herself undergoing a crucial transformation from the capricious "sylvan-princessly" personae of her early poetry (poetry which marked her as poet "for women") into the impressive monument of a female poet who stands with and mourns for all the tyrant's victims.

In this way, Akhmatova does educe a writing role for the "blessed wife," but this persona is no helpmate to a male creator. In lieu of the Christ-like traits of male artists, she enhances her role through other historical and religious analogies—the Russian boyars' wives lamenting over their slain rebel husbands and, in direct complement to the Christ figure, the mother of Christ suffering unimaginably at her son's crucifixion. According to the scenes of "Requiem," Akhmatova's gender constructs very much echo those of Mandel'shtam, although they reverse his assignation of speaking roles. In her rendering, men are depicted as the silenced, unseen victims, while the mourning women are empowered to lament and commemorate.

Section III • The Stalinist Period and World War II

SELECTED NOTES

1. See, for example, Roy A. Medvedev, *Let History Judge: The Origins and Consequences of Stalinism;* (New York: Columbia University Press, 1989); Tucker, Robert C., *Stalin in Power: The Revolution from Above, 1928-1941* (New York: Norton, 1990).
2. I base these figures on Robert Conquest's updated version of his classic *The Great Terror: A Reassessment* (New York: Oxford University Press, 1990).
3. Richard Stites notes the domestic programs of both Lenin and the famous Bolshevik woman activist, Aleksandra Kollontai. Kollontai advocated collectivizing both workplace and home, whereas Lenin specifically attacked the waste and pernicious effect of individual housekeeping.
4. Writing about women in official literature, [Xenia] Gasiorowska observes: "Women are never wreckers or saboteurs or murderers; they are not expelled from the party or sent to labor camps or even found guilty of ideological deviations. A woman's wrongdoings are possible only within the domain of morals and manners within the specific Soviet way of life. Conversely, however intelligent, educated, or dedicated a Soviet heroine may be, she does not rise above the invisible ceiling assigned to a woman's career." See her *Women in Soviet Fiction 1917-1964* (Madison, Milwaukee, and London: The University of Wisconsin Press, 1968.)
5. I preface the term masculinity with qualifiers like "conventional" or "stereotyped" so as not to settle into an artificial binary opposition of masculine and feminine. Biologists, psychologists, and social scientists have been discovering that the concepts of masculinity and femininity are actually "fuzzy sets" of attributes and behaviors which cannot be invariably applied, even though we still seem able to distinguish generally between the two. ...
6. In his pioneering book, *Mandelstam*, Clarence Brown [for further bibliographical information, see SUGGESTED FURTHER READINGS in Section Two] elabo-rates on the poet's combining of high and low references: "The epic, heroic world of Homer and the tragedies is practically never to be found without a leaven of the domestic, the low, the thoroughly Russian ..."
7. Pasternak received tangible proof of this fact. While he was writing *Zhivago*, the authorities pressured him to abandon his novel by arresting his mistress, Ol'ga Ivinskaia, and sending her to a labor camp.
8. Quoted from the translation by Max Hayward and Manya Harari, 1958 (New York: Ballantine, 1986).
9. Quoted from Mirra Ginsburg's translation of *The Master and Margarita*, 1967 (New York: Grove Press, 1978).
10. These citations are taken from the translation of *Requiem* by D. M. Thomas (London: Paul Elek, 1976).

Cultural Contexts

SOVIET LABOR CAMPS: A BRIEF HISTORY

by Leona TOKER*

....

On August 30, 1918, Fanny Kaplan shot at and wounded Lenin; the same day Leonid Kanegisser assassinated M. S. Uritskii, head of the Petrograd Cheka. The government retaliated with the "Red Terror," proclaimed by the cabinet's decree of September 5, 1918. The decree expanded the powers of the Cheka and, among other things, practically legalized the camps. In the months that followed, the camps were still a relatively minor issue, because the Cheka made prompt use of its new license not only to make arrests but also to pass and execute death sentences. About 60,000 death sentences were meted out between September 1918 and January 1920; the number of people shot or hanged summarily, especially in the territories swept by the Civil War was, apparently, much larger.

Since the right to make arrests was also exercised by other government agencies, the prisons were becoming overcrowded. There was a lack of funds to pay their staff and supply the prisoners with clothing, soap, or even sufficient amounts of food. For reasons both ideological (the expected waning

* From *Return from the Archipelago: Narratives of Gulag Survivors.* Indianapolis: Indiana University Press, 2000. Pp. 13-27.

of prisons under socialism) and economic (small budget, housing shortages), new prisons could not be built in the post-Revolution years. Instead, people formally sentenced to imprisonment, as well as those held on an administrative basis, were often transferred to supposedly temporary camps organized in available monastery or private estate buildings or in hastily constructed barracks. Whereas the makeshift character of the facilities seemed to point at the impermanence of the camps, the relative cheapness of setting them up encouraged their proliferation.

In addition to using the "places of confinement" under the jurisdiction of the Commissariat of Justice, the Cheka maintained camps of its own. The two agencies entered into a competition for funds, facilities, and inmates. In this power struggle, the Cheka stood for the expediencies of repression, whereas the Commissariat of Justice laid emphasis on Marxist legal ideals, such as re-education. The continued existence of crime after the revolution was now attributed to "relics of the capitalist past"; the agenda of the Commissariat of justice was to "re-educate" the inmates through labor. For this reason, as well as in the hope of financing the prisons and camps at least partly by deductions from the prisoners' wages, the Commissariat of Justice recommended labor, especially physical labor, for all prisoners; lighter offenders were even sentenced to forced labor without imprisonment.

The Cheka and the NKVD (the People's Commissariat of Internal Affairs), which ran most of the prisons and camps from 1922 through 1930, had more practical concerns. Whereas the NKVD favored prison labor not so much for its "educational" value as for the prospect of making the camps economically self-sufficient, the main concern of the Cheka lay with incapacitation of the "socially dangerous," especially since the widespread unemployment in the whole country in the early twenties was a stimulus for the free workers' productivity and an obstacle to the systematic development of convict labor.

In most camps from 1918 through 1920 the discipline was perfunctory, the regulations were lax, and successful escapes were numerous. The death toll was large, mainly owing to neglect and privation; in 1922 great numbers of prisoners plainly starved. In camps situated near larger cities prisoners fared better than in more distant locations, since the possibilities of interaction with the local population were greater, the mail and the provisions more regular, and the rule of the guard commanders less arbitrary. In the camps themselves manufacture was difficult to organize, and since taking the prisoners to work outside the enclosures promoted escapes, the Cheka often chose not to enforce the convict labor. The logistics lessons were, however, assimilated: in 1920, on the initiative of Feliks Dzerzhinskii, head of the Cheka, "special concentration camps" were created in the northern regions, mainly around Arkhangelsk. The remote location and rugged terrain made escape even from the work sites unpromising. The first of the camps to leave a grim trace in popular memory was set up in Kholmogory in 1921 to hold the Kronshtadt sailors who had survived the brutal suppression of their rebellion.

The Cheka was officially abolished by a decree of February 6, 1922, as a hint at a liberalization following the end of the Civil War. Its functions and its leader, however, were transferred to the State Political Administration (GPU). This new agency was supposed to run only one prison in Moscow and one in Petrograd, but Dzerzhinskii managed to keep the "special" camps as well.

In 1922-23 the inmates of the Kholmogory and Pertominsk camps near Arkhangelsk were transferred to the venerable monastery grounds of the Solovetskie Islands in the White Sea; the so-called *Solovki* then became the largest single concentration camp in the country. The prisoners included former members of the upper classes or the intractable intelligentsia, members of the suppressed political parties, White Guard soldiers and officers, clergymen, peasants who had opposed the grain requisitions, workers who had gone on strike, black-market traders, and engineers or technicians charged with "wrecking." There were also common and professional criminals; their numbers eventually grew.

Recruiting camp guards and commanders from captive White Guard officers and Chekists who had committed punishable offenses solved the question of staffing. Aware of the precariousness of their position, the former officers sought to ingratiate themselves with the new regime by emphatic zealousness; most were eventually shot anyway. The numerical disproportion between the cadre and the prisoners led to sadistic ways of maintaining control: a church on Sekirnaia Hill was converted into a torture prison and the monastery basements into execution chambers. The penal function of the Solovki was not secret, and there were rumors of atrocities; but with little concrete information in print, the threat represented by the camps was enhanced by their mysteriousness.

In the Solovki prisoners categorized as "political" were exempt from labor. This status was granted only to members of the Social Revolutionary (SR) Party, Mensheviks, and anarchists; all the other actual or "platonic" opponents of the regime were classed as "counterrevolutionaries" (later as "enemies of the people") and held together with the criminal offenders. Eventually, even members of socialist parties were denied the status of political prisoners, and the notion itself went out of official circulation.[1] Labor became mandatory throughout the camp system.

In the northern camps opponents' and delinquents' isolation from society was more efficiently combined with forced labor. Camp maintenance soon stopped being the main form of employment. Lumbering for export (much in demand) and infrastructure projects turned camp inmates into a slave labor force. The locations of new camps were now determined not by the available facilities but by the sites where such labor was needed. From the Solovki, camp metastases (Solzhenitsyn's famous metaphor) spread to the mainland.

The expansion of the network was spurred by Stalin's collectivization of agriculture, which brought hundreds of thousands of peasants into the camps, and by the great leap toward industrialization, which created a huge demand for labor. The concept of "re-education through labor" was now given a new meaning: the degree to which the prisoners were "reforged" was now measured by their production output. Certain work teams, usually made up of criminal convicts, were granted conditions that allowed them to claim miraculous productivity. Thus, ideology ceased competing with expediency and became its instrument. The shift to the so-called reforging campaign was preceded by a typically Stalinist scapegoating: in the fall of 1929 hundreds of the White Guard officers who had served as warders in the Solovki were shot, along with great numbers of their fellow officers and intellectuals from among the prisoners.

The darkest side of reforging was the new policy of using hunger as incentive. Up to 1930 the starvation of the prisoners was a by-product of the lack of funds, of the difficult food situation in the whole country, of thefts, and of plain neglect. Reforging transformed it into a disciplinary and motivational measure. Robert Conquest notes that "Stalin was well aware of Marx's economic objection to slavery" as inefficient because slaves, who got minimal subsistence irrespective of their production results, had no incentive to work; consequently, "with his usual refusal to accept precedent," he resorted to "the simple but untried method of not giving the slave a flat subsistence, but linking his rations to his output." The prisoners were divided into categories according to the percentage of the output quotas that they fulfilled, which determined the diets (the place on the food scale) that they were assigned.

....

In the early thirties labor camps spread over the territory of the USSR, especially its arctic regions. The prisoners built railways, roads, industrial complexes, and cities around them; they manned the construction works and coal, lead, and gold mines, as well as the development of whole regions, like the gold-rich frigid Kolyma. The worst lot was that of forced-labor pioneers sent to set up brand new camps and work sites: they did not have even minimal accommodations until they had built them themselves. The mortality rate on such new projects was much higher than in veteran camp sites.

....

Having demolished the left and the right opposition to the "party line" by the mid-thirties, Stalin sought to destroy the very possibility of opposition to his rule. As the Hungarian writer and Gulag survivor Joszef Lengyel would remark, the common denominator of the repression of the White Guards and the Kronshtadt sailors in the twenties and of the Old Bolsheviks or the foreign Communist refugees in Russia in the thirties was "the principle that 'He who once dared lift his hand against any ... authority, can be expected to dare to do so again'." The arrests of the late thirties were the result of vengeful and prophylactic purges—yet the fact that they swept away ordinary apolitical people was not unrelated to the demand for slave labor. Each unit of the secret police had its quotas of arrests just like every industrial plant had its production quotas. A significant percentage of arrests was made on the basis of voluntary denunciations: a person could perish in the camps because someone wanted his apartment, or her job, or a victim for career-oriented "vigilance." Yet after Kirov's assassination in December 1934, the inflow of victims was intensified by the exponential proliferation of new dossiers: each detainee was pressured (and since the summer of 1937 routinely tortured) to make depositions against several others still at large.

The dynamic of the ensuing developments in the Gulag was shaped by the fluctuations in the supply and demand of slave labor: a deadly regime periodically depleted the labor force, and since the set production targets had to be reached, the camp authorities would attempt to conserve the remaining labor force by improving the prisoners' lot. In the years of the most intense terror, 1938-1939, there was no shortage of prison labor—hence the conditions of the camp inmates were at their worst. A significant percentage of the people arrested at that time were shot in the cellars of the NKVD; a wave of in-camp trials and executions swept through the "Archipelago" as well. In many camps, however, hard labor and starvation were sufficient instruments of a somewhat slower extermination.

In 1939, after Nikolai Iezhov was replaced by Lavrentii Beria at the head of the NKVD, the number of arrests decreased, and there was even a small wave of pre-trial releases. The life of the camp inmates became somewhat less precarious: in-camp executions were discontinued, and a whole generation of their perpetrators fell, together with Iezhov himself. The attempts of the medical personnel and the more liberal of the camp authorities to keep people alive improved the balance between conservation of the work force and fulfillment of the plan. Yet the camps soon received replenishments from the eastern regions of Poland annexed to the USSR in 1939, and in 1940 from the newly annexed Baltic States and Romanian territories. After Hitler's assault on the USSR in 1941, the critical demand for an immediate output in the lumber camps led to a maximum exploitation of the labor force and a total disregard for the disabled, who were often left to die of exhaustion and pellagra. A relative relaxation followed the first Soviet victories, and American lend-lease flour improved the diet of the inmates of the Far Eastern camps. Yet during and after the war several whole nationalities were transferred to Kazakhstan and Siberia, with the weaker dying and the more prominent put behind barbed wire in the process (Conquest 1960). Great numbers of younger people were sentenced to camp terms for breaches of labor discipline. Toward the end of the war came German, Alsace-Lorrainian, Japanese, Italian, Austrian, and other POWS, and the "Vlasovites" (former Soviet soldiers who had allowed the Germans to recruit them and had served under General Vlasov); new consignments arrived from the Baltic states and Western Ukraine. At the same time many of the Soviet officers and soldiers were arrested, lest the weapons of those who had defeated Hitler should be turned against Stalin.

....

In the first year after World War II, the principle of extermination by labor was again put into practice in special-regime *katorga* camps (Solzhenitsyn, GULAG ARCHIPELAGO, GA, from now on) for people who had in various ways, willingly or unwillingly, collaborated with the Germans. After twelve working hours the prisoners were locked up in overcrowded tents or barracks, often without blankets in the coldest weather: everything was done in this closed space rather than in lavatories, dining rooms, or medical wards. A part of their rations, insufficient to begin with, was appropriated by the criminal convicts in charge of the delivery, and the time for whatever sleep their conditions allowed was reduced by roll calls and searches. On their clothing each wore an identification made up of a letter and three numerical digits. Solzhenitsyn writes that the first "alphabet" in Vorkuta (about 28,000 prisoners) was dead within a year; it must have contained particularly strong people to have lasted that long. This was the darkest hour of the Archipelago since 1938.

In other camps of the late forties, the balance between the production plans and the mortality toll was similar to that of 1939-40 and 1942-43. Most of the victims of the Great Terror were by now sick or dead. The post-war arrests had brought in people who had had contacts with foreigners, including ex officio contacts with the American personnel in charge of the wartime lend-lease transfers of the American equipment to Russia. There were great numbers of former "collaborators," both in the narrow and in the broad sense of the word, the latter including anyone who had held any job—down to street-sweeping—under the German occupation. The largest post-war "wave" was made up of Lithuanians, Latvians, Estonians, Moldavians, and Western Ukrainians.[2]

....

In the post-war years new kinds of brutalization spread over the camps. The so-called "honest thieves" regarded those professional criminals who had served in the army during the war as supporters of the regime: due to the resulting abuse, many of the latter were now converted into "bitches" with a grudge against their former associates. This led to a ruthless in-camp warfare between the "bitches" and the "honest thieves" (see Shalamov's 1959 sketch "'Such'ia voina" ["The 'Bitch' War"] 1998). The sociology of the political prisoners had also undergone changes: the place of a large percentage of the meek victims of the Great Terror was taken by yesterday's tough soldiers and by people from the recently annexed territories. The loyal supporters of the regime still remaining behind barbed wire were now outnumbered by active non-conformers. Moreover, according to Solzhenitsyn (GA 5: 2), at a certain point in the late forties the terror regime overshot its aims: the newly introduced twenty-five-year sentences left people no hope of living until their release and created a devil-may-care attitude. The massive presence of war veterans in the camps intimidated the professional criminals, and, largely under the influence of the Western Ukrainians, who tended to reject the humanistic inhibitions of veteran inmates, prisoners began to assassinate stool pigeons, thus facilitating organized disobedience. In 1952-54 strikes broke out in many camps, often leading to rebellions; they were brutally suppressed, sometimes with the use of tanks[3] though "diplomacy" was resorted to in moderate cases.

In 1952-53 Stalin was planning a new wave of mass terror, and it is quite possible that his closest associates—Beria, Kaganovich, Molotov, Khrushchev—were slated for scapegoating. Yet these people, unlike the Old Bolsheviks purged in 1937-39, knew their boss's methods. According to one theory... they may have helped him off the stage—whether immediately before or, more likely, after his stroke in early March 1953. If these conjectures are right, then despotism was destroyed by its own inner dynamics. One should not derive comfort from such a thought, yet one may find it supported by a partial analogy from the history of the Gulag. The improvement of the prisoners' diet in the early fifties (when the supply of the convict labor dwindled) actually enhanced their resistance: "Freed from the urgent day-to-day worry over food, the prisoners had time to think about other things that were wrong, and started considering their position as a whole. They quickly realized that though certain marginal improvements had been made, their fundamental predicament remained the same... The government had, quite literally, given them food for thought" (J. Scholmer). One can only speculate whether this process would have been impeded by the new mass influx of slave labor. The scenario consisted in provoking pogroms, and, in an act of, as it were, protection, deporting the Jewish population to Birobidzhan and Siberia. Instead, on March 27, Beria gave amnesty to prisoners sentenced to five years or less, thus releasing huge numbers of common criminals. The sentences of political prisoners were, at the time, seldom shorter than eight years, and the "Beria amnesty" further promoted the unrest among them.

In a bid for power, Beria also initiated the first de-Stalinization move: on April 4 the country awoke to the news that the doctors arrested during the loud anti-Semitic campaign ostensibly directed against "murderers in white gowns" were exonerated and, if still alive, released from prisons. This was generally taken for a sign that the terror would subside. In a brief struggle among Stalin's heirs, Beria was defeated and, in July 1953, executed. The victorious Khrushchev continued the liberalization. Though uprisings in the camps were suppressed with the usual brutality, it became obvious that the Gulag was facing a crisis; the uprisings were therefore followed by a dramatic improvement in camp conditions as well as by releases of individual political prisoners, especially in 1955.[4] After the Twentieth Communist Party Congress in 1956, where Khrushchev made his Secret Speech about Stalin's crimes, great numbers of Communist purge victims were exonerated. Special release commissions came to the camps: it is estimated that 8 million of the 12 million inmates were set free. A large proportion of those left behind had actually been Nazi collaborators in the wartime years (the *"politsai"*)—they would be encountered, and disdained (usually for good reason), by the dissidents imprisoned in the sixties. In the years 1956-61 the camp regime was the most humane in Gulag history.

The years of "the thaw" (1953-64) and the so-called stagnation (1964-86) have been aptly redescribed as, "enlightened Stalinism": the bureaucratic party dictatorship continued with fewer "excesses." Food shortages were no longer allowed to turn into famines: if harvests were poor, Khrushchev preferred to buy grain abroad, whereas Stalin had exported it while millions of peasants were starving in the Ukraine. The ratio of terror and goal-oriented propaganda was reversed—propaganda took priority and terror became punitive instead of prophylactic. The remaining "excesses" mostly pertained to deadly repression of "economic opposition"— not just embezzlers but also official proponents of economic reform, traders in foreign currency, and individuals whose business initiatives represented ideologically premature sprouts of a free market system.

The removal of the brutal and unpredictable Stalinist terror led to a revival of an intense intellectual and cultural life in the big cities and to renewed hopes for the future of the country, the rule of law, and human rights. These hopes were premature. The year

1956 also saw the Soviet invasion of Hungary. And 1961, the year of the open de-Stalinization campaign at the Twenty-Second Congress of the Communist Party, was also the year when the regime in concentration camps was again considerably tightened. Here the "thaw" yielded to the "squeeze" earlier than in the media.

....

In general, however, the new political prisoners of the "stagnation" period were no longer the confused chance purgees; they were actual dissidents, members of national movements or human-rights activists, and they often commanded the criminals' respect for their courage. The attitude of the rowdies to the more eminent among the dissident convicts, to those of whom they had heard in the media, was particularly friendly. In the prison narratives of dissidents, the main criticism of the criminal communities of these less hungry times concerns not their "foreign relations" but the extreme cruelty of their homosexual laws, according to which the passive homosexuals were forever stigmatized, mistreated, and turned into sexual slaves.

In 1972 political prisoners, especially those able to maintain a contact with foreign media, often with the help of bribed guards, would be moved further from Moscow, to the Perm district in the Urals. The function of political imprisonment was now perceived not as "corrective" but as *incapacitating* and *punitive* (cf. GA 7: 2). Since extensive political repression was not supposed to be necessary at the stage of developed socialism, in the mid-sixties the practice of incarcerating some of the dissidents in psychiatric institutions gained momentum (see Semen Gluzman, *On Soviet Totalitarian Psychiatry.*

....

By the eighties the long-term ineffectiveness of slave-labor economics had been reconfirmed. As a result of propaganda-related monumentalism, inflexible central planning, disregard for ecology, and, in particular, the deadly waste of know-how and intellectual resources in the Stalin years followed by a partial suppression of creative intelligence under "tired totalitarianism," the Soviet Union found itself facing an economic impasse. Stalinist terror controls over efficiency in workplaces might have delayed the decline, yet the country's growing dependence on trade relations with the West made the regime's insistence that human rights were an internal affair progressively less tenable. The dissidents of the sixties, starting with Andrei Amalrik, had learned to establish contacts with foreign journalists and diplomats; writers had found ways of publishing their works abroad; and millions of ordinary people throughout the country started listening to foreign radio broadcasts despite the government's attempts to jam the transmissions. The KGB could now get away with quietly destroying only those opponents of the regime who had remained unknown to the public: links with foreign media went a long way toward safeguarding individual dissidents' lives.

The losses in Afghanistan heightened the public discontent. Many of the returning veterans of the Afghanistan war bitterly and fearlessly rejected conformism. The nuclear disaster at Chernobyl, and the impossibility of concealing it, provided the decisive stimulus for reform favored by Mikhail Gorbachev, who, however, did not expect his wary changes to develop their own momentum and end in what is now known as the Second Russian Revolution.

The beginning of Gorbachev's *glasnost* and *perestroika* in 1986 meant also a gradual end to political imprisonment in the Soviet Union. One of the last retribution/incapacitation "model-muddle" (Robert Sommer, *The End of Imprisonment*, New York: Oxford University Press, 1976: 16-34) camps for political prisoners, Perm-35 in the Urals, seemed to be surviving on a day-to-day basis when the journalist David Remnick (*Lenin's Tomb: The Last Days of the Soviet Empire*, New York: Random House, 1994: 270-76) visited it in 1987. He found its cadre embarrassed at their dwindling prestige and looking out for their pensions.[5]

At first, individual case revisions and pardons took place in response to "contrite" appeals; later, almost any letter of appeal or any protest from the West could lead to an individual's release; the process was completed by El'tsin in 1992. Which is not, however, to imply that since the present convicts in Russian and the former Soviet Republics are common criminals, public opinion need no longer be concerned with the conditions in their penal facilities, especially those for juvenile delinquents.

....

Yet though the Gulag grew out of specific socio-political and ideological circumstances, it was a complex of moral liabilities of a general nature that allowed it to rise. Consensus-based democratic institutions can restrain the effects of such tendencies as a blank disregard for individual dignity, the treatment of people as instruments or as obstacles, a single-minded drive toward a maximization of immediate profits, blind political faith, and psychological defenses against sympathy. Yet to reverse these tendencies one needs... the individual commitment to sensitive interpersonal respect. *Sub specie aeternitatis*, literary explorations of the Gulag experience created conditions for the formation and refinement of this commitment. In their immediate social and historical context, however, these literary works played a significant role in accelerating the erosion of the Archipelago and, with it, the system that it had buttressed for seven decades.

SELECTED NOTES

[1] By the early thirties most of the Mensheviks and the SR had served prison sentences and were living in exile in the eastern regions. During the Great Terror they were rounded up and sent to the camps. By then all real and imaginary political offenses were subsumed under different paragraphs of the capacious 58th article of the criminal code, and their bearers were assigned the worst regime in the camps, the polar opposite of their erstwhile privilege.

[2] Some of these prisoners had, indeed, participated in the Nazi atrocities. After the dissolution of the Soviet Union, in the Baltic republics the exoneration was as indiscriminate as the arrests of the forties, with the real war criminals benefiting from the erstwhile injustice to the innocent victims.

[3] Solzhenitsyn's film script "Znaiut istinu tanki" ["Tanks Know the Truth"] ... is based on such events in Kengir. (*Plays and Film Scripts*), Vermont/Paris: YMCA Press.

[4] The years 1955-56 also saw reforms in the country as a whole: a minimum wage, improved pensions, elimination of tuition fees, repeal of the law that fixed workers to their places of employment, etc.

[5] Later some of the camp facilities were used for alcoholics: the wisdom of the proverb "a holy place never stands empty" was appreciated in the camps.

SOCIALIST REALISM

SOVIET LITERATURE

ADDRESS DELIVERED
TO THE FIRST ALL-UNION CONGRESS OF SOVIET WRITERS
AUGUST 17, 1934

by Maksim GOR'KII*

....

The role of the labor processes which transformed the erect animal into Man and laid down the foundations of culture has never been as thoroughly and profoundly studied as the subject deserves. That is perfectly natural, since that kind of research is not in the interests of the exploiters of labor who, though they have converted into money the raw material called the energy of the masses, have of course not been interested in enhancing the value of that raw material. Since hoary antiquity, since the time people became divided into slave-owners and slaves, the muscles of the toiling masses have been used, and are still being used, in the same way as we now use the mechanical power of rivers. Historians of culture have described

* From *Maxim Gorky On Literature: Selected Articles*. Translated by Julius Katzer. Moscow: Foreign Languages Publishing House, 1967. Pp. 228-268.

primitive men as philosophizing idealists and mystics, creators of gods and inquirers into the "meaning of life." To primitive man was attributed the mood of the shoemaker Jakob Boehme [German mystic, popular with the Russian Symbolists], who lived in the late 16th and the early 17th centuries and, among other things, indulged in the kind of philosophy dear to bourgeois mystics. This man taught that "man should meditate about heaven, the stars, the elements, and the animals that originated from them, as well as about holy angels, the devil, heaven, and hell."

You are aware that the history of primitive culture has availed itself of data supplied by archeology and the impact of ancient religions, the latter being treated in the light, and under the influence, of Christian philosophic dogmatism, which has not been alien even to atheist historians ... However, no historians of primitive and ancient culture have made use of the data of folklore, the people's oral art, or of the evidence provided by mythology, which on the whole is a reflection of natural phenomena, of the struggle against Nature, and a reflection of social life, in broad artistic generalizations.

It would be hard to imagine a biped animal, which has been exerting all its efforts in a struggle for existence, *engaged in a thinking that is divorced from labor processes and from clan and tribal problems*. It would also be hard to imagine Immanuel Kant, barefoot and clothed in animal skins, wrapped in thought about "a thing-in-itself." Abstract thought was something done by man of later times, that solitary man of whom Aristotle said in his *Politica*: "Without the bounds of Society, Man must be either a god or a brute." As a brute he sometimes compelled others to acknowledge him as a god, but he also served as material for numerous legends about animal-like men, in the same way as the first men to tame the horse and ride it provided the origin of the centaur myth.

Historians of primitive culture have been completely silent regarding the unmistakable signs of a materialist mode of thought inevitably precipitated by labor processes and by the sum of the facts of ancient man's social life. These signs have come down to us in the form of fairy-tales and myths, which carry memories of the work of taming wild animals, discovering herbs and inventing tools. Even in antiquity men dreamed of aerial flight, which can be seen in legends about Phaethon, Daedalus and his son Icarus, and the tale of the "flying carpet." Men also dreamed of high-speed travel, hence the fairy-tale about "seven-league boots," and the horse was domesticated. The desire to travel along rivers at speeds faster than their currents led to the invention of the oar and the sail, while the striving to smite foes and beasts from a distance brought about the invention of slings, and bows and arrows. Men dreamed of spinning and weaving a tremendous quantity of cloth in a single night, of building "palaces" overnight, i.e., a house fortified against any enemy. The distaff, one of the most ancient of tools, and the primitive hand-loom came into being, as did the Russian fairy-tale about Vasilisa the Wise. One could cite dozens of more proofs of the way ancient fairy-tales and myths stem from the facts of life, dozens of proofs of the far-sightedness of primitive man's thinking in terms of images and hypotheses, this already along technological lines, but a kind of thinking which has led to such present-day hypotheses as, for example, the utilization of the energy of the earth's rotation on its axis or the destruction of polar ice. All the myths and tales of antiquity are crowned, as it were, by the myth about Tantalus, who, up to his neck in water, is tormented by unquenchable thirst—an image of ancient man surrounded by phenomena of the external world which he has not yet cognized.

I have no doubt that you know these ancient tales, myths and legends, but I should like their fundamental meaning to be more profoundly understood. I have in view the striving of working men of ancient times to ease their labor, raise productivity, arm themselves against enemies, both quadruped and biped, and also to exert an influence on the hostile natural elements by means of the spoken word, by "spells" and "invocations." The latter fact is of particular importance, since it shows how profoundly men believed in the power of the spoken word, this faith stemming from the obvious and tangible advantages provided by human speech, which organizes men's social life and labor processes. They even tried to influence the gods through "invocations." This was quite natural, since all the gods of antiquity lived on earth, bore the image of human beings and behaved as such; they favored the obedient and frowned upon the disobedient, and were just as envious, vengeful and ambitious as human beings are. The fact that the gods were anthropomorphous goes to show that religious thinking did not spring from a contemplation of the phenomena of nature, but sprang from the social struggle. It is quite feasible that "notable" people of antiquity provided raw material for the invention of gods: Hercules, the "hero of labor," and "master of all skills," was eventually elevated to Olympus to sit among the gods. In the imagination of primitive men, a god was not an abstract conception or a fantastic being, but a perfectly real figure equipped with some implement of labor, skilled in one trade or another, and man's instructor and fellow-worker. A god was an artistic embodiment of successes in labor, so that "religious" thinking among the toiling masses is something that must be placed within quotation marks, since this was a purely artistic creation. Though it idealized man's abilities and was a harbinger, as it were, of their powerful development, the creation of myths was fundamentally realistic, The stimulus can easily be discerned in every flight of ancient fantasy, this always being men's striving to lighten their labor. It is quite clear that this striving originated in those engaged in physical labor, and also that no god could have appeared and existed for so long in working men's daily life were he not so highly useful to the lords of the earth, to those who exploited labor. In our country, God is so rapidly and easily falling into disuse precisely because the reason for his existence has disappeared, viz., the need to justify the power of man over man, since in our country any man is the collaborator of his fellow-men, their friend and comrade-in-arms, their teacher, but never lord over their minds and wills.

....

The period between 1907 and 1917 was one of the unbridled sway of irresponsible thought, a period of complete "creative freedom" for Russian writers. This freedom found expression in propaganda of all the Western bourgeoisie's conservative ideas, which were put into circulation at the close of the 18th century (following the French Revolution) and flared up regularly after 1848 and 1871. It was asserted that "Bergsonian philosophy marks the tremendous progress achieved in the history of human thought"; that Bergson, moreover, "expanded and deepened the theory of Berkeley"; that "the systems of Kant, Leibnitz, Descartes and Hegel are dead systems and over them, like a sun, the works of Plato shine in eternal beauty," that very Plato who founded the most pernicious fallacy of the fallacies perpetrated by a mode of thought divorced from all reality, from a reality which develops continuously and universally in processes of labor and creativity.

Dmitrii Merezhkovskii, who was an influential writer at the time, cried out:

> All is empty on this earth,
> Love and hatred, death and birth.
> Nothing matters—be what must,
> All has been and shall be dust.

Patently under the influence of Baudelaire and the so-called "damned," Sologub, following in Schopenhauer's footsteps, depicted the "cosmic absurdity of the existence of personality" with remarkable distinctness, and though his verses mourn over this, he himself lived the life of a prosperous philistine. In 1914 this man threatened the Germans with the destruction of Berlin as soon as "the snow melts in the valleys." Ideas such as "Eros in politics" and "mystical anarchism" were preached at the time; the most wily Vasilii Rozanov preached eroticism; Leonid Andreev wrote his sinister stories and plays, and Artsybashev chose a lascivious satyr in modern clothing as the hero of a novel [titled *Sanin* after the protagonist]. On the whole, the years between 1907 and 1917 fully deserved the appellation of the most shameful decade in the history of the Russian intelligentsia.

Since our democratic intelligentsia had less historical training than their Western opposite numbers, their "moral degeneration, and intellectual impoverishment proceeded more rapidly. This is a process, however, common to the petty bourgeoisie of all countries and inevitable for any intellectual without the strength of character to decisively adhere to the proletariat, which has been called upon by history to refashion the world for the common weal of all people of honest labor.

All of us—whether we are writers, factory workers, or collective farmers—are working poorly as yet, and cannot take full stock of all that has been created by and for us. Our working masses do not as yet properly understand that they are working for themselves. The consciousness is latent on all sides, but has not yet burst into a bright and cheerful flame. Nothing, however, can flare up till it has reached a certain temperature, and no one has ever been able so successfully to raise the temperature of labor's energy as the Party, organized by the genius of Vladimir Lenin, and the man who leads the Party today.

We must make labor the principal hero of our books, i.e., man as organized by labor processes, one who, in our country, is equipped with the might of modern techniques, and is, in his turn, making labor easier and more productive, and raising it to the level of an art. We must learn to understand labor as a creative act. Creativity is a concept which we writers use too often and with hardly the right to do so. Creativity is that degree of intensity in the work of the memory at which the rapidity of its operation produces from its store of knowledge and impressions the most outstanding and characteristic facts, pictures and details, and puts them into the most precise and vivid words that all can understand. Our young literature cannot yet boast of that quality. Our writers' store of impressions and knowledge is not extensive, and one does not yet discern a striving to build up and extend and deepen that store.

The main theme in 19th-century European and Russian literature was the individual, as opposed to society, the state and Nature. The chief cause of the individual's opposition to bourgeois society was the urge to amass an abundance of negative impressions contradictory to his class ideas and traditions of life. The individual felt keenly that these impressions were retarding the process of his growth and crushing him, but he had but a poor understanding of his own responsibility for the vulgarity, baseness and criminality of the foundations of bourgeois society. Jonathan Swift lashed at the whole of Europe, but the bourgeoisie of Europe believed that his satire was directed against Britain alone. By and large, the rebellious individual, who criticized the life of his society, rarely and poorly realized his responsibility for the shameful practices of society. A deep and proper understanding of social and economic causes was even more rarely the basic motive of his criticism of the existing order. His criticism sprang most frequently either from a sense of the hopelessness of his existence within the iron cage of capitalism or from a striving to avenge his failures in life, and the humiliation it inflicted. It may be said that when an individual turned to the working masses, he did not do so in the interests of the latter, but in the hope that, after destroying bourgeois society, the working class would insure his freedom of thought and willfulness of action. I repeat: the basic and chief theme in pre-revolutionary literature was the drama of the individual, whose life seemed cramped, who felt superfluous in society and sought to find some convenient place for himself; since he could not find one, he suffered and perished, either after reconciling himself to a society that was hostile to him or by taking to drink and ending up in suicide.

In our country, the Union of Soviet Socialist Republics, there must not, there cannot be, any superfluous people. Every citizen has full liberty to develop his capacities, gifts and talents. The only demand presented to the individual is that he should be honest in his attitude to the heroic work of creating a classless society.

The entire mass of the USSR's population has been called upon by the Workers' and Peasants' Government to participate in the building of a new culture. Hence each and every one of us is responsible for errors, shortcomings, spoilage in production, and all manifestations of philistine vulgarity, meanness, duplicity and unscrupulousness. This means that our criticism must be genuine self-criticism, that we must evolve a system of socialist ethics to regulate our work and mutual relations.

In describing facts that reveal the workers' intellectual development and show how the age-old petty proprietor is turning into a collective farmer, we, writers, confine ourselves to merely reporting, for it is in very inadequate terms that we depict the emotional processes underlying these changes.

We still have a poor insight into the facts of reality. Even the outer appearance of the country has changed strikingly and the poverty-stricken patchwork pattern of the land has gone. No longer do we see such scenes as a light-blue strip of land sown to oats, next to it a golden band of rye, a greenish strip of wheat, patches overgrown with weeds, and on the whole a sorry-looking expanse of parceled land. Today vast expanses of land present a single pattern and one color. Villages and towns are dominated not by churches but by big public buildings. Giant factories reflect the sun in their huge expanses of glass, while ancient churches, toylike in appearance and pagan in their motley variety, testify to our people's talents, which used to find expression in church architecture. However, the new face of our land and the striking changes in it are not reflected in our literature.

We live at a time when the old way of life is being radically refashioned, and a sense of dignity is awakening in man, who is realizing that he is a force actually changing the world. Many people are amused when they read that people have changed such names as Svinukhin [derived from "swine"], Sobakin [from "dog"], Kuteinikov [from "drunkard"], Popov [from "priest"], Svishchov [from "defect"], etc., to Lenskii [from the river "Lena," which may also have inspired the pseudonym Lenin], Novyi [from "new"], Partizanov [from "partisan"], Dedov [from "forefathers"], Stoliarov [from "shriner"], and so on. There is nothing ridiculous about that, for it goes to show a mounting dignity, since people refuse to bear names or nicknames which humiliate them by reminding them of the servile past of their grandfathers and fathers.

....

Neither the drama nor the novel has so far produced a sufficiently vivid depiction of Soviet woman, who is playing such an important part in all spheres of socialist construction. It is difficult to explain why dramatists have even tried to create as few feminine roles as possible. Although woman's social status in our country is equal to man's, and women have given full proof of the variety of their gifts and their capacity for work, this equality is very often and in many respects formal and external. Men have not yet forgotten, or perhaps have prematurely forgotten, that for dozens of centuries women were trained for sensual purposes and as domestic animals capable of "keeping house." This old standing and shameful debt of history to one-half of the world's population should be paid off by men of our country first of all, so as to set an example to all other men in the world. Here, too, literature should try to depict women's work and mentality, so that the attitude towards women should rise above the accepted philistine attitude, which has been borrowed from the lower animals.

Further, I think it necessary to point out that Soviet literature is not only Russian-language literature, but all-Union literature. Since the writers of the fraternal republics, who differ from us only in language, live and work under the impact and the beneficent influence of the idea that unites the whole world of working people which capitalism has divided, it is clear that we have no right to ignore the writings of the national minorities simply because we are more numerous. The value of art is gauged not by quantity but by quality. If we have had the giant Pushkin in our past, it does not follow that Armenians, Georgians, Tatars, Ukrainians and other nationalities are incapable of producing great masters of literature, music, painting and architecture. It should not be forgotten that, throughout the Union of Socialist Republics, a rapid renascence of the whole mass of working people is in progress towards an honest and human life, the free creation of new history and the creation of socialist culture. We can already see that the greater its advance, the more powerfully does this process reveal the gifts and talents latent in 170 million men and women.

....

After saying so much about shortcomings in our literature, I must mention its merits and achievements. I lack the time to discuss the striking difference between Western literature and our own. However, I shall say it is quite clear to any unbiased judge that our literature has out-stripped the Western in novelty of theme and, I would remind you, that many of our writers have even found higher appreciation in the West than in their own country. I spoke out loud and clear in 1930 about our literature's achievements, in an article published in the collection *On Literature*, as well as in many other articles in the same book. Four years of tense work have elapsed since then. Does that work entitle me to raise my appraisal of our literature's achievements? Yes, appreciations of a number of books that have come from our chief readers—from workers and collective farmers—entitle me to do so. You all know these books, so I shall not name them; I shall only say that we have already a goodly group of writers who can be recognized as leaders in the development of our letters.

....

The proletarian state must educate thousands of first-rate "masters of culture," and "engineers of souls." This is needed so as to return to the whole mass of working people that right to develop their minds, talents, and abilities that they have been deprived of throughout the world. This practically attainable goal imposes on us, writers, a strict responsibility for our work and social behavior. That not only places us in the position, traditional for realistic literature, of "judges of the world and of people," and "critics of life," but also entitles us to a direct participation in the construction of a new life and the process of "changing the world."

Possession of that right should inculcate in each writer a consciousness of his duty and responsibility for the whole of literature and for the things that should not be found in it.

The Union of Soviet Writers unites 1,500 members, which means one writer per 100,000 readers. This is not much, considering that at the beginning of this century the inhabitants of the Scandinavian peninsula had one writer per 230 readers. The inhabitants of the USSR are constantly and almost daily demonstrating their talents, which, however, does not mean that we will soon have 1,500 writers of genius. Let us dream of only fifty. To avoid self-deception let us plan for five writers of genius, and forty-five of great talent. I think that that will do as a beginning. The rest will consist of people who are as yet insufficiently attentive to the realities of life, organize their material poorly, and work at it carelessly. To this number we must add many hundreds of candidates for membership, and then hundreds of "beginners" in all the republics and regions. Hundreds of them engage in writing and dozens have already appeared in print. During 1933-34 about 30 collections of stories and literary almanacs carrying works by local beginners appeared in various places ranging from Khabarovsk and Komsomolsk to Rostov, Stalingrad, Tashkent, Voronezh, Kabardino-Balkaria, Tiflis [Tbilisi] and so on.

To appraise this work is the duty of our critics, who still do not notice it, though the time is ripe. This work, such as it is, demonstrates the depth of the cultural progress in the masses. When one reads these publications one sees that the authors of these verses, plays and stories are factory and rural correspondents. I suppose that there are no fewer than 10,000 young people in our country who are anxious to work in literature. Of course, the future Institute of Literature will not be able to absorb even one-tenth of this host.

I shall now ask a question: why has this Congress of Writers been organized, and what are the aims the future Union will set itself? If these aims are directed towards only the professional welfare of literary workers, then the game has hardly been worth the candle. It seems to me that the Union must set before itself not only the professional interests of writers, but the interests of literature as a whole. To a certain extent the Union must assume leadership over the host of beginners, organize them, distribute their forces on different jobs and teach them how to work on the material of both the past and the present.

Work is proceeding in our country on a *History of Factories and Mills*. It has proved very hard to draw highly qualified writers into this work. Only the poetess Shkapskaia and Maria Levberg have so far been doing good work, while the others are not doing any work on raw material and do not even find time to edit the material already prepared.

We do not know the history of our past. Work has been planned, and has in part commenced, on the history of towns once ruled by independent princes or located on the old borders, from their inception down to our days. In the form of sketches and stories this work must describe life in feudal Russia, the colonial policy of the Moscow grand dukes and tsars, the development of trade and industry, of the exploitaton of the peasantry by the princes, *voevods* (governors of provinces. Tr.), merchants, and the church, and end up with the organization of collective farms, that act of genuine and complete emancipation of the peasantry from the "power of the soil" and the yoke of property.

We must know the past history of our Union Republics. Hundreds of beginner-writers can be drawn into this works which will give them extensive opportunities of self-education and improving their qualification through collective work on raw material and mutual criticism.

We must know everything that took place in the past, not in the way that has been presented till now, but in the way it is shown in the teachings of Marx, Lenin and Stalin, and put into practice at factories and on fields by labor, which is organized and led by a new historical force—the will and reason of the proletariat of the Union of Socialist Republics.

That, in my opinion, is the problem confronting the Union of Writers. Our Congress must not only be a report to readers or a parade of our talents; it must undertake the organization of literature, the education of young writers in work of all-Union importance—the all-round cognition of the past and the present of our country.

SOCIALIST REALISM IN SOVIET LITERATURE

by Katerina CLARK*

Socialist realism was the official literary "method" or "theory" of Soviet literature virtually until the break-up of the Union in 1991. After Stalin died, however, in 1953, writers began to dismantle the tradition, pushing the limits of the possible. This process continued until, by the last decade or so of Soviet rule, most literary practice had strayed a long way from what, in the 1930s and 1940s, might have been accepted as socialist realism. Yet, at the same time, the conventions of socialist realism had become so ingrained as habits of composition that in the first decades of the post-Stalin period even dissident writers rarely broke out of its formal, as distinct from ideological, mold (the legacy of socialist realism can be found, for example, in the early novels of Solzhenitsyn). This essay, however, will discuss socialist realism only in its most classical, Stalinist version and will not treat the successive layers of complexity that accrued to the tradition in the post-Stalin years.

Not all Soviet literature is socialist realist. Not even all Stalinist, non-dissident literature is socialist realist. When discussing Soviet literature, one has to draw a distinction between at least

* From *The Routledge Companion to Russian Literature*. Edited by Neil Cornwell. New York: Routledge, 2001. Pp. 174-183.

three categories of works: those that exemplify socialist realism, those that are read as non- or anti-Soviet but which happen to have been published in the Soviet Union, and a third category, those that are representative of Soviet literature but not specifically socialist realist. Many in the latter category are (or were) even officially promoted (in, for example, the Writers' Union's "Golden List" of around a hundred classics of Soviet literature).

Socialist realism as such did not exist until the Bolshevik Revolution of 1917 was almost fifteen years old, or more precisely until after a decree as promulgated in April 1932 abolishing all independent writers' organizations and forming the single *Union of Soviet Writers*. The term itself was not presented to the Soviet public until 17 May 1932, in a speech made by [Ivan] Gronskii, the president of the new Writers' Union's Organizational Committee (legend has it that the term "socialist realism" had been thought of by Stalin in a meeting in Maksim Gor'kii's study).

Having coined the term, those in power in Soviet literature had to decide what it meant. Gor'kii (the First Secretary of the Writers' Union) and other authoritative figures began to clarify this in articles and speeches of 1932-4 and the First Plenum of the Organizational Committee, held in October 1932, was devoted to the topic. It was not, however, until August 1934, when the First Congress of the Writers' Union was held, that socialist realism acquired a canonical formulation in two keynote addresses to the Congress, one by Gor'kii, and the other by Andrei Zhdanov, the chief representative of the Party's Central Committee. Thereafter, these two speeches functioned as *the* canonical source for the definition, together with Lenin's 1905 article "Party Organization and Party Literature" and Gor'kii's articles in the book *On Literature* (*O literature*), published in 1933 (and in later redactions of the same book).

These sources identify a number of features that socialist realism should contain. Many of the stipulations are in effect taboos which, in that they have been fairly rigorously enforced over the decades, have ensured that socialist realism has, both aesthetically and thematically, been a conservative and even somewhat puritanical literature. For example, writers were enjoined to expunge from their work any trace of bald "physiologism" (read mention of sex and other such bodily functions). They were also to avoid all approaches and language that might not be accessible to the masses. This injunction has meant that socialist realism is not highbrow, but lowbrow, or at best middlebrow. Effectively, it also put an end to the literary experimentalism and modernist trends that had flowered in the 1920s.

The language to be used in socialist realism was circumscribed. There were to be no sub-standard locutions, no dialecticisms, no scatology, and no abstruse or long-winded expressions—let alone the neologisms and trans-sense language that had been favored by the Russian avant-garde. In consequence, most socialist realist writers used only a somewhat *comme il faut* version of standard Russian, resulting often in stilted dialogue (this was one of the trends that was reversed in the post-Stalin era, starting from the late 1950s).

Other proscriptions were more ideological in nature. For example, there was to be no "obscurantism"—no infusion of religious or mystical sentiment, no positive account of the occult. Needless to say, a socialist realist work was not to espouse the views of any political group that rivaled the Bolsheviks, whether of the left or of the right. Instead, literature was to serve the ideological position and policies of the Bolshevik Party, and in so doing should be "optimistic" and forward-looking (that is, it should intimate the great and glorious future).

These ideological prescriptions were contained in the doctrine of mandatory *partiinost'*, the cornerstone or *sine qua non* of socialist realism. *Partiinost'*—a term that is generally and somewhat barbarously translated into English as "party-mindedness"—is, then, ostensibly a quality inherent in a socialist realist work. It might be more accurately described, however, as a code word signaling the radical reconception of the role of the writer that is so central to socialist realism. If, before, the writer (and this was largely true even of the politically committed writer) saw himself as an original creator of texts, once socialist realism was instituted his role became much more instrumental, as is implicit in Zhdanov's famous characterization of the Soviet writer (in his speech to the First Writers' Congress) as an "engineer of human souls." Literature was now viewed in a utilitarian way (even more so than before) in terms of how it might "engineer" certain habits of thinking in the populace. Indeed, the writer was seen as rather like a trained professional, working for the government, who was to implement certain assignments or elaborate certain themes that were given to him either explicitly or implicitly (in either case, often through official speeches, articles in *Pravda*, and so on). Even then, he was not to fulfill these assignments in a freehanded way. The socialist realist writer did not really have autonomy over his own texts, which would often be rewritten several times before publication; sometimes he reworked them himself under prompting; sometimes another writer reworked them, and at other times it might be an editor at the publishing house. Such rewritings could at times be without the author's knowledge or permission.

The many injunctions contained in the official speeches to the First Congress of the Writers' Union and other authoritative sources, which determined the ultimate shape of socialist realism, do not fully define the heart of the tradition or establish its unique qualities. This is even true of the doctrine of mandatory *partiinost'* which, though it signals a purely service role for the writer, does not, after all, specify much about the kind of writing he will produce. The injunctions to the writer found in the canonical sources for socialist realism set out the parameters in which he was to operate, but provide only sketchy guidelines for what was to become a highly conventionalized literary tradition. The socialist realist writer was, in practice, not just to be politically correct; as an "engineer of human souls," he was expected to adhere to a particular code of construction.

The principal function of the Soviet socialist realist writer was to provide legitimizing myths for the state, to "show the country its heroes." In consequence, the second cornerstone of socialist realism, together with *partiinost'*, was the "positive hero," an emblematic figure whose biography was to function as a model for readers to emulate. Thus socialist realism is a version of heroic biography. Small wonder the novel, the most popular biographical genre of the modern period, became the central genre of socialist realism. The heroic conventions that were established in the socialist realist novel were used to a greater or lesser extent in most other literary genres, and in other media, such as film.

The particular conventions that define the socialist realist tradition were themselves established by exemplars. Ever since 1932, when the Writers' Union was formed and socialist realism was declared the sole method appropriate for literature, most official pronouncements on literature, and especially the addresses that opened every Writers' Congress, contained a short list of exemplars to guide the writers in their future work. Each new version of the list contained at its core the official classics of socialist realism, plus a few recently published works. No two lists were exactly the same, and those recently published works added to a given list were often omitted in subsequent lists. There is, however, a core of novels that were cited with sufficient regularity to be considered a canon. They include: Dmitrii Furmanov's *Chapaev* (1923); Aleksandr Fadeev's *The Rout* (*Razgrom*, 1927) and *The Young Guard* (*Molodaia gvardiia*) originally published in 1946, but the rewritten redaction of 1951 is the canon text; Fedor Gladkov's *Cement* (*Tsement*, 1925); Maksim Gor'kii's *The Life of Klim Samgin* (*Zhizn' Klima Samgina*, written 1925-36); Iurii Krymov's *The Tanker Derbent* (*Tanker 'Derbent'*, 1937-38); Nikolai Ostrovskii's *How the Steel Was Tempered* (*Kak zakalialas' stal'*, 1934); Aleksandr Serafimovich's *The Iron Flood* (*Zheleznyi potok*, 1924); Mikhail Sholokhov's *Quiet Flows the Don* (*Tikhii Don*, 1928-40) and *Virgin Soil Upturned* (*Podniataia tselina*, 1932-60).

These canonical works have been a crucial factor in determining the shape of all socialist realist works, but particularly of the novel. There was a good deal of external stimulus for following these exemplars besides the mere fact that they were advanced by authoritative voices. In the early 1930s, a literary institute was set up to train writers to follow the models. A preferential scale of royalty payments and other attractions such as dachas and visits to Houses of Creativity in idyllic locations were dangled before the writer as positive inducements to follow the developing official traditions of the Soviet novel. In other words, when authoritative voices cried-out "Give us more heroes like X [the hero of some model novel]," the cry did not fall on entirely deaf ears. As a result, the business of writing novels soon became comparable to the procedure followed by medieval icon painters. Just as the icon painter looked to an "original" to find the correct angle for a given saint's hands, the correct colors for a given theme, and so on, the Soviet writer could copy the gestures, facial expressions, actions, and symbols used in texts already pronounced canonical.

The Soviet writer did not merely copy isolated tropes, characters, and incidents from the exemplars. He organized the entire plot structure of his novel on the basis of patterns present in them. From the mid-1930s on, most novels were *de facto* written to a single master-plot that itself represents a synthesis of the plots of several model novels (primarily Gor'kii's *Mother* [*Mat'*, 1907] and Gladkov's *Cement*).

This shaping of the plot does not, however, account for everything in a given socialist realist novel. Despite the frequent western charge that these novels are clichéd and repetitive, it is not true that every novel is nothing more than the reworking of a single formula. In any given novel one must distinguish between, on the one hand, its overarching plot or macro-structure and, on the other, the micro-structures, the smaller units that are threaded together by this shaping formula—the digressions, sub-plots, and so on. If a novel is looked at in terms of these smaller units, much of it will be found to be somewhat journalistic and topical; it may, for instance, be geared to praising a recent Soviet achievement or to broadcasting or rationalizing a new decree.

The overarching plot of a given novel is not tied, as are these smaller units, to the particular point in time when it was written (such as to celebrating a recent decree that may be revoked subsequently). If its plot were stripped of all references to a particular time or place, or to a particular theme of the novel, it could be distilled to a highly generalized essence. The abstract version of a given novel's plot is the element that is, in effect, shaped by the master-plot.

Not all Soviet novels follow the master-plot. Not even all novels in the canon follow it completely. One will note, for example, that many of the canonical exemplars were published in the 1920s, or even earlier (like Gor'kii's *Mother*), namely, before socialist realism *per se* existed. They may from a post-1932 standpoint, however, be seen as embryonically socialist realist. In practice, once socialist realism had been instituted, aspects of earlier works that did not become conventional for socialist realism, or perhaps were even proscribed in canonical formulations of it, either became, as it were, "non-aspects" in that they were totally ignored in the criticism, or they were written out in subsequent redactions (one example of this can be found in the first, 1925 redaction of Gladkov's *Cement*, in which an apparently positive character, Badin, is a rapist!). More remarkably, one of the official classics of Soviet literature, Sholokhov's *Quiet Flows the Don*, shows only occasional traces of the master-plot, and primarily in connection with lesser characters. Statistically, however, a detectable (though hypothetical) master-plot has been followed to a greater or lesser degree in the overwhelming majority of Soviet novels from the 1930s and 1940s. Its status as a defining trait of socialist realism does not depend on the actual percentage of novels patterned on it, for the master-plot is not random or arbitrary; it illustrates major tenets of Marxism-Leninism.

The use of a formulaic plot suggests that socialist realism might be compared with other varieties of popular formulaic literature, such as detective stories and serial romances. Such comparisons have their limits, however, because the socialist realist novel is not intended to be "mere entertainment." From at least 1932-4, the time when the canon was instituted, its main function was to serve as the repository of official state myths. It had a mandatory allegorical function in that the biography of its hero was expected to stand in for the great myths of national identity.

Stalinist political culture centered on two major, and interrelated, myths of national identity, the myth (or master metaphor) of the "Great Family," and the myth of Moscow. The Great Family of Stalinist myth is essentially the Stalinist state. As a "family," it is contrasted with the "little," or nuclear, family to which individuals are expected to pay allegiance only to the extent that this nuclear family is itself subordinated to the interests of the Great Family (should any conflict between the two arise, the family that is "greater" must take priority). The Great Family, unlike the nuclear family, contains in effect only two categories of kin, both generally masculine. There are 'fathers', who are primarily represented as strong, determined leaders who are enlightened politically. Their worthy 'sons' are exemplary citizens, or citizens of extraordinary potential, whose exploits mark them out from the others but who are as yet limited in their ability to assume leadership roles (to become 'fathers') by an immaturity that is of course political, but is commonly represented in literature, film, and other cultural products reinforcing the status quo as an almost boyish hotheadedness, an impulsiveness or tendency to act on their own initiative and not be sufficiently guided by the Party. The identification between developmental and political immaturity in the "sons" is facilitated by the fact that their impetuousness is represented as a form of *stikhiinost'*. *Stikhiinost'*, which would be translated literally as "elemental-ness" since its root *stikhiia* means "the elements," can be used for a wide range of arbitrary, willful or headstrong behavior but is at the same time a technical term in Marxism for 'spontaneity'. 'Spontaneity', in one of the most abstract versions of the overall Marxist model for historical progress, is locked in dialectical conflict with political consciousness or *soznatel'nost'*.

In effect, the socialist realist novel is a kind of *Bildungsroman* with the *Bildung*, or formation of character, having more to do with public values than individual development. In the myth of the Great Family, the model "son's" spontaneity must be tempered under the guidance of an exemplary, highly conscious "father" before he can gain that status for himself. Each novel is structured as a story of how a particular model "son" (the positive hero) progresses over time as his spontaneity is tempered under the guidance of a highly conscious "father." Towards the end of the novel, in a highly charged moment, the hero's attainment of mastery is recognized in a sort of ritual of initiation that enables him to cross over to the status of a "father." Generally, what this initiation amounts to is a conversation, conducted with a particular aura, between the "son" and his moral/political mentor, his "father," who may, in addition to his homily, hand him a Party or *Komsomol* card as a form of passing on the baton. In some instances, this conversation is the last testament of a loyal communist before a heroic death (whether in revolutionary battle, or because he has ruined his own health in his tireless work for the cause).

This event (the initiation), or series of events (of encounters between the "son" and his "father") in the individual life of the hero represents the broader processes taking place in society at large. The general plot, with its emphasis on the succession by a more robust "son" to the status of his "father" who is most often shown as spent and in decline (or about to be posted elsewhere so that the son literally succeeds him in the local hierarchy), affirms that the country is progressing in a series of ever greater passages or revolutionary leaps to that end moment when it will attain a state of fully achieved communism. This moment (the initiation) is also one when the dialectical conflict between the (politically) conscious and those whose political consciousness is as yet inchoate and undisciplined, will be resolved. Then, all will be conscious politically without sacrificing spontaneity completely, and all will have attained an extra-personal identity, having jettisoned their narrow, counterproductive, self-centered identities.

In a typical socialist realist novel this general process unfolds at a deep structural level and is manifested largely only in the encounters between "father" and "son" which, in the interests of maintaining an elevated tone for such moments, are infrequent but crucial. At the surface level, the hero is otherwise shown to progress, to mature, as he undergoes all sorts of trials and tackles insurmountable obstacles, thus enhancing his stature as a true hero. Most socialist realist novels are structured around the task the hero is to perform in the public sphere (such as raise the yield of grain in the collective farm, build a bridge or a power station, exceed the plan's figures for his factory's output, or drive the enemy out of a particular town), the obstacles confronting the hero are often from the natural world. For example, as he tries to build a power station in his district, he may find the project threatened by a flood. Even more frequently, the obstacles in fact come from within the world of the hero's bureaucratic administration, or from military life, but are represented *as if* from the natural world. This is particularly the case for representing the enemies (national or class) who may be described as beasts or vipers, or as advancing like a firestorm or a flow of molten lava.

In presenting the hero principally with natural or natural-like obstacles, writers were effectively realizing the metaphor that is at the base of *stikhiinost'*. As, in a given work, the hero learns to control the "elemental" that is without, as he shows his mastery over it, this signifies his mastery of *political* consciousness. Alternatively, he may have to learn to master the seething passions within, a process that is *de facto* conflated with political mastery.

When the positive hero crosses over to a higher order of consciousness, when he makes his "great leap forward," this affirms that the country under the present leadership is on its proper course towards communism. The novel is both a primer for the Soviet Everyman to follow and a repository of myths of maintenance for the Soviet status quo.

This parabolic structure of the socialist realist novel is enabled by a common convention followed by the majority of Stalinist novels: the novel is set not in Moscow or Leningrad, but in a provincial locale. This locale, the novel's microcosm, is generally depicted as a relatively hermetic unit situated a considerable distance from these major cities. The novels that are set in Moscow or Leningrad are generally set in a particular factory or city district. The isolated, provincial locale that is the setting of most socialist realist novels functions as a 'typical' place, a microcosm in which one may see to scale the general processes taking place in society. But the microcosm is, as befits its location, more backward both politically and economically than Moscow, that higher point of orientation for all the novel's characters.

Thus the myth of Moscow was also an integral element in the socialist-realist tradition. This myth was not, however, generated only within literature and film. At more or less the same time as the doctrine of socialist realism was established, a central preoccupation of the leadership was a project for the reconstruction of the city of Moscow to make it an exemplum of the socialist city. Moscow, as capital of a highly centralized society, was to be an enhanced space, ahead of its time physically as the leaders were politically. Hence, in socialist realism the provincial setting of a given work functioned as a periphery, contrasted as such with the "center" that was Moscow.

Thus the positive hero progresses both through time (in a ritual of maturation) and through place. In so doing, he bridges the gap between "the periphery" and "Moscow," and he narrows the gap between ordinary citizens (those of the "periphery") and the country's elite.

Thus the "son" figure in a socialist realist novel, or in other words the protagonist, is both ordinary and extraordinary. For most of the novel, he appears as one of the most politically committed and inspiring representatives of the Soviet Everyman. Like most ordinary human beings, he is impulsive and subject to the passions. However, he is generally distinguished from the other characters by brimming with greater energy and initiative. Thus he can be more appealing as a model for the reader to emulate than the "father" figure who is much more perfect, disciplined, and austere than his "son" and generally appears in the novel much less (it is, after all, more difficult to organize a readable, or particularly suspenseful, novel around a model figure).

This dual identity in the positive hero (ordinary/extraordinary) is a characteristic of socialist realism. Zhdanov, in his speech to the First Writers' Congress, called for the new Soviet literature to combine "the most matter-of-fact, everyday reality and the most heroic prospects." As if in response, novels kept oscillating between realistic representation and a hyperbolically heroic world where heroes perform seemingly impossible feats. Moreover, the transition between ordinary and extraordinary is often quite unmotivated.

The lack of motivation for shifts in mode is not problematical within the system of socialist realism because each of the major characters in a given work is not really a character *per se*, so much as he (sometimes it is a she) is a sub-function of his moral/political role ("son" or "father"). Indeed, the positive heroes are marked as having that special status by a cluster of iconic traits and epithets that indicate symbolically their moral/political identity or, in other words, their function as a positive form of "consciousness" or "spontaneity" incarnate. "Consciousness," for example, is indicated by such epithets as "calm," "determined," "austere," and "stern." Another cluster of clichéd epithets and attributes indicate the position that each of the two positive characters occupies on the life cycle. Regardless of their respective ages, a character whose function is that of a "son" must be youthful and full of vigor, and a "father" figure decidedly older (possibly with a bent back or heavily lined face that reveals how much he has sacrificed himself for the cause). These small details effectively functioned as a code. Indeed, it was partly in these tiny details that, over time, one saw development in the socialist realist tradition.

Each novel was written in a context affected by change, controversy, and even the author's own position. All these factors bore upon how the code was deployed in an individual work and had the power to change its meanings. New meanings could come from within the system of signs by the slightest rearrangement, emphasis, or shading of the standard signs and sequences. Such changes may be scarcely perceptible to an outsider not schooled in the tradition, but they would be striking to most Soviet readers.

The patterns outlined here emerged in the 1930s. However, they remained generally applicable in the 1940s because of the cultural conservatism that characterized that decade. Even though the 1930s saw the worst purges of Soviet history, the 1940s enjoy the reputation of being the worst period of Soviet cultural history, known as the Zhdanov era. The era therefore took its name from Andrei Zhdanov, who had delivered one of the keynote speeches to the First Writers' Congress and who, in 1946, delivered a lecture on the journals *Zvezda* and *Leningrad* (directed also against the writers Anna Akhmatova and Mikhail Zoshchenko). This barrage, together with other speeches and newspaper attacks that appeared in its wake, signaled the end of hopes of liberalization, and a return to rigid adherence to the socialist-realist canon (which had been less strictly enforced during the war years). Consequently, there was less modification of the socialist-realist code during that period than one might otherwise have expected. However, given the stress on adherence to the conventions of socialist realism, writers, in their anxiety to prove their dedication, tended to overdo their obeisance to the master-plot. Most of its standard functions do not just occur, but are proliferated throughout a given novel. For example, a typical novel of the 1940s has not just one mentor figure as its main character, but many. Functions lost their logic and their ideological purpose in the novel's overall design and became yet another pattern of whorls in some superabundant decoration.

The two functions used with greatest extravagance in 1940s novels were the mentor's "last testament" and the scene in which he symbolically "passes the baton" to the hero. Most novels do not rest with one such scene, but contrive to introduce at least two or three. Perhaps the novel that outdoes them all in this respect is the 1951 rewritten, canonical version of Valentin Kataev's *For the Power of the Soviets* (*Za vlast'sovetov*), whose protagonist, Petia, receives so many "batons" from older, Party and partisan stalwarts (many of them entrusted as they are dying, or even posthumously) that one begins to suspect his primary function is to receive batons.

The effect of such superabundance in 1940s novels is not to reinforce the master-plot but rather to undermine it. The result is the main weakness of these novels—incongruity. Indeed, in novels published after Zhdanov's "signal" lecture the mode was tilted so far away from the "realistic" in favor of the "romantic" (the glossy or larger-than-life) that even before Stalin died (as early as 1951) critics began to complain that there was too much "varnishing of reality" (*lakirovka deistvitel'nosti*), a charge that was heard more loudly and insistently once Stalin had died in 1953.

After Stalin's death, there was a return to more realistic, less bombastic—or simply improbable—depiction of Soviet reality. Yet one should not assume that writers were merely "strait-jacketed" in the Stalin years, mere "afflati" of the official position. After all, many of them were serious intellectuals. Since the clichés of socialist realism effectively formed a code, they could be used not only to establish a given writer's political loyalty, but to hint at meanings that he might not be able to make explicit.

If a Soviet writer wanted to be sure his novel would be published, he had to use the proper language (epithets, catch phrases, stock images, and so on) and syntax (to order the events of the novel in accordance with the *de facto* master-plot). To do so was effectively a ritual act of affirmation of loyalty to the state. Once the writer had accomplished this, his novel could be called "party-minded." But he had room for some play in the ideas these standard features expressed because of the variety of potential meanings for each of the clichés. The system of signs was, simultaneously, the components of a ritual of affirmation and a surrogate for the Aesopian language to which writers resorted in tsarist times when they wanted to outwit censors. Thus, paradoxically, the very rigidity of socialist realism's formations permitted freer expression than would have been possible (given the watchful eye of the censor) if the novel had been less formulaic.

The Typology of the Nonexistent

by Boris GROYS*

* From *The Total Art of Stalinism: Avant-Garde, Aesthetic Dictatorship, and Beyond*. Translated by Charles Rougle. Princeton, New Jersey: Princeton University Press, 1992. Pp. 50-56.

To distinguish their views from the aesthetics of the avant-garde, the theorists of socialist realism usually insist on the role of art as a means of knowing reality, that is, on its mimetic function, which is what allows the method to be contrasted as "realism" with avant-garde formalism. However, Stalinist aesthetics distances itself no less emphatically from naturalism, associating it with the repudiated "ideology of bourgeois objectivism," which upon closer consideration proves to be what most observers, including the Lef theorists, meant by the term "realism"—the reflection of immediately perceived reality. Mimesis, which in the aesthetics of the Stalin period and even in the Soviet Union today is associated with the so-called Leninist theory of reflection, thus signifies something quite different from an orientation toward the traditional representational easel painting.

An analysis of this distinction must begin with a consideration of the notion of the "typical," a key concept in all socialist realist discourse. One definition that accurately reflects the mature phase in the evolution of the doctrine is in

Georgii Malenkov's report at the agenda-setting Nineteenth Party Congress [1952]:

> As our artists, writers, and performers create their artistic images, they must constantly bear in mind that the typical is not that which is encountered the most often, but that which most persuasively expresses the essence of a given social force. From the Marxist-Leninist stand-point, the typical does not signify some sort of statistical mean ... The typical is the vital sphere in which is manifested the party spirit of realistic art. The question of the typical is always a political question.

After thus quoting Malenkov the journal continues:

> Thus, in the way the typical in the life of society is brought out in the artistic representation, we can see the political attitude of the artist toward reality, social life, historical events.

Socialist realist mimesis, then, attempts to focus on the hidden essence of things rather than on phenomena. This is more reminiscent of medieval realism and its polemics with nominalism than of nineteenth-century realism. Medieval realism, however, did not observe any principle of party spirit and did not claim to provide political guidelines—not even to resist the temptations of the devil—because it focused on that which exists, on the true essence of things. Socialist realism is oriented toward that which has not yet come into being but which should be created, and in this respect it is the heir of the avant-garde, for which aesthetics and politics also are identical. The notion of the typical was based on the following statement by Stalin:

> What is most important to the dialectical method is not that which is stable at present but is already beginning to die, but rather that which is emerging and developing, even if at present it does not appear stable, since for the dialectical method only that which is emerging and developing cannot be overcome.

It is further considered that what is regarded as dialectically emerging and developing under socialism is that which corresponds to the latest party policies, and that anything that runs counter to these policies is becoming obsolete, then it is obvious that the former will eventually prevail and the latter will be destroyed. The connection between the typical and the principle of party-mindedness, or *partiinost'*, is thus clear: the portrayal of the typical refers to the visual realization of still-emerging party objectives, the ability to intuit new currents among the party leadership, to sense which way the wind is blowing. More precisely, it is the ability to anticipate the will of Stalin, who is the real creator of reality.

This explains why so many writers, artists, movie-makers, and so on were afforded access to privileged party circles and encouraged to participate directly in the Stalinist power apparatus. It was not a case of vulgar "bribe"—like everyone else, cultural figures could be made to work by intimidation. The point instead is that they were thus given the opportunity to glimpse the "typical" that they were expected to reflect in their works. That is, they were provided an insight into the process through which they belonged to this leadership; it was a process in which they could even personally participate. As party bureaucrat the Soviet artist is more an artist, more a creator of the new reality, than in the studio in front of the easel. Thus what is subject to artistic mimesis is not external visible reality, but the inner reality of the inner life of the artist, who possesses the ability to identify and fuse with the will of the party and Stalin and out of this inner fusion generates an image, or rather a model, of the reality that this will is striving to shape. This then, is why the question of the typical is a political question—an inability to identify with the party is reflected externally in the inability to select the "correct" typical and can only indicate political disagreement with the party and Stalin at some subconscious level. The artists themselves may not even be aware of such dissension, but subjectively consider themselves completely loyal. Although it might seem irrational form the viewpoint of another aesthetics, here it is quite logical to eliminate artists physically for the differences between their personal dreams and that of Stalin.

Socialist realism represents the party-minded, collective surrealism that flourished under Lenin's famous slogan "it is necessary to dream," and therein is its similarity to Western artistic currents of the 1930s and 1940s. The popular definition of the method as "the depiction of life in its revolutionary development," "national in form, socialist in content," is based on this dream realism, in which a national form conceals the new socialist content: the magnificent vision of a world built by the party, the total work of art born of the will of its true creator and artist—Stalin. Under these circumstances, to be a realist means to avoid being shot for the political crime of allowing one's personal dreams to differ from Stalin's. The mimesis of socialist realism is the mimesis of Stalin's will, the artist's emulation of Stalin, the surrender of their artistic egos in exchange for the collective efficacy of the project in which they participate. "The typical" of socialist realism is Stalin's dream made visible, a reflection of his imagination—an imagination that was perhaps not as rich as that of Salvador Dali (possibly the only Western artist recognized, albeit negatively, by contemporary Soviet critics), but was far more efficacious.

Light is also shed on the nature of the typical by specific recommendations of artists on how to achieve it. Particularly interesting in this regard is a speech by the prominent painter Boris Ioganson in which he attempts a concrete, practical interpretation of the theoretical tenets of socialist realist aesthetics. Repeating first the familiar theses that all art is partisan in nature and that "the so-called theory of art for art's sake" was devised "to seize an ideological "weapon from the progressive forces of society," Ioganson proceeds to Lenin's theory of reflection, according to which

> the eye reflects objects as they appear to us, but human cognition of the surrounding world ... depends on thought. [Thus] ... the peculiarity of the artistic image as a subjective reflection of the objective world consists in the fact that the image combines the immediacy and power of active contemplation with the universality of active thought.
> ... Herein lies the great cognitive significance of realism, the distinction between realism and naturalism in art. Absolutization of the isolated detail leads to naturalism, to a decrease in the cognitive value of art.

This thesis Ioganson illustrates with the following passage from Gor'kii:

A fact is still not the whole truth: it is merely the raw material from which the real truth of art must be smelted and extracted—the chicken must not be roasted with its feathers. This, however, is precisely what reverence for the fact results in—the accidental and inessential is mixed with the essential and typical. We must learn to pluck the fact of its inessential plumage; we must be able to extract meaning from the fact.

Unlike most other contemporary critics, however, Ioganson does not limit himself to this quotation of "the father of socialist realism" describing the typical as a "plucked chicken" and the method itself as the plucking, but goes on to make some specific recommendations. There are, he says, examples of pure naturalism:

A casually snapped color photograph in which composition and the purposeful will of the photographer are absent is pure naturalism. A color photograph taken with a definite purpose in mind and edited by the photographer's will, however, is a manifestation of conscious realism… If the formal element of execution is connected with the artist's intent, it is a realistic element … Thus the naturalistic and realistic approaches to photography can be distinguished according to the presence or absence of the will or purpose of the photographer. The will of the craftsman, artistic production, especially in the cinema (casting, make-up, etc.) is analogous to the will of the painter. Everything must contribute to expressing the basic idea of the work of art.

Thus, after decades of bloody struggle with formalism, it suddenly turns out that the "formal element of execution … is a realistic element." In this passage Ioganson is undoubtedly continuing to polemicize with avant-garde critics who maintained that socialist realist art in general and Ioganson's paintings in particular were merely color snapshots that in the age of photography had therefore become superfluous, redundant anachronisms. Art should instead work immediately with "the unplucked fact," that is, the photograph. Ioganson is alluding to the already noted naiveté of the avant-garde, which regarded photograpy, the cinema, and so on as such "facts" that had from the outset been "plucked"—directed, juggled—by the will of the artist-photographer .He agrees with his "formalist" critics that his works are little more than enlarged color photographs, but he denies they are any the less "creative" for that. Instead it is the transition from photography to painting, the change of technique that reveals the photographer's artistic will behind the factuality of the photograph. Thus socialist realism candidly formulates the principle and strategy of its mimesis: although it advocates a strictly "objective," "adequate" rendering of external reality, at the same time it stages or produces this reality. More precisely, it takes reality that has already been produced by Stalin and the party, thereby shifting the creative act onto reality itself, just as the avant-garde had demanded. This transfer is more "realistic," however, in the sense that it reflects a political pragmatism that contrasts with the naïve utopianism of the avant-garde.

The "theater" and "stagecraft" metaphor is anything but accidental in this context. As one influential critic of the time noted:

> The typical hero should possess a striking, vivid personality. Sometimes it seems that not only the spectator but even the artist has no really clear idea of the heroes of a work—their desires, their aspirations, their character traits, why they are where they are or where they are going. I think that here our artists could learn a great deal from Stanislavskii, who demanded that his actors express each separate personality even in crowd scenes; even if they uttered only two or three sentences they were required to embody a specific personality.

Thus the socialist realist painting is not primarily intended to produce a visual effect or to render "the beauty of Nature" in the manner of traditional realism. Instead it conveys the inaudible speech of the individuals it portrays, glimpses into their lives, looks for signs of good and evil, and so on. The mimetic nature of the socialist realist picture is a mere illusion, or rather yet another ideologically motivated message among the other messages making up the painting. More than a true "reflection" of reality, the work is a hieroglyphic text, an icon, or a prescriptive newspaper article. The three-dimensional visual illusion of the socialist realist painting can be broken down into discrete signs bearing a "supersensual," abstract content; it is read by spectators familiar with the appropriate codes and is evaluated on the basis of such a reading rather than on the virtue of its own visual properties. This is why the socialist realist painting judged by the traditional criteria of realistic art inevitably appears "inferior" and "bad." To the trained eye, however, it is no less rich in content than the Japanese No theater. To the viewer of the Stalin period, moreover, it offered the additional and truly aesthetic experience of terror, since an incorrect coding or decoding could mean death. Despite its surface radiance and prettiness, the socialist realist painting evokes in the Soviet citizen of especially that period the same awe that the Sphinx inspired in Oedipus, who did not know which of his interpretations would mean patricide—that is Stalinicide—and thus his own death. Happily, to the modern viewer such pictures are as trite as the Sphinx, but the fact that they must be locked up in the cellars indicates that even today they have not entirely lost their former charms.

WAR DIARY

EXCERPTS

by Vasilii GROSSMAN*

* Vasily Grossman

** From *A Writer at War: Vasily Grossman with the Red Army, 1941-1945.* Edited and translated by Antony Beevor and Luba Vinogradova. New York: Pantheon Books, 2005. Pp. 338-350.

Italics have been used for Vasilii Grossman's own diary notes and jottings to set them apart from the comments by the translators and editors of *Writer at War*, Antony Beevor and Luba Vinogradova. Similarly, in the *Afterword*, the reminiscences of Grossman's daughter have been italicized.

2 May.

The Day of Berlin's capitulation. It's difficult to describe it. A monstrous concentration of impressions. Fire and fires, smoke, smoke, smoke. Enormous crowds of (German) prisoners. Their faces are full of drama. In many faces there's sadness, not only personal suffering, but also the suffering of a citizen. This overcast, cold and rainy day is undoubtedly the day of Germany's ruin. In smoke, among the ruins, in flames, amid hundreds of corpses in the streets.

Corpses squashed by tanks, squeezed out like tubes. Almost all of them are clutching grenades and sub-machine guns in their hands. They have been killed fighting. Most of the dead men are dressed in brown shirts. They were Party activists who defended the approaches to the Reichstag and the Reichschancellery.

Prisoners-policemen, officials, old men and next to them schoolboys, almost children. Many (of the prisoners) are walking with their wives, beautiful young women. Some of the women are laughing, trying to cheer up their husbands. A young soldier with two children, a boy and a girl. Another soldier falls down and can't get up again, he is crying. Civilians are kind to them, there's grief in their faces. They are giving prisoners water and shovel bread into their hands.

A dead old woman is half sitting on a mattress by a front door, leaning her head against the wall. There's an expression of calm and sorrow on her face, she has died with this grief. A child's little legs in shoes and stockings are lying in the mud. It was a shell, apparently, or else a tank has run over her. (This was a girl.)

In the streets that are already peaceful, the ruins have been tidied. (German) women are sweeping sidewalks with brushes like those we use to sweep rooms.

The (enemy) offered to capitulate during the night over the radio. The general commanding the garrison gave the order. "Soldiers! Hitler, to whom you have given the oath, has committed suicide."[1]

I've witnessed the last shots in Berlin. Groups of SS sitting in a building on the banks of the Spree, not far from the Reichstag, refused to surrender. Huge guns were blasting yellow, dagger-like fire at the building, and everything was swamped in stone dust and black smoke.

Reichstag. Huge, powerful. Soldiers are making bonfires in the hall. They rattle their mess tins and open cans of condensed milk with their bayonets.

A seemingly empty conversation has remained in my memory. It was with a middle-aged horse-driver, who had a mustache and a dark brown wrinkled face. He was standing beside his ponies at the corner of Leipzigerstrasse. I asked him about Berlin, and whether he likes the city.

"Oh, you see," he said, "there was such a fuss yesterday in this Berlin. A battle was going on, in this very street. German shells were exploding all the time. I was standing by the horses, and my foot bandage had become loose. I bent down to redo it, and then a shell blew up! A horse got scared and ran off. This one. He's young, but a bit naughty. And I was thinking, what should I do now, retie my foot bandage or run after the horse? Well, I ran after him, the foot bandage trailing after me, shells blowing up everywhere, my horse running, and me running after him. Well, I've taken a look at this Berlin! I was running for two hours in just one street, it had no end! I was running and thinking—well, that's Berlin. It's Berlin all right, but I did catch the horse!"

Just to the west of the *Reichstag,* Grossman wandered around the *Tiergarten,* the central park in Berlin where all the trees had been blasted to pieces in the battle and the ground was churned up by shell and bomb blast. The great victory column, the *Siegessäule,* was known to Soviet troops during the battle as the "tall lady," because of the figure of winged victory on top, which Berliners called "Golden Elsa." The "fortress" he refers to below is the huge Zoo bunker, or flak tower, a vast concrete construction with anti-aircraft batteries on top and shelter inside for several thousand people. It had been Goebbels's headquarters in his role as the Reich's Commissioner for Defense, but he did not die there. Goebbels and his wife Magda had shot themselves in the Reichs-chancellery garden after Magda had killed their six children with poison.

Memorials to victory. The Siegessäule, colossal buildings and concrete fortresses, sites of Berlin's anti-aircraft defense. Here was the Defense HQ of Goebbels's residence. People say he had given orders to poison his family and killed himself. Yesterday, he shot himself. His little scorched body is lying here, too: the artificial leg, white tie.

The enormity of victory. By the huge obelisk, a spontaneous celebration is going on. The armor of tanks has disappeared under heaps of flowers and red flags. Barrels are in blossom like trunks of spring trees. Everyone is dancing, laughing, singing. Hundreds of colored rockets are shot into the air, everyone is saluting with bursts from sub-machine guns, rifle and pistol shots. (I learned later that many of those men celebrating were living corpses, having drunk a terrible poison from barrels containing an industrial chemical in the Tiergarten. This poison started to act on the third day after they drank it, and killed people mercilessly.)

The Brandenburg Gate is blocked with a wall of tree trunks and sand, two to three meters high. In the space (of the arch), like in a frame, one can see the startling panorama of Berlin burning. Even I have never seen such a picture, although I've seen thousands of fires.

Foreigners. [Forced laborers and prisoners of war.] Their suffering, their traveling, shouting, threats towards German soldiers. Top hats, whiskers. A young Frenchman said to me: "Monsieur, I love your army and that's why it is painful for me to see its attitude to girls and women. This is going to be very harmful for your propaganda."

Looting: barrels, piles of fabric, boots, leather, wine, champagne, dresses — all this is being carried on carts and vehicles, or on shoulders.

Germans: some of them are exceptionally communicative and amiable, others turn away sullenly. There are many young women crying. Apparently, they have been made to suffer by our soldiers.

It was in Germany, particularly here in Berlin, that our soldiers really started to ask themselves why did the Germans attack us so suddenly? Why did the Germans need this terrible and unfair war? Millions of our men have now seen the rich farms in East Prussia, the highly organized agriculture, the concrete sheds for livestock, spacious rooms, carpets, wardrobes full of clothes.

Millions of our soldiers have seen the well-built roads running from one village to another and German autobahns [freeways] ... *Our soldiers have seen the two-floor suburban houses with electricity, gas, bathrooms and beautifully tended gardens. Our people have seen the villas of the rich bourgeoisie in Berlin, the unbelievable luxury of castles, estates and mansions. And thousands of soldiers repeat these angry questions when they look around them in Germany: "But why did they come to us? What did they want?"*

Most soldiers flocked to the Reichstag on this day of victory. Only a few, mainly officers, appear to have found the Reichschancellery. They were allowed to wander around on the ground floor, but SMERSh operatives, under the command of General Vadis, had sealed the cellars and the bunker. They were searching desperately for Hitler's body. Grossman, who went with Efim Gekhman, collected souvenirs and Nazi memorabilia. According to Ortenberg, Grossman obtained the last souvenirs in his collection on 2 May 1945 in Berlin. Grossman and Gekhman entered Hitler's office in the morning. Grossman opened a drawer of a desk, inside were stamps saying "The Führer has confirmed," "The Führer has agreed," etc. He took several of these stamps, and they are now in the same archive as his papers.

The new Reichs-chancellery. It's a monstrous crash of the regime, ideology, plans, everything, everything. Hitler kaputt ...

Hitler's office. The reception hall. A huge foyer, in which a young Kazakh, with dark skin and broad cheekbones, is learning to ride a bicycle, falling off it now and then. Hitler's armchair and table. A huge metal globe, crushed and crumpled, plaster, planks of wood, carpets. Everything is mixed up. It's chaos. Souvenirs, books with dedicatory inscriptions to the Fuhrer, stamps, etc.

In the south-west corner of the Tiergarten, Grossman also visited Berlin's ZOO.

Hungry tigers and lions... were trying to hunt sparrows and mice that scurried in their cages.

The Zoological Garden. There was fighting here. Broken cages. Corpses of marmosets, tropical birds, bears, the island for hamadryases, their babies are holding on to their mothers' bellies with their tiny hands.

Conversation with an old man. He's been looking after the monkeys for thirty-seven years. There was the corpse of a dead gorilla in a cage.

"Was she a fierce animal?" I asked.

"No. She only roared a good deal. People are angrier," he replied.

On a bench, a wounded German soldier is hugging a girl, a nurse. They see no one. When I pass them again an hour later, they are still sitting in the same position. The world does not exist for them, they are happy.

Grossman returned to Moscow and in early June escaped to a dacha. At first he could not write. He collapsed with nervous exhaustion, a reaction which had been postponed, like for so many who returned from the war. But then, with rest, fresh air, fishing and long walks, he felt ready to start his self-imposed task—to honor in his writing the heroism of the Red Army and the memory of the countless victims of the Nazi invasion.

Afterword

The Lies of Victory

Vasilii Grossman's belief in a "ruthless truth of war" was cruelly scorned by the Soviet authorities, especially when they attempted to suppress information about the Holocaust. At first, he refused to believe that anti-Semitism could exist within the Soviet system. He had assumed that the jibes of [celebrated Soviet writer] Mikhail Sholokhov which had outraged both Erenburg and him were an isolated example of reactionary sentiments, leftovers from the pre-revolutionary past. But he was to find soon after the war that the Stalinist system itself could be deeply anti-Semitic. Much later, when writing *Life and Fate*, he made it appear to be overt during the war, but this was premature. There were warnings, but the anti-Semitism within the regime did not emerge fully until 1948. It then became virulent in 1952, with Stalin's "anti-cosmopolitan" campaign and the conspiracy theory that Jewish doctors were attempting to kill Soviet leaders. Yet Stalin's anti-Semitism was not quite the same as that of the Nazis. It was based more on xenophobic suspicion than on race hatred.

....

Grossman was convinced that under Nikita Khrushchev, the chief commissar at Stalingrad and the denouncer of Stalin at the XX Party Congress in February 1956, the way was open at last for the truth to be told. But Grossman's lack of political judgment served him badly. He failed to see that the implicit parallels between Nazism and Stalinism in his novel *Life and Fate* constituted far too harsh a reality. The heroic myths of the Great Patriotic War had taken too deep a hold. He should also have realized the full significance of the fate of the Hungarian uprising in 1956, crushed brutally by General Babadzhanian, his hero in *The People Immortal*.

Grossman completed *Life and Fate* in 1960 and submitted the manuscript. It seemed as if his novel was being sat on due to incompetence or idleness, but in fact his editors were in a state of fear and consternation. The decision was passed upwards. On 14 February 1961, three senior KGB officers arrived to seize every copy of the manuscript. They ransacked the apartments of both Grossman and his typist, taking papers and even the carbon paper and typewriter ribbons. The manuscript was passed to the Communist Party's chief ideologue, Mikhail Suslov, the immensely powerful chief of the Cultural Section of the Central Committee.[2] Suslov's verdict was that it could not be published for over two hundred years. This remark was a striking recognition of the novel's importance.

The devastation appeared complete. Grossman's previous books were withdrawn from circulation. Reduced to penury and with only a few friends prepared to risk association with him, he soon suffered from cancer of the stomach. He died in the summer of 1964, assuming that his great work had been suppressed for ever. Erenburg offered to chair a committee on Grossman's work, but the *Writers' Union* refused. In the eyes of the Soviet authorities, Vasilii Grossman was virtually a non-person in political terms.

Grossman had, however, deposited a copy of the manuscript with a friend. And this friend, who had put it in a canvas satchel, had left it hanging on a hook under some coats at his dacha. Eventually the manuscript was discovered and copied on to microfilm it is said by Andrei Sakharov, the great physicist and dissident. Vladimir Voinovich, the satirical novelist and creator of *Private Chonkin* (a Red Army equivalent of *The Good Soldier Schwejk*), then smuggled the microfilm out of the Soviet Union to Switzerland.[3] *Life and Fate* was published there and in many other countries across the world. It appeared in Russia only as communism itself collapsed. Grossman's unspoken promise to his mother was finally fulfilled. She lived again through the novel as *Anna Shtrum*. Grossman himself may have been dragged down by the wolfhound century, but his humanity and his courage have survived in his writing.

SELECTED NOTES

[1] General Helmuth Weidling, the commander of LVI Panzer Corps, had been appointed commander of Berlin on 23 April by Hitler just after the Führer, due to a misunderstanding, had ordered his arrest for cowardice. Weidling, after his surrender at General Chuikov's headquarters, prepared this announcement to encourage his men to lay down their arms and halt the bloodshed.

[2] Suslov, Mikhail (1902—1982), Soviet Central Committee ideologue who had supervised the 1937-8 purges in the Ukraine and the Urals, and then in 1944-5 directed a brutal campaign of execution and deportation against national minorities who had been under German occupation.

[3] Voinovich, Vladimir Nikolaevich (1932—), began to write poetry when in the Soviet Army between 1950 and 1955. He turned to prose and later became a dissident. His most famous book, *The Life and Amazing Adventures of Private Ivan Chonkin*, contributed to his ejection from the Writers' Union in 1974. He emigrated in 1980 and was stripped of his citizenship by Brezhnev.

WE EXIST IN A COUNTRY GROWN UNREAL AND STRANGE

by Osip MANDEL'SHTAM*

We exist in a country grown unreal and strange;
No one ten steps away hears the talk we exchange.
But when chances for half-conversations appear,
We will never omit the Kremlin mountaineer.

Each thick finger, a fattened worm, gesticulates,
And his words strike you like they were many-pound weights.
His full cockroach mustache hints a laughter benigning,
And the shafts of his boots: always spotlessly shining.

And the gang of thick-skinned leaders near him obeys;
Semi-humans are at his disposal always.
Decree after decree he incessantly coins
Which hit people on foreheads, eyebrows, eyes and groins.

He possesses the broad chest, a Georgian perfection,
And each new death for him is a berry confection.

1934

---

* 1891-1938. From *Modern Russian Poetry: An Anthology with Verse Translations*. Edited and with an Introduction by Vladimir Markov and Merrill Sparks. Macgibbon & Kee, Printed in Great Britain, 1966 P. 321.

Russia, Our Happiness. Russia, Our Light

by Georgii IVANOV*

Russia, our happiness. Russia, our light.
And what if there is no Russia in sight,

No Neva with the sunset's fading glow,
No Pushkin—wounded, dying in the snow,

No Petersburg, no Kremlin on Earth's face,
Nothing but snow and snow—and open space?

Snow, snow, it is all snow. And night goes on,
And it will never end, never be gone.

Snow, snow, it is all snow ... And dark, dark night
Will never end nor yield to dawn's bright light.

Russia is dust. And silence—crisp and clear.
And what if all that Russia is is fear?

A rope, a bullet, icy dark—and add
A music that is driving you half-mad,

A rope, a bullet, a dawn which pain inflamed
Over things that the world has not yet named?

1931

---

* *George Ivanov*
** 1894-1958. From From *Modern Russian Poetry: An Anthology with Verse Translations*. Edited and with an Introduction by Vladimir Markov and Merrill Sparks. Macgibbon & Kee, Printed in Great Britain, 1966 P. 411.

THIS THING CALLED HOMESICKNESS! A FABLE

by Marina TSVETAEVA*

This thing called homesickness! A fable
That was exploded long ago!
Because for me it does not matter
Where to be completely so

Alone, and with my bag from the market
To plod home on who cares *what* stone —
To some house (like hospital, barracks)
That doesn't know it is my own.

It doesn't matter whose — the faces,
Midst which to bristle like a pure,
Caged lion — or which human setting
To be shoved out of soon — for sure —

Into myself and my own feelings
(Kamchatka bear without his ice).
It's all the same: *where* not to get on?
Or *where* not to be treated nice?

And this about one's native language:
I'll not be fooled... though it's milk-sweet.
Who cares which mother-tongue is spoken
If not understood by those you meet!

(By readers, by the gossip milkers,
By those who gulp each paper's word ...)

They're of this century, the twentieth,
And I—ere centuries occurred!

Having grown wooden like an old log
Remaining here from some park lane.
Each person, every thing's the same thing,
And that, perhaps, which seems again

More same than all else was the dearest:
All marks, all dates, all signs of me—
Vanish as by hand-flicking magic:
A soul born—somewhere: that simply.

My native land did not sustain me
Enough so that on all my soul
Even the most thorough detective
Could find a birthmark or a mole!

Each house is strange; each church means nothing.
It's all one and the same to me.
But if a bush looms by my pathway
Especially a rowan tree...

1934

* *Marina Tsvetayeva*
** 1892-1941. From *Modern Russian Poetry, An Anthology with Verse Translations*. Edited and with an Introduction by Vladimir Markov and Merrill Sparks. Macgibbon & Kee, Printed in Great Britain, 1966 Pp. 447-449.

NO MATTER HOW THE SOVIET TINSEL GLITTERS

by Vladimir NABOKOV*

(Translated by the author)

No matter how the Soviet tinsel glitters
Upon the canvas of a battle piece;
No matter how the soul dissolves in pity,
I will not bend, I will not cease

Loathing the filth, brutality and boredom
Of silent servitude. No, no, I shout,
My spirit is still quick, still exile-hungry,
I'm still a poet, count me out!

1944, Cambridge, MA.

---

* 1899-1977. From *Modern Russian Poetry, An Anthology with Verse Translations*. Edited and with an Introduction by Vladimir Markov and Merrill Sparks. Macgibbon & Kee, printed in Great Britain, 1966 P. 479.

SONG ABOUT OUR MOTHERLAND

by Vasilii LEBEDEV-KUMACH*

O, my homeland is a spacious country:
Streams and fields and forests full and fair.
I don't know of any other country
Where a man can breathe a freer air!

All the way from Moscow to the border,
Southern peaks to northern oceans' foam
Man can walk and feel that he's the owner
Of this boundless motherland and home.
Here our life can flow as freely, broadly
As the Volga—brimming and unchecked.
Here the young will always have a roadway
And the old will always have respect.

O, my homeland is a spacious country, etc.

One can't see the end of fields that are rich
Or recall all names of towns we've heard,
But one proud word that we say, "Tovarishch",
Means much more than any other word.
With this word we are at home all places
And this word we always comprehend:
There are no more black or colored races,
For with it—the whole world is your friend.

O, my homeland is a spacious country, etc.

There is none unwelcome at our table;
He who merits it gets his reward.
We now write in golden strokes the stable
Law of Stalin in a calm accord.
These words have a greatness and a glory
Which the years cannot mar or molest:
Every man has these rights in his story:
He may work, may study and may rest.

O, my homeland is a spacious country, etc.

O, the spring wind blows across our homeland,
What a joy to be alive today!
And no one wherever he may roam can
Laugh and love in any better way.
But we'll frown our eyebrows most severely
If a foe should want to cause our fall—
Like our bride, we love our homeland dearly;
Like our mother we'll save her from all.

O, my homeland is a spacious country, etc.

1935

* *Vasily Lebedev-Kumach*
** 1898-1949. From *Modern Russian Poetry, An Anthology with Verse Translations*. Edited and with an Introduction by Vladimir Markov and Merrill Sparks. Macgibbon & Kee, printed in Great Britain, 1966 Pp. 739-741.

A Word to Comrade Stalin

by Mikhail ISAKOVSKII*

I cannot stop it. It came by itself.
It came without any call on my part.
So please allow me to tell You these words,
These simple words that rose up from my heart.

The day arrived. The time is now fulfilled.
At last the earth has found its peace again.
So I thank You for Your supreme exploit,
For Your great labors You have done for men.

Thank You—that through the years of our ordeal—
You helped us hold ground till the fight was through.
Though our belief in ourselves may have dimmed,
Comrade Stalin, we never doubted You.

You were our strength and guarantee the foe
Would not escape his punishment somehow.
So please allow me, Sir, to shake Your hand
Firmly—and bow before You this low bow.

For Your faithfulness to our Motherland,
For Your wisdom and honor, for the star
Of purity and truth of Your own life,
For Your being the great man that You are.

Thank You—that in those greatly troubled days—
In the Kremlin You thought about our worth,
That You are present everywhere with us,
That You live on this planet we call Earth.

1945

* *Mikhail Isakovsky*
** 1900-1973. From *Modern Russian Poetry, An Anthology with Verse Translations*. Edited and with an Introduction by Vladimir Markov and Merrill Sparks. Macgibbon & Kee, printed in Great Britain, 1966 P. 749.

Epilogue

AFTER WWII AND AFTER STALIN

- COMMENTS ON THE EPILOGUE SELECTIONS
- A DENUNCIATION
- MEMOIR

Comments on the Epilogue Selections

> *A special kind of denunciations—the literary—are the critical articles ...*
>
> —Irina Belobrovtseva,
> on the critical articles
> that met the Master's novel
> in Mikhail Bulgakov's
> *The Master and Margarita*

As already stated several times, hopes that the Soviet victory in WW II would lead to an end of repressions and persecutions and to a more democratic political life and a freer cultural climate, did not materialize. The so-called **"Zhdanovshchina,"** named after Andrei **Zhdanov**, Stalin's and the Party's spokesman in cultural matters until his sudden death in 1948, instead brought crack-downs on publications with liberal leanings and vilification campaigns against writers "whose work had supposedly shown too little Communist spirit" (Kees Boterbloem). Best known is his fierce attack on Anna **Akhmatova** and Mikhail **Zoshchenko** in a lengthy speech delivered at a meeting of writers and the Party Executive Committee in Leningrad in 1946. Akhmatova was berated for "the "wretchedly limited" scope of her poetry and for "mixing fornication and prayer," and also for "foaming at the mouth," while "dashing from drawing-room to chapel." Zoshchenko was attacked for his story "Adventures of a Monkey," in which a monkey is shown as "the highest judge of [Soviet] social life," according to Zhdanov, who also believed this story showed a "zoological enmity towards the Soviet state." Probably an even more serious, not mentioned, offense was Zoshchenko's autobiographical-fictionalized memoir of his struggle with depression titled *Before Sunrise*. This highly innovative work, written during the war, shows traces of Freudian ideas and these had by then been taboo for several decades in the Soviet Union. Zhdanov's final verdict on the writer is that it would be "difficult to find in the whole of our literature anything more disgusting than the morals which Zoshchenko preaches in *Before Sunrise*, portraying both the people and himself as vile and lascivious creatures who have no shame or conscience." I have given several quotes from his *Speech* to demonstrate the crudeness of the insults Zhdanov permitted himself in regard to two of the most outstanding Russian writers of the century—a crudeness which indicates the spirit of the post-war cultural climate. Included here, the "Decree" (or "Resolution") to shut down one journal (which had published the unfortunate writers) and closely supervise the other (which had done likewise), like the Speech, offers plenty of insulting defamation from the "spokesman of culture," Zhdanov.

The last item of the Reader is an excerpt from Evgenii **Evtushenko**'s *Precocious Autobiography*, which deals with the fact that even the dead Stalin "could not leave this world without spilling blood" (Edvard Radzinskii). The young poet witnessed how people, especially women and children, were crushed as "millions of mourners or celebrators jostled and pressed ever tighter against each other and against [lorries that had been put up] as crush-barriers" (Ronald Hingley) on the order of Lavrentii **Beria**. Well over a hundred people died at Stalin's funeral. The memoir provides a hopeful note, nevertheless: Evtushenko lost the love he, like millions of his countrymen, had harbored for the Great Leader for ever on this occasion, and most likely other "worshipers "did too. The **Thaw** was making an as yet timid, yet palpable, entry with the appearance of poets such as Evtushenko, Andrei **Voznesenskii** and Bella **Akhmadulina** and their increasingly popular poetry readings, which attracted mass audiences in the early 1960s. In their poetry, innovation and experimentation are valued again, as stated in Voznesenskii's programmatic "Parabolic Ballad" where the French painter Paul **Gauguin** is hailed for scorning the "straight line" to acknowledgment and fame, preferring the "parabola" to the Paris Louvre, where he now is exhibited with all the honor due to him as an innovator. As will be remembered, Gauguin went to

Tahiti and as far as Sumatra for his motifs, taking a long detour indeed to recognition as innovator in his native France. Threatened again and again by the *"revenant"* (returning ghost) of Stalin, the Thaw was not to lead to a cultural or political summer, but it did become the prologue to fruitful cultural creativity in the second half of the century, to dissidence and persecution of dissidence, to renewed protest and renewed demands for "polyphony" and "dialogism," as opposed to "monologism." This second half of the century was a time that, in spite of Brezhnev's rule of "stagnation," found innumerable ways of subverting, fighting, undermining, challenging, defying, parodying, and otherwise slowly but surely invalidating the Stalinist (and even Leninist) legacy.

SUGGESTED FURTHER READINGS

Ryan, Karen, L. *Stalin in Russian Satire, 1917-1991: The Corpse and the Revenant.* Madison: University of Wisconsin Press, 2009. Pp. 156-163.

A Denunciation

The Central Committee Resolution on the Journals Zvezda and Leningrad

by Andrei ZHDANOV*

August 14, 1946

The Central Committee of the All-Russia Communist Party notes that the literary journals *Zvezda* and *Leningrad*, published in Leningrad, are being managed in a very unsatisfactory manner.

Recently many ideologically harmful works, totally without ideas, have been appearing in the journal *Zvezda* alongside important and successful works by other Soviet writers. *Zvezda*'s grave mistake has been to offer its columns to the writer Zoshchenko, whose work is alien to Soviet literature. The editors of *Zvezda* know that Zoshchenko has long specialized in the writing of trivially commonplace, empty, and superficial things, and in preaching rotten rubbish, devoid of ideas, trivially commonplace, and apolitical, aimed at disorienting our youth and poisoning their minds. The last

* From *The Central Committee Resolution and Zhdanov's Speech on the Journals Zvezda and Leningrad*, Bilingual edition. English translation by Felicity Ashbee and Irina Tidmarsh. Royal Oak, MI: Strathcona Publishing, 1978. Pp. 41-45.

of Zoshchenko's published stories, "The Adventures of a Monkey" (*Zvezda*, No. 5-6, 1946), is a trivially commonplace lampoon on the Soviet way of life and on Soviet people.

Zoshchenko portrays the Soviet way of life and the Soviet people in a hideously caricatured form, slanderously showing them as primitive, uncultured and stupid, with philistine tastes and ways. Zoshchenko adds anti-Soviet slogans to his hooligan's malicious portrayal of our way of life.

For *Zvezda* to offer its columns to such dregs of society as Zoshchenko is the more reprehensible since the editors of *Zvezda* are well aware of Zoshchenko's real character, as well as of his unworthy conduct during the war, when instead of helping the Soviet people in their struggle against the German invaders, he wrote a work as loathsome as *Before Sunrise*, a review of which, as well as of all Zoshchenko's "creative" work, appeared in the journal *Bolshevik*.

The journal *Zvezda* is also popularizing in every way the work of the writer Akhmatova, whose literary, social, and political attitudes have long been known to Soviet society. Akhmatova's work is typically representative of a kind of ideologically empty poetry alien to our people. Her poetry, steeped in pessimism and a spirit of decline, expressing tastes like those of the former drawing-room poetry, has become ossified in a stance of bourgeois aristocratic aestheticism—of "art for art's sake"—which refuses to follow in the footsteps of the people, is harmful to our youth and cannot be tolerated in Soviet literature.

Beyond doubt, offering Akhmatova and Zoshchenko an active part in the journal has brought elements of ideological instability and disorganization into Leningrad's writing circles. Works which cultivate a spirit of servility towards current bourgeois culture of the West, and which are quite alien to the Soviet people, have begun to appear in the journal. There have begun to be published works imbued with melancholy, pessimism and disappointment in life (the poetry of Sadof'ev and Komissarova in No. 1, 1946, etc.). By allowing such work to be included in the journal, the editors have aggravated their mistakes and still further lowered the ideological level of the journal.

Having once allowed the penetration of ideologically alien works into the journal, the editors have also lowered the artistic standards required for literary material published in the journal. The journal has begun to be filled with plays and stories without talent (Iagfel'd's "The Road of Life," Stein's "The Swan Lake," etc.). Such lack of discrimination in the choice of material to be published has resulted in a lowering of the artistic level of the journal.

The Central Committee notes that the journal *Leningrad* was being especially badly run, as it constantly offered its columns to the trivially commonplace and slanderous pronouncements of Zoshchenko, and to the empty and apolitical poetry of Akhmatova. And not only the editors of the journal *Zvezda* but also the editors of the journal *Leningrad* have made grave mistakes in publishing a number of works full of a spirit of servility towards everything foreign. The journal has published a number of inadmissible works such as "The Event over Berlin" by Varshavskii and Rest, and "At the Barrier" by Slonimskii. In Khazin's poem "The Return of Onegin," in the guise of a literary parody, a slanderous attack is made on contemporary Leningrad. The material published in the journal *Leningrad* is for the most part of low standard and devoid of ideas.

How could it have happened that the journals *Zvezda* and *Leningrad*, appearing in Leningrad, the heroic city, well known for its progressive revolutionary traditions, a city which had always been the disseminator of new and progressive ideas and culture,—how could it have happened that material so apolitical and lacking in ideas has permeated their columns?

What is behind these mistakes of the editors of *Zvezda* and *Leningrad*?

The leading members of the staff of the journals, in the first place their editors, Comrades Saianov and Likharev, seem to have forgotten the maxims of Leninism, that our journals, whether they are scientific or literary, cannot be apolitical. They have forgotten that our journals are powerful weapons of the Soviet state in the education of the Soviet people and especially its youth, and that, therefore, they must be guided by what constitutes the whole basis of the Soviet system—its political theory. The Soviet state cannot tolerate the upbringing of its youth in a spirit of indifference to Soviet political theory, without ideological foundations, and with an attitude of "couldn't care less."

The power of Soviet literature, the most progressive of any literature in the world, consists in the fact that it is a literature which neither has, nor can have, any other interest besides the interest of its people and its state. The aim of Soviet literature is to help the state to bring up our youth in the right way, to help it to solve its problems, to bring up the new generation to be alert, believing in its work, fearless of any obstacles and ready to overcome them.

This is why any preaching, which lacks ideas, and is apolitical, such as "art for art's sake," is alien to Soviet literature, is harmful to the interests of the Soviet people and the state, and must not be allowed to have any space in our journals.

The lack of ideology amongst the leading members of the staff of the journals *Zvezda* and *Leningrad* has also resulted in these members putting their relationship with the writers on a friendly and personal footing only, instead of concentrating on the education of the Soviet people, and on guiding the activity of the writers into the right political channels. Because of a fear of offending friends, work of obviously low standard has been allowed to be published. This kind of liberalism which sacrifices the interest of the people and the state, and the interests of the education of our youth, to personal interests, leads to writers no longer trying to improve their work, to their losing their feeling of responsibility towards the people and the Party, and thus ceasing to advance.

All of the above proves that those directing the journals *Zvezda* and *Leningrad* were inadequate for their work, allowing serious political mistakes to be made in the direction of the journals.

The Central Committee states that the Board of the Union of Soviet Writers, and in particular its chairman, Comrade Tikhonov, did not take any steps to improve the journals *Zvezda* and *Leningrad* and not only did not lead the struggle against the harmful influence of Zoshchenko, Akhmatova and similar anti-Soviet writers on Soviet literature, but even connived to infiltrate the journals with these tendencies and customs alien to Soviet literature.

The Leningrad City Council of the All-Russian Communist Party overlooked the enormous mistakes of these journals, and stood apart from the journals' direction, thus giving opportunity to writers such as Zoshchenko and Akhmatova to assume a leading role in the journals' direction. Moreover, while aware of the Party's views on Zoshchenko and his "works," the Leningrad City Council (Comrades Kapustin and Shirokov), having no right to do so, on the 26.VI of the current year gave their sanction to the new editorial board of the journal *Zvezda*, of which Zoshchenko now became a member. This was a grave political mistake on the part of the Leningrad City Council. The paper *Leningrad Pravda* has also made a mistake in publishing a suspiciously laudatory review of Zoshchenko's work by Iurii German, which appeared in the paper on the sixth of July of the current year.

The Board of the Propaganda Department of the Central Committee of the All-Russian Communist Party has not exercised sufficient control over the work of the Leningrad journals.

The Central Committee of the All-Russian Communist Party has decreed:

> 1. To oblige the editors of the journal *Zvezda*, the Board of the Union of Soviet Writers and the Board of the Propaganda Department of the Central Committee of the All-Russia Communist Party to take all necessary measures to eliminate the mistakes and failings of the journal, pointed out in the above Decree, to correct the ideological line of the journal, ensure a high ideological and artistic standard in the journal, and to cease publication of the works of Zoshchenko, Akhmatova, and others like them.
>
> 2. Since, at present, suitable conditions for the publication of two artistic-literary journals in Leningrad do not exist, to stop the publication of the journal *Leningrad*, and concentrating the literary effort of *Leningrad* on the journal *Zvezda*.
>
> 3. In order to ensure a proper organization of the Editorial Board of the journal Zvezda, and a serious improvement

in its contents, to appoint an editor-in-chief, and a board working under him. To ensure that the editor-in-chief has full responsibility for the ideological policy of the journal, and for the quality of the published material.

4. To confirm Comrade A. M. Egolin as editor-in-chief of the journal *Zvezda*, while leaving him at his job as the second in command to the Head of the Propaganda Department of the Central Committee of the All-Russian Communist Party.

*—The paper **Culture and Life** [Kul'tura i zhizn']*
21 August 1946

Memoir

by Evgenii EVTUSHENKO*

* *Yevgeny Yevtushenko*

** *From Yevtushenko's Reader: The Spirit of Elbe; A Precocious Autobiography; Poems. Translated from the Russian by Robin Milner-Gulland and Peter Levi, S. J. Andrew, R. MacAndrew, George Reavey, C. Todd, John Updike, Stanley Kunitz, Vera Dunham, and Herbert Marshall. New York: E. P. Dutton and Co., 1972. Pp. 84-94.*

ON MARCH 5, 1953, AN EVENT TOOK PLACE WHICH shattered Russia—Stalin died. I found it almost impossible to imagine him dead, so much had he been an indispensable part of life.

A sort of general paralysis came over the country. Trained to believe that they were all in Stalin's care, people were lost and bewildered without him. All Russia wept. And so did I. We wept sincerely, tears of grief—and perhaps also tears of fear for the future.

At a meeting of the Writers' Union poets read their poems in honor of Stalin, their voices broken by sobs. Tvardovskii, a big and powerful man, recited in a trembling voice.

I WILL NEVER FORGET GOING TO SEE STALIN'S COFFIN.

I was in the crowd in Trubnaia Square. The breath of the tens of thousands of people jammed against one another rose up in a white cloud so thick that on it could be seen the swaying shadows of the bare March trees. It was a terrifying and a fantastic sight. New streams poured into this human flood from behind, increasing the pressure. The crowd turned into a monstrous whirlpool. I realized that I was being carried straight toward a traffic light. The post was coming relentlessly closer. Suddenly I saw that a young girl was being pushed against the post. Her face was distorted and she was screaming. But her screams were inaudible among all the other cries and groans. A movement of the crowd drove me against the girl; I did not hear but felt with my body the cracking of her brittle bones as they were broken on the traffic light. I closed my eyes in horror, the sight of her insanely bulging, childish blue eyes more than I could bear, and I was swept past. When I looked again the girl was no longer to be seen. The crowd must have sucked her under. Pressed against the traffic light was someone else, his body twisted and his arms outflung as on a cross. At that moment I felt I was treading on something soft. It was a human body. I picked my feet up under me and was carried along by the crowd. For a long time I was afraid to put my feet down again. The crowd closed tighter and tighter. I was saved by my height. Short people were smothered alive, falling and perishing. We were caught between the walls of houses on one side and a row of army trucks on the other.

"Get those trucks out of the way!" people howled. "Get them out of here!" "I can't do it! I have no instructions," a very young, towheaded police officer shouted back from one of the trucks, almost crying with helplessness. And people were being hurtled against the trucks by the crowd, and their heads smashed. The sides of the trucks were splashed with blood. All at once I felt a savage hatred for everything that had given birth to that "I have no instructions," shouted at a moment when people were dying because of someone's stupidity. For the first time in my life I thought with hatred of the man we were burying. He could not be innocent of the disaster. It was the "No instructions" that had caused the chaos and bloodshed at his funeral. Now I was certain, once and for all, that you must never wait for instructions if human lives are at stake—you must act.

I don't know how I did it, but working energetically with my elbows and fists, I found myself thrusting people aside and shouting: "Form chains! Form chains!" They didn't understand me.

Then I started to join neighboring hands together by force, all the while spitting out the foulest swearwords of my geological days. Some tough young men were now helping me. And now people understood. They joined hands and formed chains. The strong men and I continued to work at it. The whirlpool was slowing down. The crowd was ceasing to be a savage beast. "Women and children into the trucks!" yelled one of the young men. And women and children, passed from hand to hand, sailed over our heads into the trucks. One of the women who were being handed on was struggling hysterically and whimpering. The young police officer who received her at his end stroked her hair, clumsily trying to calm her down. She shivered a few times and suddenly froze into stillness. The officer took the cap off his straw-colored head, covered her face with it, and burst out crying.

There was another violent whirlpool further ahead. We worked our way over, the tough boys and I, and again with the help of the roughest curses and fists, made people form chains in order to save them.

The police too finally began to help us.

Everything quieted down.

"You ought to join the police, Comrade. We could use fellows like you," a police sergeant said to me, wiping his face with his handkerchief after a bout of hard work.

"Right. I'll think it over," I said grimly.

Somehow, I no longer felt like going to see Stalin's remains. Instead, I left with one of the boys who had been organizing chains. We bought a bottle of vodka and walked to our place. "Did you see Stalin?" my mother asked me.

"Yes," I said coldly, as I clinked glasses with the boy. I hadn't really lied to my mother. I had seen Stalin. Because everything that had just happened—that was Stalin.

50 WRITERS
An Anthology of 20th Century Russian Short Stories
Selected, with and Introduction by Mark LIPOVETSKY and Valentina BROUGHER
Translated and annotated by Valentina BROUGHER and Frank MILLER, with Mark LIPOVETSKY

2011   792 pages

Cloth 978-1-936235-14-8
Paper 978-1-936235-22-3
Electronic 978-1-61811-010-7

The largest, most comprehensive anthology of its kind, this volume brings together significant, representative stories from every decade of the 20th century. It includes the prose of officially recognized writers and dissidents, both well-known and neglected or forgotten, plus new authors from the end of the 20th century. The selections reflect the various literary trends and approaches to depicting reality in the 20th century: traditional realism, modernism, socialist realism, and post-modernism. Taken as a whole, the stories capture every major aspect of Russian life, history and culture in the 20th century. The rich array of themes and styles will be of tremendous interest to students and readers who want to learn about Russia through the engaging genre of the short story.

Valentina Brougher (PhD University of Kansas) is Professor Emerita, Department of Slavic Languages, Georgetown University. Her articles on twentieth-century Russian writers have been published in major academic journals, and her translations of twentieth-century prose have appeared in anthologies and special editions.

Mark Lipovetsky (PhD Ural State University, Russia) has lived in the USA since 1996 and is an associate professor of Russian studies at the University of Colorado-Boulder. He is the author of six monographs, numerous articles in major American and Russian journals, and recipient of many grants and fellowships, including a Fulbright, SSRC, and Leverhulme (UK).

Frank Miller (PhD Indiana University) is a professor of Slavic languages at Columbia University and coordinator of the Columbia-Barnard College Russian language program. He is the author or coauthor of several widely-used Russian textbooks and translator of Russian prose

"If you like the short-story genre, don't pick up this addictive collection unless you are prepared to be lost in its riches for a considerable time. These beautifully translated, haunting Russian tales, written from 1901 to 2001, almost all previously unpublished, read so smoothly that they are seductive. And, as the editors suggest, if the stories are read as they are arranged chronologically, the continuity of certain themes makes the whole lot into 'a kind of amazing meganovel, with different heroes, historical periods and situations which nevertheless resonate with one another and become intertwined...'"
—Priscilla S. Taylor, *The Washington Times*

Series: **Cultural Syllabus**

THE RUSSIAN AVANT-GARDE AND RADICAL MODERNISM
An Introductory Reader

Dennis G. IOFFE and Frederick H. WHITE

2012   500 pages

Cloth 978-1-936235-29-2
Paper 978-1-936235-45-2
Electronic 978-1-61811-142-5

The Russian avant-garde was a composite of antagonistic groups who wished to overthrow the basic aesthetics of classical realism. Modernism was the totality of these numerous aesthetic theories, which achieved a measure of coherence immediately after the First World War. This collection of essays by leading scholars examines the major figures, movements and manifestos of the period. Scholarly attention is given to literature, visual arts, cinema and theatre in an attempt to capture the complex nature of the modernist movement in Russia. This book would be especially relevant for university courses on the Russian twentieth century as well as for those looking for a comprehensive approach to the various movements and artistic expressions that constitute the Russian avant-garde.

Frederick H. White (PhD University of Southern California) is associate dean in the College of Humanities and Social Sciences at Utah Valley University. In 2006, he published *Memoirs and Madness: Leonid Andreev through the Prism of the Literary Portrait* (MQUP). Dr. White has recently completed a second book manuscript, *Neurasthenia: Constructions of Madness in the Life and Narratives of Leonid Andreev*.

Dennis Ioffe (PhD University of Amsterdam) has worked as an assistant professor of Russian and German studies at Memorial University in Newfoundland and as a research and teaching fellow at the Princess Dashkova Russian Centre at the University of Edinburgh. He has published over 50 scholarly articles and has edited or co-edited several academic collections, among them *The Discourses of Somatics and Eroticism in the Russian Culture* (2008) and *The Russian Philology under Stalin* (2008).

Series: **Cultural Syllabus**

Academic Studies Press and Bibliorossica.com present an ebook collection

Leading Russian Scholarly Publishers

A unique ebook collection, **Leading Russian Scholarly Publishers** includes the best books in different fields of scholarly along with bestsellers in other non-fiction genres from 2009 to 2012 which are made available in this electronic collection for the first time. The initial collection of more than 1000 titles of 2009-2011 as well as the most significant publications from recent years is being supplemented by the 2012 publications immediately after their release. It unites the catalogs of publishers specializing in history, philosophy, linguistics, history of culture, literature and art, sociology, anthropology, ethnography, Jewish studies, and other humanities, with an emphasis on Russian studies. It is a unique overview of the major scholarly work being created and published in a region that is even now isolated, with a book market that is traditionally slow in getting books to the outside world. **It is all that you've wanted to read in Russian but did not know where to find.**

BiblioRossica is a **continuously expanding portal for modern academic literature on the humanities, in an electronic format.** Our goal is to collect and make available, to researchers all over the world, the latest and best publications in the humanities. That's why **BiblioRossica** is an invaluable tool in teaching and research activities.

We see the book market changing right before our eyes: academic libraries are moving towards replacing more and more traditional print publications with electronic books. That's why the catalog's structure and the user interface of our website are designed to address the particular needs of research libraries, as well as the specifics of using texts in the scientific and educational contexts. Thus, the **BiblioRossica** portal provides access to the most recent publications, just released in print. Thanks to the extensive catalog of current publications and a modern user interface, the portal combines the traditions of meticulous research with the newest technologies.

All publications on the **BiblioRossica** site are licensed through direct contracts between publishers and Academic Studies Press.

All electronic publications are protected from unauthorized use and unauthorized copying.

For more information please visit us at **www.bibliorossica.com**
Contact: **support@bibliorossica.com**
+1 617 7826290

www.ingramcontent.com/pod-product-compliance
Lightning Source LLC
Chambersburg PA
CBHW061340300426
44116CB00011B/1933